Cambridge Imperial and Post-Colonial Studies

The Cambridge Imperial and Post-Colonial Studies series is a well-established collection of over 100 volumes focussing on empires in world history and on the societies and cultures that emerged from, and challenged, colonial rule. The collection includes transnational, comparative and connective studies, as well as works addressing the ways in which particular regions or nations interact with global forces. In its formative years, the series focused on the British Empire and Commonwealth, but there is now no imperial system, period of human history or part of the world that lies outside of its compass. While we particularly welcome the first monographs of young researchers, we also seek major studies by more senior scholars, and welcome collections of essays with a strong thematic focus that help to set new research agendas. As well as history, the series includes work on politics, economics, culture, archaeology, literature, science, art, medicine, and war. Our aim is to collect the most exciting new scholarship on world history and to make this available to a broad scholarly readership in a timely manner.

Colette Le Petitcorps · Marta Macedo ·
Irene Peano
Editors

Global Plantations in the Modern World

Sovereignties, Ecologies, Afterlives

palgrave
macmillan

Editors
Colette Le Petitcorps
Institute of Social Sciences
University of Lisbon
Lisbon, Portugal

Irene Peano
Institute of Social Sciences
University of Lisbon
Lisbon, Portugal

Marta Macedo
Institute of Contemporary History
NOVA School of Social Sciences
and Humanities
Lisbon, Portugal

ISSN 2635-1633 ISSN 2635-1641 (electronic)
Cambridge Imperial and Post-Colonial Studies
ISBN 978-3-031-08539-0 ISBN 978-3-031-08537-6 (eBook)
https://doi.org/10.1007/978-3-031-08537-6

Cover illustration: Kanok Sulaiman

This Palgrave Macmillan imprint is published by the registered company Springer Nature Switzerland AG
The registered company address is: Gewerbestrasse 11, 6330 Cham, Switzerland

Foreword

It is a pleasure and an honour to welcome you to this volume. I can promise your labour in reading will be rewarded as creative connections emerge from the book's plethora of case studies, analytic suggestions and conceptual discussions that will surely lead to further valuable questions. You are about to step into a collection of state-of-art research that takes the plantation as an analytic tool with which to confront the present, address the legacies of the past, and think about the future, while bringing together what anthropology, history, science and technology studies and other disciplines can do to outline the transient equations with which we attempt to frame, understand, and act upon our collective endeavours.

This is a book about the plantation-institution, about the plantation as a machine of production and devastation, the plantation as a device that generates inequalities and invents hierarchies, the plantation that persists in embodied memories and post-memories of violence for some and of entitlement for others. It is about the plantation and its afterlives of dispossession, exclusion, containment, and detention, of racialized existences, exhausted environments, improbable re-assemblages of species, and combinations of capital and labour that are increasingly about fictional capital and non-human labour. This is a book that lengthens the compact temporality of a symposium intersecting past and future—a symposium that emerged from the creative interactions between Colette Le Petitcorps, Marta Macedo, and Irene Peano while team members of the *The Colour of Labour* project, plus the enthusiastic respondents to the call for contributions—and a volume that will bind them through the afterlives of that original temporality.

The Colour of Labour: The Racialized Lives of Migrants was a daring concept that I thought might fit the "high-risk high-gain" profile of the European Research Council grant programme. I was fortunate enough to be awarded an advanced grant (ERC AdG 695573), one that enabled me to gather a team of talented young scholars interested in analysing the ways in which plantation and plantation-like economies and societies produce racialized lives in different ethnographic and historic contexts, with a focus on post-abolition contexts. The aim was to examine how the plantation as a race-making machine persisted beyond its quintessential American-Caribbean format, with its centuries of de-humanizing enslaved and trafficked Africans, in which blackness and whiteness were generated first as positional categories and later ascribed properties of nature. What other classifications and racialized hierarchies came with new arrangements in plantation labour? How did new systems of classification coexist with the established ones? We looked beyond the Atlantic trade, to the Indian and Pacific oceans, to the forced, semi-forced, and contracted routes of labour traffic and the related dynamics of diversifying and hierarchizing the labour force—whether in Hawaii, the Guianas, Mauritius, or São Tomé or in contemporary agribusiness in Europe.

In the process, we went beyond the original questions and raised new ones. With the privilege of a slow-science framework that counteracted, even if only for a while, the current trend of squeezing research outputs into a predefined spreadsheet, we were able to not only engage in actual empirical and conceptual research but also to cross-fertilize lines of research in enduring ways. It was in this environment of academic freedom that the editors of this volume called for an open-ended symposium exploring plantations and their afterlives along the lines of materialities, durabilities, and struggles. Despite the misfortunes of the year 2020, the pandemic-related postponements and the cyberization of academic meetings, it was a most accomplished venture, as this volume ably demonstrates.

In their introduction, the editors Le Petitcorps, Macedo, and Peano guide you through a comprehensive discussion of the critical literature on plantations, raise the relevant questions, and present the clusters of problems and theory that structure the volume, while also dissecting the different contributions and bringing them into dialogue with one another.

They will guide you along the axes of sovereignties, ecologies, and afterlives and into the geopolitical clusters that form the sections of the book. In the end, Deborah Thomas leaves us with the perfect coda, one that at once settles the matter and makes us want to start all over again, go back to the subject, expand the clusters and themes with a new refraction and its new kaleidoscopic combinations: modernities, mobilities, and mutualities.

Cristiana Bastos

Cristiana Bastos is a research professor of Anthropology at the Institute of Social Sciences, University of Lisbon, Portugal. She is currently leading the project "*The Colour of Labour*", awarded with an Advanced Grant by the European Research Council.

Acknowledgments

The volume springs from a symposium titled "Plantations and their afterlives: Materialities, durabilities, struggles" organized by the editors and held virtually in September 2020, but hosted by the Institute of Social Sciences at the University of Lisbon. Participants addressed plantations from multiple angles (labour, race, technologies, environments, subjectivities, resistance, ruination, memory) across different geographies and chronologies, ranging from the seventeenth century to the present. In this volume, we gathered a selection of the papers presented at the conference, together with others, revisiting some well-established themes on plantations pasts and presents under a new light. We are grateful to all the conference presenters, commentators, and audience who joined our conversation and, in many cases, kept it going well past the event. We also wish to thank Cristiana Bastos and Deborah A. Thomas for their deep engagement with this project and for their contributions to this volume.

The symposium, and the editors' work, was supported by the European Research Council-funded project "The Colour of Labour: The Racialized Lives of Migrants" (Advanced Grant n. 695573, PI Cristiana Bastos). We thank our colleagues in the project research team for the lively discussions and especially Mari Lo Bosco, Project Manager, who provided invaluable help during the entire process.

We also want to thank the anonymous reviewers for commentaries and suggestions on earlier versions of the manuscript. Finally, we owe our appreciation to Palgrave Macmillan, and particularly to Richard Drayton, together with the other editors of the "Cambridge Imperial and Post-Colonial Studies" series, who welcomed our proposal since its early stages and supported us all the way, making this book possible.

Praise for *Global Plantations in the Modern World*

"The plantation is a distinctive global institution, vital to the making of the modern world. It is hugely creative in its wealth-making potential and massively destructive in what it does to the environment and to plantation workers. This highly stimulating and provocative set of essays help us redefine and rethink what the plantation means, offering great insights into slavery and emancipation."

—Trevor G. Burnard, *Professor and Director of the Wilberforce Institute for the Study of Slavery and Emancipation, University of Hull, UK*

"A rare and relevant rethinking of plantations and their afterlives, this book powerfully intervenes in some of the most important debates of our time. The authors and editors brilliantly weave together ethnographic, archival and archaeological case studies that layer into productive critiques of colonialisms, racisms, environmental destructions, and im/mobilities. Through prisms of plantations and counterplantations and the unexpected human and more-than-human actors buttressing and resisting them, the book provides unanticipated insights into the Anthropocene, slavery, racial capitalism, industrial agriculture, migrant labour and – most importantly – possibilities for alternative futures."

—Seth M. Holmes, *Chancellor's Professor, UC Berkeley, USA*

"The common elements of plantations are the linear arrangement of monocrops and the deployment of labour on a massive scale. The other elements – racial, political, embodied, affective – are specific to their historical and geographic milieu. By placing diverse plantation worlds in conversation, the authors expose the worlds that made plantations, and the worlds plantations made and continue to make through their multivalent entanglements. The results are revelatory."

—Tania Murray Li, *University of Toronto, Canada*

Contents

Notes on Contributors

David Akwasi Mensah Abrampah is a lecturer in the Department of Archaeology and Heritages Studies, University of Ghana. He has interest in both anthropology and historical archaeology, including linguistic anthropology, the archaeology of salt mining/trading and culture contact in Ghana.

Marie Aureille is a Ph.D. candidate in anthropology at the Ecole des Hautes Etudes en Sciences Sociales (EHESS), Laboratoire d'Anthropologie Politique. Drawing on multispecies ethnography, her dissertation examines changing power relations in farming within decollectivization policies in Cuba and the production of the State through farmers and cooperatives inclusion in the planned economy.

Rodrigo C. Bulamah is a postdoctoral researcher at the Social Sciences Graduate Program, Federal University of São Paulo, working at the interface between history and anthropology. His main field is the Caribbean and he deals with themes such as colonialism, plantation legacies, religious formations, kinship, historicity, and political ecology.

Sophie Chao is Discovery Early Career Research Award (DECRA) fellow and lecturer at the Department of Anthropology, University of Sydney. Her research investigates the intersections of Indigeneity, ecology, capitalism, health, and justice in the Pacific. Chao is the author of *In the Shadow of the Palms: More-Than-Human Becomings in West Papua*

(Duke University Press, 2022) and co-editor of *The Promise of Multispecies Justice* (Duke University Press, 2022) with Eben Kirksey and Karin Bolender. She previously worked for the human rights organization Forest Peoples Programme in Indonesia, supporting the rights of forest-dwelling Indigenous peoples to their customary lands, resources, and livelihoods.

Nile Davies is a doctoral candidate in Anthropology and the Institute for Comparative Literature and Society at Columbia University. His dissertation examines the politics and sentiments of reconstruction and the aftermaths of "disaster" in post-war Sierra Leone.

Colette Le Petitcorps holds a Ph.D. in Sociology at the University of Poitiers (France). She worked as a postdoctoral researcher affiliated with the ERC Project "The Colour of Labour: The Racialized Lives of Migrants" (ICS, university Lisbon) and as a lecturer at the University of Western Brittany in Brest, and is associated with the Centre d'études en sciences sociales sur les mondes africains, américains et asiatiques (Centre for social studies on African, American, and Asian worlds) in Paris. She works on gender, labour relations, and the economy of the poor in the post-plantation, with the case of contemporary Mauritius.

Marta Macedo is a researcher at the Institute of Contemporary History, NOVA School of Social Sciences and Humanities, affiliated with the ERC Project "The Colour of Labour: Racialized Lives of Migrants", Institute of Social Sciences, University of Lisbon. Her current work focuses on the circulation of coffee and cocoa plantation systems (Brazil, São Tomé, Belgium Congo), mixing approaches from the history of science and technology, environmental history and labor studies.

Nicholas B. Miller is an assistant professor of History at Flagler College and Marie Curie individual fellow at the University of Cologne. His current Marie Curie research project adopts a history of knowledge approach to the global history of the plantation. He is also writing a global history of Hawai'i. His publications include *John Millar and the Scottish Enlightenment: Family Life and World History* (Oxford, 2017).

Sophie Sapp Moore is a Mellon Foundation postdoctoral fellow at the Humanities Research Center and the Center for Environmental Studies, Rice University. Moore is a broadly trained political ecologist with a background in critical geography, comparative literature, and postcolonial theory. Her interdisciplinary research examines how intersecting processes of political and socio-ecological transformation shape the agrarian environments of the postcolonial Caribbean.

Mariana Muaze is an associate professor in the History Department at the Federal University of the State of Rio de Janeiro (UNIRIO), with a postdoctorate at University of Michigan, and author of the book "Memórias da Viscondessa: família e poder no Brazil Império" (Zahar, 2008), which won the National Archives Research Award.

Irene Peano obtained her Ph.D. in Social Anthropology from the University of Cambridge. Since 2012, she has been researching the processes of migrant farm-labour and agribusiness organization in contemporary Italy, also with reference to multiple genealogies and particularly to histories of racialization that relate, among others, to earlier plantation economies.

Lorenzo Ravano specializes in the history of black political thought, modern political philosophy, and the history of slavery and abolition. He obtained his Ph.D. from the University of Bologna with a dissertation on black abolitionism, and he is currently based in Paris. He was visiting fellow at the Center for the Study of Slavery and Justice at Brown University and postdoctoral scholar at the Université Paris Nanterre.

Martino Sacchi is currently based in Paris and holds a co-tutored PhD in the history of political thought from the University of Bologna and the Université Paris 1 Panthéon-Sorbonne. His research interests include mobility, identity formation and nineteenth-century labour history in metropolitan France and the Antilles. He held a postdoctoral position at the Université Paris Nanterre (ESNA-Mondes Américains).

Tristan Stubbs is the author of *Masters of Violence: The Plantation Overseers of Eighteenth-Century Virginia, South Carolina, and Georgia*, published by the University of South Carolina press. The book won the Hines prize for the best first book on the history of the Lowcountry. He earned his Ph.D. in History from the University of Cambridge and is currently an affiliate faculty member of the Carolina Lowcountry and Atlantic World Program at the College of Charleston. He previously held appointments with the University of Oxford and the University of Sussex, the Colonial Williamsburg Foundation, the Virginia Historical Society, and the University of South Carolina.

Deborah A. Thomas is a professor of Anthropology in the Department of Anthropology at the University of Pennsylvania. She authored *Political Life in the Wake of the Plantation: Entanglement, Witnessing, Repair* (2020), *Exceptional Violence: Embodied Citizenship in Transnational Jamaica* (2011), and *Modern Blackness: Nationalism, Globalization, and The Politics of Culture in Jamaica* (2004) all for Duke University Press. She co-directed the films *Bad Friday: Rastafari after Coral Gardens* and *Four Days in May.*

List of Figures

List of Tables

CHAPTER 1

Introduction: Viewing Plantations at the Intersection of Political Ecologies and Multiple Space-Times

Irene Peano, Marta Macedo, and Colette Le Petitcorps

As monocultural complexes aimed at the intensive production of cash crops for the global market, plantations have played an indisputably central and persistent role in shaping the economic, socio-political, cultural and ecological setup of the modern world. Their foundational

Present Address:
I. Peano (✉) · M. Macedo · C. Le Petitcorps
Institute of Social Sciences, University of Lisbon, Lisbon, Portugal
e-mail: irene.peano@ics.ulisboa.pt

M. Macedo
e-mail: martamacedo@fcsh.unl.pt; marta.macedo@ics.ulisboa.pt

C. Le Petitcorps
e-mail: lepetit.colette@wanadoo.fr; colette.petitcorps@ics.ulisboa.pt

M. Macedo
Institute of Contemporary History, NOVA School of Social Sciences and Humanities, Lisbon, Portugal

C. Le Petitcorps et al. (eds.), *Global Plantations in the Modern World*, Cambridge Imperial and Post-Colonial Studies,
https://doi.org/10.1007/978-3-031-08537-6_1

character is reflected in (if by no means exhausted by) the plethora of discourses that have invested plantations' workings since the inception of European economic and sovereign expansion across continents. These have addressed a vast range of themes and processes—from land appropriation to production, processing and trade, through labor recruitment and management for profit extraction, taxation and regulation, political conflict and morality, sovereign rule and instruments of control and subversion, and many more—adopting multiple positions and perspectives, with disparate aims. Among such discourses, as far as scholarly engagements are concerned, over the course of the last century (and earlier), a significant number of important critical works have been produced, which it is impossible to summarize in this introduction. However, a few core bodies of literature can be identified, that have shaped our own approach in conceiving of this edited volume.

In broad strokes, we build upon conceptualizations of plantations as race-making institutions, from the publication of pioneering works such as Edgar Thompson's (1932, 1939, 1975), W.E.B. DuBois' (1899, 1911, 1935) and C.L.R. James' (1980 [1966]) onwards, also and especially in relation to political-economic frameworks, that have contextualized the role of plantations in the development of capitalism (Braudel 1992; Williams 1944), the world-system (e.g. Mintz 1960, 1968, 1985; Rubin 1959; Tomich 2004; Wolf 1982; Wallerstein 1974), colonial and post-colonial dependency and underdevelopment (Beckford 1999 [1972]; Best 1968; Rodney 1981; Smith 1967). At the same time, we are attentive to the imbrication of racism in unequal class relations investing also the spheres of gender, sexuality and intimacy (e.g. Casid 2004; Chatterjee 2001; Fox-Genovese 1988; Morgan 2004; Stolcke 1988; Stoler 1985a) and to the role of migration and its governance, its differential exclusions and segregations (e.g. Bastos 2018, 2020; Behal 2012; Moulier-Boutang 2016; Northrup 1995), in relation to the organization of plantations as productive apparatuses. Overall, such approaches have contributed to outline the role of plantations as crucial foci for both the expansion of imperial and post-imperial projects and for opposition to them—from the first slave revolts and flights to contemporary peasant, worker and community struggles.

Drawing on such established fields of critical inquiry, in recent years scholars' attention is increasingly turning to plantations' ecological dimensions, on the one hand, and on the other, to the long-term material, affective, and symbolic imprints they have left on the environments that they contributed so heavily to mold—even after seemingly epochal transformations and in some cases plantations' very demise. These stand out as particularly innovative axes of research, promising to shed light on current predicaments also by querying time-honored historical truths, their making and unmaking. In dialogue with recent scholarship on post-plantation politics and its affective archives (Thomas 2019; cf. her Afterword in this volume), on the afterlives of multiple plantation pasts (Adams 2007; Hartman 2007; McInnis 2016; McKittrick 2011, 2013; Sharpe 2016), and on eco-materialist perspectives (Allewaert 2013; Haraway 2015; Haraway et al. 2016; Haraway and Tsing 2019; Tsing 2015; Li and Semedi 2021), we seek to further articulate a nexus between plantations' more-than-human dimensions and their all-too-human (modern, imperial) dynamics of control, extraction and subversion, all the while exploring their "durabilities" (Stoler 2016). In this sense, our approach builds on reflections recently put forth by other scholars on the need to "methodologically, conceptually, and politically placing political violence and non-human entities side by side" (Navaro et al. 2021: 2), and being attuned to what Navaro and her co-authors call "reverberations" —"the lingering effects (and affects) of violence [...] including its echo, cyclical recurrence, and sporadic reoccurrence in different guises, shapes, and dimensions" (Ibid.: 10).

It is in this vein that we have identified this volume's three main axes to analyze plantations and their workings as those of ecologies, afterlives and sovereignties. While, as mentioned, both eco-materialist approaches and analyses of plantations' durabilities, hauntings and ruinations have been developed by recent scholarly works, the third theme—that of sovereignty—is perhaps the least explored in relation to plantations, despite some promising, early engagements with such nexus (cf. Thompson 1932). If currently the political philosophy underlying Westphalian, modern sovereignty is being questioned not only by reference to a present in which the nation-state appears to be giving way to new, complex and multilayered formations of power, but also by problematizing the very foundations of the modern state, no critical work has approached the theme specifically in relation to plantations. And this notwithstanding the acknowledgment, by such scholarship, of the role private (mercantilist, capitalist and industrial) enterprise played at the height of modernity in pre-figuring and effecting imperial and colonial forms of sovereignty across continents. What better context than that of plantations, among the first (together with mining) extractive projects associated with European expansion across the globe, to analyze the imbrications of political and economic power away from reified, monolithic and preempted conceptions of the modern state? Furthermore, while important work has been produced on the first two themes, very few scholars have addressed the intersections between one and the other, let alone of those two with the theme of sovereignty.

In the following sections, we engage with all authors' contributions to explore such topics through a transdisciplinary and global approach. The broad range of case studies collected here analyzes the techniques that have allowed plantations to function on multiple levels, spanning across spatiotemporal frames from a number of disciplinary perspectives. On the one hand, the very proliferation of plantations across chronologies, geographies and specific political contexts precludes universal categorizations, calling into question any monolithic notion of "the" plantation. On the other hand, common features accrue to the different processes examined in the present book. All chapters speak to the emergence and transformation of modern sovereignties, productivist labor regimes, their attendant subjectivities and environmental dimensions, defining and nuancing the contours of plantations as institutions whose internal relations have pervaded whole societies, spilling over the bounds of individual estates. These case studies thus also broaden the scope beyond the sole instance of agricultural/agro-industrial production, by including the sites and types of labor that have developed in the evolution and restructuring of plantation economies, such as those pertaining to tourism, heritage, or domestic service. At the same time, the excesses, contradictions, resistances and ruinations of mechanisms of extraction and (and by means of) control are made apparent. Through the heterogeneity of plantations, we also consider mutations, failures and deviations, providing an insight into the afterlives, specters and remnants of these systems of production, extraction and authority, also in their subjective and affective dimensions.

The book is organized into four geographical sections—the Caribbean, the Americas, West Africa and its diasporas and finally South and South-East Asia—that highlight the planetary dimension of the plantation system and its expansion through differently paced and timed political-economic and ecological projects, across the modern and post-modern period. Such breadth allows to expand the focus beyond analyses of plantations that very often have dealt with individual empires through human-centered lenses, and with the singular geographies of the slave trade or of indentured labor. This also grants for an in-depth, granular exploration of plantation ecologies, subjectivities and afterlives on the ground. The choice of this broad chronology and planetary outlook on plantations provides for an accurate assessment of how local specificities are enmeshed in transnational and trans-imperial movements, resulting from "frictions" (Tsing 2004) with global processes.

Plantation Ecologies: Environmental Degradation, Segregated Human Relations and Racial Injustice

Plantations were shaped as much by political, economic and social dynamics as by specific ecological assemblages. While sustaining and promoting imperialist projects, capitalist ventures, racialized labor regimes and anti-colonial resistances, plantations were, on a very physical level, agro-ecological systems that altered and were altered by biological processes. As such, several contributors in this volume start from the acknowledgment that plantation environments cannot be seen as mere background scenarios to human action but must be reckoned with as acting forces in their own right (see Bulamah; Moore; Stubbs; Davis; and Chao). Building upon a robust and decades-old literature attentive to environmental transformations, the centrality of individual plant species for plantations' very existence, as well as the importance of soil, air, water, fungi, insects and other animals in all their multiple interactions is considered for its role in configuring the contingent socio-ecological relations established inside and beyond plantations, past and present (Dean 1995; Fiege 2012, Ch. 3; Grove 1997; MacLennan 2014; McCook 2019; Soluri 2006; Uekötter 2014). Thus, plantations are perfect laboratories to bring together environmental and labor dimensions, as explored by inspiring early works in cultural ecology (Steward et al. 1956). Many chapters in this book make it clear that what happened "on the ground" was co-producing modern plantations' social hierarchies and power relations (cf. Bray et al. 2019; Brown and Lubock 2014; Rogers 2010; Stewart 1996; White 1996). As the breadth of collected case studies testifies, the effects of the plantation mode of agricultural production run deep in our present and are global in scope. While many regions bear the imprint of historical plantation experiences, contemporary plantations, that span across the planet, keep reproducing and feeding on imperial matrices of ecological disruption and racial inequality.

Such processes, legacies and durabilities also put the volume's case studies in dialogue with recent discussions on the notion of the Anthropocene. The term, which signals the emergence of a new geological era resulting from human activities, has gained currency in the social sciences, but the undifferentiated notion of the "Anthropos" on which it is founded also spurred criticisms for its erasure of racialized and gendered power dynamics, violence and exclusion (Yusoff 2019) and led to the emergence of a plethora of alternative concepts politicizing this new epochal shift (Bonneuil and Fressoz 2016). In fact, political ecology scholars have long argued that human activity is embedded within larger ecosystems that have had an impact on global processes of wealth accumulation, concentration and inequality, and asymmetrically distributed environmental degradation (Escobar 1999; Hornborg 2007; Robbins 2012; Ross 2017), proposing the concept of Capitalocene to merge world-system theory with earth-system science (Moore 2015, 2016).

Intervening in such geo-historical debates, the identification of our era as Plantationocene (Carney 2021; Haraway 2015; Haraway and Tsing 2019; Haraway et al. 2016; Murphy and Schroering 2020) further shifts the focus, foregrounding the importance of monocultural agro-industrial systems (Besky 2020) for our understanding of ecological devastation and the perpetuation of colonial and imperialist relations, in particular through racialized and coerced labor. Rather than feeding into discussions about a definite periodization of geological epochs, we are interested in how the empirically grounded studies that compose this collection speak to the *analytical* potential of the Plantationocene. Our goal is to examine the multiple socio-ecological interactions within which plantations are enmeshed, and identify their effects. The fine-grained approaches from post-humanist and critical race perspectives developed in this book bring to the fore the violence against humans and non-humans, the unequal power relations intrinsic to the plantation system and the possibilities for its subversion, allowing us to imagine more elaborate ways of narrating plantation regimes, and to move beyond overly simplistic binaries between exploitation and resistance.

The recurrent uprooting, selection and transplanting of different life-forms from specific ecologies was foundational to modern plantation projects (Dusinberre and Iijima 2019; Haraway et al. 2016; Tsing 2015). In the process of putting cultivators and cultivars to work, the planters and managers who engineered the ordering and disciplining of these "naturecultural" worlds also sustained specific beliefs about the superiority of plantation-style production and, attached to that, about "nature's" ideal keepers. Plantation-making was instrumental in the development of racialized discourses about local populations that did not conform to specific notions of productivity and profitability, with important political consequences: supposedly "lazy" agriculturalists, employing "backward" agricultural methods, should not be granted access to land (Li 2014), just as pastoralists and hunter-gatherers. Thus, plantation-making almost always involved the exclusion of local peoples, the destruction of their livelihoods, the denigration of their intimate and embodied knowledges, and ultimately the ruination of the very ecologies that nurtured those communities.

If making plantations demanded plans, ideal schemes, prototypes to be built based on technical expertise and hierarchical control, many case studies confirm that plantations seldom functioned according to these predefined designs. If laborers—whether enslaved, indentured or waged, in various combinations—never fully conformed to planters' disciplinary prescriptions (and in fact it was insubordination or its threat that made the constant elaboration and refining of such prescriptions necessary in the first place), local environmental conditions also challenged scientific, "rational" projects. Furthermore, when the imagined plantation was physically realized, unforeseen consequences may ensue. Plantations have always been vulnerable to forces generated from within as much as from without, and disturbances happened far more often than acknowledged (Tsing 2004).

In fact, the standardization, simplification and scaling-up processes that characterize these agricultural systems, seeking to convert plants into marketable crops and humans into labor power, occlude the transformative capacities of the other life-forms that obstinately continue to exist within plantations. Not denying the ways in which plantations have caused biodiversity loss, Chao's contribution in this volume points to the necessity of complicating our understanding of plantations' metabolisms, acknowledging the role of non-humans in countering extractive aims that stretch across unprecedented scales. This case study eloquently illustrates how monocrop regimes, while contributing to eliminate some organisms, created possibilities for the proliferation of others. Bringing to the fore fungi feasting on palm trees, fungi that established symbiotic relations with those trees, and salvific plants turned into invasives, together with the perspectives of indigenous communities working for/fighting against the oil palm sector in West Papua, Chao casts light on the interdependent if unstable relations across species that are formed in those ecologies. Besides, discussing the parallel dimensions of conflict and collaboration constitutive of this plantation experience, this chapter highlights an aspect that the study of plantations has frequently ignored, namely the constant need for maintenance. Plantations' disciplining (and policing the boundaries of) humans and "nature" has always been as much about repair and improvisation as about planning and control.

By calling attention to environmental disruptions, we can also better understand how non-human forms have impacted on the very structure and character of labor (e.g. affecting tasks and seasonal rhythms) and how the transformation of the relations between humans and other life-forms has shaped the tense social dynamics constitutive of plantation worlds. Modern agricultural regimes for the cultivation of rice, tobacco, indigo and cotton in eighteenth-century North American plantations, discussed by Stubbs, and the struggles for their implementation, provide a fertile terrain to study the open conflicts between working people (be they enslaved men and women, overseers or managers) and the planters. Planters' demands to bring Europe's "new agricultural" science to the colonies of Virginia, South Carolina and Georgia, together with their expectations regarding both the yield and quality of new crops, clashed with overseers' real or presumed competences and skills. While adaptation to specific environmental conditions and the violent disciplining of bondspeople were routinely asked of overseers, absentee landowners were disappointed when events fell outside the script. Planters' concerns over their reputation and financial returns resulted in the vilification of overseers. This chapter opens an important discussion on how scientific agricultural projects affect plantation-labor relations and hierarchies, that cut across class and racial lines.

Thus, plantation-making has always also been a matter of contention between alternative world views and agendas (cf. also Miller, this volume). But despite the violent and unequal power relations spun within and through plantations, projects for taming "the wild" and building strict social hierarchies always left "room to maneuver" for alternative livelihoods (Trouillot 2002b). Even if the plantation mode of production plays a central role in all chapters, it is important not to lose sight of how these specific socio-environmental regimes have had to negotiate their existence in relation to other communities and life-forms. Over the centuries, assemblages of humans and non-humans opened up possibilities for the subversion of plantation discipline. Bulamah's contribution explores an array of geographies in the early modern and modern Caribbean that run counter or parallel to plantation apparatuses. These geographies—inhabited by enslaved men and women, pirates, smugglers, maroons and their "companion species"—functioned as spaces of subsistence, autonomy, healing or struggle. Bulamah explores in detail the human-pig entanglements made possible inside provision grounds and in the landscapes surrounding plantations. Such crafted and nurtured environments that subaltern peoples created along with their animals helped mitigate or evade subordination in plantation spaces. Moore's chapter also highlights how the imperial and colonial imaginaries imposed onto the land and its inhabitants collide with those of local communities. It discusses precisely the (too often neglected) conflictual relation between peasant and plantation modes of production. Focused on Haïti's Central plateau during US occupation, this case study examines the efforts of both scientists and the military to transform the landscape into cotton plantations, and the struggle of Afro-Caribbean communities to defend their livelihoods. The environmental characteristics of the Central Plateau and the biological properties of the cotton plant are essential to Moore's story. The physiological features of cotton varieties and the physical qualities of this borderland, together with imperial authorities' changing perception of them, make the various elements necessary to bring a plantation into existence visible. This chapter is also a good reminder that plantations recurrently failed. In Haïti, even under the oppression of US imperialism, other forms of cultivation prevailed over cotton monocrops. However, regardless of plantations' actual workings, the racialized representations of the peasant guerrilla ("cacos") as wild, wasteful and primitive still linger in public memory, making the enduring ideological power of plantation imaginaries evident.

Yet, the plantation stories addressed in this book show that inequalities were and are more than a matter of perception: they have been inscribed on the actual bodies of workers. Labor tasks have been learned and performed by men and women involved in shaping new habitats where crops could grow. As those workers have transformed the environment, conversely, the environment has acted upon them. In his contribution, Davies places the bodies of contemporary Sierra Leonean plantation workers at the center of his narrative. By stressing the relationship between them and the spaces they inhabit, he shows how the very process of generating sugar and profit has also produced contamination and death. Pesticides with noxious effects on land and water penetrated the porous boundaries of human flesh, revealing the embodied and environmental dimensions of subordination and toxicity produced by this plantation experiment. While attempting to recover the life stories of people whom narratives of global development and international aid have forgotten, this chapter also opens up new avenues to investigate the ways in which laborers frame their identities not only in relation to kin and other relations, to land or work, but also to toxic matter and other environmental components. The nexus established between chemicals and illness also encourages a reflection on the value attributed to specific subjects and the racial contours of such metrics. The cheapness of plantation labor has multiple meanings: besides being poorly paid, it is fungible and, according to differential perceptions of physical well-being, disposable. This case study feeds into an important discussion on the role of plantations as systems of labor-power commoditization, producing and reproducing specific bodies and human groups along racial lines, in relation to the too often overlooked subjectivities of working people (Holmes 2013; Nash 2017; cf. also Miller, this volume).

The Afterlives of the Plantation: Old and New Insights

While some studies address the present of plantations' productive activities across different epochs, others focus on their afterlives. They investigate the future of the plantation system after the dismantling or transformation of its productive apparatus, that in many cases left economic and environmental ruination in its wake. The authors of this book's chapters address the afterlives of plantations from different angles, following previous scholarship on plantation futures. If the present legacy of plantation societies was a classic theme in Caribbean dependency theories (Beckford 1999 [1972]), contemporary scholars have built and expanded on those insights to analyze the ways in which "the plantation" has spun multiple futures across a range of (black) geographies, seeking also to envisage decolonial horizons (McKittrick 2011).

The durability and extensibility of plantations, as the central locus of antiblack violence and death, have been tracked most especially in the contemporary United States' prison archipelago and segregated urban areas (Davis 2003; Wacquant 2002). But the notion of "afterlives", famously adopted by Saidya Hartman in connection with (plantation) slavery to denote "skewed life chances, limited access to health and education, premature death, incarceration, and impoverishment" (2007: 6), has been productively stretched to encompass also psychic, affective and imaginary dimensions, often in connection with notions of spectrality and haunting (Adams 2007; Clukey and Wells 2016; Gilroy 1993; McPherson 2003)—that however remain mostly tethered to American (or at best Atlantic) geographies. References to the afterlives of various aspects of plantation management, relating for the most part to labor organization and discipline, have also been made across different contexts (e.g. Mintz 1985; Rosenthal 2018; Sherman 2021; Weiss 2011 - cf. the next section), but demand further exploration.

In original ways, the chapters collected in this volume examine the afterlives of plantations beyond the spatiotemporal and political-economic frames in which these durabilities are normally expected. Authors carefully analyze the restructuring of plantations in their labor-extractive and lethal aspects by means of policies whose driving ideology was in some cases anti-imperialist and alternative to capitalism: the establishment of citrus plantations in 1960s socialist Cuba (Aureille) and of Chinese-owned sugar plantations in 1970s Sierra Leone (Davies), Revolutionary Haïti's reorganizing sugar plantations by 1805, after the war of independence (Ravano and Sacchi) or the shift from Chinese-owned plantations in the nineteenth-century's native kingdom of Hawai'i to the twentieth-century white nativist rule with its attendant solidification of racial categories (Miller). The recursive use of past techniques for disciplining land and labor in order to exploit ever new territories for monocrop cultivation is evident in Moore's chapter on the United States' occupation of Haïti's hinterland for cotton production in the 1910s to 1930s. A productivist rationale can be seen to cut across plantations that otherwise resulted from opposed ideologies, from the colonial to the "native" or the anti-colonial, in some cases with similar effects on workers' conditions. The case studies gathered in this book thus highlight more complex global geographies and temporalities inherent to plantation systems than the one shaped by the transatlantic slave trade and its morphings into indenture alone.

Besides expanding the reach of such processes to planetary scales and longer histories, we seek to bring together plantations' devastating social and ecological legacies within a single framework. From this perspective, plantations are analyzed as a shared symbolic-affective reference and a haunting past that permeate present eco-material and social relations, subjects' and communities' imaginaries of the future—be it in expectations about plantations' rebirth after their material ruinations (Aureille, Davies), in nostalgias about plantations' brutally hierarchical power structures, and in disavowals of some of their localized genealogies (Peano), or rather in the constant flight from plantation-derived violence (Bulamah, Moore). As noticed by Mintz and Wolf (1957), the durability of plantation systems does not merely rest on the coercion employed to set up such enterprises, but rather on the establishment of indirect constraints that bind people to plantation labor and order. The moral economy that developed between planters and laborers in order for the latter to secure a minimum of subsistence explains the long duration of relations of dependence into the present, still expressed in racial terms. Thomas (2019) also identified a political-affective continuity between the imperialist governance of Jamaican plantations and the formation of the nation-state as a post-plantation society in the mid-twentieth century. She highlighted how contemporary social relations based on absolute loyalty to a powerful local figure—what she calls "garrison politics"—are grounded in the system of political authority first developed in sugar estates. Relations of dependence between planters and their laborers, sustained by a moral tie that indefinitely indebts the laborers to their master, are the main mechanisms reproducing the plantation system long after the abolition of slavery, and even after the cessation of monocrop cultivation. The estate hierarchy survives in post-plantation subjectivities, being a major blueprint of socialization into work for generations and up to the present. Ravano and Sacchi's chapter echoes these perspectives, demonstrating how after the insurrection of enslaved Africans, the Haïtian nation was built on the policing of former slaves' activities, mobility and access to citizenship by conditioning this latter to bonded labor in sugar plantations.

At the same time, the afterlives of plantations index the perpetual strife to make life out of spaces of death and violence. Wynter (2003) identified a constitutive tension between the dominant logic of plantations as a sovereign-making project and the internal threat to such project caused by enslaved people who maintained a conception of themselves as human subjects rather than as objectified property. This conflict pervades the post-plantation present. Analyses of these mechanisms have focused on the reproduction of slave institutions built on the edges of the plantation (Trouillot 2002a) in order to ensure everyday survival, exploring collective memories of life-making away from plantations, through provision grounds and solidarity networks that are remembered and remade also through embodied and material dynamics, in the ways in which former plantation laborers and their descendants inhabit space (Chivallon 2012). Alternatives to plantation life have often lain in the creation of an agriculture-based socio-economic system that would ensure one's own family and community subsistence. Plantations were thus also central in the emergence of oppositional and peculiar social groups, such as small black peasantries (Ibid.), which are still an important component of many contemporary societies—across the Caribbean, in the United States and in Brazil for example—playing a role in slowing down or undoing the further expansion of plantations.

Once again, the exploration of these processes reveals the extent to which plantations are precarious productive systems, far less stable than what many contemporary representations would make us believe. Furthermore, the sense of community inherited from plantation experiences and their culture-making dynamics directly unsettles the socio-political organization promoted by contemporary nation-states (Thomas 2019). These dimensions are evidence to the long-lasting legacies of the fundamentally strained relations between plantation infrastructures and communities, and of the unexpected institutions developed on their margins. It bears repeating that the unpredictability of making life out of plantations is an essential feature of social, cultural and economic systems that have developed everywhere in the margins of global plantation geographies. Plantations can be defined as hyper-exploitative systems because they ensure only the immediate, bare reproduction of their labor force, without providing for the social reproduction of laborers in the long term (Meillassoux 2018). In this context, the structuration of an Afro-American culture has been seen by Mintz and Price as "a miracle" (Mintz and Price 1992).

Everywhere in plantation systems, new social groupings have been created out of the interpersonal relations between laborers of different origins, in order to organize everyday survival and to create a modicum of space for human life. Bulamah demonstrates in his chapter how the Haïtian revolution was the direct result of enslaved people's provision grounds. In organizing daily survival, the household economy created in the margins of plantations by the unexpected association between slaves, free black persons and animals (pigs) is the main institution that made the Revolution possible according to the author. He makes use of the concept of the counter-plantation, drawn from Haïtian sociologist Jean Casimir (2008), to highlight how much the invention of a creole culture through these encounters was the expression of the opposition to the dominant culture of occupiers and plantation entrepreneurs.

If creolization processes have challenged labor and productive organization in all plantation systems, according to Casimir (ibid.), Haïtian creolity is peculiar in its structural ungovernability. The full institutionalization of an autonomous life among slaves of different origins, who organized their own social reproduction during the eighteenth century (i.e. before the fixation of racial categories by the colonial state), undermined colonial and later national attempts to create and control a unified social formation. In this view, we can interpret the militarized labor regime imposed by the newborn Haïtian nation-state, described by Ravano and Sacchi, as a panic-driven response to what was perceived as an ungovernable country. The invention of a peasant economy and society, as an afterlife of provision grounds, appears foundational in Haïtian history if we connect these studies to Moore's chapter. As we already mentioned, the author shows that the peasants of the hinterland opposed the US project to establish cotton plantations during the 1910s and up to the 1930s, and finally determined its failure and abandonment. The household economy and other strategies of survival, always readapted by plantation laborers according to the socio-economic conjunctures of plantation systems, are one of the main foci of those analyses that deal with plantation afterlives.

Reflections on "afterlives" thus question the kind of subject formation deriving from past experiences of plantation norms and values and the horizons of expectation they still entail in the present. Some chapters in this book highlight the ways in which laborers regard plantations as a "promise of development", providing welfare and social mobility (Aureille, Davies, Chao), or on the contrary as a place from which to escape (Bulamah, Moore, Chao, Peano, Miller). Yet, despite apparently antagonistic ways of internalizing the plantation system, its pasts and futurities, it remains a common symbolic and affective reference for social action in the present: even when plantations are the space that everybody runs from, nobody stops talking about them, as Toni Morrison observed (quoted in McKittrick 2013: 10). Drawing on these insights, but also opening new horizons for thinking plantation futures, the chapters in this book address the continuities of plantation infrastructures and of subjects' internalization of their set of norms through time (Ravano,

Sacchi in Haïti, Aureille in Cuba, Davies in Sierra Leone, Behal in India); the "counter-plantation" events that keep threatening plantation projects and can cause their ruination (Bulamah and Moore in Haïti, Chao in West Papua); and the complex spatiotemporal overlaps of relations of domination with social encounters that challenge our contemporary imaginaries on the fixity of plantation systems (Abrampah in Ghana, Peano in Italy, Miller in Hawai'i).

In his study of the Chinese sugar plantation at Magbass, in Sierra Leone, Davies shows that despite its managers' discourses promoting rural development, the plantation enterprise concretely created long-term precarity for its workers. The sugar plantation is chronically set for abandonment as a result of economic and political conjunctures (especially the civil war that raged between 1991 and 2002), leaving workers jobless in a wasted land. This intervention by a foreign economic actor, ostensibly in favor of the putative "rural poor" in Africa, had long-term consequences that are typical of plantation economies, what Beckford (1999) identified as persistent underdevelopment and poverty. In his perspective, the socio-economic future of plantation laborers is both blocked by the ongoing grip of export-oriented production in plantation zones and by recurring land dispossession. This last aspect is also present in Ravano and Sacchi's chapter on independent Haïti. The transition from slavery to a free labor regime was artificially set "by both limiting access to subsistence farming and by subduing freedom to labor subordination". In the same vein, the persistence—until the 1970s in most Caribbean and Indian-Ocean plantation societies, and even until today in Indian tea plantations (see the interview with Rana Behal)—of a system of remuneration based on subsistence wages, supplemented in kind, has both induced the reproduction of relations of dependence at work and the normalization of subsistence wages.

Thus, plantation afterlives display structural, economic and political as well as symbolic, material and affective dimensions. Ravano and Sacchi's chapter particularly highlights the formation of Haïtian nationhood after the war of independence, in parallel with an emerging conception of citizenship that was conditional upon work on plantations or upon army service. Work and discipline, conceived according to the old norms of colonial plantations, are necessary also to access modern citizenship. Independence, freedom and waged labor in Haïti appear then less opposed to than in continuity with slavery, plantations and the colonial regime. This important point on the direct relation of modern citizenship to plantation infrastructure, echoing other works like Thomas' (2019) on Jamaica or Williams' (1991) on Guyana, speaks of the normalization of mechanisms first introduced by plantation systems (McKittrick 2013). This aspect is particularly developed in Aureille's study. The author describes the ways in which peasants were groomed to a socialist way of life via the creation by the Cuban State of villages and agricultural communities within citrus plantations. Plantations, here as everywhere, represented an institution that governed not only production, but more broadly social life and the economy. Although citrus plantations were later dismissed and a transition to agroecology and re-peasantization was promoted in their place, former workers still framed their expectations of social mobility, recognition and protection according to the set of norms and values ordering social relations in plantations. This case study illustrates an important aspect of plantation histories: the transition from plantation systems to new political, economic and social structures is not the straightforward result of a plan. Conceptions of social justice and political legitimacy based on workers' experience of the plantation can, and often do, conflict with the imposition of a new economic order and set of norms, but they might also foster such changes actively. As Garcia (1986) showed in relation to North Eastern Brazil's historical district of sugar plantations, for example, the transition from planters' traditional domination to the introduction of labor laws and a free labor market in the 1980s was not spontaneous nor fully ordered, but the product of social tensions in which workers' conceptions of political legitimacy played an important part.

Finally, this book provides new reflections that go off the beaten track, problematizing the binary approach that pits plantation durabilities against counter-plantation dynamics. Abrampah's archaeological study of Danish plantation ruins in Ghana and Peano's analysis of the contemporary discourse on "modern slavery" applied to migrant farm labor in Italy both uncover more complex heritages of domination and social encounters on "plantation-looking landscapes" than what our contemporary imaginaries on plantations and slavery may typically foreground. In the archaeological excavation of the eighteenth-century Danish plantation house at Frederikssted, Abrampah and his collaborators found many more vestiges of local elites' settlement of the main building after its abandonment by Danish colonizers than of the latter's very short-lived occupation of the area for cotton and maize cultivation. Abrampah's archaeological findings speak both of the colonial occupation and of its aftermaths, in the adoption by African elites of various types of European material implements in their everyday life. Peano's chapter also unveils the "heterogeneous layers" of heritage (Foucault 1977: 82) behind the contemporary association between slavery and black migrant bodies in media, politicians', NGOs' and activists' discourses in Italy, but also in legal and corporate dispositifs. The author shows for example how the justification of Ethiopia's invasion with the moral necessity to abolish Abyssinian slavery by Mussolini's fascist government, and the latter's elaboration of racial theories via the rediscovery of Medieval slavery in Italy, are far more influential on contemporary conceptions of "modern slavery" and race than a "plantation elsewhere" might be. At the same time, canonical counter-plantation experiences and their legacies (most notably Rastafarian culture and its West African re-elaborations) may inform contemporary migrant farm workers' languages of resistance and refusal.

These works remind us, through the genealogy of power and social encounters they carefully trace, of the "hazardous play of dominations" (Foucault 1977: 83) that emerge, overlap, conflict and disperse, in fluid rather than fixed spaces. In this respect, according to Peano, instead of really explaining contemporary mechanisms of labor exploitation, plantation narratives and discourses on modern slavery tethered solely to the "New World" as the primal scene of exploitation tend to reproduce race-making operations, by representing migrant farm laborers as the "others", locked in black bodies without any acknowledged subjectivity. Following contributors' insights, the "afterlives of plantations" therefore also define a contemporary imaginary of race and race fixity (such as that which prevails in Hawai'i and its histories, as Miller argues), that has been the product of a long-term process of ideological elaboration, far beyond slave times.

Plantations as Sovereign Machines: Subject Formation, Relations of Patronage and the Intimacies of Power

Plantations have been viewed as displaying sovereign-like features of control and violence monopoly over land and subjects, through force as much as ideology, across a wide range of contexts and epochs. Yet, if the sovereign-making powers of plantation systems have long been flagged in the literature, they have hardly been analyzed—witness the plethora of references to "plantocracies", broadly if vaguely defined as polities reflecting "the will of the planter class" (Craton 1984: 190; cf. e.g. Breman 1989: 184–193, *passim*; Burnard and Garrigum 2018: Ch. 7; Mbembe 2013: 32, 36; Trouillot 1982; Williams 1970) and sometimes re-christened "saccharocracies" in the Cuban and wider Caribbean context (Fraginals 1964; Sandiford 2000; cf. MacLennan 2014 on "sovereign sugar" in Hawai'i). The indeterminacy and casualness with which such labels are employed in the literature is perhaps a reflection of the fact that "plantocracy" was an (often ironic and even scathing) emic category that seems to have taken hold starting from as early as the seventeenth century. It may have been employed by planters themselves, but above all it was a term wielded by their contemporary critics—among whom colonial officers and other imperial cadres figured prominently, predictably regarding the planter class's ambitions to achieve political independence from the metropole with hostility. The concept of the plantocracy has thus been largely taken for granted, but widely employed—making plantations into the unexplored index of an institution (or indeed a set of institutions).

A noteworthy, if still cursory, definition of the plantocracy can be found in Cedric Robinson's (1983) discussion of W.E.B. DuBois' *Black Reconstruction*. There, Robinson picks up on the inadequacy of Marxian thought in postulating the necessity of a bourgeois revolution to shape working-class consciousness, when such principle is applied to analyze the drivers of the North American Civil War: in such context, enslaved people had forged their own consciousness independently of the rise of the bourgeoisie and its liberal ideology (a process we referred to earlier in relation to plantation afterlives, that developed across the Americas).

> The dominant ideology of the society was that of the plantocracy, a dictatorship of labor and land with no democratic pretensions. But of more significance, the ideology of the plantocracy had not been the ideology of the slaves. The slaves had produced their own culture and their own consciousness by adapting the forms of the non-Black society to the conceptualizations derived from their own historical roots and social conditions. (Ibid.: 238)

Here, plantations are seen to create both ideological and wider operational, material dimensions of political power in the form of boundless (at least in the intention of planters and certainly in the legal underpinnings of plantations) control over land and labor. Crucially, their sovereign effects (and failure thereof) are also employed to question overly deterministic, Euro-centric, liberal and teleological views of history and politics, something we wish to pick up on here.

The most notable exception to the lack of analytical scrutiny on the links between plantations and sovereign features of power, however, remains E.T. Thompson, who famously described the plantation as "a settlement institution" (1959: 44; cf. 1932, Ch 1), *political* in character.

> [T]he central fact about the plantation is the acquisition and exercise of authority on the part of the planter in the interest of agricultural production. The plantation is a political institution; like the state it secures collective action on the basis of authority. The plantation system represents an extension of political control into the larger society whose institutions cooperate to maintain it. On the particular plantation authority is immediate and control is expressed in concrete acts of command and obedience. In the plantation system authority and control become diffuse and abstract. It becomes diffuse and abstract as the plantation extends its interests and influence beyond the concrete relations characterizing the local group into the institutions of the larger society, and the greater the span of extension the more abstract they become. [...] what is far more important [...] for the planter and his fellows is to gain control of the state. (ibid.: 55)

Further possible analytical connections between plantations and the sovereign sphere may be detected (still in wholly implicit form) in other classical works, such as Raymond Smith's (1967) definition of plantations as "total social institutions", following Goffmann and with specific reference to the Guyanese case. Similarly, a few years before Smith, Stanley Elkins (1959) had compared North American plantations to Nazi concentration camps. Yet, unlike the case of asylums analyzed by Goffmann, and unlike German *lagers*, American slave plantations were not, at least at first, the emanation of a sovereign power, or at any rate not in the same way as twentieth-century asylums or camps.

Indeed, rather than engaging in anachronistic analogies, it may be rather more productive and historically accurate to trace the genealogy of contemporary sovereign institutions of terror, discipline and segregation starting from early modern plantation systems—just as genealogies of labor management and the broader organization of production, among others, have been traced (or suggested) linking different features of plantations to later economic enterprises, such as factories (Mintz 1985; Rosenthal 2018) or diamond mines (Sherman 2021; Weiss 2011). Similarly, recent analyses have explored the long history of capital's formation and expansion across the globe through chartered companies, free ports, dependencies, trusteeships—understood as "quasi-sovereign" forms (Benton 2010; Easterling 2014; Mezzadra and Neilson 2019; Stern 2011; Stoler 2016). One could add plantations to such list.

As noted in the previous section, plantation-based genealogies of contemporary institutions have been developed with particular depth in relation to the North American context, and more specifically to the US carceral and criminalizing system (via Jim Crow, lynching, policing and ghettoization) as plantations' poisonous heritage (Davis 2003; McKittrick 2013; Wacquant 2002). In relation to Jamaica, Thomas (2019) also explored the ways in which postcolonial sovereignty (and political life more generally) has been affectively inflected by the plantation system and its disavowed archives of violence. We have addressed the genealogical dimension in more detail in relation to the theme of plantation afterlives. Here, we wish to reflect on the multifarious and context-specific ways—including but not limited to genealogy—in which plantation systems may be related to sovereign operations.

In the cases discussed by the volume's contributors, in fact, the relationships and arrangements obtaining in the space of the plantation may be analogous to, mirrors or pre-figurations of, or substitutes for the power and grip of the modern state as the locus of legitimate sovereignty. In Aureille's study, the forgone socialist plantation in Cuba represents, in the imaginaries of those living in its ruins today, an affectively charged index of state sovereignty, a metonymy of its ascending and descending parables with respect to socialist rule's perceived buoyancy, viability and effectiveness. In some ways, the chapter raises issues similar to those emerging from Stubbs's and Muaze's, centered on earlier epochs and different contexts on the American continent. In their analyses, the paternalistic and violent relations obtaining in the heyday of different plantations (in the United States and Brazil, pre- and post-independence respectively) appear as the building block and the mirror of national-imperial sovereignties. More specifically, in the eighteenth-century context examined by Stubbs, the founding fathers of the nascent liberal democracy were at the same time prominent planters, whose perceived ruling capacities were refracted across private and public domains. Planters' preoccupations with their reputation, as a mirror of their overseers' alleged skills and moral virtue, can thus be read as a metonymy or index of their alleged qualities as state leaders. Across public and private management, paternalism in this context appears as a core feature of statehood and of wider power dynamics (cf. Thomas 2019). Similarly, and in an even more univocal relation, in the nineteenth century plantations were the foundation of the newly independent Brazilian empire. As Muaze shows, the ruling planter class invested heavily in the cultivation of hierarchical and paternalistic distinction as a marker of its claim to power. All three cases push us to question the necessity of linkages between (and the content of) bourgeois institutions and ideologies, modern sovereignty and class consciousness in relation to plantation economies. Whether through socialism or in the upholding of slave-based production systems, modern sovereignty built through the plantation is seen to exceed the limits of liberal bourgeois citizenship and subjectivity, problematizing any uniform progressions and historical linearities.

Analyses of plantocratic regimes also question other grounding assumptions of theories of sovereignty. If the institution of private property is foundational not only to modern sovereignty but also to self-sovereignty, where the latter epitomizes the possessive individual of the liberal sort and is often the precondition to accessing citizenship and its constellation of entitlements, the extent to which plantocratic regimes made sovereignty distinct from property may be up for discussion. Should the distinction between sovereignty and property remain a necessary, definitional feature of modern political organization, as political philosophers argue (cf. Blaufarb 2016; Tomba 2019), where would this leave nineteenth-century plantocracies such as the antebellum United States or the Brazilian empire? Could they be simply relegated to pre- or early modern anachronisms? Or could the contiguities between one and the other be ascribed to something akin to, but more complex than, Marx and Engels' classic definition of the modern state as "a committee for managing the common affairs of the whole bourgeoisie"?

At the same time, if in practice plantocratic sovereignty may be akin to a form of (colonial) property, ideas of the sovereign individual as the double (and the keystone) of the sovereign polity/plantation are closely associated with the emergence of a sharp distinction between a private and a public sphere, where the former was as tightly codified as the latter, as Muaze describes for nineteenth-century Brazil (cf. Lowe 2015; Stoler 1995). This was in turn mapped upon distinctions between lesser and higher legal personhood, along the lines of gender and class as well as of race, which constituted the ground for free or enslaved status. In early nineteenth-century Haïti, property represented the precondition for the birth of modern citizenship, together with labor (and hence the alienation of one's powers, again the outcome of a possessive individualist conception of the subject), as both Bulamah and Ravano and Sacchi highlight in their respective chapters. Indeed, the very notion of freedom in post-revolutionary Haïti was founded on the twin discourses of labor and property. Similarly, in the case of Hawai'i discussed by Miller, the mid-nineteenth-century institution of fee-title property and contract labor, facilitated by the concomitant establishment of common-law courts (later administered by the planter elite), paved the way to the establishment of sugar plantations on the archipelago, and hence to its progressive loss of autonomous sovereignty, in a reverse process from those of the independent Caribbean islands. By contrast to Haïtian ideals of freedom, however, in the Cuban case analyzed by Aureille individual, property-based subjectivity applies to those who resisted the socialist project of expropriation in the 1960s, and thus to marginalized subjects. Yet, an act of property expropriation asserted socialist state sovereignty as much as founding the post-revolutionary Haïtian state-building process described by Ravano and Sacchi. Finally, in the late twentieth-century Sierra Leonean context discussed by Davies, while notions of hard work and self-making do appear, it is less self-property than one of its corollaries, namely self-exertion, that signals the mastery of individual and collective destinies, in line with the neoliberal ethos and the concomitant erosion of modern citizenship (an evanescent ideal to start with).

In Sierra Leone, furthermore, the presence of a Chinese-run sugar-making facility was violently questioned by civil-war rebels in a controversial bid to protect national and peasant interests. After the end of the conflict, a perceived failure of sovereignty led to the encouragement of foreign investments, and to new arrangements in which Chinese state capitalism gave way to a straightforwardly corporate model that took advantage of tax exemptions and gained sovereign control of the plantation and factory premises—signaling Sierra Leone's nominally willful, though possibly obligated, sovereign retreat. Relations of dependency at inter-state level resonate across epochs and point to the imbrication of subjectivity and sovereignty, where one constitutes the ground for the other and vice versa. Just as subjects and other, non-human life-forms are hierarchically dependent on one another, so are putatively sovereign states. These recursive relations of dependency are grounded in plantations as either the original locus in which they were first experienced, refined and institutionalized, or as the site where they are re-elaborated, re-enacted, re-activated.

Finally, and in relation to hierarchies and subjugation, plantations can act as the discursive counterpoint for assertions of sovereignty *cum* racialized domination, as in the case described by Peano. In Italy, appeals against "slavery", associated to the transatlantic trade, have served present as well as past sovereign (and sovereign-*ist*) manifestations with more or less explicit racist, colonial/anti-immigration purposes, while a supposedly "milder" system of enslavement has been used to differentiate a country seeking to style itself as more "civilized" than its trans-Atlantic and European imperial counterparts. Indeed, the control of movement, foundational to modern sovereign claims, has in the plantation one of its original experimental grounds: not only did the demand for plantation labor in the wake of slavery abolition in the British colonies (1834) occasion the birth of the indenture system as the origin of sovereign control on mobility, pointing to the colonial genealogy of the modern state (Mongia 2018; cf. Miller, this volume). The regulation of slaves' mobility also represented a laboratory for the generalization of migration regulation in subsequent epochs (Browne 2015; O'Connell Davidson 2015; Parenti 2003), when it has invested freed slaves' and so-called "new slaves'"—and more generally racialized and criminalized subjects' (cf. Peano, Ravano and Sacchi).

In all cases, plantations appear as a sovereign-making machine, a workshop in (or against) which tools of both domination and resistance are forged, through the making of subjects and the shaping of their capacities, intimacies and relations. Of course, sovereign (and proprietory) claims in all these contexts were far from smooth, conflict-free affairs, not only on account of overt resistance by the oppressed, but also as a result of partly diverging interests within dominant groups (as the employment of the very notion of "plantocracy" to which we referred earlier testifies; cf. Stoler 1985b).

In the present moment, state sovereignty is often perceived to be undergoing a terminal process of ruination, which however leads to renewed—and in some cases even fortified—forms of control and governance (Brown 2010; cf. Mezzadra and Neilson 2013 on the concept of a "sovereign machine of governmentality", which of course draws and expands on Foucault's seminal work on the subject). Sovereignties, inside and outside old and new plantation forms, are not fading so much as transforming within and beyond the nation-state framework, through their failures, as it were. The decline of modern state sovereignty has also been read as the potentially transformative withering away of hegemonic political forms, that had their foundations in plantation slavery, colonialism and racism (Thomas 2018). Yet, the nostalgia that accompanies the ruination of plantations and their sovereign frameworks, which some chapters clearly point to (Davies, Aureille), is an indication that life in the ruins of plantations and of nation-building may indeed feel harder and less hopeful.

The temporalities of this process are also problematic, for the nation-state has been depending all along on more-than-national sovereign entanglements, as many of the chapters clearly illustrate. In the Cuban as much as in the Sierra Leonean and Haïtian cases, export-oriented production has bound these polities to the world market and to several foreign interferences since the inception (cf. Ravano and Sacchi; Moore; Aureille; Davies)—if from the diametrically opposed ideological premises of socialist internationalism, that crucially supported the developmental project in Cuba, or of the discourse of fraternity and mutualism that accompanied Chinese investment in West African countries as in many others (and whose current retreat does not necessarily lead to a strengthening of national sovereignty), on the one hand, as opposed to the naked for-profit trade of capitalist markets (that may however at times be bound to discourses on "development") on the other hand. Hence, a question arises about these emerging forms of sovereignty in the ruins of plantations: what directions are sovereign forms of power and control taking, and how do they speak to the past? How can we understand current transformations in the light of historical plantations as sovereign sites, which therefore both constituted the ground for and exceeded the nation-state framework? As mentioned, the graduated sovereignties and lateral citizenships of neoliberal exceptionalism (Ong 2006) may be seen to traverse the political history of the capitalist world-system from the inception, with plantations as one of their original sites of development. Indeed, plantations and other economic enterprises that displayed proto- or quasi-sovereign prerogatives were in many cases the building blocks of imperial projects (Cf. Behal, Miller, Moore, Muaze, Stubbs in this volume), where the latter intersected in complex ways with other, pre-existing kinds of assemblages of sovereignty, ownership and personhood (Bulamah; Miller; cf. Allewaert 2013; Chatterjee 2001; Hansen 2021). In this sense, a deepened understanding of plantations' sovereign qualities can contribute in crucial ways to the problematization of liberal, modernist and Eurocentric conceptions of (Westphalian) sovereignty, its ideological grip and genealogies.

All chapters addressing the theme of sovereignty in relation to the plantation point on the one hand to the productive and subject-making aspect of such forms of power (tied for example to the notions of modernity and development, and in the Cuban case also to the construction of "the new man" and the skilled worker). On the other hand, of course, they refer to the multiple exclusions and erasures sovereignty is founded upon: in Aureille's, Davis', Bulamah's, Miller's, Peano's and Chao's chapters, we learn about forced displacements, the eradication of biodiversity, the debilitation and exposure of multiple life forms to various kinds of hazards and the hyper-exploitative conditions of workers in old and new agrocapitalist ventures—all invariably accompanied by resistance, refusal, sabotage or flight. Indeed, in the Americas, "the notion of control of a whole territory and no longer a single plantation historically went hand in hand with the systematic formation of a national guard, very much directed against the possibility of a general slave uprising, rather than an exterior enemy of foreign powers" (Moulier-Boutang 2016: 41). Hence, the play of control and resistance, of production and subversion and their complex entanglements emerge as features of power relations in the space of the plantation, which put the production of subjectivities in connection with other life-forms and their diminution as much as with their thriving or flight.

Acknowledgments Most of the research and analysis for this piece was carried out between 2017 and 2022, within the ERC Advanced Grant project "The Color of Labor: The racialized lives of migrants" (grant no. 695573, PI Cristiana Bastos). Since 2021 Irene Peano's work has been supported by a grant from the Portuguese Foundation for Science and Technology (FCT), grant no. 2020.01002.CEECIND/CP1615/CT0009.

References

Adams, J. 2007. *Wounds of Returning: Race, Memory, and Property on the Postslavery Plantation*. Chapel Hill: The University of North Carolina Press.

Allewaert, M. 2013. *Ariel's Ecology: Plantations, Personhood, and Colonialism in the American Tropics*. Minneapolis: University of Minnesota Press.

Bastos, C. 2018. "Portuguese in the Cane: The Racialization of Labour in Hawaiian Plantations." In *Changing Societies: Legacies and Challenges, Vol. 1, Ambiguous Inclusions: Inside Out, Inside In*, ed. S. Aboim, P. Granjo, and A. Ramos, 65–96. Lisbon: Imprensa de Ciências Sociais.

Bastos, C. 2020. "Plantation Memories, Labor Identities, and the Celebration of Heritage: The case of Hawaii Plantation Village Museum Worlds." *Advances in Research* 8: 25–45.

Beckford, G. 1999 [1972]. *Persistent Poverty: Underdevelopment in Plantation Economies of the Third World*. Kingston: University of the West Indies Press.

Behal, R. 2012. *One Hundred Years of Servitude: Political Economy of Tea Plantations in Colonial Assam*. New Delhi: Tulika Books.

Benton, L. 2010. *A Search for Sovereignty: Law and Geography in European Empires, 1400–1900*. Cambridge: Cambridge University Press.

Besky, S. 2020. "Monoculture." In *Anthropocene Unseen: A Lexicon*, ed. C. Howe and A. Pandian, 277–280. Punctum books.

Best, L. 1968. "Outlines of a Model of Pure Plantation Economy." *Social and Economic Studies* 17 (3): 283–326.

Blaufarb, R. 2016. *The Great Demarcation: The French Revolution and the Invention of Modern Property*. Oxford: Oxford University Press.

Bonneuil, C., and J.-B. Fressoz. 2016. *The Shock of the Anthropocene*. London: Verso.

Braudel, F. 1992. *Civilization and Capitalism, 15th–18th Century, Vol. 2: The Wheels of Commerce*. Los Angeles: University of California Press.

Bray, F., B. Hahn, J. B. Lourdusamy, and T. Saraiva. 2019. "Cropscapes and History: Reflections on Rootedness and Mobility." *Transfers* 9 (1): 20–41.

Breman, J. 1989. *Taming the Coolie Beast: Plantation Society and the Colonial Order in Southeast Asia*. Delhi: Oxford University Press.

Brown, W. 2010. *Walled States, Waning Sovereignty*. New York: Zone Books.

Brown, Kate, and T. Thomas Klubock. 2014. "Environment and Labor: (Special Issue)". *International Labor and Working-Class History*: 85.

Browne, S. 2015. *Dark Matters: On the Surveillance of Blackness*. Durham: Duke University Press.

Burnard, T., and J. Garrigus. 2018. *The Plantation Machine: Atlantic Capitalism in French Saint-Domingue and British Jamaica*. Philadelphia: University of Pennsylvania Press.

Carney, J.A. 2021. "Subsistence in the Plantationocene: Dooryard Gardens, Agrobiodiversity, and the Subaltern Economies of Slavery." *The Journal of Peasant Studies* 48 (5): 1075–1099.

Casid, J. 2004. *Sowing Empire: Landscape and Colonization*. Minneapolis: Minnesota University Press.

Casimir, J. 2008. "Haïti et sa créolité." *Worlds and Knowledges Otherwise* 2 (3): 2–8.

Chatterjee, P. 2001. *A Time for Tea: Women, Labour and Postcolonial Politics on an Indian Plantation*. Durham: Duke University Press.

Chivallon, C. 2012. *L'esclavage, du souvenir à la mémoire: Contribution à une anthropologie de la Caraïbe*. Paris: Karthala.

Clukey, A., and J. Wells. 2016. "Introduction: Plantation Modernity." *The Global South* 10 (2): 1–10.

Craton, M. 1984. "The Historical Roots of the Plantation Model." *Slavery & Abolition* 5 (3): 189–221.

Davis, A. 2003. *Are Prisons Obsolete?* New York: Seven Stories Press.

Dean, W. 1995. *With Broadax and Firebrand: The Destruction of the Brazilian Atlantic Rainforest*. Berkeley: University of California Press.

Du Bois, W.E.B. 1899. *The Philadelphia Negro: A Social Study*. New York: Schocken.

Du Bois, W.E.B. 1911. "The Social Evolution of the Black South." *American Negro Monographs* 1: 4.

Du Bois, W.E.B. 1935. *Black Reconstruction*. Rahway: Harcourt, Brace and Company.

Dusinberre, M., and M. Iijima. 2019. "Transplantation: Sugar and Imperial Practice in Japan's Pacific." *Historische Anthropologie* 27 (3): 325–335.

Easterling, K. 2014. *Extrastatecraft: The Power of Infrastructure Space*. London: Verso.

Elkins, S. 1959. *Slavery: A Problem in American Institutional and Intellectual Life*. Chicago: University of Chicago Press.

Escobar, A. 1999. "After Nature: Steps to an Antiessentialist Political Ecology." *Current Anthropology* 40 (1): 1–30.

Fiege, M. 2012. *The Republic of Nature: An Environmental History of the United States*. Seattle: University of Washingtom Press.

Fox-Genovese, E. 1988. *Within the Plantation Household: Black and White Women of the Old South*. Chapel Hill: University of North Carolina Press.

Foucault, M. 1977. "Nietzsche, Genealogy, History." In *Language, Counter-Memory, Practice: Selected Essays and Interviews*, ed. D.F. Bouchard, 139–164. Ithaca: Cornell University Press.

Fraginals, M. 1964. *El Ingenio: Complejo Económico Social Cubano del Azúcar*. Habana: Editorial Crítica.

Garcia, A. 1986. "Libres et assujettis." *Actes de la recherche en sciences sociales* 65: 14–40.

Gilroy, P. 1993. *The Black Atlantic: Modernity and Double Consciousness*. Cambridge: Harvard University Press.

Grove, R. 1997. *Ecology, Climate and Empire: Colonialism and Global Environmental History, 1400–1940*. London: White Horse Press.

Hansen, T. 2021. "Sovereignty in a Minor Key." *Public Culture* 33 (1): 41–61.

Haraway, D. 2015. "Anthropocene, Capitalocene, Plantationocene, Chthulucene: Making Kin." *Environmental Humanities* 6 (1): 159–165.

Haraway, D., and A. Tsing. 2019. "Reflections on the Plantationocene: A Conversation with Donna Haraway and Anna Tsing Moderated by Gregg Mitman." *Edge Effects*, June 18.

Haraway, D., N. Ishikawa, S.F. Gilbert, K. Olwig, A.L. Tsing, and N. Bubandt. 2016. "Anthropologists Are Talking—About the Anthropocene." *Ethnos* 81 (3): 535–564.

Hartman, S. 2007. *Lose Your Mother: A Journey Along the Atlantic Slave Route*. New York: Farrar, Straus and Giroux.

Holmes, S. 2013. *Fresh Fruit, Broken Bodies: Migrant Farmworkers in the United States*. Berkeley: University of California Press.

Hornborg, A. 2007. "Introduction: Environmental History as Political Ecology." In *Rethinking Environmental History: World-System History and Global Environmental Change*, ed. A. Hornborg, J.R. McNeill, and J. Martinez-Alier, 1–24. Lanham: AltaMira.

James, C.L.R. 1980 [1966]. "The Making of the Caribbean People." In *Spheres of Existence: Selected Writings*, ed. C.L.R. James, 173–190. London: Allison and Busby.

Li, T.M. 2014. *Land's End: Capitalist Relations on an Indigenous Frontier*. Durham: Duke University Press.

Li, T.M., and P. Semedi. 2021. *Plantation Life: Corporate Occupation in Indonesia's Oil Palm Zone*. Durham: Duke University Press.

Lowe, L. 2015. *The Intimacies of Four Continents*. Durham: Duke University Press.

MacLennan, C.A. 2014. *Sovereign Sugar: Industry and Environment in Hawai'i*. Honolulu: University of Hawai'i Press.

Mbembe, A. 2013. *Critique de la raison nègre*. Paris: La Découverte.

McCook, S. 2019. *Coffee Is Not Forever: A Global History of the Coffee Leaf Rust*. Athens: Ohio University Press.

McInnis, J. 2016. ""Behold the Land": W. E. B. Du Bois, Cotton Futures, and the Afterlife of the Plantation in the US South." *The Global South* 10 (2): 70–98.

McKittrick, K. 2011. "On Plantations, Prisons, and a Black Sense of Place." *Social and Cultural Geography* 12 (8): 947–963.

McKittrick, K. 2013. "Plantation Futures." *SMall Axe* 42: 1–15.

McPherson, T. 2003. *Reconstructing Dixie: Race, Gender, and Nostalgia in the Imagined South*. Durham: Duke University Press.

Meillassoux, C. 2018. *Femmes, greniers et capitaux*. Paris: L'Harmattan.

Mezzadra, S., and B. Neilson. 2013. *Border as Method, or, the Multiplication of Labor*. Durham: Duke University Press.

Mezzadra, S., and B. Neilson. 2019. *The Politics of Operations: Excavating Contemporary Capitalism*. Durham: Duke University Press.
Mintz, S. 1960. *Worker in the Cane: A Puerto Rican Life History*. New Haven: Yale University Press.
Mintz, S. 1968. "Caribbean Society." *International Encyclopedia of the Social Sciences* 2: 306–319.
Mintz, S. 1985. *Sweetness and Power: The Place of Sugar in Modern History*. New York: Penguin.
Mintz, S., and R. Price. 1992. *The Birth of African-American Culture: An Anthropological Perspective*. London: Routledge.
Mintz, S., and E. Wolf. 1957. "Haciendas and Plantations in Middle Americas and the Antilles." *Social and Economic Studies* 6 (3): 380–412.
Mongia, R. 2018. *Indian Migration and Empire: A Colonial Genealogy of the Modern State*. Durham: Duke University Press.
Moore, J.W. 2015. *Capitalism in the Web of Life: Ecology and the Accumulation of Capital*. London: Verso.
Moore, J.W., ed. 2016. *Anthropocene or Capitalocene? Nature, History, and the Crisis of Capitalism*. Oakland: PM Press.
Morgan, J. 2004. *Laboring Women: Reproduction and Gender in New World Slavery*. Philadelphia: University of Pennsylvania Press.
Moulier Boutang, Y. 2016. "Agency and Transnational Perspectives on the Constitution of Waged,Unfree, and Free Labor: The Role of Mobility in the Nineteenth Century." In *New Frontiers of Slavery*, ed. D. Tomich. Albany: State University of New York Press.
Murphy, M.W., and C. Schroering. 2020. "Refiguring the Plantationocene: Racial Capitalism, World-Systems Analysis, and Global Socioecological Transformation." *Journal of World-Systems Research* 26 (2): 400–415.
Nash, L. 2017. *Inescapable Ecologies: A History of Environment, Disease, and Knowledge*. Berkeley: University of California Press.
Navaro-Yashin, Y. 2012. *The Make-Believe Space: Affective Geography in a Post-War Polity*. Durham: Duke University Press.
Navaro, Y., Z. Biner, A. von Bieberstein, and S. Altuğ, eds. 2021. *Reverberations: Violence Across Time and Space*. Philadelphia: University of Pennsylvania Press.
Northrup, D. 1995. *Indentured Labor in the Age of Imperialism, 1834–1922*. Cambridge: Cambridge University Press.
O'Connell Davidson, J. 2015. *Modern Slavery: The Margins of Freedom*. London: Palgrave Macmillan.
Ong, A. 2006. *Neoliberalism as Exception: Mutations in Citizenship and Sovereignty*. Durham: Duke University Press.
Parenti, C. 2003. *The Soft Cage: Surveillance in America from Slavery to the War on Terror*. New York: Basic Books.
Robbins, P. 2012. *Political Ecology: A Critical Introduction*. Chichester: Wiley.

Robinson, C. 1983. *Black Marxism: The Making of the Black Radical Tradition*. Chapel Hill: University of North Carolina Press.
Rodney, W. 1981. "Plantation Society in Guyana." *Review (Fernand Braudel Center)* 4 (4): 643–666.
Rogers, T. 2010. *The Deepest Wounds: A Labor and Environmental History of Sugar in Northeast Brazil*. Chapel Hill: University of North Carolina Press.
Rosenthal, C. 2018. *Accounting for Slavery: Masters and Management*. Cambridge: Harvard University Press.
Ross, C. 2017. *Ecology and Power in the Age of Empire: Europe and the Transformation of the Tropical World*. Oxford: Oxford University Press.
Rubin, V., ed. 1959. *Plantation Systems of the New World*. Washington: Pan American Union.
Sandiford, K. 2000. *The Cultural Politics of Sugar: Caribbean Slavery and Narratives of Colonialism*. Cambridge: Cambridge University Press.
Sharpe, C. 2016. *In the Wake: On Blackness and Being*. Durham: Duke University Press.
Sherman, Z. 2021. "Infrastructures and the Ontological Question of Race." https://www.e-flux.com/architecture/coloniality-infrastructure/411239/infrastructures-and-the-ontological-question-of-race/.
Smith, R.T. 1967. "Social Stratification, Cultural Pluralism and Integration in West Indian Societies." In *Caribbean Integration*, ed. Lewis and T.G. Mathews, 228–256. Puerto ico: Institute of Caribbean Studies.
Soluri, J. 2006. *Banana Cultures: Agriculture, Consumption, and Environmental Change in Honduras and the United States*. Austin: University of Texas Press.
Stern, P. 2011. *The Company-State: Corporate Sovereignty and the Early Modern Foundations of the British Empire in India*. New York: Oxford University Press.
Stewart, M.A. 1996. *'What Nature Suffers to Groe': Life, Labor, and Landscape on the Georgia Coast, 1680–1920*. Athens: University of Georgia Press.
Steward, J.H., et al. 1956. *The People of Puerto Rico: A Study in Social Anthropology*. Urbana: Universidty of Illinois Press.
Stolcke, V. 1988. *Coffee Planters, Workers and Wives: Class Conflict and Gender Relations on Sao Paulo Coffee Plantations, 1850–1980*. Basingstoke: Macmillan.
Stoler, A. 1985a. *Capitalism and Confrontation in Sumatra's Plantation Belt, 1870–1979*. New Haven: Yale University Press.
Stoler, A. 1985b. "Perceptions of Protest: Defining the Dangerous in Colonial Sumatra." *American Ethnologist* 12 (4): 642–658.
Stoler, A. 1995. *Race and the Education of Desire: Foucault's History of Sexuality and the Colonial Order of Things*. Durham: Duke University Press.
Stoler, A. 2016. *Duress: Imperial Durabilities in Our Times*. Durham: Duke University Press.

Thomas, D.A. 2018. "The End of the West and the Future of Us All." *African Diaspora* 11 (1–2): 123–143.

Thomas, D.A. 2019. *Political Life in the Wake of the Plantation: Sovereignty, Witnessing, Repair*. Durham: Duke University Press.

Thompson, E. 1932. *The Plantation*. Chicago: University of Chicago Press.

Thompson, E. 1939. ''The Plantation: The Physical Basis of Traditional Race Relations". In *Race Relations and the Race Problem*, ed. E. Thompson. Durham: Duke University Press.

Thompson, E. 1975. *Plantation Societies, Race Relations, and the South: The Regimentation of Populations: Selected Papers of Edgar T. Thompson*. Durham: Duke University Press.

Tomba, M. 2019. *Insurgent Universality: An Alternative Legacy of Modernity*. New York: Oxford University Press.

Tomich, D.W. 2004. *Through the Prism of Slavery: Labor, Capital, and World Economy*. London: Rowman & Littlefield Publishers.

Trouillot, M.-R. 1982. "Motion in the System: Coffee, Color, and Slavery in Eighteenth-Century Saint-Domingue." *Review (Fernand Braudel Center)* 5 (3): 331–388.

Trouillot, M.-R. 2002a. "Culture on the edges. Caribbean Creolization in Historical Context." In *From the Margin: Historical Anthropology and Its Futures*, ed. K.A. Brian, 189–210. Durham: Duke University Press.

Trouillot, M.-R. 2002b. "North Atlantic Universals: Analytical Fictions, 1492–1945." *The South Atlantic Quarterly* 101 (4): 839–858.

Tsing, A. 2004. *Friction: An Ethnography of Global Connection*. Princeton: Princeton University Press.

Tsing, A. 2015. *The Mushroom at the End of the World: On the Possibility of Life in Capitalist Ruins*. Princeton: Princeton University Press.

Uekötter, F. 2014. "Introduction." In *Comparing Apples, Oranges, and Cotton: Environmental Histories of the Global Plantation*, ed. F. Uekötter, 7–25. Frankfurt am Main: Campus Verlag.

Wacquant, L. 2002. "From Slavery to Mass Incarceration: Rethinking the 'Race Question' in the US." *New Left Review* 13: 41–60.

Wallerstein, I. 1974. *The Modern World System I: Capitalist Agriculture and the Origins of the European World-Economy in the Sixteenth Century*. New York: Academic Press.

Weiss, L. 2011. "Exceptional Space: Concentration Camps and Labor Compounds in Late Nineteenth-Century South Africa." In *Archaeologies of Internment*, ed. A. Myers and G. Moshenska, 106–118. New York: Springer.

White, R. 1996. "Are You an Environmentalist or Do You Work for a Living?" In *Uncommon Ground: Rethinking the Human Place in Nature*, ed. W. Cronon, 171–85. New York: W. W. Norton.

Williams, B. 1991. *Stains on My Name, War in My Veins. Guyana and the Politics of Cultural Struggle*. Durham: Duke University Press.

Williams, E. 1944. *Capitalism and Slavery*. Chapel Hill: University of North Carolina Press.

Williams, E. 1970. *From Columbus to Castro: The History of the Caribbean 1492–1969*. New York: Harper & Row.

Wolf, E. 1982. *Europe and the People Without History*. Berkeley: University of California Press.

Wynter, S. 2003. "Unsettling the Coloniality of Being/Power/Truth/Freedom: Towards the Human, After Man, Its Overrepresentation—An Argument." *The New Centennial Review* 3 (3): 257–337.

Yusoff, K. 2019. *A Billion Black Anthropocenes or None*. Minneapolis: University of Minnesota Press.

PART I

Revisiting the Caribbean: Genealogies for the Plantationocene

CHAPTER 2

From Marrons to Kreyòl: Human-Animal Relations in Early Caribbean

Rodrigo C. Bulamah

Introduction[1]

Many scholars agree that the Caribbean was the first place to set the stage for Western modernity (James 1989; Scott 2004; Mintz 1996). In a concise definition, Sidney Mintz (1996) has argued that in the Caribbean case, "the tragedy and glory of the encounter of the entire non-Western

[1] Previous versions of this article were presented at VII ReACT (Reunião de Antropologia da Ciência e da Tecnologia, Universidade Federal de Santa Catarina, 2019), Plantations and their Afterlives Symposium (Universidade de Lisboa, 2020), and the Global Scholars Academy Writing Workshop (Harvard Law School and The Graduate Institute of Geneva, 2021). I have benefited from thoughtful suggestions from Carlos Sautchuk, Felipe Vander Velden, Irene Peano, Marta Macedo, Colette Le Petitcorps, Vydia Kumar, Rene Urueña, and Carlos Andrés Baquero-Díaz. I am also grateful to Ludmila Maia, Guilherme Moura Fagundes, Rosa Vieira, Caetano Sordi, Alyne Costa, Marcelo Mello, Omar Ribeiro Thomaz, and Federico Neiburg for their insightful comments. As they should be, mistakes or inconsistencies are my own. This research was supported by the São Paulo Research Foundation (FAPESP), grant no. 2019/04170-4.

R. C. Bulamah (✉)
Federal University of São Paulo, São Paulo, Brazil
e-mail: rbulamah@unifesp.br

C. Le Petitcorps et al. (eds.), *Global Plantations in the Modern World*, Cambridge Imperial and Post-Colonial Studies,
https://doi.org/10.1007/978-3-031-08537-6_2

world with the West (…) happened long before it did anywhere else, and under conditions that would prevent its awful novelty from being recognized for what it was: a modernity that predated the modern" (ibid.: 305). An infrastructure that epitomized modern life, as C. L. R. James famously argued, the plantation was the institution that granted life in the New World its most modern features, particularly for those who were kidnapped, deported, and enslaved (James 1989: 392). At the same time, in runaway communities as well as in certain spaces of the plantation itself, many enslaved Africans and their descendants found a place in which to produce their own food and raise their own animals, while also feeding the great house and sometimes attaining a surplus that was enough to be sold at local markets.

In the complex landscapes of the colonies such as Saint-Domingue, for instance, it was possible for enslaved people to experience a certain autonomy and formulate ideas of freedom that were crucial in inspiring the series of revolts that would later lead to what we now call the Haitian Revolution. By looking at plantations as infrastructure, I wish to develop a figure–ground reversal in which the plantation is not taken for granted but assumed in its complexity. Through mobilizing a selection of historical sources, from written documents to oral histories, gathered during archival and ethnographic research in Haiti and France, I want to uncover the materiality of freedom that inspired broad demands for liberty.

For many Caribbean scholars, the small portions of land that planters granted the enslaved Africans and their descendants to reduce the operative costs of the colonial plantations, known as provision grounds, were spaces in which enslaved people could produce their own food while also developing techniques, practices, and concepts that worked both in complementarity and in opposition to the plantation. In his pioneering study about the formation of Haiti, Polish historian Tadeusz Lepkowski (1970) formulated the concept of the "peasant breach" after observing a fracture in the plantation economy in which enslaved people, while working in these provision grounds, were protagonists of "another alternative to the rural development of the country" (ibid.: 61).

Haitian sociologist Jean Casimir (1992) calls this system the "counter-plantation", wherein not only a new economic system was established but a new world based on the creative force of creolization. For Sylvia Wynter (1971), the ambivalent relationship between the "plantation system" and what she names the "plot system", centered around the provision grounds, constitutes the main theme of Caribbean history, arguing that "[it] is at once the root cause of our alienation, and the possibility of our salvation" (ibid.: 99). More recently, new scholarship combining historiography and literary studies has shown the richness of Casimir's and Wynter's concepts in shedding new light on the daily life of Africans and their descendants in the colonial and postcolonial Caribbean (DeLoughrey 2011; Castellano 2021; Dubois and Turits 2019). Inspired by this literature, I want to stress how human-animal alliances played an important role in ontogenetic processes, such as creolization, that shaped new collectivities in the Caribbean.

If until very recently the Haitian Revolution remained unthinkable for most of Western historiography (Trouillot 1995), the multiple alliances that made it possible are still very much unknown. In the north of Haiti, where I did most of my ethnographic fieldwork, oral histories emphasize, on one side, an association between ancient slaves and free Blacks that reveals a great nostalgia for a time of unity (see also Aureille, this volume). On the other hand, other alliances, such as those between humans and animals, appear in narratives that stress how Creole pigs were the "source of life" for peasants and poor people (*sous lavi malere yo*). By analyzing the plantation as infrastructure and the struggles staged in colonial landscapes with a focus on associations between humans and other-than-humans, my goal here is to look at the new ecologies that were created through relational practices, mutuality, and political affects.

Although greatly inspired by Sidney Mintz's (1985) important study on how sugar created global connections between labor, capital, and culinary habits, I aim here to understand the ecological entanglements in which animals, humans, and other beings took part. By "bringing animals back in", as Robin Derby (2011) provocatively puts it, I also want to go beyond metaphors that compare human and animal conditions. Much like Benedicte Boisseron in her fascinating book *Afro-Dog: Blackness and the Animal Question* (2018), I am not interested exclusively in comparing human and animal forms of subjection and humiliation, but in understanding how humans and other-than-humans defied the colonial order through forging "defiant alliances". By doing so, I wish to engage with the new grand narrative that sees human agency as a geological force, epitomized by the idea of the Anthropocene, questioning its limits and what we can do with it to finally reflect on the afterlives of enslaved people's provision grounds.

Inaugural Multispecies Encounters

"From these eight female pigs", wrote the well-known Dominican friar Bartolomé de Las Casas in his famous *Historia de las Indias* (1957 [1559]), "were born all the pigs that until today have lived and live in all the *Indias*, which have been and are endless" (ibid., vol. 1: 246). His hyperbolic commentary describes an important event associated with Columbus's second trip to the West Indies. In 1493, the Genovese traveler brought eight female pigs (*Sus scrofa*), among other animals, to the Caribbean from La Gomera in the Canary Islands. As the first pigs to populate the New World, these specimens gave rise, in Las Casas's biblical world view, to all the herds of pigs in the following centuries. In fact, the arrival of these animals in the Caribbean happened irregularly and was marked by escapes, disputes for spaces with other beings, and by their establishment as feral populations.

These "creatures of empire" (Anderson 2004) were crucial to the formative moments of European expansion and the subsequent Conquest, taking part in what Alfred Crosby (1972) famously dubbed the "Columbian exchange". The first pigs arrived in the island of Hispaniola, site of the first European colonial settlement in the Americas, and were part of the initial phase of the "Atlantic moment" defined by Trouillot (2003) as "a first moment of globality", in which we can witness the "continuous centrality of the Atlantic as the revolving door of major global flows over four centuries" (ibid.: 29).

During the period of European voyages to the Caribbean and the Americas, vessels carried some food for crewmembers, who spent long periods on the high seas traveling from port to port. With the emergence of European settlements in the region, animals from the Old Continent were taken to the New World. Dogs, for example, were used for hunting and protection, and pigs became the first livestock, serving to Europeanize landscapes, by transforming them into something increasingly familiar to colonizers (Alves 2011; Crosby 1986; Johnson 2012). Native animals by contrast were objects of fascination, subject to detailed descriptions that contributed to the construction of an Edenic vision of the New World (Paravisini-Gebert 2008). However, hunting and animal husbandry were the main paradigms in these human–animal interactions. According to historian Marcy Norton (2013), in an extension of practices common to Europe, the native fauna of the Caribbean and the Americas at the beginning of Spanish expansion was viewed according to two prisms: hunting, a noble and elite activity, and livestock husbandry, an activity relegated to the plebeian level. Animal adoption, an Amerindian interspecies practice frequently described by travelers and colonial agents was therefore an enigma, one sometimes understood as husbandry. As Norton states, "Amerindian adoption was a cognate to forms of social life and intergroup conflict as European hunting and breeding were to rule and warfare" (ibid.: 22). Nonetheless, these multispecies encounters also gave rise, as we will see, to new ecologies and interactions in those landscapes that empires tried to domesticate and control.

Pigs were particularly well-suited to the long sea voyages to the New World, as they constituted important sources of meat and fat and were omnivorous, requiring no special food. Furthermore, even though they were subjected to intense forms of confinement, discomfort and suffering, they were hardy enough to survive (Donkin 1985). As Abbot Guillaume-Thomas Raynal (1770) noted at the end of the eighteenth century,

> America, at the time of the discovery, had no pigs, sheep, oxen, horses, or even any domestic animals. Columbus brought some of these useful animals to Saint-Domingue, where they spread everywhere (...). They have multiplied there prodigiously. There are thousands of horned animals, whose skins have become the object of considerable exportation. The horses have degenerated, but the quality is compensated by the number. The lard of pigs is a substitute for butter. (ibid.: 53)

In Saint-Domingue, the French name for the island of Hispaniola, the abundance of animals mentioned by Las Casas, or what Raynal described as the "prodigious multiplication", occurred in large part between the sixteenth and seventeenth centuries, when the entire island was under Spanish rule. Herds of animals such as pigs, goats, oxen, horses, and dogs became feral after being abandoned or running away.[2] Classified by the chroniclers of the time as *marrons*, *maroons* or *cimarróns* or even *montarazes* (from the Spanish *montes*), these animals multiplied, above all, due to favorable interactions with the new landscapes. The mountain geography of the island's interior was less suitable for large plantation, and this, coupled with the lack of natural predators and presence of dense

[2] On feralization and invasive species, see Caetano Sordi (2020).

forests, played a notable role in this expansion.[3] *Marron* (or maroon), as explained by Tardieu (2006), is a term derived from Arawak language whose original meaning was "fugitive", but it was incorporated into the colonial lexicon of different empires to define native plants and animals that defied European domination both in practical and ontological terms as something external to the European order.

Over time, the term *marronage* also came to be used to define people who evaded captivity, as in the French expression *partir marron*, used in newspaper advertisements to search for enslaved runaways.[4] This linguistic contiguity between animals and enslaved Africans is an evidence of how domestication, in the strict sense of the term, operated as "the archetypal pattern of other kinds of social subordination" (Thomas 1983: 46). In fact, such semantic extension is an example of the "generalized domestication" defined by Ghassan Hage (2017) as a colonial way of inhabiting the world that operates through metaphors of animalization guiding contemporary expressions of racism and ways of exploiting nature. For Hage, more than just revealing a classificatory system, "metaphors embody a practical orientation" (ibid.: 10). In this sense, while immobility of labore was at the center of the slave system and the plantation, conceiving black men and women as feral beings (*marron*) naturalized their hunting, capture, punishment, and death (Brown 2010).

As in other Spanish colonies in the Caribbean, the productive activities undertaken on Hispaniola moved away from an initial focus on gold mining—employing native Arawak forced labor and Europeans under indentured contracts and later enslaved Africans—to a small sugar production cycle that lasted until the beginning of the seventeenth century (Mintz 1996; see also Williams 1994). The effective transition to a plantation economy happened later in these domains than in the other colonial territories of the Caribbean and Americas. In the Spanish colonial settlements, the exploitation of animal products, whether from herds or hunting, pearl fishing, growing ginger and tobacco, extracting salt to produce salted herring from the Baltic Sea, and producing timber were more important than cultivating sugar. Yet, despite sparse occupations,

[3] For careful research on recent plantation experiments in central Haiti, see Moore, this volume.

[4] For a wide range of documents about *marronage*, see the website for the "Le marronage dans le monde atlantique" project (Université de Sherbrooke): www.marronnage.info/fr/index.html.

the Caribbean was the target of constant attention from the Spanish Crown due to the immense flow of wealth that connected its territories there to Europe, Africa, and Asia (Giusti-Cordero 2009).

Variations, conflicts, and fractures in the processes of occupation and the subsequent intensification of production, as well as a long list of diseases and a plurality of beings from diverse origins, eventually led to the development of a diverse Creole landscape in which the plantation could thrive (McNeill 2010). While dogs were trained to hunt runaway enslaved people, revealing a historical proximity between animalization and racialization, as Boisseron (2018) argues, European pigs, along with other non-humans, became part of a pool of "commons" that oriented early occupations as well as rhythms of settlement and colonization. Indeed, animals became part and parcel of a form of life that Malcom Ferdinand (2019) names "colonial dwelling" (*l'habiter colonial*), a way of inhabiting the planet based in a form of racial violence in which the plantation was the organizing infrastructure. In fact, the French name for plantation, *habitation*, stresses exactly this exclusionary dimension, as only the white European settlers were subjects with rights—as Sybille Fischer (2016) reminds us—and therefore allowed to have proper life in the colonial setting, hence their designation as *habitans* (settlers). Paradoxically, as Creole animals that forged colonial landscapes in the New World, pigs gave rise to new forms of life based exactly in what was "uncommon" (de la Cadena and Blaser 2018), establishing new sociotechnical ecologies on the margins of the plantation machine.

Despite the social and economic prevalence of slavery and monoculture, the colonial landscape was also open to the forging of new landscapes in the margins of, or even against, the plantation. In fact, the agro-industrial order of Caribbean plantation went far beyond the generalized control and alienation efforts that define some classic and contemporary readings of the plantation. Anna Tsing (2015), for instance, uses the sugarcane plantation that sustained colonial Brazil as a prototypical example that illustrates her definition of "scalability": a project that could reproduce itself in different scales precisely because of its immutable frame, as it depended on "few interspecies relations" and "was comparatively self-contained [and] oblivious to encounter" (ibid.: 39). More than that, continues the author, the enslaved Africans in this project "had no local social relations and thus no established routes for escape". "Like the cane itself", Tsing concludes, "which had no history of either companion species or disease relations in the New World, [the enslaved people] *were isolated*" (idem, emphasis added). By looking at historical sources, however, we can see that even in the face of immeasurable forms of violence and alienation, people found ways to recreate their lives and their ecologies even within the pervasiveness of the plantation.[5]

Across the whole Caribbean in the seventeenth and eighteenth centuries, wealth assumed many forms, and the hunting of feral animals attracted the attention of pirates, smugglers, traders, adventurers, and other actors named "a masterless class" by Julius Scott (2018). There was great ambiguity in the practices of theft and smuggling, which always occupied an unstable position between legality and illegality, and *rescate* (as these activities were called) became profitable to the point of guiding exchanges, circulations, conflicts, and wars in the region (Andrews 1978; Brown 2020). Known as buccaneers, due to their habit of smoking game meat in a wood grill (from *boucan*, in French), or filibusters (possibly derived from "light boats", *vrijbuiter*, in Dutch), pirates and merchants occupied specific islands and regions of the archipelago for long periods of time. Among those islands was Tortuga, off the northwest coast of Saint-Domingue. Jules Lecomte's (1837) historical novel *L'Île de la Tortue: Roman Maritime* illustrates this moment pretty well, describing hunting customs, same-sex marriages, and exchanges between pirates, privateers, and merchants who, at the time, could or could not be linked to great European empires. Comparing them with the *habitans*, Lecomte highlights (ibid.: 18–20, emphasis added):

> Settlers [*habitants*] were those whose aptitude seemed more peculiar to constructions and plantations; people of peaceful morals and mood. The Buccaneers declared themselves hunters; the pursuit of oxen and wild boars in the woods of Saint-Domingue, *the preparation of hides and salted meats which constituted their daily occupations, later offered society the first elements of its trade and commerce.* (…) Finally, the Filibusters or Corsairs, formed the third class of Adventurers by increasing their chase after Spanish ships.

The hunting of feral pigs and cows and the trade in their hides, meat and fat constituted the central activities of pirates and adventurers.

[5] More interesting is Anna Tsing's idea of "feral geographies", which she has talked about in recent conferences and developed more carefully in her ongoing collective work "Feral Atlas". See: feralatlas.org (last accessed 10/02/2021).

Extending Alida Metcalf's (2005) concept of "go-betweens" to non-humans, we could state that pigs, cows, and other animals were active mediators of relationships between Europeans and native populations in the Caribbean islands and the American continent (see also Velden 2018). Escape, adaptation, and husbandry of European species led effectively to the occupation and formation of living settlements and trading posts in different parts of the region. Concurrent with the genocide and assimilation of Amerindian populations, the presence of these animals also motivated the settlement of buccaneers and corsairs, who started to raise animals for meat and use in transport and traction engines and thereby became settlers (Oexmelín 1930, chapter 5). It was exactly the establishment of villages in the western part of Hispaniola, mainly by groups of Frenchmen, which motivated the concession of a third share of the colony to the French Crown by the Treaty of Ryswick in 1697. However, between the two colonies, the circulation of traders, animals, and wealth remained intense.

Traveling in Hispaniola in the late eighteenth century, the famous Martinique-born lawyer and writer Louis-Élie Moreau de Saint-Méry (1958 [1796]) noted that, particularly along the northern coast of Saint-Domingue, "forests are refuge for feral pigs [*cochons marons*]" before adding a geographical description of the north of the island and of its occupation. Except for villages such as Monte-Cristi, Puerto-Plata, and Samaná, he writes, "the northern share of the Spanish part is almost uninhabited" (ibid.: 207). "However", he continued, "every land close to the sea is granted [by the Crown], not in small lots, (...) but in large portions. In a way, it is for fishing that such concessions are requested, ***but even more for hunting the feral pig***" (idem, my emphasis). The interactions between hunters, dogs, pigs, and plants attracted Moreau de St-Méry's attention, and he described them in detail (ibid.: 207–208, emphasis removed):

> The time of this hunt is defined by the moment when a species of palm produces its seeds, which form a cluster and which the animal is extremely fond of. A Spaniard, if he is alone with some dogs goes armed with a spear, a machete, and a knife in the parts of the wood which contain the palm. When he sees a feral pig, the dogs circle it and distract it by barking until the hunter comes to kill him with his spear. The beast is then opened and emptied, the head and feet are thrown away, and the hunter takes care of the body, which he sometimes cuts to facilitate transport.

When hunters went to the forest collectively, Moreau de St-Méry's remarked (ibid.: 208, emphasis in the original):

> they choose a place where they believe the prey would be abundant; they build a small hut or *ajoupa* there, covered with stains or palm leaves, and they place several forks with crossbars to salt and dry the feral pig halves or to pile them up when they are ready. Quite often transportation is by sea at least if the result is a considerable game.

Whether individually or collectively organized, this dynamic of hunting, drying, and salting the meat, as well as its transportation and trade, dominated the economy of northern Hispaniola, making the border between Saint-Domingue and the Spanish Captaincy General of Santo Domingo a very fluid landscape. Moreau de St-Méry brings to light the poverty in the Spanish portion of the island, quite unlike the thriving colonial society that he saw on the Western side. Observing the town of Cotuy, close to the gold mines of the Cibao province, he states that the region "as the Spanish portion in general, was not in a situation of less neglect and misery" at the beginning of the eighteenth century (ibid.: 213). The poor settlers of Cibao, "descendants of primitive European owners", most of them French, were known as *actionnaires* on account of their being in possession of a deed of concession (*acte de concession*) and were rarely counted in colonial censuses.

The topographical formation of the eastern part of the island made it poorly adapted to large-scale agriculture, unlike the northwestern part, where Cap Français or Le Cap, the capital of French Saint-Domingue, was located in the Plaine du Nord. For the residents of the central and northeastern region, their only option was to care for their herds, which they could own in limited quantities, and go hunting (*monteria*), which was allowed only on certain days.

"It is to the education of animals, especially pigs that the inhabitants of Cotuy dedicate themselves almost exclusively, and these animals need intense care" (ibid.: 214), highlights Moreau de St-Méry, calling our attention to the constant tension between domestication and feralization. Even with dedicated attention to food and care, pigs "were attracted to the woods with the hope of finding roots, fruits, and insects (...) but they did not always return [home] at night, going far away to the point of becoming feral and, at times, in high numbers" (ibid.: 215). The miserable fate of those that raised them was to be "constantly betrayed in his wait … limited to hunting those he once believed were domesticated" (idem). These accounts reveal that domestication was indeed as practical a problem as it was a metaphysical one during those early times in the Atlantic. Domestication was (and is) an unstable practice, rather difficult to define when it comes to human–animal ecologies. Although some authors tend to dismiss the concept due to its Eurocentric genealogy, I agree with recent efforts that call for a more empirical critique of human–animal encounters that can amplify domestication's semantic field (see, for instance, Vander Velden 2012; Norton 2015; Sautchuk 2018).

Instabilities between domestication and feralization, expressed in tensions between breeding and hunting, helped shape a fundamental part of the economy of the Caribbean that was not centered on the plantation but was associated with it through circuits of provision both at sea, in exchange circuits between the islands, and on land, as in the case of the divided island of Hispaniola. This disparity between plantation colonies and provision territories has been seen by many historians as an indication of a particular type of backwardness in Spanish colonies in the Caribbean. Having not moved toward the "plantation complex" that Philip Curtin (1990) talks about or gone through the "plantation revolution" identified by Ira Berlin (1998), these colonies, especially between the seventeenth and eighteenth centuries, seem to have been left out of history (or historiography), as Juan Giusti-Cordero (2009) convincingly argues.[6] Animals and their interactions with humans reveal the limits of these overly schematic conclusions, which sometimes leave aside the trans-colonial connections and flows that linked different spaces without necessarily involving the metropolis (Johnson 2012). Even though not initially oriented toward the plantation, the economic importance of the Spanish Caribbean and its animal economies, prompted attempted raids, wars, and invasions by other European imperial powers. And such initiatives did not go unanswered by the Spanish Crown.

[6] It is a consensus among historians that the plantation finds its place in the Spanish Caribbean only later if compared to the British, French, and Dutch colonies. In Cuba, this occurred only at the end of the eighteenth century; in Puerto Rico from 1820; and in the Dominican Republic, which had no direct relationship with Atlantic slavery, at the beginning of the twentieth century (Giusti-Cordero 2009: 59–60).

Provision Grounds and the Ambiguous Materiality of Freedom

In describing the French settlers in the north of Saint-Domingue, Moreau de Saint-Méry (1958 [1796], vol. 1) speaks of a "disapproval of the coarse customs and the non-social character" of Cotuy's inhabitants. "Perhaps", he continues, "the habit of a life whose care almost always has animals as an object makes it acquire a certain rudeness that shocks those who do not share it" (ibid.: 216). But this trait may still have been the result of a history of disputes over territories, something that was acquired through the participation of animals as agents in this geography of warfare. "Maybe there is still a precaution in this judgment, proper to the Frenchman who still remember, a century later, the massacre of his countrymen in Samaná" (idem) suggests Moreau de St-Méry, referring to the *ravages* or *devastaciones*—the massacres of animal livestock with the aim of relocating or expelling settlers—that took place in the region at the end of seventeenth century (see Moya Pons 2007: 40–43). The result of these *ravages*, however, has always proved to be quite insufficient (Giusti-Cordero 2014: 20).

These same French settlements were established to produce tobacco, whose production lasted until the end of the seventeenth century, when, after the decisive assignment of the western part of the island to France in 1697, sugar production assumed an increasing importance. Thus, the many landscapes of Hispaniola were shaped from a set of social, material, and ecological interactions in which animals were used in transportation and mechanical work in the plantation and, with the help of hunting, supplied meat and leather to the colonies and, not uncommonly, to European cities as well. At the beginning of the eighteenth century, as stated by the governor of Cap Français, Monsieur de Charitte, "[The Spaniards] know that, in relation to our sugar plantations, we cannot do without their cattle, since our herds are not sufficiently populated to supply what we need…" (cited in Moya Pons 1977: 233).[7]

[7] As historian Moya Pons remarks in another work (Moya Pons 2007: 94), "In 1702 the Spanish exports of livestock, horses, and hides to the French colony increased to 50,000 *escudos* annually. This trade defined the relationship between the two colonies for the next ninety years and helped foster the sugar revolution in Saint-Domingue in the eighteenth century".

As we have seen, pigs and other beings played a central role in the production of this Creole landscape and influenced travelers, pirates, settlers, captives, Europeans, and Africans, motivating occupations and disputes and interacting in different ways with colonial society and the class and racial divides that came to be a central part of it. But these interactions went far beyond the plantation. At the end of the eighteenth century, in opposing the abolitionist theses of the newly created Society of Friends of Blacks in Paris (*Société des Amis des Noirs de Paris*), Crublier de Saint-Cyran (1790) describes the houses and parcels of land managed by slave families in Saint-Domingue, saying that their working conditions were "generally less harsh than that of workers in France" (ibid.: 4). He further adds, "there is no [enslaved person] who does not have a house and land for himself and his family, who does not have chickens, pigs, and other properties, which are always carefully respected by the master…" (ibid.: 5).

Reports by colonial officials or travelers like Saint-Cyran should be read with caution. Produced in a period that saw conditions of extreme violence, animalization, and dispossession of Black people, such reports had specific political goals within the abolitionist debate that was taking place in different parts of the Atlantic. However, it is in the cracks of these historical sources that we can find important descriptions that, when read against, as well as along, the grain (Stoler 2009), provide fragments of the forms of sociality, conceptions, and daily practices of enslaved people. More than that, such documents not only help us to understand the changing attitudes of different human groups toward the "natural world", as Keith Thomas (1996) famously put it, but also the way in which animals shared an experience of place while materially creating new agrarian landscapes within but also against the plantation.

Saint-Cyran's quick description of the houses and plots designated to enslaved people in Saint-Domingue confirms a general policy in the French, Spanish, and British colonies of granting portions of land that would serve to produce food for subsistence and, sometimes, for commercial exchange in regional markets, allowing the enslaved a form of social mobility. At the same time, the concession of a space for growing food and raising animals largely benefited the plantation economy and served the colonial system by promoting the immobility of enslaved people and preventing them from becoming *marrons*. "Nothing is more adequate to retain [the enslaved] and prevent them from escaping than to provide them with something from which they can derive some benefit, such as birds, pigs, a tobacco plantation, cotton, herbs or the like", noted the Reverend Jean-Baptiste Labat (1724, tome 2: 50), writing from the French colony of Martinique at the beginning of the eighteenth century. He then added that "the seizure [of these lands and animals] is sufficient to prevent, perhaps for good, that all Blacks on a plantation try such an escape" (idem).

Within the socioeconomic order of plantations, these lands, named "provision grounds" (*habitation* or *place à vivres*, in French, and *conucos*, in Spanish), enabled the development of labor techniques, agricultural practices, and forms of exchange between enslaved and free people. They helped shape what Lepkowski (1970) calls the "peasant breach" in his classical study of colonial Saint-Domingue, understood as a collective experience distinct from the slave order, an experience that, even if it "united them to the plantation and prevented escapes", can be seen as reflecting "cracks in the apparent solid edifice of the slave agro-industrial system" (ibid.: 62; see also Tomich 2004). As Mintz (1989: 236, emphasis added) remarks,

> estate slaves commonly grew their own subsistence on plantation uplands, using lands judged unsuitable for the major plantation crops. It was on such lands that the slaves acquired or perfected their horticultural skill, developed their own standardized agricultural practices, learned the characteristics of Caribbean soils, mastered the cultivation of new crops, and otherwise prepared themselves for their *reconstitution as peasantries*.

Variations in the size of the plantation, its geography and its main culture (which determined the quantity and seasonality of labor) could still confer a greater or lesser degree of productive autonomy to the enslaved, as compellingly argued by Trouillot (1993) of the coffee plantations in Saint-Domingue. For this reason, it was exactly on the outskirts of the plains where sugar flourished, in the mountain and marginal landscapes surrounding the plantation geography, that such techniques and skills were developed during slavery, both among the enslaved people who were guaranteed the chance to plant in this steep terrain, unsuitable for sugarcane, and among the maroon communities that thrived in the colony's interior (Price 1979). Mintz's argument focused, above all, on agricultural practices, from soil preparation to harvest and, from there, to the processing, storage, conservation, and selection of seeds; it left aside the technical knowledge developed in relation to game animals or husbandry. The historical source that Mintz used in his analysis was the well-known travel account of John Stewart (1823), whose observations centered on colonial Jamaica. The passage of particular interest to Sidney Mintz was as follows (Stewart 1823: 267, quoted in Mintz 1989: 187, emphasis added):

> Adjoining to the [enslaved] house is usually a small spot of ground, laid out into a sort of garden, and shaded by various fruit-trees. Here the family deposit their dead, to whose memory they invariably, if they can afford it, erect a rude tomb. Each slave has besides this spot, a piece of ground (about half an acre) allotted to him as a *provision-ground.*

In these provision grounds, enslaved people grew roots, bananas, fruits, and peppers. Any surplus was destined for local exchanges and for sale in the markets, which guaranteed the enslaved access to cash and therefore to some social mobility, particularly in the case of enslaved women. But in or close to these spaces, creatures such as pigs and birds also coexisted. John Stewart continued his account of the provision grounds in Jamaica (1823: 267, quoted in Mintz 1989: 187, emphasis added):

> This is the principal means of [slave's] support; and so productive is the soil, where it is good and the seasons regular, that this plot will not only furnish him with sufficient food for his own consumption, but an over-plus to carry to market. By means of this ground, as of the *hogs and poultry* which he may raise (*most of which he sells*), an industrious negro may not only support himself comfortably but save something.[8]

Stewart notes that other species, such as horses, cows, sheep, and, on most estates, goats, were forbidden to people subjected to slavery. This is explained, possibly, both by the high value of these animals and by the space and intensive care they needed. Pigs, however, were forbidden to walk freely on the land under the planters rules; but, like birds, they

[8] See also, Chapter 5 from the traveler's account (Stewart 1823) where he talks about wild animals: "Hunting the wild boar was a favourite diversion both of the hardy active white creole of the interior *and of the Maroons*" (ibid.: 74, emphasis added; spelling as in the original).

played a crucial role on the provision grounds.[9] Thus, it is remarkable that throughout the Caribbean, as Mintz (1989) states, common social histories produced countless similarities among these early peasantries, and, due to their diversity of traditions and cultural influences, "originated in good measure from a common history of slavery and forced labor, the domination of the plantation system, and the narrow range of economic alternatives available to those who resisted that system by developing life-styles outside it" (ibid.: 225).

Through the study of cultural practices in the early Caribbean, Sidney Mintz and Richard Price (1976) developed a very influential theory about the sociotechnical genesis of African-American cultures that became known as "creolization". With a strong materialist approach combined with the cultural ecology discussions of the time, the authors renewed perspectives on cultural and social formations in the Atlantic basin.[10] I argue here—adding something distinct to the creolization thesis—that human–animal alliances were crucial to the new life-worlds forged inside the provision grounds. In these gray zones on the margins of, and within, the plantation itself, spaces and techniques of cultivation and animal husbandry ensured other-than-human encounters in which new political horizons gave rise to what Wynter (1971) termed the "plot system" that, in opposition to the plantation, was "the focus of resistance to the market system and market values" (ibid.: 99). Similar to what Casimir (2018) called the "counter-plantation", the plot (or the provision ground) was oriented "towards the protection and regeneration of the community" (ibid.: 101).

In a context where property was extremely racialized and social mobility was restricted, people who lived under the burden of captivity experienced, even if in very limited forms, degrees of freedom through affective and material ensembles, recalling notions of dignity and autonomy that were not lost in the Middle Passage and forging—in a sort

[9] Also interesting is Stewart's observation that hogs and poultry were mostly raised to be sold, a practice that is still common nowadays in Haiti and that reveals a certain taboo related to direct consumption of domestic animals raised in a family's household.

[10] Mintz and Price generalizations have been challenged by Africanists since the 1990s, but their empirical approach prompted further developments about cultural contact and ethnogenesis not only in the Americas but also in pre-colonial Africa and Europe. For a recent appreciation of this debate, see Sidbury and Cañizares-Esguerra (2011).

of "becoming with", to borrow a proposition from Haraway (2010)—new landscapes, futures, and possibilities of life. It was at this point that the peasant breach made possible the emergence of new ecologies from practices, affects, and techniques developed in the relationship with land, plants as well as game and livestock animals, particularly pigs. "Furthermore", notes Trouillot (1990: 39),

> as the richer planters became increasingly involved in sugar, and as the coffee revolution absorbed both those whites with more limited resources and those free blacks who had hitherto engaged in foodstuff production, ever larger segments of the growing population came to depend on the agricultural and craft products of slave families.

With slave uprisings gaining momentum in the north of the colony, "rebelling slaves did not ask for an end to slavery, but merely for additional days to cultivate their plots" (idem). In this process, the use of land and its property was closely related to the notion of freedom; or, as historian Carolyn Fick (1990) puts it, for the black laborers, "a personal claim to the land upon which one labored and from which to derive and express one's individuality was (…) a necessary and an essential element in their vision of freedom". "For without this concrete economic and social reality", the author concludes, "freedom for the ex-slaves was little more than a legal abstraction" (ibid.: 249).

From the beginning, in the set of events that would lead to the Haitian Revolution, redefining the cartography of Atlantic warfare for good, "defiant alliances" with other-than-human agents inside provision grounds played an important role (Boisseron 2018).[11] Organized on the outskirts of the city of Le Cap, between mid and late August 1791, the *Bwa Kayman* ceremony is the event that prefigures the Haitian Revolution (Fick 1990; Dubois 2004: 99–102). In this ceremony, a great alliance was sealed involving enslaved Africans and their descendants, freedmen (*affranchis*) and free people of color (*gens de couleur*). In an act of sacrifice, they killed a pig in a service to the spirits known as the *lwa*.

[11] Malcom Ferdinand (2019: 377–378) describes three types of interspecies alliances that opposed the colonial dwelling—the inconvenient beings, the killers of colonial armies, and the anticolonial diplomats. To this, we can add a fourth that looks exactly at those living beings that were important for the colonial enterprise but that also granted the possibility of other forms of inhabiting the world, working in the fine line that separates accommodation and resistance.

For Maurice Etienne, a popular historian I met during my fieldwork in northern Haiti, that was a moment of awareness for the enslaved Africans, "an achievement of conscience" that created the possibility of revolt: "to acquire the morale they needed, they sacrificed a pig and believed that if they drank his blood, the pig would make them invincible". With this sacrifice, pigs mediated an alliance with spirits, and those fighting for freedom gained strength to carry out a counter-plantation project, destabilizing the institution of slavery, reversing the Atlantic colonial order, and creating the path to the country's independence (Fig. 2.1).

In the image above, the painter Jean-Baptiste Jean reproduces the celebration of 200 years of *Bwa Kayman*: a pig is sacrificed in a great ceremony surrounded by people dressed in handkerchiefs that, when tied on the heads or waist, reveal possession by a spirit. Three drums are beaten

Fig. 2.1 "Celebration of 200 years of the Bois-Caïman, 1791–1991", Jean-Baptiste Jean, 1993. Author's collection

while a man blows a shell, the main symbol for collective action in Haiti. People dance and Haitian flags appear in the hands of some. A bowl of blood is placed on the floor, reflecting the sacrifice of the pig in the story of the ceremony. In the center of the painting, a reproduction of the original scene appears in a curious *mise en abîme*. In the ritual that gave birth to an independent country, pigs that were once *marrons* became *kreyòl* (Creole), a term that came to define the cuisine, the language, and society of Haiti as a whole. The creole pigs were, as Michelet Delima, a senior peasant from the north of Haiti, once told me, the backbone of the house economy (*se sou kochon kreyòl ke lekonomi lakay te chita*) (Bulamah 2020). Through this process, the plantation or the *habitation* was subverted, and those who were once denied the right to inhabit finally became known, in Haitian Creole, as the new *abitan* (Fischer 2016).

Counter-Plantation and Its Afterlives

In 2000, Crutzen and Stoermer proposed a new geological marker that could take into account the effective force of humankind as a geophysical force redefining not only human history but also the history of the planet as a whole (Crutzen and Stoermer 2000). We have reached the Anthropocene. Although many scientists had already recognized the geological and morphological impacts of human activity, the effect of Crutzen and Stoermer's proposition was felt in many academic fields and has been particularly fruitful in the Humanities and Social Sciences. For the authors, the onset of the Anthropocene could be located around "the latter part of the eighteenth century", coinciding with James Watt's invention of the steam engine, symbol of the industrial revolution (2000: 17–18). For other scholars, however, a more appropriate name for this new era would be the Plantationocene, a concept that would shed light on colonization and the plantation infrastructure as the model and motor of modern forms of extracting Earth's resources that shaped our contemporary world (Haraway et al. 2016; see also Mathews 2020).

As I have argued here, the plantation was, in itself, an enterprise viscerally linked to a wide range of other-than-human beings, including the land itself, plants, animals, and spirits. On the one hand, while the hunting of wild and feral animals and animal husbandry played an important role in the formation of new landscapes by pirates and settlers, colonial society depended on controlling the lives of animals, fungi, and plants, as their labor was crucial in monoculture production. On the other hand, Africans and their descendants, enslaved or runaways, interacted with these and other beings inside and outside the plantation, either in the provision grounds and animal pens or in the maroon communities, producing forms of counter-plantation alliances that materially defined territories, lives, and futures beyond the plantation. In post-revolutionary Haiti, these provision grounds and the small family compounds known as *lakou* became the center of a new Creole landscape (Bastien 1951; Dubois 2012: 107–109).

If the history of our world is in a way the history of the plantation, we should consider the role of more-than-human beings in forging new alliances and alternative futures. Pigs as well as other beings, with their own intentions and projects, played a crucial role in the technogenesis of these agrarian landscapes and in the ontogenesis of modern ideas such as freedom, understood here not only as a sociological dimension of peasantry as a class, but as a fundamental value of modernity. Therefore, if modern infrastructures, such as the plantation, have a crucial role in contemporary forms of inhabiting the world, we cannot disregard the many counter-plantation practices and the plot systems that created other forms of dwelling. To bring Casimir (2018) and Wynter (1971) back to our conversation, these practices protected and regenerated not only the community but also the world at large. They were not only forms of resistance but the materialization of new ecologies in practice: a work of regeneration for a time that we now know as the Anthropocene.

References

Alves, A.A. 2011. *The Animals of Spain: An Introduction to Imperial Perceptions and Human Interaction with Other Animals, 1492–1826*. Boston: Brill.

Anderson, V. 2004. *Creatures of Empire: How Domestic Animals Transformed Early America*. New York: Oxford University Press.

Andrews, K.R. 1978. *The Spanish Caribbean: Trade and Plunder, 1530–1630*. New Haven: Yale University Press.

Bastien, R. 1951. *La familia rural haitiana, Valle de Marbial*. México: Libra.

Berlin, I. 1998. *Many Thousands Gone. The First Two Centuries of Slavery in North America*. Cambridge: Belknap Press.

Boisseron, B. 2018. *Afro-Dog: Blackness and the Animal Question*. New York: Columbia University Press.

Brown, V. 2010. *The Reaper's Garden: Death and Power in the World of Atlantic Slavery*. Cambridge: Harvard University Press.

Brown, V. 2020. *Tacky's Revolt: The Story of an Atlantic Slave War*. Cambridge: Harvard University Press.

Bulamah, R.C. 2020. Pode Um Porco Falar? Doença, Sistemas e Sacrifício No Caribe. *Horizontes Antropológicos* 26 (57): 57–92.

Cadena, M., and M. Blaser, eds. 2018. *A World of Many Worlds*. Illustrated. Durham: Duke University Press.

Casimir, J. 1992. *The Caribbean: One and Divisible*. Santiago, Chile: United Nations, Economic Commission for Latin America and the Caribbean.

Casimir, J. 2018. Une Lecture Décoloniale de l'histoire Du Peuple Haïtien de 1697 à 1915. *Rencontre* 34: 95–105.

Castellano, K. 2021. "Provision Grounds Against the Plantation: Robert Wedderburn's Axe Laid to the Root." *Small Axe: A Caribbean Journal of Criticism* 25 (1 (64)): 15–27.

Crosby, A.W. 1972. *The Columbian Exchange: Biological and Cultural Consequences of 1492*. Westport: Greenwood Pub. Co.

Crosby, A.W. 1986. *Ecological Imperialism: The Biological Expansion of Europe, 900–1900*. Cambridge: Cambridge University Press.

Crublier de Saint-Cyran, P.-E. 1790. *Réfutation Du Projet Des Amis Des Noirs, Sur La Suppression de La Traite Des Nègres et Sur l'abolition de l'esclavage Dans Nos Colonies*. Paris: Imprimerie de Devaux.

Crutzen, P., and E. Stoermer. 2000. "The 'Anthropocene'." *Global Change Newsletter*, 2000, 41 edition.

Curtin, P.D. 1990. *The Rise and Fall of the Plantation Complex: Essays in Atlantic History*. Cambridge: Cambridge University Press.

DeLoughrey, E. 2011. Yam, Roots, and Rot: Allegories of the Provision Grounds. *Small Axe* 15 (1): 58–75.

Derby, L. 2011. "Bringing the Animals Back in: Writing Quadrupeds into the Environmental History of Latin America and the Caribbean." *History Compass* 9 (8): 602–621.

Donkin, R.A. 1985. *The Peccary: With Observations on the Introduction of Pigs to the New World*. Philadelphia: The American philosophical Society.

Dubois, L. 2004. *Avengers of the New World: The Story of the Haitian Revolution*. Cambridge: Belknap Press of Harvard University Press.

Dubois, L. 2012. *Haiti: The Aftershocks of History*. New York: Picador.

Dubois, L., and R.L. Turits. 2019. *Freedom Roots: Histories from the Caribbean*. Chapel Hill: University of North Carolina Press.

Ferdinand, M. 2019. *Une écologie décoloniale: Penser l'écologie depuis le monde caribéen*. Paris: Éditions du Seuil.

Fick, C.E. 1990. *The Making of Haiti: The Saint Domingue Revolution from Below*. Knoxville: University of Tennessee Press.

Fischer, S. 2016. Inhabiting Rights. *L'esprit Créateur* 56 (1): 52–67.

Giusti-Cordero, J. 2009. "Beyond Sugar Revolutions: Rethinking the Spanish Caribbean in the Seventeenth and Eighteenth Century." In *Empirical Futures: Anthropologists and Historians Engage the Work of Sidney W. Mintz*, ed. A.

Khan, G. Baca, and S. Palmié, 58–83. Chapel Hill: University of North Carolina Press.
———. 2014. "Sugar and Livestock: Contraband Networks in Hispaniola and the Continental Caribbean in the Eighteenth Century." *Revista Brasileira do Caribe* XV (29): 13–41.
Hage, G. 2017. *Is Racism an Environmental Threat?* Malden: Polity.
Haraway, D., N. Ishikawa, S.F. Gilbert, K. Olwig, A.L. Tsing, and N. Bubandt. 2016. Anthropologists Are Talking—About the Anthropocene. *Ethnos* 81 (3): 535–564.
Haraway, D.J. 2010. *When Species Meet*. Minneapolis: University of Minnesota Press.
James, C.L.R. 1989. *The Black Jacobins: Toussaint L'Ouverture and the San Domingo Revolution*. New York: Vintage Books.
Johnson, S.E. 2012. *The Fear of French Negroes: Transcolonial Collaboration in the Revolutionary Americas*. Berkeley: University of California Press.
Labat, J.-B. 1724. *Nouveau Voyage Aux Isles de l'Amérique*. Haia: P. Husson editeur.
Las Casas, B. de. 1957. *História de Las Indias. 2 Vols.*, ed. J. Pérez de Tudela and Emílio Lopez Oto. Madri: Biblioteca de Autores Españoles.
Lecomte, J. 1837. *L'Île de la Tortue: roman maritime, vol. 1 - Histoire des flibustiers*. Paris: Hyppolite Souverain.
Lepkowski, T. 1970. *Haiti*. La Habana: Casa de las Américas.
Mathews, A.S. 2020. Anthropology and the Anthropocene: Criticisms, Experiments, and Collaborations. *Annual Review of Anthropology* 49 (1): 67–82.
McNeill, J.R. 2010. *Mosquito Empires: Ecology and War in the Greater Caribbean, 1620–1914*. New Approaches to the Americas. New York: Cambridge University Press.
Metcalf, A.C. 2005. *Go-Betweens and the Colonization of Brazil, 1500–1600*. Austin: University of Texas Press.
Mintz, S.W. 1985. *Sweetness and Power: The Place of Sugar in Modern History*. New York: Penguin.
Mintz, S.W. 1989. *Caribbean Transformations*. New York: Columbia University Press.
Mintz, S.W. 1996. Enduring Substances, Trying Theories: The Caribbean Region as Oikoumene. *The Journal of the Royal Anthropological Institute* 2 (2): 289–311.
Mintz, S.W., and R. Price. 1976. *An Anthropological Approach to the Afro-American Past: A Caribbean Perspective*. Philadelphia: ISHI.
Moreau de Saint-Méry, M.L.E. 1958. *Description Topographique, Physique, Civile, Politique et Histoire de La Partie Française de l'Isle Saint-Domingue. Tomo I*. Paris: Société de l'Histoire des Colonies Françaises et Librarie Larose.

Moya Pons, F. 1977. *Historia colonial de Santo Domingo*. Santiago, RD: Universidad Católica Madre y Maestra.

Moya Pons, F. 2007. *History of the Caribbean: Plantations, Trade, and War in the Atlantic World*. Princeton: Markus Wiener Publishers.

Norton, M. 2013. Animals in Spain and Spanish Americas. In *Lexikon of the Hispanic Baroque: Transatlantic Exchange and Transformation*, ed. K. Mills and E. Levy, 17–23. Austin: University of Texas Press.

Norton, M. 2015. The Chicken or the Iegue: Human-Animal Relationships and the Columbian Exchange. *The American Historical Review* 120 (1): 28–60.

Oexmelín, A. 1930. *Les Aventuriers et les Boucaniers d'Amérique, par Alexandre Oexmelín, chirurgien des aventuriers de 1666 à 1672*, ed. Bertrand Guégan. Paris: Aux Editions du Carrefour.

Paravisini-Gebert, L. 2008. Endangered Species: Caribbean Ecology and the Discourse of the Nation. In *Displacements and Transformations in Caribbean Cultures*, ed. L. Paravisini-Gebert and I. Romero-Cesareo, 8–23. Gainesville: University Press of Florida.

Price, R. 1979. *Maroon Societies: Rebel Slave Communities in the Americas*. Baltimore: The Johns Hopkins University Press.

Raynal, G.-T. 1770. *Histoire Philosophique et Politique Des Établissemens et Du Commerce Des Européens Dans Les Deux Indes. Tomo 3*. Vol. A. Amsterdam: s.n.

Sautchuk, C.E. 2018. "Os Antropólogos e a Domesticação: Derivações e Ressurgências de Um Conceito." In *Políticas Etnográficas No Campo Da Ciência e Das Tecnologias Da Vida*, ed. J. Segata and T. Rifiotis, 85–108. Porto Alegre: Editora da UFRGS.

Scott, D. 2004. Modernity That Predated the Modern: Sidney Mintz's Caribbean. *History Workshop Journal* 58: 191–210.

Scott, J.S. 2018. *The Common Wind: Afro-American Currents in the Age of the Haitian Revolution*. London: Verso.

Sidbury, J., and J. Cañizares-Esguerra. 2011. Mapping Ethnogenesis in the Early Modern Atlantic. *The William and Mary Quarterly* 68 (2): 181–208.

Sordi, C. 2020. Bicho Bandido: Wild Boars, Biological Invasions and Landscape Transformations on the Brazilian-Uruguayan Border (Pampas Region). *Social Anthropology* 28 (3): 614–628.

Stewart, J. 1823. *View of the Past and Present State of the Island of Jamaica with Remarks of the Moral and Physical Conditions of the Slaves, and on the Abolition of Slavery in the Colonies. Edinburgh: Oliver & Boid, Tweeddale-House*. Edinburgh: Oliver & Boid, Tweeddale-House.

Stoler, A.L. 2009. *Along the Archival Grain: Epistemic Anxieties and Colonial Common Sense*. Princeton: Princeton University Press.

Tardieu, J.-P. 2006. Cimarrón-Maroon-Marron: Note Épistemologique. *Outres-Mers* 93 (350–351): 237–247.

Thomas, K. 1983. *Man and the Natural World: A History of the Modern Sensibility*. Pantheon Books.
———. 1996. *Homem e o mundo natural: mudanças de atitude em relação as plantas e aos animais (1500–1800)*, trans. João Roberto Martins Filho. São Paulo: Companhia das Letras.
Tomich, D. 2004. *Through the Prism of Slavery: Labor, Capital, and World Economy*. Lanham: Rowman & Littlefield.
Trouillot, M.-R. 1990. *Haiti, State Against Nation: The Origins and Legacy of Duvalierism*. New York: Monthly Review.
Trouillot, M.-R. 1993. Coffee Planters and Coffee Slaves in the Antilles: The Impact of a Secondary Crop. In *Cultivation and Culture: Labor and the Shaping of Slave Life in the Americas*, ed. I. Berlin and P. Morgan, 124–137. Charlottesville; London: University Press of Virginia.
Trouillot, M.-R. 1995. *Silencing the Past: Power and the Production of History*. Boston: Beacon Press.
Trouillot, M.-R. 2003. *Global Transformations: Anthropology and the Modern World*. New York: Palgrave Macmillan.
Tsing, A.L. 2015. *Mushroom at the End of the World: On the Possibilities of Life in Capitalist Ruins*. Princeton: Princeton University Press.
Velden, F.F.V. 2012. As galinhas incontáveis. Tupis, europeus e aves domésticas na conquista no Brasil. *Journal de la Société des Américanistes* 98 (2): 97–104.
Velden, F.F.V. 2018. Os primeiros cachorros: Encontros interétnicos e multiespecíficos no Sudoeste da Amazônia. *Revista Brasileira de Ciências Sociais* 33 (July): 1–23.
Williams, E. 1994. *Capitalism and Slavery*. Chapel Hill: The University of North Carolina Press.
Wynter, S. 1971. Novel and History, Plot and Plantation. *Savacou* 5: 95–102.

CHAPTER 3

The Rise and Fall of Caporalisme Agraire in Haiti (1789–1806): Labor Perspectives Through the Plantation Complex

Martino Sacchi and Lorenzo Ravano

Introduction

In this chapter, we analyze the government of emancipated slaves and the reorganization of plantation labor during the Haitian Revolution. The chronology of the revolution is generally divided into four phases: the struggle of free people of color against racial discrimination (1789–1792), the armed insurrection of the enslaved Africans that led to the abolition of slavery (1791–1793), the reorganization of the colony after emancipation under the leadership the black general Toussaint Louverture (1794–1801), and the war of independence ended in the foundation

M. Sacchi
Università di Bologna, Bologna, Italy
e-mail: martino.sacchilandriani@gmail.com

L. Ravano (✉)
Liceo di Lugano 1, Lugano, Switzerland
e-mail: lorenzo.ravano@edu.ti.ch

C. Le Petitcorps et al. (eds.), *Global Plantations in the Modern World*, Cambridge Imperial and Post-Colonial Studies,
https://doi.org/10.1007/978-3-031-08537-6_3

of the State of Haiti (1802–1805). Although the abolition of slavery is evidently a central event in the history of the Haitian Revolution (Dubois 2004; Nesbitt 2008; Popkin 2010; Bogues 2010), in this chapter we will approach the question of plantation labor by analyzing the constant restructuring of the subordination of black workers. Rather than focusing on the classic conceptual couple slavery/freedom, we then address the problem around the concepts of *dependency* and *independence*. By showing both the continuities and discontinuities of labor codes, we consider the resilience of the plantation system beyond juridical innovations that characterized slave emancipation and national independence. First, we outline the main features of the plantation regime at the eve of the Revolution. Secondly, we transversally read the rural codes issued from the abolition of slavery (1793–1794) to national independence (1804). We argue that different discourses on citizenship, ranging from western political economy to radical black nationalism, should be read against the grain of police measures granting export-oriented economy through an increasingly militarized agriculture. In the last paragraph, we consider the fall of militarize agriculture to address the issue of "plantations afterlives".

The plantation regime stands at the core of the double dimension of dependency, which must be considered both as a personal relationship between laborers and masters, and as a systemic relation derived from export-oriented production. From this perspective, it is possible to trace continuities beyond the formal abolition of slavery and to look at intertwining histories of labor and citizenship in the colonial and postcolonial context.

Policing Emancipation, Preserving Plantation

To eighteenth century European observers, colonies were far from being peripheral sites. As the Abbé Raynal famously stated in his 1770 account on the West Indies, they "can be regarded as the principal cause of the rapid movement which stirs de universe" (Duffy 1987: 6). Indeed, at the eve of the Revolution, Saint-Domingue, the so-called pearl of the Antilles, was the world's leading producer of both sugar and coffee. It had a total of about 8000 plantations (moreover sugar, coffee, indigo, and a small number of cotton plantations), generating two-fifths of France's overseas trade. According to the mercantilist economic policy of the so-called *Exclusif* (i.e., France's monopoly on colonial trade), almost three-quarters of the crops produced in the French Antilles were exported to the metropole, and then re-exported to other European markets. Nevertheless, a conspicuous amount was directly smuggled to other Caribbean and North American colonies. In addition to this value produced by colonial trade, it is important to notice that the enslaved people in all French colonies represented an estimated capital investment of one billion of *livres tournois* (Geggus 1993: 73–98; Dubois 2004: 24–30). Contemporary historiography has clearly demonstrated that Caribbean and American plantations were one of the foundation of capitalism: a worldly embedded socio-economic system based on the exploitation of African men and women, integrated in the emerging Western banks and stock markets, and operating on a global scale within international trade (Beckert and Rockman 2016).

More precisely, the plantation complex implied a peculiar organization of the productive process, characterized by concentration of land and labor. Differently from the Brazilian methods originally imported to the Antilles, the agri-manufacturing model integrated farming and processing activities within a single cycle (Mintz 1986). Such an integrated model necessitated a concentration of capitals as well as of laborers to be organized in slave gangs. Rather than assigning individual tasks to specific slaves, field laborers proceeded in rows, grouped according to their physical capacity to endure different tasks: harvesting, trimming, weeding, or clearing the field from stones (Fick 1990: 27–33). As Garrigus and Burnard noted, the gang system allowed to synchronize cultivation with the tight manufacturing schedules imposed by mills and boiling houses, although such overall functioning was historically precarious (Burnard and Garrigus 2016; Cheney 2017). Planters' manuals expressed the importance of timing and discipline metaphorically describing the plantation as a "machine" articulating different activities under a common organizational principle (Martin 1765; Burnard and Garrigus 2016: 5). Consequently, violence came to be clearly conceived as an economic rationale logic too. Since Louis XIV's Edict of 1685, known as the *Code Noir*, the Monarchy attempted to preserve the plantation system by regulating the master–slave relationship founded on violence (Ghachem 2012). Nonetheless, this set of rules was never rigidly enforced and the slaves remained basically subordinated to the absolute power of their masters. But similar preoccupations on the regulation of master–slave relationship appeared in the writings of planters and colonial administrators. On the one hand, colonial administrators feared that the masters' violence would foment slave rebellions, producing the collapse of colonial order (Cazzola and Ravano 2020). On the other hand, many planters reasoned about how the use of violence on the plantation should be managed, in part because of the high death rates among slaves that implied the continuous import of enslaved Africans in Saint-Domingue through the Atlantic slave trade. As we can read in the manual on coffee plantations written by Pierre Joseph Laborie to instruct the English army who occupied the southern province of Saint-Domingue from 1793 to 1798, masters "must extract from the negro all the work he can reasonably perform, and use every means to prolong his life" (Laborie 1797: 159–160). In this sense, violence should be calibrated to push the slaves' bodies to the limits of their work capability: whipping and other forms of torture should be exercised on the very thin threshold between life and death in order to impose the maximum degree of obedience and efficiency and, at the same time, the maximum extension a slave's productive lifetime.

Aside from the increasing rationalization of the production process, colonial society was less strictly compartmentalized than we may expect: its internal frontiers were continuously challenged by slave mobility. Marronage was constitutive of plantation society and since the mid-eighteenth century it became increasingly associated with slave uprisings: the poisoning wave that affected the white population of Saint-Domingue from 1757 to 1758, and for which the maroon leader François Mackandal was executed, has been considered an important antecedent to the 1791 revolution (Fick 1990: 46–75). But marronage did not necessarily imply a mass escape or revolt. It was also an everyday and individual form of resistance (the so-called *petit marronage*), which could take different geographical directions, such as rural, urban and maritime, and different timings (days, weeks, months). Indeed, statistically speaking most of Saint-Domingue slaves left for small periods of time, in response to conjunctural reasons inherent to their plantation, while other slaves aimed also to reach port cities, where they could find new employment as seamen, or left the island to reach other colonies (Debien 1974; Fouchard 1981; Thompson 2006; Scott 2018; Gonzalez 2019). Moreover, exchanges between the internal world of the plantation and the rest of society did include not only escape but also personal relations and petty markets. Within the plantations' population, the number of informally free blacks (*libres de savanne*) grew in parallel to taxation imposed to planters in order to discourage manumissions. These undocumented but free blacks autonomously farmed small plots on the estates of their former masters (Debien 1967). In conclusion, the violence of the plantation society curiously coexisted with its relatively porous borders: in terms of both mobility and of property regimes. The Revolution provided the framework in which long-term social conflicts would explode these borders, temporarily fragmenting the social unit of the plantation.

Indeed, when the insurrection of the enslaved Africans broke out in August 1791 in the Northern province of Saint-Domingue, labor organization rapidly occupied a pivotal position among the many governmental issues imposed to the French Civil Commissioners sent by Paris to the colony to restore the public order and economic production. In this regard, it is worth to recall the fact that Jacobin Commissioners Léger-Félicité Sonthonax and Étienne Polverel, who issued the first decrees of emancipation in August and October 1793, originally landed in the colony with the sole project of preserving plantation productivity and enforcing the decree of 4 April 1792, which extended full citizenship rights to so-called free people of color. As we mentioned above, the colonial crisis had in fact exploded with the struggle of free people of color—many of whom were also plantation owners—against racial discrimination that excluded them from citizenship rights defined by the National Assembly from 1789 to the proclamation of the Constitution in 1791. In the decades before, and especially after the Seven Years War, racial norms had fragmented the social group of slave owners. Local administrative measures formally forbade to members of the colored wealthy class to hold relevant public office, to practice medical professions, as well as carry weapons and dress European-style clothing. As John D. Garrigus has shown, Frenchness was increasingly based on whiteness, so that colonial authorities reclassified as colored some Creole people previously considered as members of white families. At the eve of slave insurrection, the National Assembly looked with apprehension at this "aristocracy of the skin" and met the demands of the right to property (including that of slaves) made by free people of color (Garrigus 2006; Gauthier 2007). Colonial social unrest at the eve of the Revolution thus reflected the overlapping of different forms of social differentiation, ranging from racial discrimination of a sector of the free population to the tension between the universalist discourse on equality and the structural role of slavery in the colonial economy. In this context, when slave armies, organized by black leaders such as Biassou, Jean-François and Toussaint Louverture, forced Sonthonax and Polverel to declare emancipation, the organization of labor came to the forefront of political debates. The

Jacobin Commissioners presented the formal inclusion of former slaves into citizenship as a *concession* strictly connected to civic *duties*: plantation labor or military service. The first labor codes made clear that the specificity of colonial agriculture strongly influenced this nexus between recognition, work compulsion, and subordination:

> The agriculture in France gives only the raw products: each of its farms employed few arms and few instruments of ploughing. They have nothing in common with the factories intended to valorize the raw materials. [...] These plantations [of Santo Domingo], are both agricultural and manufacturing. They produce the raw materials, shape them and develop them. One family is not enough as in France to form a plantation. Each plantation forms a numerous population, there are several, whose population surpasses that of our villages and small towns of Europe; and it is to free hands, to voluntary work that these important plantations will owe their existence and their activity.[1]

With these words, Polverel let it transpire that maintaining the agro-industrial complex of the plantation under a free labor regime determined numerous governmental problems. Indeed, soon after the flight of many white planters, who reached Europe, the United States, and other colonies such as Martinique, slaves reshaped colonial geographies occupying more land for subsistence farming or moving elsewhere (Barthélemy 1990; Fick 1990: 249–250). From then on, all leading factions (French, blacks and mulattoes) will attempt to restore the previous social fabric. The export-oriented plantation economy was then the common *material* ground on which conflicting political projects were deployed on the stage of the Revolution.

Revolutionary Citizenship Through Militarized Agriculture

Desertions and occupations of land by former slaves had both practical and theoretical implications on revolutionary citizenship. How to legitimize coercion within the formal frame of emancipation? At first,

[1] E. Polverel. *Règlement de police sur la culture et les cultivateurs, fait sur la petite habitation Oshiell, Plaine du fond de l'Isle à Vache le 28 février 1794, l'an troisième de la République française, signé Polverel*. In *Revue d'histoire des colonies*, 36 (127–128), 1949: 402.

Polverel mobilized a main argument of European discourses on pauperism (Oudin-Bastide and Steiner 2015). According to this, poor people are in a sort of eternal servitude: they may change their master, but they will always be remain "slaves of their needs" and be dependent on someone else to make a living.

> I see only two differences between them and the slaves: for the latter slavery is perpetual, while the servitude of the wage workers is only temporary; the slaves have not even received the price of their liberty, instead of the wage workers receiving it in detail, every year, every month or every day. But these differences are only apparent. The wage workers, always commanded by their needs, leaves one master only to sell themselves to another; they change master but their servitude is eternal[2]

From this perspective, the liberation of labor from despotic ties was put in relation to the fragile condition of the "free" wage worker. The liberal critique of European corporate regulations and of colonial slavery historically interacted with a supposed anthropological incapability of self-government of the working poor, characterized by objective dependency. This argument, which would shape nineteenth century France's discourse on the so-called social question (Castel 2003), showed its inconsistencies when transplanted into colonial social relations. Since plantation production implied a strong concentration of land and labor, it soon became evident that specific measures had to be set in place to actively produce the citizen at the intersection of social relations of dependency. Policing emancipation would imply to artificially set the external conditions for a "free" labor regime by both limiting access to subsistence farming and subduing freedom to labor subordination. As we will see, the transition from liberal discourse to black nationalism would radicalize this position by superimposing military and labor hierarchies. We can thus read the concept of citizenship against the grain of the rural codes and trace the metamorphosis of "personal dependency" and "international dependency" beyond emancipation projects and constitutional watersheds making Haiti an independent State.

[2] Ibid.

Land Concentration

In the first place, drops in colonial production must be contained by avoiding land parcellation. Against slaves' claims to petty property, land concentration prevailed both at emancipation (1793) and at the time of national independence (1804). While suggesting a system of *cultivation portionnaire*, Polverel clearly stated that properties remained indivisible until the end of war (art. 8). Former slaves will never cease to oppose this measure, since any redistribution of vacant plantations among soldiers and farmers meant very little to them if the work on large estates remained mandatory. Ongoing resistance would eventually contribute to a general reorientation of production toward coffee, necessitating comparatively less labor discipline than sugar (Moral 1961: 20–21). In contrast, the control of plantations became the pivotal stake among competing elites: French administrators, colored former planters and military officers, and the black officers who ranked the revolutionary army (Casimir 2009).

In the first period after emancipation, Toussaint Louverture supported the French general Étienne Laveaux against the mulattoes controlling southern estates, making this alliance the starting point to distribute plantations among black generals. This trend would remain in place when the conflict progressively took an anti-colonial dimension. In 1801, Louverture forbid to sell lands of less than 50 *carreaux*, and strove also to avoid abuses on land management, with the decree of May 7th.[3] Similarly, after having defeated French armies, the new leader of independent Haiti Jean-Jacques Dessalines attacked the mulatto elite, invalidating past land transactions and subordinating new ones to state authorization.[4] Overall, the main issue was that of bridging the gap between factual appropriations having taken place throughout the war by both mulatto élites and black peasants and a process of bordering via property titles managed by the State. This set of measures was part of a broader nationalist anti-colonial

[3] Toussaint Louverture, *Règlement relatif aux revenus des habitations*, au Port-Républicain, le 13 prairial an VIII. In ANOM, CC9B/18.

[4] *Arrêté qui règle quelques points importants du service militaire et de l'administration*, Quartier-Général les Cayes, le 7 Février 1804 an 1. In M. Nau and D. Telhomme (dir.) 1930. *Recueuil général des lois et actes du gouvernement d'Haiti*. Imprimerie Nemours Telhomme: 5; J. J. Dessalines. *Décret Impérial, 2 Mai 1806, an III de l'indépendance*. In *Lois et Actes sous le règne de Jean-Jacques Dessalines*. 2006. Port-au-Prince: Editions Presses nationales d'Haiti: 10–11.

project. The first Constitution of independent Haiti stated the inviolability of property and, at the same time, the prohibition to any "white person, of whatever nationality [to] set foot on this territory in the role of master or proprietor nor in future acquire any property [in Haiti]" (Dubois et al. 2013: 64). Race was now framed as a political category, rather than as a phenotypical one. Witness the fact that all Haitians will be "known by the generic denomination of blacks" but women, Germans, and Poles (who presumably deserted foreign armies) may be naturalized as such (Dubois et al. 2013: 64).

Parallel to the reorganization of labor, at stake was the very notion of universalism inherent to the French Revolution: a conflicting redefinition of its boundaries and, consequently, of the historical actors who were meant to realize the universalist project itself. On the one hand, in the first years of the Haitian Revolution, the free people of color had used the French revolutionary discourse to claim the removal of all racial discrimination and their own inclusion into French citizenship. In fact, being free proprietors and taxpayers, and in some cases also slave owners, such as the leader Julien Raimond, the free people of color considered themselves part of the Third Estate. Such inclusion did not question the existence of slavery: by using both the *Declaration of the Rights of Man and of the Citizen* and the article 59 of the *Code Noir*, they argued that the only legitimate statutory differentiation should be that opposing free people to slaves, in contrast to further discriminations based on color (Ghachem 2012: 7–18; Semley 2017; Ravano 2021). On the other hand, Dessalines' Constitution posed blackness itself as the main vector of universalism. Countering the western idea of a linear expansion of modernity from the European center to its colonial peripheries, the political mobilization of color meant to show and reverse the partiality of western universalism and to reverse the geographical partition between modernity and pre-modernity (Fisher 2004). However, as the Haitian historian Claude Moïse already noted, the constitutional article instituting the formal equality of "black" citizens at the time of independence was another (although reversed) juridical camouflage of the material reality of Haitian society (Moïse 1988: 32–33). Behind the formal unity of the "black people" of Haiti declared in the Constitution laid the material difference between former African slaves employed on plantations and the military elites that ruled the Haitian State and economy. We shall thus move to the social and productive level to see how this new Haitian citizenship was historically manufactured through labor policies. Violence forged this connection between dependent labor and freedom, shaping what Michel-Rolph Trouillot defined a "war within the war" between black peasants and the revolutionary élite (Trouillot 1995: 40).

Limitations to Mobility

The temporary fading of plantation borders led to undisciplined mobilities that threatened the reproduction of plantation economy. As Commissioner Polverel stated, former slaves were mainly interested in the concrete dimension of emancipation: they wanted to "live their freedom" and to verify "that they were free to decide not to work, and that they could go wherever they wanted".[5] Formally speaking, black peasants were indeed now free to choose their masters and to have labor disputes heard by tribunals. Nevertheless, it became imperative to channel former slaves' movements toward wage labor and to retain them on plantations. Repressing vagrancy and the breach of contracts was thus a pivotal task of rural police since emancipation in 1793. Sonthonax introduced the felony of vagrancy for those peasants found outside plantations and general Gabriel d'Hédouville (governor from April to October 1798) enforced it through more severe detention periods.[6] With production being at the core of mobility policies, the judges of colonial tribunals were authorized to release people convicted to more than six months of imprisonment in case they accept to sign a work contract. In order to retain labor on plantations, a minimum length was set for contracts, progressively increased from one year in 1793 to three years in 1798. Any switch from a plantation to another one was subordinated to the obtention of an authorization, so that the emergence of the colonial labor market was rigidly compartmented. Penalties for breach of contract were also hardened, adding six months of prison detention for cultivators to Polverel's withholding of wages (crop shares), as well as fining landowners

[5] E. Polverel, *Règlement sur les proportions du travail et de la récompense, sur le partage des produits de la culture entre les propriétaires et les cultivateurs. Fait sur la petite habitation Oshiell du Fond de l'Isle à Vache le 7 février 1794, l'an 3 de la République Française.* In *Revue d'histoire des colonies*, cit.: 391.

[6] In August 1793, detention range from 1 to 3 months in case of recidivism (art. 3–11; 32–36), while in 1798 Hédouville brings them to 6 months (art. 20): G. d'Hédouville, *Arrêté concernant la police des habitations et les obligations réciproques des propriétaires ou fermiers et des cultivateurs*, 6 thermidor an VI (July 24, 1798). In AN AF/III/210, dossier 963, n. 44.

not being able to provide the contracts of all their workers. Hédouville was particularly accurate in underlining that any unjustified absence from a plantation in order to cultivate kitchen plots would not be considered as "work" and consequently fined.[7] Large-scale rebellions occurred against these policies. When Hédouville ordered to capture black general Moïse in September 1798, peasants in Fort-Liberté delivered a petition threatening a halt to production and a general flight from plantations: "We don't want to work anymore; we prefer to die, if General Hédouville does not leave the colony; we don't want to be engaged anymore: we will rather stay in the woods all our life, if he does not leave".[8] Louverture's intervention in this regard would strategically play on both the internal and external fronts of the revolution. On the one hand, Louverture pushed for a repatriation of Hédouville criticizing his policies and countered metropolitan arguments on the impossibility to establish a free labor regime on plantations.[9] On the other hand, he enforced previous norms through a militarized agriculture regime known as *caporalisme agraire*. The full doctrine of militarized agriculture was set by the *Règlement relative à la culture* (12 October 1800). It formalized the equivalence between army hierarchies and plantation production:

> Considering that a soldier, without incurring the most severe punishment, cannot leave his company, his battalion or his half-brigade to go to another, without a permission (...) it must also be forbidden to the peasants to leave their plantation to go to reside in another, without a legal permission, (...) since they change plantation at will, come and go and do not occupy themselves in any way with the cultivation of the land.[10]

[7] Ibid., art. 17.

[8] *Extrait des Pièces originales déposées du Greffe de la Municipalité de Toussaint Louverture*, in *Arrêté des différentes communes de la colonie de St.-Domingue adressées à l'Agent particulier du Directoire*, Cap-Français, P. Roux, 1799: 6.

[9] Toussaint Louverture, *Rapport, fait par Toussaint Louverture, général en chef de l'Armée de St.-Domingue, au Directoire exécutif, le 22 Brumaire an 7*, Cap-Français, P. Roux, 1799; Toussaint Louverture, *Réfutation de quelques assertions d'un discours prononcé au Corps Legislatif le 10 prairial, an cinq, par V. Vaublanc. Toussaint Louverture, général en chef de l'armée de Saint-Domingue, au Directoire exécutif*, Cap-Français, P. Roux, 1797.

[10] Toussaint Louverture, *Règlement relatif à la culture*, Port-au-Prince, le 20 vendémiaire an IX (October 12, 1800), In ANOM, CC9B/9.

The code specifically targeted that part of the young population not having experienced slave labor and now reclaiming the right to roam as constitutive to their freedom. "The security of freedom" demanded discipline: military hierarchy must inform the division of labor. Such overlapping of regimes was far from being metaphoric, since cultivators are explicitly punished through the same penalties of rank-and-file soldiers (art. 1, 2) and plantation managers are placed under the surveillance of local army generals (art. 7).[11] *Caporalisme agraire* revealed more effective than previous codes in fostering production increases, showing the intimate connection between coercion and productivity (Lundhal 1979). General Leclerc, leading Napoleonic troops to Saint-Domingue in 1802, considered it useful to maintain Toussaint's system instead of reestablishing slavery as in nearby Guadeloupe (Girard 2009). These ambiguous connections between discipline, labor, and freedom directly structured Haitian revolutionary nationhood: Toussaint's 1801 Constitution defined the plantation farm as the foundational paternalistic unit of the new society (Dubois et al. 2013: 54).

Furthermore, the re-bordering of labor mobility was constantly enforced through an attempt at rationalizing identification and registration. Deserting soldiers and vagrant paupers already constituted a laboratory to the emergence of identification cards in XVIII century France parallel to the falling apart of the corporate system of the Old Regime (Denis 2008). As soon as Sonthonax and Polverel arrived in Saint-Domingue, they mandated plantation registers to be delivered to military commands under the threat of periodical controls by the general governor.[12] The control of port cities—having always been considered as opaque spaces for slaves where to hide or from which to embark as sailors— becomes a fundamental stake of the rural police. On 10 September 1793, Civil Commissioners impose the registration of all Africans living in the cities as skilled workers or domestic slaves, stating their name, place of birth, age, sex, health condition, residence, and skills.[13] After the abolition of slavery, mobility was subordinated to authorization as it was for the *billet d'esclave*: cultivators were allowed to

[11] Ibid., artt. 1, 2, 7.

[12] L. -F. Sonthonax, E. Polverel, *Proclamation relative à la discipline des esclaves*, Port-au-Prince, le 5 mai 1793. In *Revue d'histoire des colonies*, cit.: 37.

[13] E. Polverel, *Proclamation aux Africains et descendants d'Africains, qui ne sont employés ni à la culture des terres, ni au service militaire*, fait au Port-au-Prince, le 10

circulate within their municipality only with the plantation manager's permission, while having to provide an internal passport to move outside the municipal territory.[14] In this regard, the organization of "free" labor in Saint-Domingue/Haiti provided an important antecedent for the government of mobility in the aftermath of the 1848 abolition (Sacchi Landriani 2021). Cities were at the core of Toussaint's surveillance since militarized agriculture imposed a dual partition of society into soldiers and peasants. "So-called domestics" trying to escape into towns from the labor police are particularly targeted, explicitly stating that "peasants cannot be domestics".[15] What is at stake with such a statement is the redefinition of the difference between work and non-work as it was previously sketched by French commissioners and governors. Under Louverture's government, citizens must prove they were engaged in a "useful activity". In practice, any activity outside the long-term contracts on plantations and domestic services, or the enlistment in the army, was not considered as "useful" and could be legitimately pursued as vagrancy.[16] When peasant revolts against the enforcement of militarized agriculture shook the colony, such as the vast rebellion in the northern province in 1801 leading to the execution of the black general Moïse by Louverture's order (Dubois 2004: 247–249), this set of identification measures was recoded as a means of surveillance of internal enemies through *cartes de sureté*.[17]

Discipline and Labor Exploitation

Labor discipline was the third aspect connecting all the rural codes from slavery abolition to national independence. Plantation gangs were re-established along with the pivotal figure of the work foremen.

septembre 1793, l'an deuxième de la République. In *Revue d'histoire des colonies*, cit.: 358–359.

[14] See art. 35 and 36 of Hédouville's *Arrêté concernant la police des habitations*.

[15] See art. 11 of Toussaint's *Règlement relatif à la culture*.

[16] Ibid., art. 3.

[17] Toussaint Louverture, *Proclamation. 4 frimaire an X* (25 Novembre 1801) in *Journal de débat et loix du pouvoir législatif, et des actes du gouvernement*, Paris, Imprimerie de le Normant, 29 pluviôse an X (18 February 1802): 1–3. According to art. 7, certificates were valid for six months, they were delivered by municipal administration to local inhabitants and they were validated by the major and by the police.

The ex-slave drivers, called *conducteurs*, were the main agents of the internal police of plantations. According to Polverel's February 1794 code, they were supposed to wear a red, white, and blue hat symbolizing the new republican order, and they could be elected by the community of cultivators. Not surprisingly, this vague idea of democratization disappeared in all subsequent proclamations. As a matter of fact, the division between work foremen and simple laborers inherited the violence of the previous slave regime, as well as its gendered structure. Since most skilled positions on plantations, such as boiling, were not available to slave women, after emancipation *conducteurs* were usually creole men, while cultivators were especially African-born women (Sheller 2013: 157–179). All rural codes differentiated salaries on the base of age and gender, usually assigning adult women half the share of men. At the same time, as the war decimated the male population, women constituted the very backbone of production. All moralizing measures—such as the repression of a "dissolute" lifestyle, the forbidding of divorce, and the enforcement of the catholic family—were thus consistent with labor regimes.[18]

The Fall of Caporalisme Agraire *and the Plantation Afterlives*

Between 1793 and 1805, rural police measures involved both the organization of production on the farms and the organization of society. The disruption of the already porous borders of the slave society had brought to the foreground the necessity to fabricate the citizen through a process of re-bordering. We talk about "re-bordering" as both a material and epistemic process necessary to insert large-scale plantation economy within the formal frame of emancipation. Rural police aimed to materially trace lines securing private property, the citizens' personal rights (such as the inviolability of the household) and labor positions across the productive chain. At the same time, such policing presupposed a process of definition. It differentiated what was "work" from the realm of activities to be considered as "non-work"; it distinguished the factual "use" of land made by peasants from its "property"; it enforced disciplined "freedom" repressing unregulated interpretations of that freedom. In this sense, the task of rural police was to actively produce the partial citizen—the

[18] Toussaint Louverture, *Proclamation, 4 Frimaire an X*, cit.: 1.

poor—in order to subsequently force her or him to reach full freedom through the division of labor. For all these reasons, plantations should be envisaged both as economic and political: they constitute the laboratory in which both export crops are produced, and modern citizens are "manufactured" through the nexus between liberty, work, and discipline. While ex-slaves claimed independence from the plantation, Toussaint and Dessalines looked for political and economic independence through the plantation regime itself as the only means to face continuous threats of invasion. Therefore, the *caporalisme agraire* forged Haitian nationhood through a military organized plantation-State, which may constitute a vantage point from which to consider its "afterlives".

Militarized agriculture would progressively fall apart after the end of Dessaline's reign. From 1806 to 1820, in the Northern part of the island the constitutional monarchy of the king Christophe continued the military regime, while Pétion's Republic in the South begun parceling land to coopt the mass of black peasants and maintain political stability. Although large estates will not disappear, a new configuration of land property did emerge especially under the government of Jean-Pierre Boyer that reunified Haiti in 1820 (Lacerte 1978; Fick 2000; Girard 2019). The plantation regime, as it was known during the seventeenth century, became marginal. Nevertheless, the issue of its "afterlives" has always haunted historical research and political thinking. For instance, Trouillot noted the persistence of an extractive logic that kept shaping internal and international relations of dependency throughout the nineteenth century. Firstly, taxation soon became a pivotal instrument for the subordination of the countryside to parasitic cities, establishing "a dialectic of separation and complementarity" (Trouillot 1990: 59, 82). Secondly, this internal relation participated to a broader form of dependency: commercial penetration by Britain and the US, along with the debt of independence imposed to Haiti by Charles X in 1825, subordinated the newborn nation to market imperatives (Dubois 2012). The history of Haitian labor codes thus contributes to rethink the conceptual couples through which we think our present, such as freedom/slavery or autonomy/coercion, intertwining different layers of dependency. While the forms of integration in the world market push to consider plantations as a constitutive element of global capitalism, the forms of labor coercion cease to appear as residual elements of a pre-modern past. Considered as a theoretical site, plantations thus stand at the core of multiple lines of reflection, connecting the critique of linear readings of modernity and development, the deconstruction of the western norm of "free" wage labor, and the recodification of racial difference in global capitalism (Robinson 2002; van der Linden 2008).

References

Barthélemy, G. 1990. *L'univers rural haitien. Le pays an dehors*. Paris: L'Harmattan.

Beckert, S., and S. Rockman. 2016. *Slavery's Capitalism. A New History of American Economic Development*. Philadelphia: University of Pennsylvania Press.

Bogues, A. 2010. The Dual Haitian Revolution as An Archive of Freedom. *BIM* 3 (2): 26–34.

Burnard, T., and J. Garrigus. 2016. *The Plantation Machine. Atlantic Capitalism in French Saint-Domingue and British Jamaica*. Philadelphia: University of Pennsylvania Press.

Casimir, J. 2009. *Haïti et ses élites. L'interminable dialogue de sourds*. Port-au-Prince: Les Edition de l'Université d'Etat d'Haïti.

Castel, R. 2003. *From Manual Workers to Wage Laborers: Transformation of the Social Question*. New Brunswick: Transaction Publishers.

Cazzola, M., and L. Ravano. 2020. Plantation Society in the Age of Revolution: Edward Long, Pierre-Victor Malouet and the Problem of Slave Government. *Slavery and Abolition* 41 (2): 234–255.

Cheney, P. 2017. *Cul de Sac: Patrimony, Capitalism, and Slavery in French Saint-Domingue*. Chicago: University of Chicago Press.

Debien, G. 1967. Les affranchissements aux antilles françaises aux XVII et XVIII siècles. *Anuario de estudos americanos* VVIII: 1194–1197.

Debien, G. 1974. *Les Esclaves aux Antilles françaises: XVIIe-XVIIIe siècles*. Basse-Terre: Société d'Histoire de la Guadeloupe et de la Martinique.

Denis, V. 2008. *Une Histoire de l'Identité: France, 1715–1815*. Seyssel: Editions Champ Vallon.

Dubois, L. 2004. *Avengers of the New World. The Story of the Haitian Revolution*. Cambridge: Harvard University Press.

Dubois, L. 2012. *Haiti: The Aftershocks of History*. New York: Metropolitan Books.

Dubois, L., J. Gaffield, and M. Acacia. 2013. *Documents constitutionnels d'Haïti, 1790–1860*. New York: De Gruyter.

Duffy, M. 1987. *Soldiers, Sugar and Seapower: The British Expeditions to the West Indies and the War against Revolutionary France*. Oxford: Clarendon Press.

Fick, C. 2000. Emancipation in Haiti: From Plantation Labour to Peasant Proprietorship. *Slavery and Abolition* 21 (2): 11–40.

Fick, C.E. 1990. *The Making of Haiti: The Revolution of Saint Domingue from Below*. Knoxville: University of Tennessee Press.

Fisher, S. 2004. *Modernity Disavowed. Haiti and the Cultures of Slavery in the Age of Revolution*. Durham: Duke University Press.

Fouchard, J. 1981. *The Haitian Maroons: Liberty or Death*. New York: E.W. Blyden Press.

Garrigus, J. D. 2006. *Before Haiti: Race and Citizenship in French Saint-Domingue*. Palgrave Macmillan.

Gauthier, F. 2007. *L'aristocratie de l'épiderme. Le combat de la Société des Citoyens de Couleur, 1789–1791*. Paris: Editions CNRS.

Geggus, P.D. 1993. Sugar and Coffee Cultivation in Saint Domingue and the Shaping of the Slave Labor Force. In *Cultivation and Culture: Labor and the Shaping of Afro-American Culture in the Americas*, ed. I. Berlin and P. Morgan, 73–98. Charlottesville: University Press of Virginia.

Ghachem, M.W. 2012. *The Old Regime and the Haitian Revolution*. Cambridge: Cambridge University Press.

Girard, P. 2009. Napoléon Bonaparte and the Emancipation Issue in Saint-Domingue, 1799–1803. *French Historical Studies* 32 (4): 587–618.

Girard, P. 2019. Making Freedom Work: the Long Transition from Slavery to Freedom during the Haitian Revolution. *Slavery and Abolition* 40 (1): 87–108.

Gonzalez, J. 2019. *Maroon Nation. A History of Revolutionary Haiti*. New Haven: Yale University Press.

Laborie, P. J. 1797. *The Coffee planter of Saint Domingo; with an appendix Containing a View of the Constitution, Government, Laws, and State of that Colony, previous to the Year 1789*. T. Cadell, W. Davies.

Lacerte, R.K. 1978. The Evolution of Land and Labor in the Haitian Revolution, 1791–1820. *The Americas* 34 (4): 449–459.

Lundhal, M. 1979. *Peasants and Poverty: A Study of Haïti*. London: Croom Helm.

Martin, S. 1765. *An Essay Upon Plantership: Humbly Inscribed to His Excellency George Thomas Esq., Chief Governor of all the Leeward Islands*. A. Millar.

Mintz, S.W. 1986. *Sweetness and Power. The Place of Sugar in Modern History*. New York: Penguin.

Moïse, C. 1988. *Constitutions et luttes de pouvoir en Haïti, 1804–1805: la faillite des classes dirigeantes*. Edition du CIDIHCA.

Moral, P. 1961. *Le Paysan Haïtien. Etude sur la vie rurale en Haïti*. Paris: Maisonneuve & La Rose.

Nesbitt, N. 2008. *Universal Emancipation: The Haitian Revolution and the Radical Enlightenment*. Charlottesville: University of Virginia Press.

Oudin-Bastide, C., and P. Steiner. 2015. *Calcul et morale. Coûts de l'esclavage et valeur de l'émancipation (XVIIIe–XIXe siècles)*. Paris: Albin Michel.

Popkin, J. 2010. *You Are All Free: The Haitian Revolution and the Abolition of Slavery*. New York: Cambridge University Press.
Ravano, L. 2021. The Borders of Citizenship in the Haitian Revolution. *Political Theory* 49 (5): 717–742.
Robinson, C.J. 2002. *Black Marxism. The Making of the Black Radical Tradition*. Chapel Hill: The University of North Carolina Press.
Sacchi Landriani, M. 2021. The Politics of Identification in Post-Emancipation Martinique: Civil Status, Internal Passports, Workers' Booklets, and Immigration Cards. *Slavery and Abolition* 42 (3): 545–566.
Scott, J. 2018. *The Common Wind: Afro-American Currents in the Age of the Haitian Revolution*. London: Verso.
Semley, L. 2017. *To Be Free and French: Citizenship in France's Atlantic Empire*. Cambridge: Cambridge University Press.
Sheller, M. 2013. Sword-Bearing Citizens: Militarism and Manhood in Nineteenth Century Haiti. In *Haitian History. New Perspectives*, ed. A. G. Sepinwall, 157–179. London: Routledge.
Thompson, A.O. 2006. *Flight to Freedom: African Runaways and Maroons in the Americas*. Kingston: University of the West Indies Press.
Trouillot, M.-R. 1990. *Haiti: State against Nation. The Origins and Legacy of Duvalierism*. New York: Monthly Review Press.
Trouillot, M.-R. 1995. *Silencing the Past: Power and the Production of History*. Boston: Beacon Press.
van der Linden, M. 2008. *Workers of the World. Essays Toward a Global Labor History*. Leiden: Brill.

CHAPTER 4

Cacos and Cotton: Unmaking Imperial Geographies on Haiti's Central Plateau

Sophie Sapp Moore

Introduction

I am walking in the hills above the Guayamouc River in central Haiti when a flash of white catches my eye. I turn to the side of the dirt path and seek out what has called my attention—a yellow-white puff blown out from one thin red-brown stem of a bush about the height of my shoulders. The white flash catches my eye on a path I have walked dozens of times because it is the dry season, and I am surrounded by ochre yellow, siena brown, the gray of rock exposed by the last season's rains. Nothing stays white in the dry season, a thin layer of dust settling on every surface despite near-constant washing and sweeping. No one else is on the path, and I reach into the scratchy nest of branches and pinch the white puff between two fingers, the dry brown leaves scraping my hand. The puff is

S. S. Moore (✉)
Rice University, Center for Environmental Studies and Humanities Research Center, Houston, TX, USA
e-mail: slm17@rice.edu

C. Le Petitcorps et al. (eds.), *Global Plantations in the Modern World*, Cambridge Imperial and Post-Colonial Studies,
https://doi.org/10.1007/978-3-031-08537-6_4

denser than I expect. I pull a little and find it firmly attached to a thin, hard stem, surrounded by stiff points.

I only know this is cotton because it is white, or whitish, though I learn later that cotton is in the same family as okra and hibiscus. If the plant had been flowering, I would have noticed the yellow flowers' affinity with those I have seen at the end of long graceful okra stems and the red blooms that decorate front yards all over the village. This plant is growing amidst twisting vines and cactus hedges, its thin, flat, five-pointed leaves drab and drooping in the relentless winter sun. I am too hot and tried to exert effort to pull the boll from the stem, but I think about it as I keep walking down the dusty path, wide enough for three people to walk side by side in the dry season, but only one in the wet, when the path is overgrown with reaching leaves and tendrils. The scraggly bush stays in my mind's eye; I feel unsettled to have encountered cotton here. The sparse bush looks nothing like the pictures I have seen of cotton plantations in the U.S. South, the dense, low rows thickly constellated with the bright white of the heavy four-chambered bolls of *Gossypium hirsutum*, the upland cotton most commonly grown in the twentieth- and twenty-first- century Americas.

The cotton plant that scrapes my hands is not exactly wild. Its presence here in the hills, indeed, puts into question the very idea of "wildness" in agrarian places like Haiti's hinterland. Ninety years ago, there had been a cotton plantation in Saint-Michel de L'Attalaye, about 60 km to the Northwest of where I am walking. I don't know how this plant got here, if the wind carried its seed to the hills from long-ago fields planted in a nearby valley, or whether it is the "hardy indigenous plant" described by foreign botanists in the 1920s. It grows outside the bounds of any fence, but along a path well-traveled by farmers, market women, livestock, and all the other residents of this cluster of villages between the Samanà and Guayamouc Rivers in Haiti's interior. It's the first cotton plant I have ever seen in Haiti. In my friends' fields, I see patch-worked plots of manioc, maize, beans, peanuts, pumpkin, and sugarcane. When I visit their gardens, we stand in the shade of banana and coconut palms and the glossy leaves of the huge mango trees that groan with fruit in May. But perhaps I simply did not notice it, or its kin, in this place where many harvest and few gather.

Writers including Sidney Mintz and Eric Williams have told the story of colonialism in the Caribbean through sugarcane. But it is cotton that carries the story of American empire, from the Caribbean to the Sea

Islands to the Mississippi Delta and back again. In that story, Haiti's interior is one nexus of a "tropic of cotton" that connects the geographies of U.S. empire.[1] Here I pick up one thread of the story of the expansion of U.S. empire in twentieth-century Haiti: the circulation, cultivation, and creation of knowledge around cotton. In this chapter, I look at how cotton enabled the circulation of racial capital, the particular forms of empire that resulted, and how Afro-Americans have contested those imperial geographies. Key actors in this story include USDA scientists, U.S. Marines, Haitian peasants, and the rural militias of the interior, as well as two cultivars of cotton: *G. Barbadense* and *G. Hirsutum*. The story begins on Haiti's high Central Plateau, a semi-arid region between Hispaniola's two biggest mountain ranges, running along today's border with the Dominican Republic.

Andeyò

The high Central Plateau was never planted with sugarcane, cotton, coffee, or tobacco in the colonial period, before Haiti won its independence in 1804. The rugged geography of the region, its distance from the colony's port cities, and the problems posed by a lack of access to irrigation all contributed to the concentration of plantation agriculture on coastal plains. Nonetheless, the Central Plateau's transformation into an agrarian geography was as important to the making of the Haitian state as it was to the making of U.S. empire. Today's provincial capital of Hinche is one of Hispaniola's oldest continuous settlements, founded in 1504 in Spanish territory. National Route #3 leads from Port-au-Prince to Hinche. Heading north over the hills from Mirebalais on Route #3, the landscape becomes noticeably less green as the Péligre Lake recedes behind. Agricultural fields are smaller, and the soil rockier. Footpaths trod by people and animals wind through unfenced grasslands dotted with trees. A red sign bearing the name of mobile provider Digicel marks entry to each village, with pink-and-blue painted wooden slat houses set

[1] This story maps a different geography than that at the center of Sven Beckert's *Empire of Cotton: A Global History* (2014), which shows how the transformation of cotton into a global commodity drove the expansion of European empire. While the expansion of U.S. empire likewise folded imperial subjects into "the global cotton-growing complex by constructing infrastructure, creating new labor regimes, and recasting local social structures" (343), the history of racial slavery in North America and the Caribbean shaped the geography of that empire in ways unique to the hemisphere.

close by the cobblestoned or dirt streets. Cement arches, painted blue and white, mark the entry points to larger towns like Mirebalais and Hinche.

In the three centuries that followed the establishment of the first Spanish settlements, the borderlands remained a place where free people of color, maroons, fugitives, and other travelers circulated more or less freely. They raised cattle and other livestock, which moved as freely as their people around the borderlands. After 1804, the center-island region, which was still a part of Spanish Santo Domingo, occupied an unstable position between the Northern Kingdom and the Southern Republic of Haiti. In 1822, President Jean-Pierre Boyer (1818–1843) unified the country's Northern and Southern states and occupied Spanish Santo Domingo. For the first time, the Central Plateau came under the state's administrative control when the region was ceded to Haiti at Dominican independence in 1844. Despite its isolation (or perhaps because of it), the Central Plateau has long been a stronghold for the Haitian army, as it would be for the U.S. Marines who occupied the country from 1915 to 1934.

Jean Casimir (1981) describes the central borderlands as a site of continuing tensions between various forms of free and fugitive life and the plantation regime in the nineteenth century. It was in this region, Casimir argues that the mode of rural socio-political organization he terms the "counter plantation" emerged. In 1860, Casimir notes, fugitives were still being captured in the mountainous Bahoruco region (1981: 60). Such outlaws were known as "cacos" by the Spaniards who encountered them before 1804 (*kakos* in Haitian Kreyòl). The term would eventually come to encompass rural militants more generally. David Nicholls likewise traces the roots of the *kakos*' anti-state politics to the 1860s, noting an uprising in the Central Plateau town of Hinche in 1868 (1985: 179). Before the U.S. Occupation began in 1915, opposition candidates mobilized *kakos* primarily against internal enemies, which has led some scholars to emphasize their role as political mercenaries.

Casimir dates the span of the Caco Wars between 1867 and 1929, a period in which rural guerrillas proved amenable to fighting for political candidates for a certain price. The pacification of the borderlands in the late nineteenth century involved a struggle between the plantation and counter plantation systems, waged in ideological as well as material terms. On the high Central Plateau, a region historically understood as a harbor for fugitives opposed to the national project, the plantation-counter plantation frontier provided the social and structural frame for rural dwellers' ongoing struggle. Casimir traces the derivation of *kako* to the fierce native *taco* birds of prey, who find the large *zandolite* lizards tasty. He characterizes the *kako* struggle as one against the forces of order (the rule of law), the army, or the government (the lizards! he makes sure to note), even if the *kakos* had brought those very "lizards" to power. Casimir contradicts dominant associations between the *kakos* and mercenaries of the colonial period, however, insisting that we should conceive of the *kakos* not as cheap mercenaries, but as fighting of their own free will (1981: 177).

Kakos' allegiances were intimately tied to their agrarian roots. Greenburg writes that *kakos* "were peasant guerillas operating in a long tradition dating back to 'harassing the French' during the Revolution. In the nineteenth century, the phrase cacos came to identify a group of small-holding peasants who took up arms to challenge the Salnave government in 1867. Through the rest of the century, the cacos were called upon by rural chiefs to undertake revolutionary activity against the national government in Port-au-Prince" (2016: 54). Rural people refer to the countryside as *andeyò*, "outside," and to themselves as *peyizan* (peasants), a term that signals a political position as well as economic and social attachments to an agrarian way of life. The isolation of Hispaniola's interior from both of the island's capitals—Port-au-Prince and Santo Domingo—well into the twentieth century reinforced the importance of autonomy and mobility to the region's residents. Mercenary tendencies notwithstanding, *kakos'* anti-state politics and opposition to projects of national development were grounded in their identity as smallholding or landless peasants living and defending a largely self-sufficient agrarian life. Indeed, a widespread rural tradition of armed struggle often blurred the line between organized *kako* and armed peasant. Rural dwellers in the interior were accustomed to taking up arms to defend their hard-won freedoms. Until the Occupation began a campaign of disarmament in 1918, peasants were habitually armed with weapons including machetes, knives, pistols, and rifles, even if they were not active in insurgent networks.

While *kakos'* shifting allegiances had at times aligned with national political interests, their final mobilization was decidedly anti-imperial in nature. On 27 July 1915, U.S. Marines disembarked in Haiti's capital city of Port-au-Prince, on the order of President Woodrow Wilson. Their presence initiated an Occupation that would last for the next 19 years. The invasion was ostensibly motivated by political instability in the country, which had come to a head with the assassination of President Vilbrun Guillaume Sam, who had sought to promote U.S. commercial interests in Haiti. Sam's opponents wanted to replace him with Rosalvo Bobo, a Northern nationalist who had strong support amongst the *kakos*. Bobo had denounced Sam's collaboration with U.S. interests, and in 1915 the *kako* forces he had mobilized in the North were already marching south with the intention to overthrow Sam when Bobo received news that Sam had been killed in the capitol (Chochotte 2017: 39–40). His assassination motivated the Occupation's installation of their puppet, Phillippe Dartiguenave, whose leadership, such as it was, unfailingly advanced U.S. economic and political interests. While President Dartiguenave rarely ventured from the National Palace in Port-au-Prince, the Occupation set up a military stronghold in the country's interior, most particularly by establishing the Gendarmerie, a military force manned by Haitians and commanded by U.S. officers.

The Occupation of the hinterland demanded the constant surveillance of the border, across which rural dwellers were accustomed to free travel and trade. Like the colonial agents of rural discipline who had come before them, the officers tasked with controlling the hinterland associated the high degree of mobility that border dwellers habitually practiced with the widespread "banditry" that they thought endemic to the borderlands (see Sacchi and Ravano, this volume).[2] As such, their pacification campaign targeted fighters and civilians indiscriminately, considering all forms of free movement dangerous to the aims of the Occupation. Already aware of the defiance of the *kakos* and the free movement of guerrillas and fugitives across the border in 1916, one U.S

[2] The association between free movement and 'banditry' was long-standing and had been formalized in law since at least 1826. A revised English translation of the 1826 Code Rural, the legal statute that governed agrarian life, was issued to U.S. Marines. Its provisions were particularly focused on the criminalization of mobility and the obligation to cultivate the soil. One article reads: "Throughout the extent of the localities under their direction, rural police officers should be on the lookout to see that no one lives in idleness... if these individuals cannot give a good account of themselves, they will be considered vagrants, and arrested as vagabonds." Using the same language of banditry and vagabondage that had been the official descriptor of non-compliant rural dwellers since the eighteenth century, the Occupiers' Code restricted peasants' freedom of movement as well as their economic activities, requiring that any cultivator found outside his district on a non-market day "explain where he lives or whether he is employed by one of the proprietors of the section, or [provide] a paper proving his identity, [or else he] will be considered a vagabond" and prosecuted as such. Like the vagrancy laws that were part of the black codes and, later, Jim Crow in the U.S. South (see Alexander 2012: 28, 31), such a conviction could warrant permanent surveillance by the police, handily supplying an unwilling labor force for the work gangs of the *corvée* (Chochotte 2017: 56, n100).

Marine reported that "forty or fifty Haitian men from the interior town daily cross frontier into San Domingo urgently recommend that the old permit system be reestablished to control exodus. I recommend same for Ouanaminthe and Hinche" (Chochotte 2017: 63). While the border had been a matter of national concern since the partition of the island in 1844, it was during the U.S. Occupation that the infrastructure for surveillance and control of the hinterland was established, including military outposts, roads and water systems, and, of course, a network of spies and informants. Chochotte writes: "the U.S. suppression of caco insurgent networks represented the real first disruption to this transnational borderland culture that supported a martial life on both sides of the border. Now under U.S. repression, restrictions were placed on the mobility of Haitians traveling to the Dominican Republic to rearm themselves" (2017: 63).

Although Casimir dates the *kako* struggle as lasting through 1929, the *kako* army's last major revolt against the Occupation was in 1919, led by a Hinche landowner named Charles Péralte. "There were supposed to be five thousand cacos in the field with twelve thousand more available. Opposing them at first were possibly two thousand gendarmes and one thousand marines, most of whom were needed elsewhere for police duty. The insurrection was concentrated in the interior areas of Hinche, Mirebalais, and Lascahobas at first but the gendarmerie proved incapable of suppressing the rebels. The uprising spread toward the capital with the encouragement of political opponents of the occupation" (Posner 1964: 262). In 1919, Péralte's forces mounted significant attacks against the Occupation forces in and around Hinche, but were defeated after Péralte's assassination (by Marines in blackface) in 1919. Hans Schmidt calls the *kakos* "part time military adventurers and conscripts recruited and loosely organized by local military strongmen" (1995: 42). But what does the 1918–1919 conflict—the last *kako* war—signify in the context of a country that is itself under military occupation?

Occupation Infrastructure

Although the uprising that killed President Sam provided a pretext for the U.S. invasion of Haiti, the Occupation had in fact been planned for years. In November 1914, U.S. officials had drawn up the "Plan for Landing and Occupying Haiti the City of Port-au-Prince" warning that "five thousands soldiers and civilian mobs" threatened foreign interests in the country (Chochotte 2017: 42). The economic motivation of the Occupation was explicit, with a clear focus on the development of large-scale agricultural commodity production as a means to settle Haiti's external debts and stabilize its internal financial markets. In the early part of the twentieth century, the now-ubiquitous narrative about Haiti's environmental degradation was not yet in effect. Rather, observers emphasized the agricultural promise of the interior, marveling at its fertile soils and riotous tropical flora. Infrastructure would be crucial to the exploitation of that tropical abundance. One observer, an anonymous "American Resident" notes that railroads "will facilitate the transportation of coffee, cotton, sugarcane, and castor beans, all of which flourish in practically a wild state. [...] It may be said that Haiti's greatest wealth lies in the fertility of her soil" (1919: 26). Occupiers' plans to develop the interior thus envisioned infrastructure as the scaffolding of the hinterland's transformation into a zone of large-scale commodity crop cultivation.

In the first years of the Occupation, USDA scientists, botanical adventurers, and American concessionaires ventured into the interior. While they commended the alluvial soils they found in the plains and valleys of the center-island region, they found it hard going, with those few roads suitable for vehicular travel dating back to the colonial period. Infrastructural development, and road-building, in particular, was thought to be the necessary precursor to the exploitation of the interior's agricultural promise. The military administration of the Gendarmerie facilitated the extension of Occupation infrastructure into the hinterland, including the building of roads, railroads, aqueducts, irrigation infrastructure, and so on, much of which resurrected the colonial infrastructure that imperial observers viewed with such nostalgia.[3] By 1922, the Occupation had overseen the construction of 385 miles of new road, and the repair of over 200 miles of existing roadway (Millspaugh 1931: 92). American Gendarmerie commander Butler opines: "We were all embued [*sic*] with the fact that we were trustees of a huge estate that belonged to minors [...] and that we were endeavoring to develop and make for them a rich and productive property" (Schmidt 1995: 89). Occupation observers note the presence of peasants in the interior, but their subsistence cultivation practices barely register as agricultural production to plantation

[3] In Haiti as elsewhere across the globe, the use of infrastructural development has long been and remains a tool of colonization and imperial expansion. See, for example, Cowen (2019) and the 2021 *e-flux* collaboration edited by Axel et al.

prospectors. Rural dwellers were perceived as at once politically unruly and economically dormant.

Since the 1600s, colonial observers had seen the island's interior as unproductive, threatening, and inaccessible—in any case, mostly unpromising for the kind of large-scale cultivation that came to define the plantation system as it spread through the Americas. Nonetheless, by the twentieth century, the center-island region's relatively sparse population, large proportion of uncultivated land, significant state landholdings, and saturation with U.S. military presence made it an appealing target for agricultural development under the Occupation. Occupiers' single-minded focus on intensive commodity crop cultivation as the best means to both pacify and extract value from the hinterland depended upon the same colonial economic logic that had transformed Haiti's coastal plains into sugarcane plantations before the Revolution. The denizens of the interior, however, were no longer the Taíno Amerindian, African, and Creole fugitives that had populated the region when it had been a part of Spanish Santo Domingo. Peasants in the interior had, until the Occupation, been citizens of a sovereign nation that had been free for over a century. Occupiers' imposition of plantation logics on the interior now more explicitly pursued both political and economic aims.

It was on the high Central Plateau that the Occupation's disciplinary and extractive objectives converged. Rural development, in this context, served a dual purpose, as the means to both political pacification and intensification of economic activity. Observers' writing equates the tradition of rural militancy endemic to the hinterland with its presumed "wildness:" "In those detached regions revolutions grew up and spread just as malaria grows and spreads in marshy districts. And as malaria is stamped out by clearing and draining, so revolution has been eradicated by opening up the regions where it formerly was bred" (Weatherly 1926: 359). The infrastructural work of transforming the interior into a plantation zone was crucial to realizing the political objectives of the Occupation as well as developing its economic interests:

> In this process the road-builder has played a leading part. Regions about Mirebalais and Hinche, former strongholds of the Cacos, are now in easy communication with the rest of the republic. The telegraph and telephone have brought isolated districts into intimate touch not only with government officials but with the general public. It usually happens that roads originally built for military use prove equally advantageous for general

> social purposes, as was proved in the case of the great Roman roads and those built by Napoleon. But in a mountainous country like Haiti main highways by themselves would be like bodies without limbs. Most of the people live in rough districts inaccessible to highways; for them trails are the vital need. Over these trails the peasant carries his little crops to market, and over them also the gendarmes pass freely to remote posts and outposts. By means of them sanitary and agricultural agents, penetrating to the most remote hamlets, have been able to bring every part of the country under official oversight. (Weatherly 1926: 359)

The American officers who commanded the Gendarmerie built on the legacy of Haiti's nineteenth-century *police rurale* (see Sacchi and Ravano, this volume) to enforce rural discipline and govern public works projects like road building and the clearing of land. Crucial to their enforcement effort was the reinstatement of the *corvée*,[4] beginning in 1918. The *corvée* was a legal order that compelled rural residents to work on road building in their district for a certain period of time each year. Although rarely used, the *corvée* had existed in practice since the French colonial period, and in law since 1863. The Gendarmerie was tasked with enforcing the *corvée*, which proved difficult—peasants overwhelmingly perceived the order as equivalent to the reinstatement of slavery (Posner 1964: 262–263). They fled to the hills, where the *kakos* were gathering recruits to rise up against the Occupation. Those who resisted the *corvée* were subject to retaliatory violence by the Gendarmerie. Installed far from Port-au-Prince in a territory known for rural militancy, American officers were notorious for meting out vigilante justice and ignoring disciplinary standards imposed in the far-away capital.

They also regularly welcomed delegations of scientists, surveyors, and agricultural entrepreneurs from the United States. Commander Frederick Baker, who managed the cotton plantation in Saint-Michel, was one such player in the Occupation's vanguard. He had an assignment with the USDA Division of Cotton, Rubber, and Other Tropical Plants, at Port-au-Prince, where he was working on rubber tree agricultural research (Francisco-Ortega et al. 2017: 15). Although biographical information for Baker is scarce, it seems that he had been working in Haiti since at least 1914. While rubber cultivation in Haiti would come into play during

[4] Or *kovè* in Kreyòl, a word that, after the Occupation, came to more generally signify one of the many forms of collective labor still practiced voluntarily in the countryside today.

the Second World War,[5] Baker's work also focused on the development of large-scale cash-cropping of cotton and sisal in Haiti's interior.

Throughout the Occupation, Baker hosted numerous visitors to Haiti, including the famous collector David Fairchild on his 1933 expedition (Francisco-Ortega et al. 2017: 15, 17). Collectors like Fairchild characterized the interior as a "wild" zone, with many undocumented species of botanical interest. But for agricultural scientists like Baker, the flora of the interior were incidental to the promise its "uncultivated" lands held as potential plantations. As such, USDA scientists like Baker played a crucial role in integrating the "civilizing mission" of U.S. imperial expansion with the techno-political framework of agricultural development. We know that Baker managed the cotton plantation at Saint-Michel because of the Senate Hearings conducted in 1921 and 1922, an "Inquiry Into Occupation and Administration of Haiti and Santo Domingo." In these hearings, witnesses testify to Baker's oversight of atrocities committed by Gendarmes against Haitians in the interior. These included extrajudicial killings, forced labor, the burning of crops, and imprisonment without trial. It was against such brutal acts that the *kakos* mobilized.

The *kako* uprising that surged in 1918 intervened at the conjuncture between militarized occupation and the science of empire. Militants were motivated not only by the brutality of the Occupation, but also by a deep commitment to agrarian autonomy, mobility, and self-determination that cut across boundaries of class and color. As such, the *kako* struggle was one element of a broader counter plantation strategy through which rural dwellers refused and undermined the Occupation's plan to "civilize" the interior through agricultural development. The Saint-Michel endeavor was part of a project of pacification of Haiti's hinterland that explicitly reproduced plantation power. Agricultural science, and particularly USDA scientists, played a key role in making the Caribbean into an experimental space for the expansion of U.S. empire. Cotton appears most frequently in archival sources from the 1920s and 1930s, well into the American Occupation, but before it became apparent that large-scale

[5] Indeed, commodity production overall (including coffee, cacao, rubber, and sisal as well as cotton) ramped up significantly to support World War II production demands. That increase depended upon the plantation infrastructure set in place on the Central Plateau during the U.S. Occupation. Post-Occupation presidents, in particular Elie Lescot (1941–1946), remained sympathetic to U.S. interests and subject to the influence of U.S. foreign policy.

export production would ultimately be untenable. This timing was not, of course, an accident.

Tropic of Cotton

In the late nineteenth and early twentieth centuries, the variety of *Gossypium barbadense* grown in the Sea Islands was the gold standard for cotton. Planters prized this low-country cotton for its silky fibers and bright white color; it dominated the global market until the Civil War. But between 1892 and 1932, the boll weevil ravaged the U.S. South. At the same time, the abolition of slavery reduced the population of skilled laborers who tended the finicky crop. By the first decade of the twentieth century, planters were already trying to figure out how to cultivate Sea Island cotton in other territories. Ironically, *G. Barbadense* had in fact come originally from the West Indies. In the early 1900s, it returned to the Caribbean. Sea Island cotton seeds were shipped to the Caribbean for planting, where they found some success. But the boll weevil (and its kin the bollworm) posed a persistent threat. In 1918, the boll weevil reached the East Coast of the United States. In 1919, a U.S. enterprise established Haiti's first experimental cotton plantation at Saint-Michel (Erasmus 1952: 24; Woodring et al. 1924: 73).

Experimental, in that planters wanted to combine the esthetic qualities of *G. Barbadense* with the hardiness of *G. Hirsutum*, the variety that grew wild in Haiti and on other Caribbean islands. In a 1929 Annual Report of the American High Commissioner at Port Au Prince to the U.S. Secretary of State, one observer details the experiment:

> "Realizing that sea-island cotton originally came from the West Indies, and finding in Haiti a hardy cotton tree that indicated a relationship to the sea-island variety, experiments were undertaken to develop a type of sea-island cotton from the hardy indigenous plant. These experiments have been so ably and successfully conducted that they have developed a strain of native cotton resembling long sea-island cotton, and it is anticipated by the Haitian Government that in a few years it will be able to establish the production of this cotton in Haiti in such quantities as to make it commercially attractive." (1929 Annual Report: 8–9)

The report invites the question: at what point is Sea Island cotton no longer Sea Island cotton? When its seeds have crossed the Caribbean?

When its shoots push up through Haitian soil? When Haitian hands pluck the bolls from the stems? When it adopts *G. Hirsutum*'s apparent resistance to the bollworm and the boll weevil? For observers like the Occupation's High Commissioner, the taxonomy of Sea Island cotton depended as much on *how* the plant was cultivated as on qualities inherent to the plant itself. The system that the Occupation wanted to establish was explicitly in conflict with Haiti's customary patterns of land use and agricultural production.

In the same 1929 report, the High Commissioner expresses frustration at peasants' "minimum cultivation" of potentially valuable commodity crops. He criticizes peasants' flexible approach to harvesting "as nature allows" (ibid.: 180). This position was consistent with other outsiders' perceptions at the time. Even sympathetic observers marveled at what they saw as Haitians' waste of the abundant resources that surrounded them. One representative of a U.S. delegation (which ultimately argued for a swift end to the Occupation) observes that:

> Their cultivation is very primitive and many people will tell you that they gather rather than cultivate, and subsist mainly on freely growing fruit like bananas, mangos, breadfruit, etc., and from the sale of products, such as coffee and cotton gathered from plants which are the almost untended descendants of the old French plantings. (Balch 1927: 59)

Imperial observers continually make a point of distinguishing gathering from harvesting, favorably associating cultivation with the legacy of French colonialism in Haiti and the "civilizing mission" of empire. In response, the High Commissioner advocates what Hans Schmidt calls the latifundia solution, "abolishing the Haitian system whereby each peasant owned and farmed his little plot of land in favor of establishing large plantations owned by foreigners" (Schmidt 1995: 178).

The distinction that U.S. observers made between wild and cultivated cotton, then, reflected much more deeply held principles mandating agricultural productivity and maximum exploitation of resources for the global market. Charles Millspaugh, though a botanist by training, remarked in particular on the "primitive" mode of cultivation he observed in his collecting expeditions into Haiti's interior. He exclaims that in 1915 "there was not a single plantation in the country, and in spite of relatively prosperous periods agriculture and peasant life in general had remained at a primitive level" (1931: 15). Millspaugh and others explicitly valorize plantation production as the ideal form of cultivation, a form that they see as embedded in Western civilizational ideals. In contrast, they emphasize what they see as the haphazard, seasonal, opportunistic qualities of peasants' relationship with the land. They see plantation production as the only legitimate agricultural form; land not cultivated as such is characterized as "wild," even though peasants are making a living from it. These principles—which scaffolded the formation of power and capital that geographer Clyde Woods calls the plantation bloc—fundamentally shaped how foreign entities intervened in Haiti during the Occupation and after.

Scientists like George Wolcott (an entomologist) and Wendell Woodring (a geologist) were concerned not only with the taxonomy of cotton, but also with the role it played in the political ecology of the hinterland. Their descriptions highlight the useful, unique, and marketable qualities of the plant, while insisting again and again that Haitians are not exploiting it to its full potential. They challenge peasants' economic logic, seeming to marvel at the nonchalance of their strategy. At stake in their framing is a fundamental justification of the Occupation as an agricultural enterprise intended to insert Haiti into global markets. Wolcott writes:

> Agriculturally, cotton can scarcely be called a cultivated crop in Haiti. Under the most favourable conditions it grows like a weed, being self-seeded and crowding out other vegetation if given half a chance. The great bulk of the crop receives little more attention from the grower than picking and transportation to a market. (1927: 79–80)

A few years earlier, Woodring had expressed very similar sentiments:

> Cotton is indigenous to the West Indies and in the island of Haiti it grows as a perennial shrub attaining a height of 3 to 5 meters. It grows wild but when desired for market is generally cultivated in a crude way. [...] The native plant seems to have supplied practically all the cotton exported by both the colony and the Republic. [...] Cotton is now generally cultivated in about the same way and to the same extent as in colonial days. (1924: 73)

Scientists and entrepreneurs made key distinctions between wild and cultivated cotton; between cotton that was gathered and that which was harvested; and between cotton that could be readily transformed into capital and that which could or would not. The imperial science that sustained the Occupation depended fundamentally upon this racist and paternalistic discourse of distinction around commodity agriculture.

"An American Resident" places particular weight on cotton cultivation: "Cotton, it is believed, will be one of the greatest agricultural products of Haiti. Over $1,000,000 worth of cotton was exported from October 1, 1918 to June 30, 1919. [...] One strong American company is devoting its agricultural efforts almost exclusively to cotton, and will this year plant not less than three thousand acres, and expects to extend this acreage in 2021" (1919: 26). Contemporaneous sources do not, unfortunately, name that "strong American company," but Millspaugh (1931: 93) refers to a "pretentious but unsuccessful agricultural project." The plantation Millspaugh describes is likely the one started as a USDA experimental station by Commander Baker.

Of note is the statistic about cotton exported between 1918 and 1919. With the majority of cotton production located on the high Central Plateau, it appears that the height of occupied Haiti's export trade in cotton overlapped with the *kako* uprising in the interior. Since Baker had been in country since 1914, and the St-Michel enterprise he managed is the only cotton plantation noted in the record, it is likely that the endeavor became a viable commercial enterprise within the first five years of the Occupation. Posner (1964: 246) even suggests that the St-Michel cotton plantation pre-existed the Occupation, although it is not possible to confirm his claim. Erasmus writes: "In about 1919 a foreign company came to St. Michel to plant cotton on a large commercial basis. Around 1926, this company was replaced by another which operated a tobacco-growing project until 1930" (1952: 24). Erasmus's account suggests that the St-Michel plantation existed in some form from at least 1917 through 1930. Cotton exports continued to rise (in USD) between 1917 and 1922, almost tripling in U.S.-dollar value.[6] Lundahl situates this spike in production in broader context, noting that American enterprises' selection for perennial cotton augmented export production through the 1930s, but ultimately made the crop more susceptible to the Mexican boll weevil, which had already ravaged North American plantations. Haiti's

[6] The data are patchy, but Schmidt notes an increase of $485,199 to $1,547,205 in export value between 1917 and 1922 (1995: 79). By 1941, cotton's total export value had stabilized at $2,359,852 annually (Holly 1955: 76).

cotton exports remained relatively minimal until the 1960s, when USDA scientists introduced new, hardier varieties (Lundahl 1979: 43).[7]

The *kako* uprising and the subsequent revelations of the Senate Inquiry of 1921–1922 motivated a shift in the Occupation's focus. Greenburg writes, "this new phase of occupation saw the introduction of public health and education programs under the Service Technique and the Service d'Hygiene. This turn toward public health and education demonstrates the emergence of development as a technology of rule in the face of harsh international criticism of violence, racism, and torture. Militarized development emerged in reaction to the ways in which military violence threatened to undermine the project of occupation" (2016: 56). The *Service Technique d'Agriculture et de l'Enseignement Professionnel*, or the *Service Technique*—the Occupation's technical and agricultural training program—was the nexus of the Occupation's shift toward agricultural and vocational education. The Service Technique operated as part of the Haitian Department of Agriculture beginning in 1922. The undertaking established a flagship campus at Damien, just outside of Port-au-Prince, where students trained in such subjects as animal pathology, botany, chemistry, sugar production, and carpentry.

The Faculté d'Agronomie still operates out of the Damien campus as part of the Université de l'Etat d'Haiti, the state university. A constellation of rural farm schools supported the Damien campus, and the *Service* established demonstration farms, crop and livestock experiment stations, a dairy, demonstration coffee mills, and veterinary clinics across the countryside. This shift to agricultural education suggests that the *kakos'* struggle, though ultimately suppressed, nonetheless transformed the Occupation's mode of engagement with the hinterland and contributed to setting new limits on U.S. intervention. The experimental geography of the Occupation's cotton venture provided the structure for a more pervasive restructuring of agrarian life in Haiti. Chapman writes, "the economic development of Haiti depends upon agriculture, and it may fairly be said that every other factor in the national life, social, political, and perhaps even intellectual, rests ultimately upon it. [...] Just as in the case of the other departments, the republic has been mapped out from

[7] Such introductions are part of a broader genealogy of U.S.-led Green Revolution interventions intended to increase yields of commodity and food staple crops across the Global South. See, e.g., Moore and Koski-Karell, forthcoming (2022); Evenson and Gollin 2003; Shiva 1991.

an agricultural standpoint, and agricultural schools, experiment stations, and research laboratories have already been established or planned for the near future" (1927: 314).

Nonetheless, the Occupation seems to have buried its plantation dreams on the Central Plateau by the 1930s. That shift coincides with changing perceptions of the hinterland, which—before exploitation attempts—had been characterized as fertile and wild. The failure of the cotton plantations is taken to reflect the "failure" of the agrarian landscape of the hinterland more generally. By the 1930s: "The Central Plain is, unfortunately, of little productive benefit to the nation, because it consists largely of savannas entirely covered with a grass locally known as Madame Michel" (Dorsinville 1933: 668). This observer, writing in the last years of the Occupation, no longer lauds the fertile soils of the interior, but rather points to the region's ecological unsuitability for cultivation. The failure of large-scale cotton production, specifically, seems to mark that shift in perspective. Through imperial eyes, the hinterland had become again a wilderness or a wasteland.

Observers emphasize that the "improvement" of the interior failed for biological, social, and political reasons: "for about five to seven years, beginning in 1929, the work of selection [for cotton production] was carried out carefully, intelligently, and, in the experimental fields, successfully. A steady improvement went on in the length, texture, and other qualities of the fiber. But the Haitian peasant, apart from the selected seeds which he received now and then, was quite indifferent to what was happening. And unfortunately in the middle thirties, the work of selection, which was still incomplete, was practically ruined by the appearance in Haiti of the Mexican boll weevil, the most destructive cotton pest for which no successful remedy is yet known" (Holly 1955: 75–76). Holly points to multiple forms of refusal and resistance that stymied cotton production in the interior. In addition to the incursion of the boll weevil, Holly notes that "the Haitian peasant, used to his perennial cotton of easy and effortless cultivation, was not ready to accept an annual cotton that required a great deal of work every year" (1955: 80). While Holly makes no reference to the political reasons peasants might refuse to do "a great deal of work" to participate in the production of cotton for export, his analysis suggests the fundamental incompatibility of plantation cotton production with peasants' agrarian way of life.

Transformations: The Land of Milk and Honey

The "wild" cotton that grows alongside the red dirt footpaths that cross the hills of the interior is just one marker of the persistent unmaking of the Occupation's imperial geographies. What does liberation look like in the tropic of cotton? The USDA's participation in the military occupation of Haiti shows how relations between plants, place, and power make imperial geographies. But what the *kako* struggle shows is also how imperial geographies are *unmade*. Agrarian struggle establishes a horizon for the future, roots a certain kind of futurity in land and in relations around it. My friends on the high Central Plateau hold close a vision of an abundant earth. Many of them are organized in a Via Campesina peasants' movement called the Mouvman Peyizan Papay (MPP), which has been active in the region since 1973. Their vision is at once of a fruitful future to come, and of an agrarian world in the making. For militants in the borderlands, the struggle continues *jiska viktwa final la*: until the final victory. When I ask what such a victory might entail, my friend Wilson laughs, smiling broadly and sweeping a hand in a wide arc in front of him: "why, it's the land of milk and honey!".

One afternoon in April, a few weeks into the Spring rainy season, I hurry across a steep hillside behind my friend Jonas. His garden spreads across a small valley surrounded by raw-faced cliffs and the greenery that hangs over the ankle-deep Samanà River. It is far from the road, tucked into a narrow crease between the hills. Jonas has carefully fenced around the whole plot, looping wire around posts stuck in the rocky, ochre-colored earth. The valley is quiet, with just a few bird sounds and the rustle of a slight breeze. The flattest part of the valley is inter-cropped with maize, okra, pumpkin, shiny dark-leafed peppers, and banana palms. The steep hillsides are waiting for the hardy, woody plants: beans and manioc.

Jonas shows me how to poke a stick into the clumped earth, and to place in it a manioc cutting, a smooth, straight stick about three inches long. Jonas chops at the rocky soil with his hoe, moving steadily across the hillside, the divots evenly and effortlessly spaced. I shuffle behind him, barefoot and sweating in the hot mid-morning sun, crouching as I place each cutting. I am nervously making sure the tiny points that will become each plant's branches are pointing up, so they can reach for the sun. The soil is still damp from yesterday's rain, and our bare feet are sticky with reddish earth. When each hole is filled with a trio of knobbed sticks, resting just barely below the earth's surface, we gather, sweating, under the mango tree and drink warm sweet coffee, a little sickly with canned milk. We head down the hillside, back toward the road, Jonas carrying an armful of *elefan* grass for his goats.

We weave between stands of banana, mango, and papaya trees as we make our way through carpets of dark-green yam leaves and delicate peanut plants in the sandy soil by the water. Jonas's house is about twenty minutes' walk from his garden. This, too, is surrounded by green. Around his house, Jonas grows eggplants, onions, peppers, and tomatoes, as well as forage for his goats. We sit in straight-backed chairs in his small front room and eat boiled manioc root from the last season's crop off tin plates. We are eating the same food that Jonas's ancestors planted in provision grounds and maroon gardens, on the land that Jonas's father inherited from his father. When Jonas shows me how to loosen the sticky clay soil to give the manioc space to grow, he teaches me to listen for the life of the soil, to imagine this red earth as once and future freedom's ground.

Conclusion

What grows in the place of imperial geographies? The puff of white that caught my eye along the red dirt path on that hot afternoon is a testament to the plantation's unmaking as an ongoing process. The legacy of the Occupation still marks the Central Plateau, in the bouldered roads that cross the hills and in the decrepit campus of Fem Leta, the "state farm" that was the Service Technique's outpost across the river from Hinche. The Gendarmes who enforced the Occupation's rural discipline would become the feared Tonton Makout, the secret police of the Duvalier dictatorship (1957–1986), for which the Occupation laid the groundwork. The "failures" of the Occupation meant that the promised railroad never reached Hinche, that the roads constructed by the *corvée* crumbled, and that irrigation canals never extended into the high Central Plateau from the fertile plains of the Artibonite.

Yet the Occupation of the hinterland did not manage to extinguish the forms of agrarian life that had existed in the borderlands for centuries. Jonas's garden belies the characterizations of Hispaniola's interior as an agricultural wasteland that have persisted since the failure of the Occupation's cotton plantations. The diversified small-plot cultivation that Jonas practices is typical for the region, as are the large expanses of uncultivated grassland where peasants gather forage for their livestock. The riotous abundance of Jonas's garden is antithetical to the plantation discipline that Occupation forces tried to enforce in the borderlands. Liberation, for Jonas and his neighbors, both hearkens to the agrarian past of the borderlands, and imagines for the region an abundant future. The Central Plateau may yet be, as Dorsinville remarked in 1933, "of little productive benefit to the nation" (668). But nonetheless, the land of milk and honey is here, in the making.

References

Alexander, M. 2012. *The New Jim Crow: Mass Incarceration in the Age of Colorblindness*. New York: The New Press.

An American Resident. 1919. "The Record of Progress in Haiti Since 1915." In *The South American: A Journal for All Interested in Latin American Affairs*. New York: South American Publishing Company, Incorporated.

Axel, N., K. Cupers, and N. Hirsch, Eds. 2021. "Coloniality of Infrastructure." E-Flux. https://www.e-flux.com/architecture/coloniality-infrastructure/.

Balch, E.G., ed. 1927. *Occupied Haiti: Being the Report of a Committee of Six Disinterested Americans Representing Organizations Exclusively American, Who, Having Personally Studied Conditions in Haiti in 1926, Favor the Restoration of the Independence of the Negro Republic*. New York: The Writer's Publishing Company.

Beckert, S. 2014. *Empire of Cotton: A Global History*. New York: Vintage.

Casimir, J. 1981. *La Culture Opprimée*. Delmas, Haiti: Lakay.

Chapman, C.E. 1927. The Development of the Intervention in Haiti. *The Hispanic American Historical Review* 7 (3): 299–319.

Chochotte, M. 2017. "The History of Peasants, Tonton Makouts, and the Rise and Fall of the Duvalier Dictatorship in Haiti." Ph.D. Thesis University of Michigan.

Cowen, D. 2019. Following the Infrastructures of Empire: Notes on Cities, Settler Colonialism, and Method. *Urban Geography* 41 (4): 469–486.

Dorsinville, L. 1933. The Plains of Haiti. *Bulletin of the Pan American Union* 67: 668–673.

Erasmus, C.J. 1952. Agricultural Changes in Haiti: Patterns of Resistance and Acceptance. *Human Organization* 11 (4): 20–26.

Evenson, R.E., and D. Gollin. 2003. Assessing the Impact of the Green Revolution, 1960 to 2000. *Science* 300 (5620): 758–762.

Francisco-Ortega, J., M. Swan, W. Cinea, N. Beaussejour, N. Korber, J. Mosely Latham, and B. Jestrow. 2017. "David Fairchild's Plant Hunting Expeditions in Haiti (LACC Working Paper No. 2/2017)." Kimberly Green Latin American and Caribbean Center, Florida International University.

Greenburg, J. 2016. 'The One Who Bears the Scars Remembers': Haiti and the Historical Geography of US Militarized Development. *Journal of Historical Geography* 51: 52–63.

Holly, M.A. 1955. *Agriculture in Haiti: With Special Reference to Rural Economy and Agricultural Education*. New York: Vantage Press.

Lundahl, M. 1979. *Peasants and Poverty: A Study of Haiti*. New York: Routledge Revivals.

Millspaugh, A.C. 1931. *Haiti Under American Control, 1915–1930*. Boston: World Peace Foundation.

Moore, S. S. and V. Koski-Karell. 2022 [forthcoming]. "Geographies of Empire: Infrastructure and Agricultural Intensification in Haiti". *The Geographical Journal*.

Nicholls, D. 1985. "Rural Protest and Peasant Revolt, 1804–1869." In *Haiti in Caribbean Context*, 167–85. St Antony's Series. London: Palgrave Macmillan.

Posner, W.H. 1964. American Marines in Haiti, 1915–1922. *The Americas* 20 (3): 231–266.

Schmidt, H. 1995. *The United States Occupation of Haiti, 1915–1934*. Reprint. New Brunswick, N.J: Rutgers University Press.

Shiva, V. 1991. *The Violence of the Green Revolution: Third World Agriculture, Ecology and Politics*. London: Zed Books.

United States Congress Senate Select Committee on Haiti and Santo Domingo. 1922. *Inquiry Into Occupation and Administration of Haiti and Santo Domingo: Hearing[s] Before a Select Committee on Haiti and Santo Domingo, United States Senate, Sixty-Seventh Congress, First Session, Pursuant to S. Res. 112 Authorizing a Special Committee to Inquire Into the Occupation and Administration of the Territories of the Republic of Haiti and the Dominican Republic*. Washington, DC: U.S. Government Printing Office.

United States High Commissioner to Haiti. 1929. *Annual Report of the American High Commissioner at Port Au Prince, Haiti, to the Secretary of State*. U.S: Government Printing Office.

Weatherly, U.G. 1926. Haiti: An Experiment in Pragmatism. *American Journal of Sociology* 32 (3): 353–366.

Wolcott, G.N. 1927. Haitian Cotton and the Pink Bollworm. *Bulletin of Entomological Research* 18 (1): 79–82.

Woodring, W.P., J.S. Brown, and W.S. Burbank. 1924. *Geology of the Republic of Haiti*. Port-au-Prince, Haiti: Lord Baltimore Press.

Woods, C.A. 2017. *Development Arrested: The Blues and Plantation Power in the Mississippi Delta*. London: Verso.

CHAPTER 5

Nostalgia for Oranges: Plantations as a Development Promise in Socialist Cuba

Marie Aureille

"Welcome to Arenas, where the Cuban sun sets" (*Bienvenidos a Arenas, donde se esconde el sol de Cuba*). This welcoming message on a concrete sign marking the entrance to the municipality comes with hand-painted sunset over the sea. If it wasn't for this indication, there is no way one could guess that the sea was so close. On either side of the wide, carefully maintained road that leads to La Victoria, the capital city of the municipality, vegetation is mostly impenetrable. There are a few patches of young eucalyptus, then a patch of mango trees—the size of their trunks and the tortuous majesty of their branches indicating their old age. The dominant species is a thorny shrub with dark green foliage, sometimes several metres high, called *marabú*. This invasive species proliferates in agricultural wastelands. In Cuba, it is a symbol of the crisis in the agricultural sector.

M. Aureille (✉)
Laboratoire d'Anthropologie Politique, Ecole Des Hautes Etudes en Sciences Sociales, Paris, France
e-mail: marie.aureille@gmail.com

C. Le Petitcorps et al. (eds.), *Global Plantations in the Modern World*, Cambridge Imperial and Post-Colonial Studies,
https://doi.org/10.1007/978-3-031-08537-6_5

During my fieldwork,[1] contemplating the landscape has often triggered narratives about the past of the municipality, which was a modern citrus plantation and an example of socialist rural development only fifteen years ago. My interlocutors were determined to teach me how to read this landscape, which was "pregnant with the past" (Ingold 2002: 189), to guide me through the material and vegetal ruins of a large socialist plantation. They wanted to show me that Arenas had not always been like this. As they recalled the municipality's glorious past, the eyes of my various interlocutors would start to shine. They eagerly described huge, clean, and well-kept cultivations, the countless paths, as well as fruit-laden trees with juicy oranges waiting to be tasted. They spoke of abundance, of the sweet taste of oranges and the beauty of the landscape. However, I could only imagine these plantations as my own mouth watered at the evocation of the orange treat. Nowadays the orange groves have disappeared, invaded by the *marabú* that has closed the paths and obstructed the landscape. Abandoned buildings emerge occasionally from the canopy. Nostalgia about Arenas's glorious past permeates all the accounts I have heard beyond generational, social or political positionings.

These descriptions of a paradise of industrial monoculture contrast with the literature on Cuban agriculture which, since the 1990s, has been focusing on the transition of the farming system towards agroecology (Muíño 2017; Rosset and Benjamin 1994; Wright 2009), and the policies of "repeasantization" (Figueroa Albelo 2005; Valdés Paz 2009) through the distribution of land in usufruct (Leyva Remón and Arias Guevara 2000) and the development of cooperatives (Harnecker 2011). The widespread adoption of these ideas outside the island by the non-Cuban press (Wright 2009), as well as by anti-globalization and environmental movements (Muiño 2014) contributed to foster a vision of Cuba as one of the most advanced countries in the transition towards

[1] I draw on an ethnographic fieldwork conducted in Arenas during 16 months from 2016 to 2018 and shorter visits in 2019 and 2022, archives from Pinar del Rio Historical Archives, the State's Departments of Agriculture and Spatial Planning in Pinar del Rio and private collections owned by my interlocutors in Arenas. All names and locations have been anonymized to protect my informants whom I thank for their trust and help. To avoid putting them at risk, some of their distinctive social features and part of their stories were modified in such a way that do not affect the general argument of the paper. I would like to thank Marta Macedo, Irene Peano, Colette Le Petitcorps, Birgit Müller, Marie-Laure Geoffray, Felix Traoré, Kateryna Soroka, Gala Aguero, Benoit de L'Estoile for their insights and feedbacks on earlier versions of this chapter.

small-scale and ecological farming, setting an example for peasant movements around the world (Thivet 2014). Little has been said about the sociotechnical legacies of the dominant form of agriculture organization until 1993, i.e. the state farm, and the difficult transformation of technologically advanced and export-oriented mono-crop systems, to small scale, diversified and poorly mechanized farming intended for local and national consumption.

The literature on (post)socialism has mainly studied agriculture through the lens of (de)collectivization. The emphasis on the question of property and central planning (Verdery 2003) has also pushed the sociotechnical issue of industrialized agriculture into the background. Under the threat of "land grabbing", plantations have received a renewed attention which explicitly linked the analysis of their economic and power structure to their infrastructural (Li 2017b) and sociotechnical characteristics, pictured as alienating for both human and non-human actors (Haraway 2015; Tsing 2015). Indeed, the plantation system is usually conceived alongside capitalist relations. Plantations are seen as a precursor form of capitalism (Haraway 2015; Mintz 1986: 58) as its most exemplary outcome (Braudel 1982: 272) for they rely on different "labour regimes" that share common features like the alienation of workers (Li 2017a) and the production or reproduction of racial, ethnic or gender discrimination. However, capitalist plantation systems and socialist agriculture share common features, such as high modernist schemes (Scott 1998) based on productivism, gigantism, and the control and supervision over workers' lives. In socialist Cuba, plantations are state farms. Without overlooking structural differences between socialist and capitalist systems, I suggest that considering these shared characteristics is crucial to understand the nostalgia and aspirations of the people of Arenas, their views on the plantation collapse and on the Cuban Revolution.

Following the nostalgia of Arenas' inhabitants and former plantation workers, this chapter explores memories and narratives of the vanished plantations and what they say about the present. How has the plantation shaped these subjects' environment, their life experiences, and their representations of a desirable life?

In Arenas, I argue, plantations stand as the materialization of State sovereignty and as the promise of development, modernity, and social progress held by Cuban socialism. Although the plantation has disappeared, norms and aspirations for a better life shaped by the experience of living in the plantations remain. They define a lost normality, a frame of reference which keep shaping social relations.

The concept of State sovereignty has been used to define and create the juridical fiction of western Nation-States, as the legitimate and ultimate power of the State to act upon a territory and its population (Dardot & Laval 2020). Through ethnographic accounts, anthropologists have underlined that sovereignty is not a given but an incomplete and contested process (Humphrey 2007). Sovereignty needs political work to come into existence. It might be materialized through concrete actions such as building borders, monuments, naming, and mapping places (Navaro-Yashin 2012: 43–50) or be shared as a more intangible set of norms and rules actively (re)produced in daily interactions (Latham 2000: 7). In such accounts, the focus is not so much on state sovereignty as the ultimate authority that comes from above (the power over life and death according to Foucault or the power to ban for Agamben) but as the actual power to structure social existence, to create an "everyday frame of life" (Humphrey 2007: 428).

From 1959 in Arenas, the Revolutionary State has built its sovereignty through the creation of plantations organized as state farms. The socialist "frame of life" that emerged entailed new conceptions of reciprocity and autonomy, values and promises of modernity that were experienced through collectivization and the experience of becoming a plantation worker. I begin with demonstrating how plantations came to embody State presence in Arenas through a rapid and radical transformation of the territory. Secondly, I focus on how State sovereignty is enforced through boundary drawing and exclusion–inclusion processes that crystallize around the constitution of state property and state farms. Then, I show how the plantation has transformed people's lives and working conditions, linking new norms and values to personal experiences of upward mobility. Finally, I underline how diverging accounts of the plantation collapse keep asserting State Sovereignty as a form of vanished normality.

The Socialist Plantation, a Matrix for a New Society

Plantations as a coercive form of labour organization and capital concentration have been widely criticized in Cuba in the twentieth century. Progressive and revolutionary movements have insisted, since the 1930s, on breaking away from the *latifundio* model, the large-scale private ownership of land (Swanger 2015). The capitalist sugar plantations owned by foreign investors and the Cuban bourgeoisie were amongst the first targets of the revolutionary government, which took power in 1959. However, revolutionaries never called into question the plantations as a socio-technical apparatus. The system of state farms devoted to monoculture established in the 1960s partly inherited the existing plantation model, understood as "large, profit-driven plant production complexes that focus primarily on one commodity and cater to distant markets" (Uekötter 2014: 13). Indeed, the regime did not question the continuous orientation of the Cuban economy towards exporting agricultural raw materials, as well as the sociotechnical system of intensive monoculture and the wage-based labour organization. The State, as the chief actor in the revolutionary economic system, was seeking to maximize foreign currency earnings to fund its redistribution system, which remained dependent on imports. The plantation model was even extended by implementing central planning. Guided by high-modernist schemes (Scott 1998), the revolutionary leaders wanted to develop productive capacities throughout the territory in order to correct the inequalities generated by the capitalist economy and to take advantage of all the island's resources (Segre 1970). Mono-cropping and plantations as agricultural modernization projects were at the core of the economic and social development plan of revolutionary leaders. In their view, the plantations' problem was solved from the moment they became state property in the name of and for "the people".

Many stretches of land became plantations in the 1960s and 1970s. This was the case of the municipality of Arenas: a marginal, sparsely populated, and loosely exploited forest plain in western Cuba[2] It became a

[2] In the following section, I rely on unpublished manuscripts written by historians of the municipality. The historian (*el historiador*) of the municipality is a civil servant, usually holding a degree in history and closely linked to the municipal section of the Communist Party. From the 1980s, the Cuban Communist Party gave orientation to create working

huge citrus plantation and a symbol of socialist rural development in the 1960s. Local historians say that Fidel Castro and the leaders in charge of the Land Reform decided the fate of this territory during a helicopter flight over the region in September 1959, when they outlined the main directions of the agricultural development plans in the area. In this region, most of the land was owned by big Cuban landowners, who were only partially exploiting it. The two agrarian reforms of 1959 and 1963, which limited the size of farms to 67 ha, led to their expropriation and the nationalization of the land. The National Institute for Land Reform (INRA) set up State farms (*granjas estatales*) and ordered to bulldoze the forest savannahs covered with endemic vegetation (pine and palm trees) to be substituted by mango and citrus trees.[3] The state farms under the command of the INRA's regional delegation and the Revolutionary Army were the first institutions that took over the organization of daily life and implemented reforms. The INRA enforced iconic policies such as the literacy campaign or the quick creation of hospitals in rural areas. Political organizations that would become the pillars of revolutionary life, such as local Communist Party committees, emerged within the new state farms. In the beginning of the 1960s, working at a state farm meant actively participating in the Revolution and socializing to its values and institutions.

The Agricultural Plan designed for the region rapidly reshaped the territory and its infrastructures. The plantation also instituted a new temporal framing marked by quick and radical changes in the short term, 5–20 years' growth planning for the middle term and the futuristic promise of creating a radically new society in the long term, those three temporal framings reinforcing one another. A new city, La Victoria,

groups under the supervision of the municipal historians to gather testimonies and archives and to write down the history of each *municipio*. In Arenas, several manuscripts were written from the beginning of the 1990s and the end of the 2000s by several *historiadores* and sometimes, their team of volunteers. To preserve anonymity of the location and of the other informants, I cannot cite their writings here although I am grateful for their precious work.

[3] In 1964, the plan designed for the area forecast the development of 16,000 ha of citrus trees and 2000 ha of mango trees. In 1970, "198 caballerias" of citrus trees (around 2650 ha) were reported to have been planted according to the municipal historians. By the mid-1980's, Arenas's citrus plantations covered around 20,000 ha (measure taken from satellite maps and maps from the archives of the Dirección Provincial de Planificación Física de Pinar del Río). The main production were oranges, and to a lesser extent grapefruit and limes (Nova González 1996; see also Ríos Hernández 2014).

was built in record time by political prisoners and peasants who had been displaced from the Escambray Mountains, where a counter-revolutionary war was raging.[4] Inaugurated in 1965, the city was conceived as an example of a new type of "agricultural conglomerate" (Segre 1970: 122–123) that would bring together displaced families, local peasants and technical and political staff. Its architect claimed that he had conceived a "peasant's city" (*una ciudad de campesinos*) in line with the political goal to break the urban/rural divide and to bring urban living standards to isolated areas. The infrastructures were designed to create the conditions for Che Guevara's "new man" to emerge, and to re-educate and socialize the populations of peasants and counter-revolutionaries to the "socialist way of life".

The creation of large fruit plantations brought about profound changes in the lifestyles of Arenas's residents. The construction of large-scale hydraulic facilities to irrigate the plantations led to population displacements. In 1967, an 'agricultural community' called '26 de Julio' was created 6 km from La Victoria right in the middle of the plantation in order to relocate sixteen families and enable the construction of a dam and a vast water reservoir for irrigation. Caridad, whose family was amongst the displaced, says it was Celia Sanchez herself, a revolutionary close to Fidel Castro, who came to talk to them about the need to move to a new village created especially for them, where they could live with "all the conditions", i.e. modern standards of housings. Each family received a "concrete house", a set of furniture, and a small plot of land to ensure their subsistence. The village had a row of almost identical single-family houses built along the road, a small school, a state store (*bodega*), and a medical consultation room. In her story, Caridad focuses on the pride to have received direct attention from a leading figure of the Revolution and

[4] From 1961 to 1965, a counter-revolutionary war took place in the Escambray Mountains, in the centre of the Island. Johanna Swanger argues that the insurrection aroused and gained support within the peasants of the area, a mainly white population, amidst fears that the Land Reform would be reverted, that the State would collectivize land threatening property rights and destroy the values of a white and patriarchal society promoting women education, racial equality, or homosexuality and interracial marriages. The revolutionary government, arguing that it was an attempt of the CIA to overthrow the newly instated Revolution severely fought against the insurrection. In 1963, revolutionary authorities enforced massive displacements to cut the insurgents from local supports and sent entire villages to camps. Alongside the victory of the Bay of Pigs, the "Battle of the Escambray" became a founding moment in the official history of the Revolutionary fight against US imperialism (Swanger 2015).

puts emphasis on what she sees as privileged living conditions rather than on the fact of displacement itself.

The citrus plantations, which were only partially mechanized, had huge labour needs. The national plan for citrus development designed a standard blueprint which organized the plantations around *escuelas al campo*, secondary schools where the curriculum included both study and agricultural work. Becoming widespread in the 1970s, this type of school was meant to speed up the revolutionary socialization of young people and "free them from family ties"—as families were thought to convey values that were still too traditional—whilst allowing parents to fully devote themselves to their work (Segre 1970: 64). Like other citrus-production areas across the country, Arenas's plantations relied on the free labour of the *escuelas al campo* students, who carried out most of the manual tasks of maintaining the plots and harvesting the fruit. More than 30 schools, each with 500 boarding students, were created in Arenas's plantations. The first 24 schools were built in record time between 1971 and 1975, sometimes by the students themselves.

These rapid transformations relied on mass mobilizations of students, urban workers, and peasant families under the catchword of "participation". Narratives of participation and self-sacrifice effectively mobilized millions of Cubans. Revolutionary leaders presented mass participation as the only way to secure Cuban's sovereignty and to produce radical changes (Guerra 2012: 9).

Technical assessments over productive choices in the plantation were caught in the national atmosphere of "popular participation" of the 1960s, resulting in spectacular achievements but also countless mistakes because of the lack of training or previous analysis, incoherence in the planning designs and the allocation of resources etc. (Dumont 1970). The National Citrus Plan entailed enormous investments with little knowledge about citrus cultivation, which was barely developed in Cuba before the 1960s.[5] The first programs of varietal selection and nurseries

[5] The commercial cultivation of citrus fruits in Cuba was introduced by American settlers at the end of the nineteenth century, following frosts that strongly affected production in Florida. The crop was intended above all for export to North America. However, its development in Cuba was limited throughout the first half of the twentieth century due to the significant increase in production in Florida and California, which were in direct competition with Cuban exports (Jiménez Villasuso and Zamora Rodriguez 2010; Ríos Hernández 2014: 113). Technical assessment for the crop was not properly structured and little research had been conducted on variety selection before the 1970s.

conducted in the 1960s gave poor results and ended with the spread of the *Phytochtora* fungi, a plague affecting rootstocks (Jiménez Villasuso and Zamora Rodriguez 2010). The varieties used were mainly from the United States, some were introduced by American settlers since the end of the nineteenth century and during the first half of the twentieth, others were imported by the Revolutionary government in 1968. In the 1970s, Cuba started its own variety selection program. In the end, the main cultivars used in the plantations were hybrids of the most widely used varieties in commercial plantations worldwide: the "Valencia" variety for orange, "Lima Persa" for limes and "Marsh" for grapefruits (FAO 2003).

The plantations of Pinar del Rio province were amongst the first to be installed in the early 1960s. However, the sandy soils proved to be unsuitable, and the state plans for citrus production gradually concentrated investments in more productive areas, especially in the province of Matanzas (Jagüey Grande). Despite being one of the first plantations, Arenas ended up amongst the last to be equipped with a citrus processing plant for export in 1980s. The yields of these plantations were low compared to the national average, around 4 t/ha against 9 t/ha at the national level and 10–11 t/ha for the great citrus pole of Jagüey Grande, and even Cuba's best yield remained well below the average of the main exporting countries at the time (Nova González 1996).

The plantations in Arenas embodied the socialist State and its ambition to govern overall production, economy, and social life. The socialist government designed plantations infrastructure as the matrix for a new society. Radical transformation of the territory, its social relations, and ecosystem was part of the formation of Revolutionary State sovereignty as a set of norms and values ordering new social and economic relations. The concept of "state property" was an essential tool for local INRA leaders to institute State sovereignty as both a process of inclusion and exclusion.

The Scope of the Plantation: State Property as Revolutionary Sovereignty

In socialist states, property has been a central element of assessing state sovereignty and Cuba is no exception. The founding act of the Cuban revolutionary system was the 1959 Land Reform, which triggered expropriations of large landowners. Revolutionary leaders presented the Land Reform as an act of regaining national sovereignty "for the people" against capitalist and foreign interests. In these first years, expropriation led to land and housing redistribution to current tenants. Later on, from the proclamation of "the socialist character of the Revolution" in 1961 until the 1968 "Revolutionary Offensive", most of the land and the economic activities became "state property".

The Cuban government designed a property system similar to Eastern-European socialist countries and the USSR, which defined a hierarchy of legitimate property forms with state property on top, followed by cooperative property, personal property and in the end, private property which was the most undesirable (Verdery 2003, 2007). As Katherine Verdery explains, under socialism property "was less a legal and more an administrative matter" (2007: 23) which organized a set of boundaries and networks of circulation of goods within the "unitary fund" of state property. Property was linked to the identity of the tenant, which gave access to certain rights and goods (Humphrey 1998: 4–5).

Displacement and expropriation were central to the establishment of the new state plantations. It started with large landowners, but also small tenants such as those moved to the 26 de Julio settlements after the construction of a dam. In the 1970s, as the Citrus Plan grew, local authorities encouraged all small farmers who owned land within the perimeter of the plantations to hand over their land to the State. In exchange, they would be given modern housing in the new town of La Victoria, as well as a pension for older farmers or a job in the state farm for the younger ones.

Renouncing private property was presented as a revolutionary act. In the ideological rhetoric of that time, the peasantry (*el campesinado*), which perpetuated private property and individualism, had to disappear, and the peasants had to join the most advanced revolutionary class: the working class. The transformation of peasant owners into agricultural workers was also a substantial status change. The farmer had to give up self-sufficiency and the power to decide over the land at his disposal. Becoming a wage worker, he had to embrace a new set of reciprocal relations with "the State". Indeed, it was a condition for access to new forms of social protection (retirement, paid holidays, maternity leave for women), from which peasants were then excluded, although they already benefited from access to healthcare and education, considered as fundamental and unconditional rights since the beginning of the Revolution (Espina Prieto 2008: 138). Becoming a state farm worker also allowed former peasants to receive desirable goods such as household appliances, trips within Cuba or abroad, housing or vehicles, that were periodically distributed by the trade union to deserving workers within the "socialist emulation" process (*emulación socialista*) (Rosendahl 1997: 37–38). This type of measure was not specific to the plantations of Arenas, since it applied to all agricultural regions where the State was implementing major modernization projects (Deere et al. 1998; Valdés Paz 2009).

Most of the small owners of Arenas ceded their land. Some did so out of revolutionary fervour, but most agreed to do so because they were getting older and did not plan on passing land to their children, to whom mass access to education was offering prospects for social advancement as an alternative to hard manual work in the fields.

A small minority refused and managed to remain on their farms. José, a 45-year-old farmer, likes to tell of how his father strongly opposed the pressure of Party officials in the 1970s to give the family land to the State. His father Santiago supported revolutionary groups in the 1950s, but he was strongly attached to the hard-won land he had inherited from his own father, himself from a family of black farmers[6] who had succeeded to buy land in the 1930s. In a context where Afro-Cubans had a long history of poverty, segregation, and exclusion from property rights, preserving this inheritance was important. Since 1959, revolutionary leaders had banned racism and segregation as a particular feature of the "class society" the Revolution sought to destroy. However, the performative act of declaring that racism had disappeared with the end of "bourgeois society" did not erase the memories of discrimination and the racist representations that kept pervading social relations (Núñez González et al. 2011).

Now that the plantation has disappeared and that the government is distributing state land in usufruct to small farmers to restart production, José proudly claims that his father was right to refuse to cede his land. José underlines how, despite the promises made by state officials that the Revolution would secure everything they needed, those who ceded their land and went to live in La Victoria have suffered from food shortages and scarcity. Indeed, unlike the inhabitants of "26 de Julio", those who handed over their land to the State did not keep a plot of land for self-subsistence and therefore depended entirely on their salary, retirement pension, and the State food distribution system, which, since the 1960s,

[6] Skin colour and race are mentioned here as they are integral to people's self-identification in Arenas's social space alongside gender or age. I use the categories people used in my presence to talk about themselves.

has suffered from repeated shortages (Dumont 1964). José mentions the case of the grandson of one peasant who has asked for his grandfather's plot in usufruct and recently moved to the land. The grandfather was a fervent Party member who was one of the first to hand over his land. "All of this to get there", concludes José. José and his father are known in the area for being outspoken critics of revolutionary policies. However, local leaders largely dismiss and ignore their criticism, considering them "backward peasants" whose "lack of education" does not allow them to properly understand the issues at stake.

José's accounts of his father's resistance to collectivization, underline the new values and reciprocity regime that was implemented in the 1960s and 1970s. In revolutionary discourses, each Cuban was supposed to fully participate in the Revolution, i.e. in the construction of a new egalitarian, fair and modern society. This discourse emphasized "self-sacrifice" for the sake of all and complete trust in the revolutionary leaders' vision (Guerra 2012). In Arenas, it meant working for the state in the plantations, participating in political activities and, for some, renouncing private property over land. In exchange, the State would provide Cubans with everything they needed: food, health, education, leisure, goods, etc. This discourse on the reciprocity relation between each Cuban citizen and the Revolution was materialized in the labour regime of the plantation in housing and infrastructure policies and in the socialist welfare system at large. Refusing to participate meant being marginalized from the new community. Idalia, the wife of another peasant in a similar situation, said that the three households that kept living on their farms were connected to the electricity only after the 2000s when two hurricanes destroyed the municipality. She sees this exclusion as an unofficial punishment for not handing over the land. The grid that supplied the nearby state farm ran very close from the houses, she explains, but they were not connected until after the hurricanes when they were included amongst the natural disaster victims.

As Caroline Humphrey recalls (2007), sovereignty as a set of norms, rules, and values consists in boundaries' production and the power of exclusion. One such boundary was established in the 1960s and 1970s between state property, materialized in Arenas by the plantation, and private property, in this case peasant property over the land. However, this was not an absolute ban. Those who managed to keep their farms did not live outside the plantation system but only on its margins. Many worked for some time on the plantation which ensured them a regular salary.

José's father, Santiago, worked several years as a guard for the plantation plots in front of his house. He switched the irrigation system during the night and watched for potential thieves.

Although state property was at the core of the Revolutionary system, the Cuban leaders always insisted that collectivization had to be voluntary. "Peasants" (*campesinos*) held an ambiguous position within ideological discourses: they were portrayed as remnants of the individualistic bourgeois society and at the same time as revolutionaries whose support to Fidel Castro's guerrilla in the Sierra Maestra campaign was crucial to secure victory. The peasant families displaced from the Escambray Mountains to build the city of La Victoria have also benefited from this ambiguous status: singled out as counterrevolutionaries that helped the CIA-funded insurrection, they were also presented as victims whose displacement was the only way the State could protect them. The municipal historians of Arenas simultaneously portrayed them as prisoners not allowed to leave the municipality and enthusiastic actors of the construction of the city and the plantation.

Local revolutionary leaders in Arenas instituted State Sovereignty through the rhetoric of participation and the idea that Revolution is a process towards the creation of a new society. State property and its "labour regime" (Li 2017a) were pivotal elements of Revolutionary Sovereignty as they allowed Party leaders and State officials to ban and marginalize those who did not fit in the new social and economic organization of society. The State plantation based on these revolutionary principles also created possibilities for redemption and integration within the new society through work and political participation. In Arenas, local peasants who resisted expropriation and displaced people from the Escambray were caught in this exclusion–inclusion process, which came to frame their daily life for decades.

Exclusion and marginalization are bitterly remembered by those who endured them, who are, nevertheless, a minority. Indeed, Arenas counted few landowning peasants in the first place—as most of the land belonged to large landlords before 1959—and still fewer who opposed expropriation. Most of the people displaced from the Escambray Mountains left Arenas in the 1970s and 1980s: some obtained political asylum in the United States and fled the country, others went back to Santa Clara province once their travel restrictions were lifted. Today, for most of Arenas inhabitants, this is old history. When asked about these events, some remember that people from the Escambray had a harsh time when they arrived, but that local peasants helped them and that there was a lot of solidarity. Members of the Communist Party insist that "the Revolution treated them well", they obtained a house, a job, an opportunity for their children to study and become doctors and teachers: "no one was left behind".

Tasting "Development" in Citrus Plantations

By the end of the 1970s, most of Arenas inhabitants worked in something related to the plantations. Working "for the Revolution" in state enterprises and administrations was a strong injunction which was difficult to evade. Besides agricultural work, the boarding schools employed a wide variety of persons: teachers, administrative staff, cooks, guardians, monitors, storekeepers, etc. Women were encouraged to study and work for the plantation, and they some were included in what was considered masculine works such as agricultural work, although they remained a minority.

The memories of the plantations that my interlocutors spontaneously shared with me were about modernity, progress, skilled work, and upward mobility. My interlocutors describe the 1960–1980s period as a time of emancipation during which their living conditions improved significantly, and they were feeling the taste of development (*desarrollo*). *Desarrollo* functions both as a positive value and as a grid to interpret the social world (Ferguson 1994) that combines revolutionary ideals and representations with the concrete experiences of Arenas's inhabitants. Revolutionary leaders presented modernizing schemes—including export monoculture, universal access to health and education, collective housing scattered between the fields, incorporating women into the workforce, the official ban of racial segregation—as the first steps to get out of *subdesarrollo* (the condition of "underdeveloped country"). Settlers experienced modernity and development not only through their social trajectories and their living and working conditions, but also as an aesthetic and sensory experience.

"From here to Cortés, it was full of *cítricos* … it was nice, when you took the road to La Victoria, to see all those beautiful fields, well-tended, clean. Sometimes I didn't eat lunch, I just ate sweet and juicy oranges in the fields" recalls 82-years-old Celestino. His children benefited from mass access to primary and secondary school. His two eldest children became teachers and worked in the *escuelas al campo*. One of his younger daughters joined the army and the other trained as livestock technician. His younger son, who dropped out of school, became a tractor operator in the plantation. For Celestino, who comes from a black peasant family, his children's social advancement is a genuine source of pride. His eldest son, who joined the Communist Party's ranks at a very early age, encouraged him to work on the plantations, first as an instructor for students and then as an agricultural worker in the irrigation department. Celestino recalls building agricultural machinery and modern irrigation systems with nostalgia and pride.

In the state farms, manual labour and time-consuming tasks such as weeding, harvesting, and pruning trees were mainly left to students under the supervision of instructors. The official purpose of hard manual tasks was to inculcate a socialist work ethic into the young students who managed the plantations. As illustrated by Celestino's experience, agricultural workers would either supervise the students or take on skilled tasks that required specific know-how, such as grafting, maintaining irrigation systems, applying fertilizers, herbicides and insecticides, and operating tractors. The workers were organized in specialized brigades in charge of irrigation, grafting, pest management, fertilization, and mechanized units. The managers (head of plot, head of production, head of a technical division) usually hold a technician degree and the top leaders of the state farm a diploma in agronomy or in economy.

This qualified work, and the specialized skills that workers developed, were a source of social recognition. Workers were encouraged to study in special programs at night and in the weekends. Grades and diploma were reinforced as one of the most legitimate forms of social hierarchy in the revolutionary society alongside militancy. Silverio, for instance, a 70-year-old black man and a former agricultural technician, was introduced to me by his daughter-in-law as "someone who knows how to do grafting" and who knows a lot about citrus cultivation. He cheerfully discussed the different varieties of orange trees, the evolution of grafting techniques, as well as the most disease-resistant grafts. Silverio also proudly remembered the orderly linear landscapes and the impeccable quality of the oranges produced in the plantation. As we were passing by a ruined warehouse one day, he mentioned that it used to be an old citrus packing plant (*el combinado*). He stressed the gradual increase in production standards and the technicalities of the equipment that determined the quality of the juice and the grading of the oranges. He enthusiastically recounted that the oranges that came out of the *combinado* were difficult to recognize for they looked very different from the one in the fields, they were perfect: "I wish you could have seen that, they were all clean and stainless, with a shiny skin". That it took part in the production of such quality fruit, meeting international standards for export is still a real source of pride for Silverio.

Many former workers perceive access to modern techniques, as well as the mechanization of specific tasks and sophisticated equipment, as a significant improvement in their working conditions and in output quality. The technical and aesthetic standards of the industrial plantation became the standards of a well-done job.

Skills and education were at the core of the revolutionary upward mobility system. The state farm managers, engineers, and technicians were children of peasants who had benefited from generalized access to secondary and technical education since the beginning of the Revolution. Francisco, for example, a white man born in the 1950s in a small-scale family of tobacco farmers in a nearby municipality, was sent to Arenas after completing his education as an agricultural technician. Graduates did not choose where they were going to work. They were placed in state farms wherever they were needed. As a result, many young people from Pinar del Rio Province landed on the Arenas plantations. Francisco soon took up positions of responsibility within the state farm and continued to take evening classes to become an agronomist. He also received training in the Communist Party School for cadres (*cuadros*). He is very proud to be a "professional" (*un professional*), which is an administrative category designing people holding college degrees and management positions. Francisco says that Arenas was a small town where life was enjoyable, especially for young people. There was a cinema, a theatre, a sports complex, bars, and a restaurant. Concerts and parties were held regularly. He would never go back to work on his father's farm, slaving (*pasando trabajo*) under the sun. He rejects manual work and speaks proudly of his responsibilities as a technician and as a manager on the state farms: "I didn't study to go back there [on his father's land]. If I had wanted to stay, I wouldn't have devoted my time and energy to studying". Besides participating in the Revolution, living and working in Arenas was a genuine opportunity for him to emancipate himself from paternal tutelage and from hard work on the land. He considers his upward mobility as a just reward for his education and his commitment to the Revolution as a state-farm manager and a Party militant.

The full-employment policy, the low wage differentiation or access to certain goods and services based on merit have played an important role in social homogenization and the reduction of racial and gender inequalities. The new labour regime and social protection system established by the Revolutionary State offered new opportunities for the emancipation of women. For Marta, a 70-year-old *mulata* (mestizo) woman, moving to Arenas was a real liberation. The daughter of local peasants, she married at 17 to a peasant whose family owned a farm nearby. A few years later, as a mother of four children, she decided to divorce. She went back to live with her elderly father, who then "retired from the land" (*se jubiló por la tierra*) thanks to the incentive scheme encouraging owners to give up their land to allow the expansion of the plantation. Her father has received a retirement pension for his land and a four-room apartment in a building in Arenas where he moved in with his daughter and grandchildren. The relocation was a real liberation for Marta. She was able to start working as a cleaner and cook in various state institutions and to become financially independent. She enjoyed the new friendships she made in her building and neighbourhood, access to the cinema, the comfort of her apartment supplied with electricity, running water, and television. This new life contrasts with the isolation and austerity of the peasant life she had known until then. Women were also employed as agricultural workers and trained as technicians and agronomists.

These diverse experiences demonstrate that in just a few decades revolutionary discourses on technical and social progress did correspond to material processes. Upward mobility and improvements on living and working conditions have created hopes (Jansen 2021), a community of aspiration (Hetherington 2014), a relatively shared vision of what *desarollo* should be. These new desirable ways of life, mechanized work standards, the aesthetics of plantations, the pride to be able to export quality products abroad, the value of education, skills, and merit in upward mobility are integral to Revolutionary State Sovereignty and serve to legitimate it. The crisis of the 1990s which followed the fall of the Soviet bloc, and the gradual disintegration of the plantation system, challenged these aspirations, values, and the revolutionary reciprocity system. Nowadays, the ruins of plantations in Arenas stand as reminders of decline, of the vanishing development promises that shaped the landscape and people life's from the 1960s to the 1980s.

Longing for Plantations, Desiring Normality

Today, citrus plantations have disappeared, and *marabú,* the thorny and invasive shrub, dominates the landscape. The plantation grid is only perceivable from satellite images, but even from space, the dark green spots of the invasive plant gradually erode the perpendicular lines of the large, modern blueprint. On the ground, one can no longer distinguish the geometry of the plantations. Only the four-storey buildings of the abandoned *escuelas al campo* emerge from the vegetation. Marabú has closed off secondary roads and only paying great attention one can find the small trunks of dry orange trees amongst the thorny massifs. Yet the plantation still exists as a memory of abundance and as a spatial frame of reference. Arenas's inhabitants keep naming places and giving directions referring to the numbers of the *escuelas al campo.*

The plantation collapse was a result of a combination of political, economic, social, and ecological factors that since the 1990s have weakened the set of relationships constitutive of the plantations. Not all stakeholders rank these factors in the same way. Exploring these divergent understandings of the plantations' decline may allow to understand how the state sovereignty built since the 1960s still pervades social norms, moral assessments, and aspirations in Arenas, as well as defining what a "normal life" should be.

The fall of the USSR meant Cuba lost its major trading partner. Its economic model—based on the export of agricultural raw materials and the import of food, oil, and manufactured goods—plunged the country into a serious economic and food crisis.[7] In 1990, Fidel Castro euphemistically referred to the crisis as the "Special Period in Peacetime" and called for a boost in the struggle to defend the Revolution and adapt to these new circumstances without giving up on its principles. In the following years, however, the government launched structural reforms and ideological reorientations, which deeply altered the reciprocity agreements that were at the core of the state-based production system. The State incited Cubans to produce their own food and to build their own houses, implicitly acknowledging that it was not able to provide for the livelihoods of its workers in exchange for hard work and sacrifice any more. The Special Period affected the material grounds of existence

[7] Imports fell by 75% for oil, 78% for fertilizers and pesticides, and 50% for food (Wright 2009: 67).

that had supported revolutionary state sovereignty in two fundamental aspects. The input and oil shortage jeopardized the metabolic subsistence of the plantation, whilst the economic crisis and the food shortage led to the redefinition of the principles of reciprocity and participation, which sustained revolutionary morality and daily life.

Whilst the lack of oil, fertilizers, and herbicides was weakening Arenas' plantations in the 1990s, both workers and managers were devoting more and more energy to feeding themselves and maintaining plots for their subsistence. They informally appropriated some plots in the interstices of the plantations. However, as early as 1993, the government allowed the distribution of small plots of 0.25 ha in usufruct for self-consumption. The State gradually outsourced responsibility for food production to individuals and cooperatives. This emerging process of decollectivization and the urgency of the crisis led many workers to hijack, appropriate or resell some parts of the plantation equipment in order to cultivate their fields or to make money to buy food on the black market where prices had rocketed.

Olegario, a white man in his seventies, worked as an accountant in the citrus plantation's mechanization unit. He used to carry out the inventories of tractors. He remembers: "In the 1980s, we had about 280 Soviet tractors in the inventory, we took care of all of Arenas' plantations". Whenever a tractor broke down, he explains, the tractor was removed from the inventory (*se daba baja al tractor*) and dismantled. "Anyone who has a tractor today got it like that… people managed to obtain (*resolvian*) a frame, they legalized it and then they rebuilt it piece by piece". During the special period, as there were no more spare parts, nor new tractors coming from the USSR, there was a real haemorrhage of tractors: "people used to come at night, they talked to the guard, and they took away a chassis or the working tractor altogether". As Olegario recounts, the misappropriation of tractors and other state resources was a common practice in the 1980s, but it was not too detrimental, as imports from the USSR replaced the missing parts. During the Special Period, with the rise of individualized food production, these practices increased with much more dramatic consequences. The "underlife" of the plantation and its "informal accommodations" (Goffman 1961 cited by Li 2017a: 261) then escalated and came out of the shadows. In the 1990s, these coping practices fell under the polysemic term of *la lucha* (the struggle), meaning both the individual struggle to survive in daily life and the struggle to defend the Cuban system, which was presented by its rulers as a citadel under siege. As Cuban leaders connected the fight for one's survival with the fight to defend the Revolution, informal and illegal practices were morally neutralized and trivialized and came to constitute the core of everyday life (Bloch 2018).

However, as Olegario underlines, workers' mundane hijacking practices took an active part in the plantations' loss of productive capacity. He deplores the individualistic behaviour of all those involved in the misappropriation of the spare parts, which he deemed detrimental to the common good, and the absurdity of certain accounting standards that allowed it. Here, smuggling should not only be seen as weakening the State's ability to control the economy, but also as a sign that State sovereignty as norms and values still structure social relations. Informal practices are wrapped in secrecy, a sense of moral unease ("that's not how things should be") and need justifications that are framed within revolutionary principles: the necessity of assuring one's subsistence, the failure of the state to provide for basic needs but also for legal ways to acquire goods. These practices have also built a sense of "enforced presentism", losing mid-term planning, and blurring the "fantasy futurism" (Guyer 2007) that characterized the revolutionary temporal framework since the 1960s. The feeling of being stuck in crisis reactivates the sense of a lost normality, that Revolutionary values and imaginary had shaped.

Besides, the input shortages and the haemorrhaging of material have gradually weakened the care relationships with the trees in the plantations. Former state-farm leaders and party members I met were pointing to the US' economic blockade, hardened in the 1990s, to the difficulties of the special period plunging the country into crisis, as well as to Cuba's dependency on USSR support. They also explained that the *coup de grâce* came with a citrus disease in the 2000s, which they suspect to be a bacteriological attack (a deliberate introduction of the virus into Cuba from the United States). Indeed, in 2008, a citrus disease called citrus greening caused by the *huanglongbling* virus, which is transmitted by a tiny insect (*Asian citrus psyllid*) was detected in Cuba. The virus was spreading to most citrus-growing regions, including Florida. The aging plantations of Arenas, already weakened by the lack of fertilization and maintenance, quickly became infected and had to be abandoned, said former plantation managers, as there was no cure for this virus. In Cuba, the health authorities had insufficient quantities of insecticide to control the vector insect. The only way to deal with it was to uproot infected trees and replant, which meant significant investments. This solution was adopted in Cuba's most productive citrus plantation in Matanzas province, which allowed part of its production to continue. The Jagüey Grande state farm was able to do so for it formed a joint venture with an Israeli company in the 1990s. In Arenas, however, the citrus plantations were officially abandoned as of 2004/2005, i.e. three years before the identification of the disease.

Some workers such as Anita, a 58-year-old white farmworker, blame national politics and local state leaders for their incompetence and the bad decision which led to the plantations neglect. Indeed, the State organized the shrinking of its providing capacity and the increasing devolution of responsibilities to non-state actors such as individuals, cooperatives, and families through policy changes on the national level. During the 1990s and 2000s, the authorities gradually closed the *escuelas al campo* and relocated the education centres to the cities where the students could stay with their parents. The plantations have thus lost the student labour force that performed most of the maintenance tasks.

The plantations also suffered from organizational and economic reforms. In 1993, the government transformed state farms into autonomous production cooperatives (Unidades Básicas de Producción Cooperativa—UBPCs) to reduce subsidies and losses in the agricultural sector (McCormack Bequer & Balbel Pérez, 2018). However, the new cooperatives were required to be profitable whilst incurring in debt because the state-owned enterprises sold them machinery and other assets they used on credit (Villegas Chadez 2017). Whilst input shortages already constrained production, many of these cooperatives were struggling to reach economic balance amid the crisis. In Arenas, 10 UBPCs replaced the state farm in 1994. In 1998, half of them had closed down or merged. Former UBPC leaders remember the contradictory injunction of being productive and profitable whilst most of the crucial decision were still made by State enterprises who remained at the top of the hierarchy. Although the cooperatives were deemed "autonomous" and democratically organized, previous hierarchies from the state farms endured. As Anita, who works in one of Arenas's two last UBPC, explains: "It was called *granja*, then *lote*,[8] then it became a *granja* again and then a UBPC, it doesn't make any difference". She bitterly states that managers from the

[8] *Granja* and *lote* are designations that referred to different ways of organizing state farms between the 1960s and 1990s when the main concern was the adequate size of the "production units".

state farm became cooperative leaders and that state-farm engineers and party officials kept interfering in every aspect of their work. Anita has been working on the plantations since she was 16. In her opinion, the decline of plantations is mainly due to mismanagement. The aging trees were not replaced on time. When they were, incompetent state-farm engineers gave them the wrong indications and did not listen to experienced workers, so much so that the trees had to be replanted twice or three times. Anita often says that "citrus is all my life". As she witnessed the plantation's destruction by the vertical and hierarchical management of state farms, she became increasingly disenchanted with the socialist ideals embraced in her youth: "I was a communist" (*yo era comunista*), she says, accentuating the past tense.

Whilst everyone I met seem to be nostalgic about the plantations, explanations of why they disappeared are rather controversial. Communist Party members, still occupying leading positions, focus on external factors (the citrus disease, the embargo, the fall of the USSR) or on the destructive behaviour of workers. Grassroot members of the Party such as the citrus technician Silverio have always evaded answering my questions stating "you know how things work here". Carmen, a 50-year-old colleague of Olegario's, who at the time of my fieldwork had just entered the Communist Party, explained that the problem was the "underdevelopment" (*subdesarrollo*) of the country: "you have to understand, it is not easy, even with the best intentions, to bring a country out of *subdesarrollo*". Non-party members such as Olegario blamed individualism. Anita pointed to the arrogance of state-farm leaders. José, who inherited the land his father refused to hand over to the state in the 1970s, sees the collapse of the plantations as a sign of the general failure of the Revolution, unable to fulfil its promises of a better life.

However, none of them has ever questioned the modernist schemes underlying the plantation. They miss the abundance, the perspectives that life in an industrial plantation gave them in terms of comfort and upward mobility. They long for the return of mechanized work in agriculture, of "technologies", of investment. They consider all this as normal living and working conditions. They point to the failure of the State to fulfil its promise (be it dysfunctional or impeded by contingencies), not of the promise itself. In 2016, many discussions would revolve around young people leaving the country by boat to get to the United States. Arenas' coast had recently become a departure point for networks of smugglers that carried immigrants through Mexico to the US. Every week, Arenas's inhabitants commented the news of a new departure; everyone knew someone who had left. Many agree that there were few opportunities for youngsters in Arenas and that they were right to go after a chance to live a better life in the US.

In 2018, rumours spread in Arenas that a new mega-tourism project would be built in the municipality, arousing genuine enthusiasm. Although some doubted that the project would effectively succeed, everyone thought it was great news and rejoiced whilst talking about the project. Several months later, a national leader made an official announcement: a joint venture between the state and a Spanish company would allow the edification of luxurious hotels.

An official billboard was placed on the main road. It did not display a revolutionary slogan but a golf player and a yacht like any advertisement for a tropical tourist destination. A 30-year-old professor leaving in the "26 de Julio" settlement published a picture of the billboard on his Facebook page with the following message: "for those who have left, development has come to Arenas". Local party officials also rejoiced, telling me how this tourism project would stimulate Arenas' agricultural sector, which according to the plan, would be in charge of producing fresh fruits and vegetables for the tourists, driving prospects of state investments in tractors and irrigation systems. Cooperative workers discussed job opportunities in the new tourism facility, hoping for a better salary.

The unanimous enthusiasm for such project reflects the way in which Arenas' inhabitants keep hoping for a huge state masterplan to bring modernity and development. Both state leaders and agricultural workers in Arenas seem to consider the small-scale agriculture without inputs practiced since the end of the plantations as transitory and a reflection of crisis. The prospect of a mega-tourism project and new farming opportunities for the export trade reinvigorates desires for what they deem normal and deserved and arouses enthusiasm linked with the feeling of reconnecting with the global world, to a concrete path towards a desired future.

Conclusion

Like many plantations around the world and over the centuries, Arenas' citrus plantations were based on a precarious economic, ecological, and social balance that went through a cycle of "boom and bust"

(Uekötter 2014: 8). The rise of the plantations followed great modernization plans and was achieved through bulldozing, massive land clearing, the reshaping of the water system, expropriations, and large population displacements involving counterrevolutionaries, students, and young managers. Cuban socialist plantations relied on the alienation of humans and non-humans, as well as on the abstraction and standardization of the territory and its ecology, on the massive impetus of wage labour and on insertion into globalized commercialization circuits. However, far from depictions of plantations as enforcing modern slavery, Arenas' inhabitants are nostalgic of plantations they associate with abundance.

Plantations in Arenas materialized the revolutionary ambitions of development, modernity, and social transformation. They embodied the socialist State and its will to take control over production, economy, and social life. The plantation as a territorial project, a socio-technical system, and a labour regime was the concrete support which gave shape to State sovereignty in Arenas. Revolutionary sovereignty instituted a set of norms and values, the conditions in which people could be included or marginalized but also redemptive pathways through participation. It defined how upward mobility should take place, ideal working conditions and standards for a well-done job, representations of what modernity and development look like and a particular relation to time through mid-term planning and ideological futurism. For 30 years, my interlocutors in Arenas experienced how promises and ideological speculations were somehow translated into material improvements in living and working conditions and upward mobility for people (peasants and their children, black people, women) who had few opportunities of emancipation before 1959. Then, for another 30 years, they experienced the downfall of revolutionary promises. The Special Period crisis and the collapse of the plantation jeopardized the material grounds on which State sovereignty stood, and especially the reciprocity framework within which the State provided its workers with all their needs in exchange for giving up their autonomy and their property over land. Scarcity, the necessity to "invent" solutions to replace all of what is missing and the daily struggle to make ends meet are experienced as development, modernity, and progress being postponed.

Nostalgia does not mean Arenas inhabitants are uncritical of the state plantation system and the Revolution. Indeed, strong and diverse criticism arises when explaining how the plantation collapsed. It also certainly leads my interlocutors to embellish this glorious past. Nostalgia, however, indexes Revolutionary sovereignty as a form of lost normality. Former workers compare their actual living and working conditions to the plantation, which serves as a standard. State sovereignty keeps being reinterpreted and stated according to the lived experience of the plantation. The norms and values that framed daily life keep being mobilized to show how abnormal is life now. Eventually hope and euphoria arise when a new project feeds projections towards a near future of re-encountering state-managed modernity and development. Although Arenas' inhabitants have developed many other ways of living over the last 20 years, their imagination of a "good life" and a future relies on the norms, values, and imaginaries forged in the plantations.

References

Bloch, V. 2018. *La lutte : Cuba après l'effondrement de l'URSS*. Paris: Vendémiaire.

Braudel, F. 1982. *Civilization and Capitalism, 15th-18th Century, vol. II : The Wheels of Commerce*. New York: William Collins Sons & Co Ltd.

Calá González, M.M. 1992. "La Revolución en el Poder." In *Monografía sobre la historia municipal de Arenas*, ed. G. Ortega Rodríguez, 229–195. (Unreleased).

Dardot, P., and C. Laval. 2020. *Dominer. Enquête sur la souveraineté de l'État en Occident*. Paris: La Découverte.

Dumont, R. 1964. *Cuba socialisme et développement*. Paris: Editions du Seuil.

Dumont, R. 1970. *Cuba est-il socialiste?* Paris: Editions du Seuil.

Deere, C.D., N. Pérez Rojas, C. Torres Vila, M. Garcia Aguiar, and E. Gonzalez Mastrapa. 1998. *Guines, Santo Domingo, Majibacoa: Sobre sus historias agrarias*. La Habana: Editorial de Ciencias Sociales.

Espina Prieto, M.P. 2008. *Políticas de atención a la pobreza y la desigualdad: examinando el rol del Estado en la experiencia cubana*. Buenos Aires: Clacso.

FAO. 2003. *Industria citrícola de Cuba : Crecimiento y perspectivas de mercado* (CCP: CI 03/9; p. 12). Grupo intergubernamental sobre frutos cítricos. https://www.fao.org/publications/card/es/c/798d9b8a-b593-5e8b-95a3-864c4144015f/.

Ferguson, J. 1994. *The Anti-Politics Machine: "development," depoliticization, and bureaucratic power in lesotho*. Minneapolis: University of Minnesota Press.

Figueroa Albelo, V. 2005. "Los campesinos en el proyecto social cubano." *Revista Temas* 44: 13–25.

Guerra, L. 2012. *Visions of Power in Cuba: Revolution, Redemption, and Resistance, 1959–1971*. Chapel Hill: University of North Carolina Press.

Guyer, J. I. 2007. "Prophecy and the Near Future : Thoughts on Macroeconomic, Evangelical, and Punctuated Time." *American Ethnologist* 34 (3): 409–421.

Haraway, D. 2015. "Anthropocene, capitalocene, plantationocene, chthulucene : Making kin." *Environmental humanities* 6 (1): 159–165.

Haraway, D., N. Ishikawa, S.F. Gilbert, K. Olwig, A.L. Tsing and N. Bubandt. 2016. "Anthropologists Are Talking–About the Anthropocene." *Ethnos* 81 (3): 535–564.

Harnecker, C.P. 2011. *Cooperativas y socialismo: Una mirada desde Cuba*. La Habana: Editorial Caminos.

Hetherington, K. 2014. "Waiting for the Surveyor : Development Promises and the Temporality of Infrastructure."*The Journal of Latin American and Caribbean Anthropology* 19 (2): 195–211.

Humphrey, C. 1998. *Marx Went AWAY–But Karl Stayed Behind. Updated Edition of Karl Marx Collective: Economy, Society and Religion in a Siberian Collective Farm*. Ann Arbor: University of Michigan Press.

Humphrey, C. 2007. "Sovereignty." In *A Companion to the Anthropology of Politics*, ed. D. Nugent and J. Vincent, 418–436. Malden: Blackwell Publishing.

Ingold, T. 2002. *The Perception of the Environment Essays on Livelihood, Dwelling and Skill*. London: Routledge.

Jansen, S. 2021. "The Anthropology of Hope."*Oxford Research Encyclopedias*. https://doi.org/10.1093/acrefore/9780190854584.013.182.

Jiménez Villasuso, R., and V. Zamora Rodriguez. 2010. "Principales cultivares y patrones utilizados en la citricultura." *Red Interamericana de Citricos (RIAC), Taller Regional sobre viveros de citricos 2010*.

Latham, R. 2000. "Social Sovereignty." *Theory, Culture & Society* 17 (4): 1–18.

Leyva Remón, A. and M.A. Arias Guevara. 2000. "Nuevos productores usufructuarios: Hacia un estudio de su estructura interna." In *Cambios tecnológicos, sustentabilidad y participación*, ed. N. Pérez Rojas, E. González Mastrapa and M. Garcia Aguiar, 185–197. La Habana: Universidad de La Habana.

Li, T.M. 2017a. "The Price of Un/Freedom: Indonesia's Colonial and Contemporary Plantation Labor Regimes." *Comparative Studies in Society and History* 59 (2): 245–276.

Li, T.M. 2017b. "After the Land Grab: Infrastructural Violence and the "Mafia System" in Indonesia's Oil Palm Plantation Zones."*Geoforum* 96: 328–337.

McCormack Bequer, M. and M.A. Balbel Pérez. 2018. "Unidades Básicas de Producción Cooperativa. Una variante de producción cooperativa en tierras de propiedad estatal." In *El Cooperativismo en Cuba. Situación actual y propuestas para su regulación y fomento*, ed. G. Fajardo García and M. Moreno Cruz, 81–95. Valencia: CIRIEC España.

Mintz, S.W. 1986. *Sweetness and Power: The Place of Sugar in Modern History*. New York: Penguin.
Muiño, E.S. 2014. "Obstáculos para la transición socio-ecológica: El caso de Cuba en el «período especial»." *Revista de Economía Crítica* 17: 118–135.
Muíño, E.S. 2017. *Opción Cero. El reverdecimiento forzoso de la Revolución cubana*. Madrid: Catarata.
Navaro-Yashin, Y. 2012. *The Make-Believe Space: Affective Geography in a Postwar Polity*. Durham: Duke University Press.
Nova González, A. 1996. The Citrus Industries in Cuba and Florida. *University of Florida, Institute of Food and Agricultural Sciences, International working paper series*(IW96-2). https://ufdc.ufl.edu/AA00067338/00001/25x.
Núñez González, N., P. Rodríguez Ruiz, M. Pérez Alvarez and O. Buscarón Ochoa. 2011. *Las relaciones raciales en Cuba. Estudios contemporáneos*. La Habana: Fundación Fernando Ortiz.
Ríos Hernández, A. 2014. *La Agricultura en Cuba*. La Habana: Editorial INFOIMA.
Rosendahl, M. 1997. *Inside the revolution: Everyday life in socialist Cuba*. Ithaca: Cornell University Press.
Rosset, P., and M. Benjamin. 1994. *The Greening of the Revolution: Cuba's Experiment with Organic Agriculture*. Melbourne: Ocean Press.
Scott, J.C. 1998. *Seeing Like a State : How Certain Schemes to Improve the Human Condition Have Failed*. New Haven: Yale University Press.
Segre, R. 1970. *Diez años de arquitectura en Cuba revolucionaria*. La Habana: Ediciones Union.
Swanger, J. 2015. *Rebel Lands of Cuba: The Campesino Struggles of Oriente and Escambray, 1934–1974*. Lanham: Lexington Books.
Thivet, D. 2014. "La Via Campesina et l'appropriation de l'agroécologie." In *Dynamiques des agricultures biologiques*, ed. A. Cardona, F. Chrétien, B. Leroux, F. Ripoll, and D. Thivet, 75–92. Versailles: Editions Quae & Educagri éditions.
Tsing, A.L. 2015. *The Mushroom at the End of the World : On the Possibility of Life in Capitalist Ruins*. Princeton: Princeton University Press.
Uekötter, F. 2014. *Comparing Apples, Oranges, and Cotton : Environmental Histories of the Global Plantation*. Frankfurt: Campus Verlag.
Valdés Paz, J. 2009. *Los procesos de organización agraria en Cuba, 1959–2006*. s.l.: Fundación Antonio Núñez Jiménez de la Naturaleza y el Hombre.
Verdery, K. 2003. *The Vanishing Hectare : Property and Value in Postsocialist Transylvania*. Ithaca: Cornell University Press.
Verdery, K. 2007. "After Socialism." In *A Companion to the Anthropology of Politics*, ed. D. Nugent and J. Vincent, 21–36. Malden: Blackwell Publishing.
Villegas Chadez, R. 2017. "Esencia y perfeccionamiento de las UBPC en el proceso de actualización del modelo económico cubano." In *Políticas públicas y procesos rurales en Cuba. Aproximaciones desde las Ciencias Sociales*, ed. A.

Leyva Remón and D. Echevarría León. Panamá: Ruth Casa Editorial, Editorial de Ciencias Sociales.

Wright, J. 2009. *Sustainable Agriculture and Food Security in an Era of Oil Scarcity: Lessons from Cuba*. London: Earthscan.

PART II

Continental and Pacific Americas: Multiple Subjectivities Between Control and Resistance

CHAPTER 6

'[A] Continual Exercise of…Patience and Economy': Plantation Overseers, Agricultural Innovation, and State Formation in Eighteenth-Century North America

Tristan Stubbs

Introduction

In eighteenth-century North America, plantation owners typically hired overseers to manage their landholdings. These men supervised crop production and dispensed punishment to the bondmen and women who worked under their command. Responsibility for maximizing profits through increased productivity therefore fell to overseers, the most important intermediaries between enslaved people and the men and women who enslaved them.

By the end of the 1700s, slaveholders—often the fount of social and cultural thought in North America—had begun to vilify overseers for

T. Stubbs (✉)
Affiliate Faculty Member, College of Charleston, USA
e-mail: tristanstubbs@hotmail.com

C. Le Petitcorps et al. (eds.), *Global Plantations in the Modern World*, Cambridge Imperial and Post-Colonial Studies,
https://doi.org/10.1007/978-3-031-08537-6_6

their perceived incompetence. In the earliest decades of the century they were subjected to little similar criticism. This shift in opinion grew out of an expectation of more profitable yields on the part of large plantation owners, who had invested significant capital in the tricky late-century agricultural innovations of the Agricultural Revolution.

In response to such attempts to homogenize them, overseers sought to champion to their employers an alternative cultural understanding of oversight that stressed the capacities of individuals as effective plantation managers. They stressed a growing notion that they were proud members of a worthy profession, a stance that provided a foundation for the later professionalization of the profession.

Schooled in the voguish tenets of classical republicanism, planters also fretted that overseers lacked sufficient judgment for the balanced rule of enslaved people, and would resort instead to extreme violence. On their plantations the leaders of the American Revolution asked similar questions about the positioning of authority to those that they posed during the Constitutional debates. Late eighteenth-century prejudices against the overseeing profession reflected republican fears that absentee landholders had yielded too much authority to overseers as much as they reflected skepticism about the agricultural competence of these men.

The Development of a Stereotype

By the end of the 1700s plantation overseers in the nascent United States faced widespread stigmatization as implacably violent brutalizers of enslaved people, and this is the stereotype that historians have traditionally called upon (Stubbs 2018).[1] But contemporary southerners leveled a further denunciation: that these men were incompetent agriculturists. In the short period between his tenures as governor of Virginia, secretary of state, and vice president, Thomas Jefferson grumbled in a letter to George Washington that the abandonment of his lands for the previous ten years had given "the unprincipled ravages of overseers" free rein.[2] Other slaveholders, only slightly more kindly, favored a distinction between the few competent and the far larger number of "common overseers."[3]

[1] This chapter draws in particular on Chapters 1 and 4, and the epilogue.

[2] Thomas Jefferson to George Washington, 14 May 1794, Notes (Jefferson 1904).

[3] George Washington to Arthur Young, 18 June 1792 (Washington 1970).

Overseers were also deemed untrustworthy. In 1776, slaveholder Matthew Marable reported in the *Virginia Gazette* that he could no longer trust a "set of people calling themselves *overseers*" with the management of his "plantations and slaves" because this never produced "anything but ruin and destruction," and so had resolved to split up his land into tenements.[4] George Washington advised that the overseers be moved off the plantation of his niece, Frances B. Washington, and replaced by a farmer and two ploughboys.[5] These prejudices held such widespread credibility that Marable felt no need to cite the source of his grievances, prompting a correspondent—calling himself "Overseer"—to ask a month later, "[w]hy did not mr. [sic] Marable inform that *wealthy fraternity* [of overseers] of the grievous complaints he had to lay against them at the bar of the publick?".[6]

Such characterizations appear to have developed only in the later 1700s (Schmidt 1994).[7] There is little evidence of comparable prejudices existing earlier. In fact, the opposite was sometimes the case. Robert Beverley, a historian of colonial Virginia, instead ascribed positive normative characteristics. He described in 1705 how overseers had "the Skill and Character of...experienced Planter[s]" (Beverley 1947: 272). A slightly later commentator presented a career in overseeing as a reward for the "expert, industrious, and careful" (Jones 1724: 54).

Structural changes to the plantation system fueled this transformation in opinions. Increasing absentee landholding in Virginia, South Carolina, and Georgia (the colonies—later states—on which this chapter focuses) disbarred slave owners from the personal control that they had once enjoyed over their plantations. The latter half of the century also saw some plantation owners experiment with the expensive innovations of the English Agricultural Revolution. But as overseers' responsibilities grew, many struggled to cope. Overseers themselves were acutely aware of the newly minted prejudices: Matthew Marable's interlocutor claimed that

[4] *Virginia Gazette* (Purdie), 2 February 1776 (italics original).

[5] George Washington to Frances B. Washington, 18 August 1793 (Washington 1970).

[6] *Virginia Gazette* (Purdie), 5 April 1776 (italics original).

[7] The nineteenth-century salience of overseers' reputation for incompetence is evidenced by the large number of times that this prejudice appeared in industrial lawsuits.

the slaveholder's fulmination was indicative of a "new mode of libeling a whole society of men"; and questioned why such libel was not "severely punishable by the laws."[8]

A Changing Agricultural Context

The overseer's principal responsibility was to force enslaved people to produce cash crops. In eighteenth-century Virginia, most plantations focused on tobacco, but corn and livestock could be raised alongside. Many Virginian overseers needed to understand the cultivation of all three (Rutman and Rutman 1984: 43; Mullin 1972: 50). Indeed, a good number of plantation owners took the decision to grow corn in favor of tobacco, based largely on their experiences of the changeable market in Virginia's traditional cash crop. In 1680 nearly every family in the Chesapeake grew tobacco; but many had abandoned it by 1740, especially in the Tidewater region, where the lowest-quality plants grew. In 1750, after two severe price depressions, the number of Chesapeake householders still growing tobacco decreased by a quarter. (Kulikoff 1986: 100). The vagaries of the trade encouraged the Virginian assembly to introduce statutes that required the planting of hemp and flax as a further alternative to tobacco (Hening 1823, I: 218; II: 120, 306; III: 81; IV: 96–97, 136).[9]

The changing face of Virginian agriculture represented a challenge for the overseer—he had to adapt to new crops as quickly as plantation owners responded to the market. As slaveholders diversified, so did the overseer's work: in March 1776, Robert Gutritch was ordered to "[n]ow sow all kinds of pease and seeds, plant broad French beans, set out cabbages and colewarts, the slips of raspberries, and gooseberries, thyme, sage," and fourteen other herbs and vegetables.[10] Diversification was particularly common in this Enlightenment age, as educated planters began to introduce scientific innovation and experimentation. Thomas Jefferson and George Washington wished to increase yields through agricultural innovation; both recorded experiments with grain and buckwheat

[8] *Virginia Gazette* (Purdie), 5 April 1776 (italics original).

[9] *Virginia Gazette* (Purdie and Dixon), 14 January 1768: 3.

[10] Entry for March 1776, John Page diary, Manuscripts Department, Earl Gregg Swem Library, College of William and Mary, Williamsburg, Virginia. See also entries for April, May, June, August, September, October, and November 1776.

and the introduction of high-yield breeds of sheep and cattle.[11] The damage to his soils caused by a tobacco monoculture led Washington to remark just after the Revolutionary War that he never rode his plantations "without seeing something which makes me regret having [continued] so long in the ruinous mode of farming which we are in."[12] Washington was prescient—as cotton cultivation became more widespread toward the end of the century and in the early 1800s it supplanted tobacco's status as the most valuable cash crop for Virginians.

The "New Agriculture" of the English Agricultural Revolution strongly influenced the agricultural experiments of noteworthy Virginians. This transformation moved agriculture away from a traditional three-year crop rotation and, in a system pioneered by Jethro Tull, introduced to the rotation forage crops, roots, and "artificial," or non-native grasses. In 1760, Washington was already a practitioner of Tull's horse-hoeing husbandry; by the late 1700s he was following the more sophisticated example of Arthur Young and practicing his own seven-year rotation (Washington 1976–1979, I: xviii). Washington corresponded frequently with Jefferson and other Virginian slaveholders such as the younger Landon Carter about their agricultural experiments. Jefferson was a correspondent of the English agriculturist William Pearce, as Washington was of Young.[13] In his determination to move away from tobacco Washington raised well over sixty alternative crops, including barley, carrots, millet, pumpkins, and wheat; he also researched manures for fertilizer, including animal dung and marl (Washington 1976–1979, I: xxx–xxxiii).

In South Carolina and Georgia, the most significant agricultural development at mid-century was the introduction of indigo, and its production became one of the most important aspects of plantation work for many overseers there. The commodity was so highly prized by customers in the New World and metropolitan Britain that, although it was never

[11] Thomas Jefferson to George Washington, 14 May 1794 (Jefferson 1904); entry for 2 August 1762 (Washington 1976–1979, I: 304); Thomas Jefferson to George Washington, 18 June 1792 (Jefferson 1904).

[12] Washington (1976–1979, I: xviii); Tobias Lear to Alexander Robertson, 16 December 1792 (Washington 1970).

[13] Thomas Jefferson to George Washington, 14 May 1794 (Jefferson 1904); entry for 2 August 1762 (Washington 1976–1979, I: 304); Thomas Jefferson to George Washington, 18 June 1792 (Jefferson 1904); Carter, "Landon Carter's crop book," 282; Thomas Jefferson to William Pearce, 15 December 1792 (Jefferson 1904).

more than a marginal crop in the middle colonies, overseers who were skilled in indigo manufacture were much in demand.[14] Production of the crop spread widely and quickly, with growers apparently learning how to grow it by word of mouth, and often from enslaved people (Klingsberg 1941: 90; Berlin 1980: 56). Although some slaveholders worried about overseers "slid[ing] into" African ways, indigo cultivation was perhaps the most significant matter on which bondpeople shared knowledge with their supervisors (Sobel 1987: 47). Enslaved people were valued highly for their competence: in South Carolina, a "woman named Hagar" was "strongly recommended for…her great care of Indigo."[15] Planters sometimes acknowledged bondpeople's greater experience with indigo ahead of that of their overseers, resulting in an upheaval of the plantation authority structure. The South Carolinian Peter Gourdin placed so much value in a gifted bondman that his will insisted that the man never be forced to do fieldwork—or, significantly, be answerable to an overseer. The bondman was also to gain his freedom after the death of Gourdin's son (Morgan 1998: 164). In this case at least, the commercial value that provided relative autonomy on the plantation away from a supervisor's gaze might one day have translated into real and tangible freedom.

Rice was even more important than indigo. Its long growth period meant that overseers in South Carolina had different tasks to their counterparts in Virginia. And the labor- and capital-intensive nature of rice cultivation on the whole discouraged rice planters from devoting valuable resources to experimenting with unproved innovations, especially since they were obliged by the second half of the century to invest in large-scale irrigation schemes if they were to compete with other growers. But novel agricultural technologies were introduced here as well. Overseer John Pressley was recompensed "for making a New Rice Machine" in 1777; South Carolinian planter Henry Laurens imitated "painstaking" Chinese methods of rice hand transplanting and cultivation; others experimented with automatic rice milling (Chaplin 1992: 48, 49).[16]

[14] Henry Laurens to Richard Oswald & Co., 26 May 1756 (Laurens 1970–1974, II: 203).

[15] Henry Laurens to John Smith, 9 May 1766 (Laurens 1970–1974, V: 125).

[16] Entry for 3 February 1777, Margaret Colleton account, 25 September 1776 to 28 August 1780, Margaret Colleton papers, folder 5, South Caroliniana Library, University of South Carolina, Columbia, South Carolina.

Indigo's profitability was short-lived. Overseas competition, unsuitable weather, and attacks by pests meant that by the closing decades of the 1700s, planters in the United States—who had lost easy access to British markets and the subsidies offered by the Crown—had largely abandoned the plant for Sea Island cotton and other crops (Stubbs forthcoming).[17] Rice, too, began to lose favor once Eli Whitney's cotton gin made that crop more viable. But this shift began to occur only at the end of the century. For most of the 1700s in South Carolina and Georgia, overseers' primary responsibilities centered on the production of rice, or indigo, or both.

Not every eighteenth-century planter tried new approaches: Landon Carter, for instance, believed that his overseers would become "lazy" if they used ploughs (Carter 1965, I: 21). Yet those who disdained overseers' incompetence in managing agricultural innovations carried influence as pioneers. And aside from creating more work, the new technologies expanded overseer responsibilities in various ways. Firstly, innovation increased employers' expectations for higher returns from a smaller relative expenditure of capital and labor, even though the new techniques did little to enhance yields—and especially in the Chesapeake (Walsh 1989: 393). Secondly, since many planters were the drivers of agricultural improvement, they considered themselves more proficient in the application of the new methods than their overseers.

Such men were in an unenviable position for another reason. Because many overseers were contracted for just a year they had insufficient time to learn even the most basic agricultural innovations, let alone a seven-year crop rotation. The English tradition of long-held tenancy contracts, often passed down through generations, encouraged tenant farmers there to research and invest in agricultural technologies, and render them profitable. These tenants developed many of the innovations that crossed the Atlantic (Jones 1974).

The agricultural transformation was therefore a moment of rupture for overseers: it magnified their responsibilities and reshaped the ways in which their performance was evaluated. The link between an increasing

[17] John Hampton to John Bynum, Richard Hampton papers, folder: Major John Hampton, 1743–1808, South Caroliniana Library, University of South Carolina, Columbia, South Carolina; John Couturier to John Ewing Colhoun, 17 April 1792, John Ewing Colhoun papers, South Caroliniana Library, University of South Carolina, Columbia, South Carolina.

interest in new technologies and growing prejudice against overseers stands out in George Washington's writings. Continuing his experiments after the Revolution, Washington wrote to Arthur Young about selective sheep breeding. The president acknowledged that "Bakewells [sic] breed of Sheep are much celebrated…but if entrusted to a common Bailiff (or what with us is called an Overseer) would, I should apprehend, soon degenerate."[18] Discussing a new threshing machine, he claimed that "the utility of it among…ignorant Overseers will depend absolutely on the simplicity of the Constructn."[19] Washington's clearest denunciation of overseer capabilities appears in his missives to his relative Lund Washington, who acted as his agent. Exasperated at the state of his plantations, he desired an "English bailiff" who understood the management of a plantation, and who would be able to apply the "New Agriculture" better than any overseer.[20]

While oversight was transformed by agricultural innovations and the introduction of crops like indigo, a related pressure derived from employers' desire to be seen as "men of improvement." Acting according to this "plantation ethos" meant matching Enlightenment efforts to improve manners and morals with a studied program to tame, regulate—and perfect—the American landscape (Greene 1992: 174, 104–105, 132; Chaplin 1992: 35). Countervailing ideological currents also flowed across the eighteenth-century southern plantation. Even as they took inspiration from a "rationalist spirit of improvement to reshape their region," slaveholders revived bucolic ideals, feeling "early pangs of romantic melancholy over the loss of an untouched, natural order" (Chaplin 1992: 60–61). When patriarchs feared the "ravages of overseers" on their lands, their rhetorical attacks expressed a degree of sadness for this lost pastoral idyll. Their subordinates were charged with executing improvements that slaveholders both welcomed and feared.

A further cultural imperative affected the overseer's image. In the years before the Revolution, Chesapeake tobacco planters became "almost pathologically concerned" that their counterparts would judge their crop negatively. These men and women seemed to have cultivated tobacco as much to gain the respect of merchants and neighbors "as to please the

[18] George Washington to Arthur Young, 18 June 1792 (Washington 1970).

[19] George Washington to Henry Lee, 16 October 1793 (Washington 1970).

[20] George Washington to Arthur Young, 18 June 1792 (Washington 1970).

anonymous chewers, smokers and snuffers who ultimately purchased the staple in Europe" (Breen 1985: 65–9). Early in the century, following a number of consignments of poor-quality tobacco, the Virginian Robert Bristow complained that they had left "a lasting disreputation" to Bristow's tobacco mark.[21] Crop quality was a particular concern for absentee slaveholders: the Virginian Joseph Ball wrote from England how criticism of his tobacco "very much Chagrins me...for when I lived in Virginia, my Tobacco was so far from being accounted the worst, that it was always very well liked, and sought after."[22] The sentiment was reflected in their relationship with overseers: Landon Carter criticized one for causing a neighbor to scorn Carter's crop (Breen 1985, 16). Reputational damage could lead to reduced earnings. Edward Ambler bemoaned "the great Faults the Merchants find with my Tobacco, they say it is not only smoaked [sic] to a great degree, but [that] the Overseers [pack it] ...in a slovenly & unsightly manner."[23]

The link between reputation and crop quality extended south, too (Sandy and Phillips 2021). The South Carolinian Pierce Butler wrote to London merchant Thomas Fraser that he could not express "how much I feel hurt that...the little rice that was made on my Estate fell short of my [overseer's] expectations...this disappointment...subjects me to a temporary embarrassment...I feel doubly hurt that at the Commencement of Our Correspondence there should be an appearance of defficiency [sic] on my part."[24] Slaveholders also faced competition from producers outside North America. South Carolinian slave owner and politician John Lloyd thanked Bristol merchant John Champion "for the samples of East India

[21] Robert Bristow to Thomas Booth, 30 September 1719, Robert Bristow copybook, Library of Virginia, Richmond, Virginia, 758.

[22] Joseph Ball to Joseph Chinn, 15 March 1755, Joseph Ball letterbook, John D. Rockefeller Library, Colonial Williamsburg Foundation, Williamsburg, Virginia.

[23] Edward Ambler to Charles Dabney, 14 July 1767, Charles William Dabney papers, 1715–1845, folder 9, box 1, subseries 1.1: 1716–1775, Manuscripts Department, Southern Historical Collection, University of North Carolina, Chapel Hill, North Carolina.

[24] Pierce Butler to Messrs Thomas Fraser & Co., 13 April 1787, Butler plantation papers, folder 9, box 2, collection 1447; Pierce Butler to Messrs Simpson & Davison, 14 July 1787, Butler plantation papers, folder 9, box 2, collection 1447.

rice," and added smugly, "it afforded me a satisfaction to see that the quality is very inferior to that which is produced in this country."[25]

Although in both regions plantations were diverse, risky, and highly competitive businesses, by imbuing economic relations with affective qualities slaveholders went beyond commercial calculus. Because their reputations were linked directly to the quality and commercial value of the crops that they raised, economic setbacks had a psychological impact. Though poorer yields and smaller economies of scale meant that Virginian plantation owners were hit harder by vacillations in cash crop prices than those in South Carolina and Georgia, the fear of financial ruin animated planters across North America. The New World had promised great returns for modest investment, and new freedoms for humble men. Yet the reality for many slaveholders was a cycle of low profit margins and shortages. Owners intervened in overseers' work because bankruptcy and loss of their own status were a real and persistent threat (Morgan 1998: 35–39).

As they did with agricultural innovation, slave owners also believed that they were more knowledgeable than their overseers about the requirements of their lands and bondpeople. Just after the Revolutionary War, the Virginian William Lee wrote that he could not "conceive there is any land in Virg[ini]a so bad," that "with tolerable managem[en]t" would fail to make a profit; therefore the blame for any agricultural disappointments must lie with "the Overseers."[26] Though Henry Laurens had only recently become a planter, in 1763 he saw himself as better informed than his overseer when allocating large quantities of foodstuffs. He warned James Lawrence that the enslaved people "will soon consume your little Stock of Corn & pease[,] therefore enquire immediately where I may be supplyed with a sufficient quantity to carry them thro the Year."[27] His South Carolinian counterpart William Ancrum directed overseer Marlow

[25] John Lloyd to George Champion, 28 September 1796, John Lloyd papers, folder 1, South Caroliniana Library, University of South Carolina, Columbia, South Carolina.

[26] William Lee letterbook, 5 August 1783 to 1 April 1787, Lee family papers, 1638–1867, Virginia Historical Society, Richmond, Virginia, 295.

[27] Henry Laurens to James Lawrence, 1 January 1763 (Laurens 1970–1974, III: 203).

Pryor to "prepare for next Years [sic] planting in the Manner you think best until I see you."[28]

Caring for enslaved men and women's health called for this putatively greater wisdom. Laurens gave very specific directions and sent medicines. Timothy Creamer, another of his overseers, received "1 Bottle infused Rhubarb to give in Case of Looseness or Cholics..., 2 bottles of...Rum, to rub in cases of pains & bruses & sometimes for the Cholic and belly ach."[29] Even minor ailments could incite protests by bondpeople or, at the very least, cause the plantation to lose money if enslaved people needed to take time off to recuperate.

Owners often contrasted their own behavior toward enslaved pregnant women with their overseers' (Morgan 2004: 164–165). Laurens advised James Lawrence to "be very careful" with "the Women with Child" owing to the value of their progeny.[30] William Lee warned his overseer that "the Woman with Child shou'd never be hard worked or oppressed in any manner & the Children sh[oul]d always be plentifully fed and have necessary cloathing."[31] Fellow Virginian Robert Carter III counseled that Criss, who had fallen ill while pregnant, should "take a vomit of Ippacacuena [ipecacuana—a medicinal root] in case She is not near her time of delivery."[32]

Concerns about political economy also encouraged slaveholders to intervene in plantation affairs wherever they could. The eighteenth-century South was a "remarkably underinstitutionalized world" (Morgan 1998: 275). Long before diffuse political power was subsumed into the modern centralized state, throughout the Anglophone world much political authority and legitimacy derived from the idealized figure of the household patriarch (Kulikoff 1986: 9). A well-regulated plantation was deemed as important as a well-regulated household: in this sense, the

[28] William Ancrum to Marlow Pryor, 30 October 1776; cf. William Ancrum to Marlow Pryor, 4 October 1776, William Ancrum account book and letterbook, South Caroliniana Library, University of South Carolina, Columbia, South Carolina.

[29] Henry Laurens to Timothy Creamer, 25 January 1765 (Laurens 1970–1974, IV: 570).

[30] Henry Laurens to James Lawrence, 1 January 1763 (Laurens 1970–1974, III: 203).

[31] William Lee to Mr. Ellis, 24 June 1778, William Lee's letterbook, 1769–1793, Lee family papers, 1638–1867, Virginia Historical Society, Richmond, Virginia, 265.

[32] William Lee to Mr. Ellis, 24 June 1778, William Lee's letterbook, 1769–1793, Lee family papers, 1638–1867, Virginia Historical Society, Richmond, Virginia, 265.

household and plantation acted as metonymies of each other (Morgan 1998: 276).

Plantation management was therefore both a key indicator of a patriarch's worth and a justification of the patriarchal model of political economy. Success in agriculture was a proxy for good government of a slaveholder's own affairs and those of his subordinates. Leading planters spoke of themselves as "managers;" many viewed their involvement in allocating plantation tasks as essential to patriarchism (Breen 1985: 65–69; Mullin 1972: 25). One Virginian promised a merchant in London that his tobacco was "exceeding good" because "it was made on the plantation w[here] I live & therefore as I saw to the whole mana[age]ment of it my self [sic] can with authority recomend [sic] it."[33] It followed that an ideal overseer was one whom Jefferson described late in the century: this overseer seemed "as if he would be docile, so that I hope to get my own outlines followed by him."[34] Intervention in plantation affairs at an overseer's expense was part of patriarchal self-fashioning because it combined a visible exhibition of the importance of successful cultivation with a demonstrable act of dominion over subordinates.

Absentee slaveholders were as anxious about outlying quarters as about their home plantations, and their correspondence with overseers attempted to reconstruct personal contact. William Lee acknowledged the hurdles that absenteeism presented: he prefaced a letter to an overseer with "[i]t is not in my power at this distance to be very particular." But he proceeded with very particular instructions about livestock, mulberry trees, fencing, ironworkers, bricklayers, and the care of enslaved people.[35] James Habersham, a large slaveholder in Georgia, visited his rice fields only once a season yet took a keen interest "in every facet of his agricultural operations."[36] The South Carolinian agricultural agent Josiah Smith corresponded frequently with his employer, George Austin, in Shropshire, England. Smith kept Austin informed because he suspected the slave

[33] Henry Fitzhugh to James Buchanan, 22 April 1755, Henry Fitzhugh papers, 1746-69, Duke University Perkins Special Collections Library, Durham, North Carolina.

[34] Thomas Jefferson to Thomas Mann Randolph Jr., 24 June 1793 Notes (Jefferson 1904: XI).

[35] William Lee to Mr. Ellis, 24 June 1778, William Lee's letterbook, 1769–1793, Lee family papers, 1638–1867, Virginia Historical Society, Richmond, Virginia, 265.

[36] Habersham cited in (Wood 1984: 138).

owner to be "[a]nxious respecting the fate of [his] planting Interest."[37] There was a belief that absentee plantations were less profitable than those with a resident owner. Smith wrote to Austin that it could not be "expected that Plantations own'd by Persons who are non residents, should produce so much profit as those constantly under the Inspection of Proprietors who reside on the Spot, & at the same time are able Planters, who are ever employ'd in contriving every thing [sic] that can make for their Advantage."[38]

The Revolutionary War did not prevent George Washington from indulging his own interest in agriculture. Throughout the Revolution Lund Washington wrote to him every month, "detailing minutely all the events that occurred on the plantations."[39] Even after the war, as president, Washington was never disconnected from his plantation operations. In 1789, he sent a lengthy and detailed letter to his overseers, designed to provide "a full and comprehensive view of my designs."[40] 1793 would bring diplomatic relations with France almost to breaking point, yet Washington still found time to pore over weekly reports from Mount Vernon and send off directives (Mullin 1972: 22).

In similar fashion, the Virginian Robert Carter of Nomini Hall left specific "observations on ye Quality & management of part of my crop of Tobacco, to ye end [tha]^t my overseers may follow [the]^m for ye future."[41] Because letters were a vital conduit of plantation intelligence, employers depended on responses. Based in London, Joseph Ball was especially troubled by informational deficiencies. He urged Joseph Chinn, "I beg of you...to read over all...of my Letters of Instructions from the

[37] Josiah Smith to George Austin, 30 July 1772, Josiah Smith, Jr. lettercopy book, 1771–1784, Manuscripts Department, Southern Historical Collection, University of North Carolina, Chapel Hill, North Carolina, 105.

[38] Josiah Smith to George Austin, 22 July 1773, Josiah Smith, Jr. lettercopy book, 1771–1784, Manuscripts Department, Southern Historical Collection, University of North Carolina, Chapel Hill, North Carolina, 227.

[39] George Washington to Lund Washington, 26 November 1775 (Washington 1970, n. 18).

[40] George Washington. "A view of the work at the several plantations in the year 1789 and general directions for the execution of it," Virginia Historical Society, Richmond, Virginia.

[41] Robert Carter III to Edward Hunt & Son, 13 May 1765, letterbook of Robert Carter III of Nomini Hall, 1760–1764, Colonial Williamsburg Foundation, Williamsburg, Virginia.

beginning Ever since I left Virginia and see whether you have comply'd with them all."[42] Robert Carter implored his overseer in 1767 to "execute [my] instructions, & to write to me a state of my affairs frequently for an inattention to either will certainly distress me."[43] The year before, Henry Laurens had berated Abraham Schad for failing to correspond: "[l]ast Night came down Seven Negroes from Wambaw but no Letter from you. Therefore I am at a loss to know why the eight [bondpeople] that were intended did not come."[44] His fellow South Carolinian William Ancrum complained to one of his overseers that he had not heard "frequently from You during the whole Season...such Indolence & Neglect in You are inexcusable."[45]

Certain slaveholders divined a commercial advantage in publicizing successful overseers. These men thereby became further exemplars of their employers' success in plantation management: praise for their subordinates burnished patriarchs' own credentials. In 1768 the Virginian Henry Fitzhugh boasted that his tobacco was "made in fresh rich Land by Overseers that I get from the frontiers of James River, where the best tob[acc]o is made."[46] And a South Carolinian slaveholder, John Palmer, recommended an overseer who was "a Pritty nice Planter of Indigo."[47]

Criticisms of Overseers and Overseer Responses

But criticism of overseers was much more common than praise. The most common criticisms centered on agricultural failings. In 1726, the Virginian Robert "King" Carter, on finding his overseer's tobacco "basely

[42] Joseph Ball to Joseph Chinn, 30 June 1749, Joseph Ball letterbook, John D. Rockefeller Library, Colonial Williamsburg Foundation, Williamsburg, Virginia.

[43] Robert Carter to Edward Ransdale, 24 June 1767, Robert Carter of Nomini Hall letterbook, 9 vols., Chauvenet collection, John D. Rockefeller Library, Colonial Williamsburg Foundation, Williamsburg, Virginia, 63.

[44] Henry Laurens to Abraham Schad, 18 April 1766, in Laurens, *Papers of Henry Laurens*, V, 101.

[45] William Ancrum to Mr. Geeving, 17 October 1778, William Ancrum account book and letterbook, South Caroliniana Library, University of South Carolina, Columbia, South Carolina.

[46] Henry Fitzhugh to John Bland, 11 August 1768, Henry Fitzhugh to John Bland, October 1763, Henry Fitzhugh papers, 1746–1769, Duke University Perkins Special Collections Library, Durham, North Carolina.

[47] John Palmer to John Ewing Colhoun, 23 May 1792, John Ewing Colhoun papers, South Caroliniana Library, University of South Carolina, Columbia, South Carolina.

handled...corrected him for it."[48] Joseph Ball, hearing that his overseers had failed to provide adequate fencing and often left the plantation, described them as "slubbering sons of bitches."[49] Thirty years later, John Harrower related how a Virginian slave owner lambasted an overseer for wastefulness: "[t]his day the Col[onel] finding more wheat left among the straw then [sic] should be[,] blamed Mr. Lewis the overseer for his carelessness" (Harrower 1900: 92). Henry Laurens, too, was quick to rebuke those who jeopardized plantation efficiency: the overseer Mark Noble caused him "the loss of my Canoe, Horses, cattle, tools, etc. etc."[50] His South Carolinian counterpart John Ewing Colhoun berated another overseer: "I doubt you are not frugal in the distribution of Provisions, if you are, you certainly made a Very trifling Crop."[51]

Given the degree of interference and criticism that overseers faced, tensions often developed with their employers. The two parties argued about a host of issues, ranging from disagreements about payment to the unsatisfactory upkeep of plantations. Since few letters survive from overseers themselves, and there is virtually no personal reminiscence, it is difficult to ascertain their opinions about their employers. Yet it seems clear that tensions were higher on resident plantations because of greater slaveholder involvement, and because overseers resented the dilution of their authority that this entailed (Baird 1999: 120–128). Though the performance of overseers on absentee plantations was more likely to have been misunderstood by planters, the closeness between the two parties on home quarters would have made disagreements more frequent, and more trying (Scarborough 1966: 72).

Whether they were on home or absentee plantations, overseers rarely accepted criticism of their agricultural competence. The earliest years of Virginia's plantation economy saw the first stirrings of their defiance. At the end of the seventeenth century, John Clayton, a parson from Middlesex County, argued with his overseer, Lewis, in favor of a new agricultural technique. Affronted, the overseer replied that Clayton "understood better how to make a Sermon than managing Tobacco," and

[48] Robert Carter Diary (Carter 1701–1732).

[49] 17 July 1745, Joseph Ball letterbook, John D. Rockefeller Library, Colonial Williamsburg Foundation, Williamsburg, Virginia.

[50] Henry Laurens cited in (Wood 1984: 140).

[51] A. Norris to H. Keylor, 23 January 1795, John Ewing Colhoun papers, South Caroliniana Library, University of South Carolina, Columbia, South Carolina.

walked away (Virginia Browne 1939: 22). Much later, a similar reaction greeted the Virginian Colonel Dangerfield when he rebuked his overseer, another Lewis, for leaving "more wheat...among the straw." This reproof made "Mr. Lewis verry much enraged for being spoke to and [he] verry sawcily threw up all the keys he had in charge and went off" (Harrower 1963: 84). Following the extension of absenteeism, overseers grew more aware of their centrality to plantation functions and more confident in using oppositional strategies. In 1766 H. Laurens explained how "[o]verseers will not be directed by any body but good planters &...bad ones will make a handle of directions from ignorant Masters in order to impose on them."[52]

In response to the widespread stigmatization that developed in the latter part of the 1700s some overseers stressed a bond—recall how Matthew Marable's correspondent in the *Virginia Gazette* deplored his calumny of this "wealthy fraternity." Rather than causing fissures between them, slaveholder tactics in fact cemented a developing notion among such overseers of their shared professional aptitude, providing a foundation for the full-on professionalization of the upper tiers of plantation management during the following century (Scarborough 1966). In Georgia, overseer Jacob Fendin claimed that the merchant and future governor Edward Telfair should be "[s]ensible of [Fendin's] Capacity In the Planting Business."[53] Thomas Mitchell, overseer to the Virginian Francis Jerdone, in 1789 worried that adverse weather would cause him to "loose [sic] [his] character as an overseer."[54] William Ancrum asked overseer Marlow Pryor whether Pryor's "Indico making answers your Reputation."[55] Because of the link between reputed agricultural ability

[52] Henry Laurens to John Jackson, 19 March 1766 (Laurens 1970–1974, V: 90).

[53] Jacob Fendin to Edward Telfair, 20 March 1774, Edward Telfair papers, 1762–1831, Duke University Perkins Special Collections Library, Durham, North Carolina.

[54] Thomas Mitchell to Francis Jerdone, 9 July 1789, Jerdone family papers, folder 2, box 2, Manuscripts Department, Earl Gregg Swem Library, College of William and Mary, Williamsburg, Virginia.

[55] William Ancrum to Marlow Pryor, 27 March 1776, William Ancrum account book and letterbook, South Caroliniana Library, University of South Carolina, Columbia, South Carolina. Cf. Josiah Smith to George Austin, 20 September 1771; Josiah Smith to James Poyas, 3 September 1779, Josiah Smith, Jr. lettercopy book, 1771–1784, Manuscripts Department, Southern Historical Collection, University of North Carolina, Chapel Hill, North Carolina, 25, 115.

and an esteemed social status, such overseers presented themselves as worthy of their employers' respect (Baird 1999: 20).

The widespread vilification of overseer competence is reason enough to view early attempts to professionalize overseeing as a form of defiance to stigmatization. Such overseers wished to champion an alternative cultural understanding of their profession that stressed the capacities of individuals and resisted slaveholder attempts to homogenize them. Yet employers' prejudices very likely hardened against this new and more vocal degree of confidence. They combined with others, such as those prejudices that accused overseers of an overweening addiction to violence, to create the long-lasting stereotypes that condemned the profession to historiographical ignominy.

Overseer Violence and State Formation

The stereotype that denounced overseers as incompetent therefore sat alongside and reinforced the traditional image of the overseer as a merciless torturer of enslaved men and women. Much as they did when intervening in agricultural decisions, patriarchs transformed the discipline of bondpeople into a site in which they attempted to reassert their dominion over the plantation and everyone on it, and in which overseers strove to assert their own position within that hierarchy. This contest served to confirm slaveholders' negative perceptions of overseers, and solidified overseers' desire to resist this image.

Though fearful of overseers' perceived violent tendencies, Robert Carter III nevertheless sanctioned violent punishment. But he set limits. Carter wrote to overseer Thomas Olive during the Revolutionary War: "[s]ir-When you undertook the management of my plantation...I submitted the conduct of the negroes, there, to your consideration & empowered you to rebuke and inflict corporal punishment as you might Judge necessary—and the same authority has been continued till now—but I do herein take from you part of the aforesaid power and I do forbid you to correct, in any manner what ever, either old or young negro belonging to me."[56] Carter thereby attempted to reset the delicate hierarchical balance by reclaiming some of the authority that wartime absenteeism had required him to cede.

As an enlightened citizen of an emerging republic, Carter understood the difficulties inherent in the granting and positioning of authority. The year that the Revolution began, he was studying Montesquieu's *Spirit of the Laws*, the Enlightenment tract that held that liberty was only possible through the separation of powers.[57] In 1798 John Adams, by then president, wrote to a group of young Georgians that it was "a gratification to my pride to see you boast of a well balanced republic—the essence of a free republic is in the balance—the security of Liberty, property, Character and Life depends every moment upon its preservation, and…America will be scourged by the Rods of Vengeance if they will not study and preserve Balance, as the only ark of Safety."[58] On the plantation, as in a republic, balance was all. As the primary unit of social control, at least in the south, the plantation played a practical role in dampening enslaved resistance and a metonymical role in reflecting elites' aspirations for a well-governed society. Capricious overseer violence was undesirable partly because it exposed balanced plantation government as a myth.

Thomas Jefferson went further: he believed that overseers introduced toxic corrupting influences that undermined civic balance. He wrote that of all the social ranks in Virginian society, the "last and lowest [is] a seculum of beings called overseers…furnishing materials for the exercise of their…spirit of domination."[59] In South Carolina, Henry Laurens worried about the "tyranny and villainy of overseers" and their "vicious designs."[60] Many of the great slaveholders of Virginia, South Carolina and Georgia fought against British tyranny and corruption; many were

[56] Robert Carter to Thomas Olive, 8 May 1781, Robert Carter of Nomini Hall letterbook, Chauvenet collection, John D. Rockefeller Library, Colonial Williamsburg Foundation, Williamsburg, Virginia, VIII, 75.

[57] Rutledge cited in Schwartz, *A History of the Supreme Court*, 5; 22 April 1776, Robert Carter of Nomini Hall letterbook, Chauvenet collection, John D. Rockefeller Library, Colonial Williamsburg Foundation, Williamsburg, Virginia, III, 18.

[58] Copy of Letter from Young Men of Augusta, Georgia to President Adams, 2 July 1798, Colonial Dames Collection, folder 94, box 10, Georgia Historical Society, Savannah, Georgia.

[59] Thomas Jefferson to William Wirt, 5 August 1815 (Jefferson 1904: XI).

[60] Laurens cited in (Sandy 2014: 365).

involved in the framing of a Constitution designed to thwart the repeat of such evils, by setting a virtuous citizenship and balanced constitution against the threat of anarchy. On their plantations they posed analogous questions about the correct uses of political authority, feared the tyranny and despotism that incorrectly used authority could entrain and, by establishing overseers as antithetical to republican society, had them play an important scapegoat role as Americans began the political formation of a new country.

This sentiment posed obstacles for overseers. Solomon Betton, overseer to John Mercer in Virginia, found that his ability to punish recalcitrant bondpeople was obstructed. In September 1791 he reported: "Davey has made his escape this Morning." Davey had reacted strongly to Betton's punishment of another bondman, Valentine; when Betton attempted to whip Davey in response, he fled, saying that he was heading to Mercer. Betton acknowledged that it was Mercer's prerogative to decide how best to discipline Davey should he appear, but worried that Mercer would give too much credence to Davey's tales. The overseer wrote, "you will know what is proper to be done—[i]f one [bondperson] is countenanced, all will expect the same."[61]

Enslaved people understood the prejudices that many slaveholders held against overseers. They drew on such prejudices when appealing to their captors above overseers' heads. Betton understood that such talebearing had the potential to disrupt his regime. "Countenancing" enslaved criticism put bondpeople's complaints ahead of his right to rule them. Planters may have made claims to balance, but overseers like Betton clove to more brutal modalities. "You may rest assured of my humanity toward them, but that they all, shall pay disregard to my orders, and commands, let it be given whenever it may—and that an offence of this kind, shall be punished with many stripes, let him come whenever he may—An oppen [sic] opposition to any authority, is such a piece of boldness as cannot be overlooked, and then to run away is equally bad, as one is directly and the other in directly [sic] setting my commands and authority at naught."[62] For this overseer, who believed all of his charges "to be rogues," enslaved people's discipline rested on an unadorned equation:

[61] Solomon Betton to John Mercer, 6 September 1791, letters from Solomon Betton, Mercer papers, Virginia Historical Society, Richmond, Virginia.

[62] Solomon Betton to John Mercer, 6 September 1791, letters from Solomon Betton, Mercer papers, Virginia Historical Society, Richmond, Virginia.

"[i]f they behave well, they will be treated well—If not, their treatment will vary accordingly."[63]

Thomas Olive also felt that harsh violence was an integral part of management, and the right to punish bondpeople a central plank of his authority. Robert Carter continued to employ Olive for some years after his wartime rebuke, but Olive's relationships with enslaved men and women did not go smoothly. Carter recounted: "Abraham, foreman, Tom, Tom, boy, Cartman...were with me this morning—Mr Tho[ma]^{s} Olive also—he informed me that he lately ordered Vincent to strip himself to be Scourged—Abraham, foreman, did not fall in with the propriety of the whipping intended, therefore he did not aid Mr Olive therein." Olive's petition to Carter suggests he felt shame at his weakened position: "[t]he Overseer asked in the presence of Abraham if he had not full power & Authority to beat strip & whip all the Negroes at Billingsgate Q[uarte]‾I answered Mr Olive that I did not allow him to use his pleasure in such a manner—that I apprehended he was as violent, now, as formerly, when I took the power of Correction from him."[64]

Like Davey, Abraham gained strength from Carter's stance on plantation justice, and in questioning the "propriety" of Olive's planned discipline used notably similar arguments to the slave owner's. Thereafter, Carter began to insist that all violent punishment be reported to him so that he could "Interfere" if necessary; Olive left Carter's employ at the end of that year (Morgan 1998: 327).[65] The difficulties faced by Betton and Olive derived from their position at the stress point between rhetoric and reality. Their individual struggles to establish authority underlined the limits of their own liberty to punish bondpeople—and of the liberty that, after the Revolution, white men of all classes had a claim to share.

Inspired by Revolutionary ideas, overseers also invoked the current language of freedom and despotism with vigor—though they employed it to support their claims to the subordination of enslaved people. John Irby complained to Virginian slaveholder Henry Banks about the "almighty

[63] Solomon Betton to John Mercer, 19 September 1791, letters from Solomon Betton, Mercer papers, Virginia Historical Society, Richmond, Virginia.

[64] Entry for 9 September 1784, daybook, VI, 31, Robert Carter papers, 1772–1794, Duke University Perkins Special Collections Library, Durham, North Carolina.

[65] Robert Carter to Newyear Branson, 16 April 1785, daybook, VI, 138; entry for 22 April 1785, daybook, VI, 194, Robert Carter papers, 1772–1794, Duke University Perkins Special Collections Library, Durham, North Carolina.

and plenipotentiary...Mr John Hargrave," his superior. Hargrave had "accused [Irby] of not having answered his Letters," claiming that the overseer had "a number of hands not engaged." These suggestions so infuriated Irby that even though his "sentiments [were] not altogether consistent with the necessary obedience incumbent on me, in my situation, if this should be an objection I can only excuse myself in this way, that it is a fault in my nature, which prompts me to believe, that to be as free as the wind of Heaven is my birth right, and that I will defend and maintain it through out [sic] life, is as certen [sic] as I now have an existence, this its [sic] likely would disconcert the despotic Law of Mr. Hargrave." The overseer warned that if Banks continued to "countenance [the] impudence" of this "bloted [sic] and suspicious man," he would "no longer than Christm[a]s continue in [Banks's] service."[66] Irby's outrage reveals a personal struggle deriving from his wish to be seen as competent and protective of his employer's interests, and to overcome his inferior position in the plantation hierarchy.

Overseers represented the antithesis of every notion of ordered liberty that Revolutionary Americans held. Republican ideals highlighted the paradox that lowly overseers exercised capricious powers over the bondpeople on whose backbreaking labor southern elites' wealth rested—a wealth that gave slaveholders the prestige to influence the prejudices of a new nation.

Conclusion

In a 1770 letter to George Washington, the Virginian planter Jonathon Boucher took prejudices against overseers to a new rhetorical level. Discussing the improvement of the human spirit, he presented an image of a plantation owner who would only "unwillingly apply to any Improvemts. Either in Arts or Sciences." The result of this? "Sunk in unmanly Sloth, his Estate will [be] left to ye. Management of some worthless Overseer." Boucher's tale opposed one of the main ideological focuses of the time—improvement—with a metonymical overseer, the harbinger of moral corruption.[67]

[66] John Irby to Henry Banks, 7 November 1797, Banks papers, 1781–1817, section 1, "John Irby" folder, Virginia Historical Society, Richmond, Virginia.

[67] Jonathon Boucher to George Washington, 21 May 1770, in (Washington 1970).

Overseers were useful cyphers for slave owners' frustrations about unreliable profits and truculent bondpeople. When agricultural schemes failed, overseers—and particularly those on absentee plantations—were the most obvious target of their employers' ire. When enslaved men and women resisted their oppression, or when they complained to their captors about their treatment by overseers, they confirmed planters' worst fears about the consequences of yielding significant responsibility and authority to these men. This confluence of ideas about status, authority, and freedom led overseers to continue to face stigmatization for their agricultural incompetence and inherent violence throughout the closing decades of the 1700s and into the fateful nineteenth century.

References

Baird, J. 1999. "Between Slavery and Independence: Power Relations Between Dependent White Men and Their Superiors in Late Colonial and Early National Virginia with Particular Reference to the Overseer-Employer Relationship." PhD thesis Johns Hopkins University.

Banks papers, Virginia Historical Society, Richmond, Virginia.

Berlin, I. 1980. "Time, Space and the Evolution of Afro-American Society on British Mainland North America." *The American Historical Review* 85 (1): 44–78.

Beverley, R. 1947. *The History and Present State of Virginia*, ed. Louis B. Wright. Chapel Hill: University of North Carolina Press.

Breen, T.H. 1985. *Tobacco Culture: The Mentality of the Great Tidewater Planters on the Eve of Revolution*. Princeton: Princeton University Press.

Butler plantation papers—The Papers of Pierce Butler (1744–1822) and Successors (microfilm), University Library, University of Cambridge, Cambridge, United Kingdom.

Carter, L. 1965. *The Diary of Colonel Landon Carter of Sabine Hall, 1752–1778*, ed. Jack P. Greene. 2 vols. Charlottesville: University Press of Virginia.

Carter, R. *The Diary, Correspondence, and Papers of Robert "King" Carter of Virginia, 1701–1732*, ed. Edmund Berkeley Jr., https://christchurch1735.org/robert-king-carter-papers/ (accessed 1 June 2021).

Chaplin, J.E. 1992. "Tidal Rice Cultivation and the Problem of Slavery in South Carolina, 1760–1815." *William and Mary Quarterly* XLIX (1): 29–61.

Charles William Dabney papers, Manuscripts Department, Southern Historical Collection, University of North Carolina, Chapel Hill, North Carolina.

Colonial Dames Collection, Georgia Historical Society, Savannah, Georgia.

Greene, J.P. 1992. *Imperatives, Behaviors and Identities: Essays in Early American Cultural History*. Charlottesville and London: University Press of Virginia.

Harrower, J. 1900. "Diary of John Harrower, 1773-1776." *The American Historical Review* VI (1): 65–107.

Harrower, J. 1963. *The Journal of John Harrower: An Indentured Servant in the Colony of Virginia, 1773–1776*, ed. Edward Miles Riley. New York: Holt, Rinehart and Winston.

Hening, W.W., ed. 1823. *The Statutes at Large, Being a Collection of All the Laws of Virginia, from the First Session of the Legislature, in the Year 1619*. 18 vols. New York: R. &. W. &. G. Bartow.

Henry Fitzhugh papers, Duke University Perkins Special Collections Library, Durham, North Carolina.

Jefferson, T. 1904. *The Works of Thomas Jefferson in Twelve Volumes*, ed. Paul Leicester Ford. 12 vols. New York and London: The Knickerbocker Press.

Jerdone Family Papers, folder 2, box 2, Manuscripts Department, Earl Gregg Swem Library, College of William and Mary, Williamsburg, Virginia.

John Lloyd Papers, South Caroliniana Library, University of South Carolina, Columbia, South Carolina.

John Ewing Colhoun papers, South Caroliniana Library, University of South Carolina, Columbia, South Carolina.

John Page Diary, Manuscripts Department, Earl Gregg Swem Library, College of William and Mary, Williamsburg, Virginia.

Jones, E.L. 1974. *Agriculture and the Industrial Revolution*. Oxford: Oxford University Press.

Jones, H. 1724. *The Present State of Virginia*. London.

Joseph Ball letterbook, John D. Rockefeller Library, Colonial Williamsburg Foundation, Williamsburg, Virginia.

Josiah Smith, Jr. lettercopy book, 1771–84, Manuscripts Department, Southern Historical Collection, University of North Carolina, Chapel Hill, North Carolina.

Klingsberg, F.J. 1941. *An Appraisal of the Negro in Colonial South Carolina*. Washington: The Associated Publishers.

Kulikoff, A. 1986. *Tobacco and Slaves: The Development of Southern Cultures in the Chesapeake, 1680–1800*. Chapel Hill: University of North Carolina Press.

Laurens, H. 1970–1974. *Papers of Henry Laurens*, ed. P.M. Hamer. 4 vols. Columbia: University of South Carolina Press.

Lee Family Papers, Virginia Historical Society, Richmond, Virginia.

Letterbook of Robert Carter III of Nomini Hall, 1760–64 (typescript), John D. Rockefeller Library, Colonial Williamsburg Foundation, Williamsburg, Virginia.

Morgan, J.L. 2004. *Laboring Women: Reproduction and Gender in New World Slavery*. Philadelphia: University of Pennsylvania Press.

Morgan, P.D. 1998. *Slave Counterpoint: Black Culture in the Eighteenth-Century Chesapeake and Low Country*. Chapel Hill: University of North Carolina Press.

Mullin, G.W. 1972. *Flight and Rebellion: Slave Resistance in Eighteenth-Century Virginia*. New York: Oxford University Press.

Robert Bristow Copybook, Library of Virginia, Richmond, Virginia.

Robert Carter papers (typescript), Duke University Perkins Special Collections Library, Durham, North Carolina.

Robert Carter of Nomini Hall letterbook, 9 vols., Chauvenet collection, John D. Rockefeller Library, Colonial Williamsburg Foundation, Williamsburg, Virginia.

Rutman, D.B., and A.H. Rutman. 1984. *A Place in Time: Middlesex County, Virginia, 1650–1750*. New York: W. W. Norton & Company.

Sandy, L. 2014. "Divided Loyalties in a 'Predatory War': Plantation Overseers and Slavery During the American Revolution." *Journal of American Studies* 48 (2): 357–392.

Sandy, L., and G. Phillips. 2021. "Reputation and 'Reputational Entrepreneurship' in the Colonial South and Early Republic: the Case of Plantation Overseers." *Historical Research* 94 (263): 96–116.

Scarborough, W.K. 1966. *The Overseer: Plantation Management in the Old South*. Baton Rouge: Louisiana State University Press.

Schmidt, J.D. 1994. "Overseers and the Nature of Southern Labor Contracts." In *Race, Class and Community in Southern Labor History*, ed. Gary M. Fink and Merl E. Reed, 87–96. Tuscaloosa: University of Alabama Press.

Schwartz, B. 1995. *A History of the Supreme Court*. Oxford: Oxford University Press.

Sobel, M. 1987. *The World They Made Together: Black and White Values in Eighteenth-Century Virginia*. Princeton: Princeton University Press.

Stubbs, T. 2018. *Masters of Violence: The Plantation Overseers of Eighteenth-Century Virginia, South Carolina, and Georgia*. Columbia: University of South Carolina Press.

Stubbs, T. forthcoming. "Indigo." In *The Encyclopedia of Slavery in the Americas*, ed. Edward E. Baptist. New York: Facts on File Inc.

Edward Telfair papers, Duke University Perkins Special Collections Library, Durham, North Carolina.

Virginia Browne, C.A. 1939. "Reverend Dr. John Clayton and His Early Map of Jamestown." *William and Mary College Quarterly Historical Magazine*, 2nd Ser., XVIIII (1): 1–7.

Virginia Gazette (Purdie).

Walsh, L.S. 1989. "Plantation Management in the Chesapeake, 1620–1820." *The Journal of Economic History* XLIX (2): 393–406.

Washington, George. 1976–1979. *The Diaries of George Washington*, ed. Donald Jackson and Dorothy Twohig. 6 vols. Charlottesville, VA: University Press of Virginia.

Washington, G. 1970. *The Writings of Washington from the Original Manuscript Sources, 1745–1799*, ed. John C. Fitzpatrick. 36 vols. New York: Greenwood Press.

William Ancrum Account Book and Letterbook, South Caroliniana Library, University of South Carolina, Columbia, South Carolina.

Wood, B. 1984. *Slavery in Colonial Georgia, 1730–1775*. Athens, GA: University of Georgia Press.

CHAPTER 7

Inside the Big House: Slavery, Rationalization of Domestic Labor and the Construction of a New *Habitus* on Brazilian Coffee Plantations During the Second Slavery

Mariana Muaze

The Fig. 7.1 displays the grandeur achieved by the coffee plantations of the Paraíba Valley during the period of the second slavery, when planters responded to the commodities demand generated by industrial capitalism by intensifying the exploitation of enslaved laborers.[1] From the beginning of the 1830s to the end of the 1880s, the Brazilian Empire was

M. Muaze (✉)
Department of History, Universidade Federal do Estado do Rio de Janeiro (UNIRIO), Rio de Janeiro, Brazil
e-mail: mariana.muaze@unirio.br

[1] The second slavery is a concept created by Dale Tomich (2004) to describe the slave regimes that flourished in the Americas in the nineteenth century, above all in the US South, Brazil, and Cuba in the years 1800–1860. Tomich calls attention to the different experiences of slavery across times and places and reinterprets the relationship between slavery and capitalism (Tomich 2018: 477). For Tomich, the first slavery started

C. Le Petitcorps et al. (eds.), *Global Plantations in the Modern World*, Cambridge Imperial and Post-Colonial Studies,
https://doi.org/10.1007/978-3-031-08537-6_7

Fig. 7.1 Big house, slave quarters, and coffee patios. Campo Alegre Farm, Marc Ferrez, 1880s (*Source* Instituto Moreira Salles Collection)

the world's largest coffee producer.[2] Almost all the production of *coffea arabica* in the country came from large farms located near the Paraíba

in America during the European colonization of the sixteenth and seventeenth centuries. "This first epoch of New World slavery received great impetus from colonial rivalry and early capitalism, with the former focused on silver, the latter on plantation products, especially sugar and tobacco" (Blackburn 2017: 1). The second slavery refers to the increase in slave trade (internal and external traffic, legal and illegal) during the period of independent state formation and the rise of industrial capitalism in the Americas, when high levels of labor exploitation generated immense profits for planters who responded to the vast demand for commodities such as sugar, coffee, and cotton in the international market during the nineteenth century. Concisely, the second slavery represented a more autonomous, durable, and productive slave regime, "capable of withstanding the onslaught of the Age of Revolution and of meeting the rising demand for plantation produce" (Blackburn 2017: 6).

[2] Brazil was a Portuguese Colony from 1500 to 1822, when it became an independent Empire. The Brazilian Empire ended on November 15th, 1889, one year after the abolition of slavery, which was decreed on May 13th, 1888.

do Sul river and its tributaries in the provinces of São Paulo, Rio de Janeiro and Minas Gerais. The Campo Alegre Plantation (pictured) and several other coffee properties developed in this region were organized around the so-called functional quadrilateral[3] and used primarily enslaved laborers from Africa and their descendants in their productive process. By exploiting the labor of millions of legally and illegally enslaved individuals, the Paraíba Valley region became the economic mainstay of the Brazilian Empire and the main *locus* of its ruling class.

During the construction of the Imperial State (1822–1840) and aligned with the ideals of monarchy, the owners of large coffee farms and their families shared common experiences and worldviews, based on social hierarchy and slave ownership, and made up a powerful faction of the ruling class with enormous political and economic influence at the local and national levels (Mattos 1987; Muaze 2008; Salles 2008). In addition to their enormous wealth and power, these agents began to value their particular way of life, a social *habitus*,[4] inspired by the behavior of the European bourgeoisie without, however, giving up slavery. These "coffee barons" and other wealthy enslavers and landowners valued ideas of *civilization* understood as etiquette, good manners, and refinement inspired especially by French *savoir vivre*, and shared a notion of *order* viewed as the maintenance of slavery in Brazil (Mattos 1987).[5] Consequently, little by little, colonial customs, such as very limited education and insular

[3] The functional quadrilateral organized the geography of coffee plantations and was composed of: the big house, granary, barn, slave houses (in line or in court), drying patio, processing mill, hospital or slave ward, and animal corral, with small variations among properties (Stein 1957). Different arrangements of coffee quadrilaterals can be found at: http://www.institutocidadeviva.org.br/inventarios/sistema.

[4] In this paper I work with the concept of habitus as defined by Norbert Elias (1978, 2006) for whom *habitus* is a non-reflective way of feeling and acting, similar to a second nature that gradually, and through self-conditioning, becomes a part of the individual's personality. Based on this notion, I believe that during the Brazilian Empire the master class was shaping and being shaped by a profoundly hierarchical and aristocratic feeling, affecting their *views of the world* and how they *saw themselves in the world*, therefore establishing a *slavocratic habitus* shared by slaveholders (Muaze 2008).

[5] The idea of civilization applied is also based on Nobert Elias's description of the civilizing process "that underlines the connections between changes in the structure of society [in the case studied the rise of the Vale do Paraíba slaveholders and the forging of the nation] and changes in the structure of people's behavior and psychical habitus" (Elias 1978: xiii).

family life, were replaced by values such as etiquette, education, instruction, courtesy, and hygiene, in addition to the consumption of luxury goods and valorization of social life. Thus, as the fortunes generated by coffee production expanded, an increasingly refined *habitus* was shared among the families of the master class. Seen as elements of prestige and social distinction, these forms of behavior and consumption worked both to consolidate identities among slaveholders and to outline differences in relation to non-hegemonic social groups (Elias 1978).

The main members of the dominant class of the Empire were the "mega-owners," farmers who held more than 100 enslaved individuals, and the so-called "large owners," enslavers of 50 to 99 captives. Together, they controlled more than 70% of the total enslaved population of the Paraíba Valley (Salles 2008).[6] The concentration of slaves and wealth was even greater if we consider extended family holdings rather than individual farms. In Vassouras, the municipality with the second-highest captive population in the middle Paraíba Valley, for example, seven of the ten richest farmers were related to one another. Extended families of planters such as this one built large agrarian empires[7] and coffee complexes[8] by exploiting the work of hundreds of enslaved Africans and afro-descendants (Salles and Muaze 2022).

[6] In Vassouras, research on post-mortem inventories (probate records) revealed patterns of slave property-holding that were at once dispersed and very concentrated. Many farmers owned between one and five enslaved persons, did not own the land they cultivated, and lived together with their captives. Some of these small-time slave owners had once been captives themselves, before gaining freedom from their former masters. At the other extreme of the pyramid, there were planters who owned two, three, four or more plantations and held hundreds of people as slaves (Salles 2008). Without considering the 2% who did not own slave, the estates can be classified as follows: mini-owners (1 to 4 slaves), small owners (5 to 19), medium owners (20 to 49), large owners (50 to 99), and mega owners (100 or more slaves) (Salles 2008: 168).

[7] Historian William Kauffman Scarborough (2006) coined the expression Agrarian Empire when analyzing the slave-owning elite in the United States South, based on nineteenth-century agrarian censuses. He used a minimum of 250 slaves to define an agrarian empire in the Antebellum US. In the context of second slavery, however, the forms of concentrated wealth varied from one slave regime to the next, so that, in relation to Rio de Janeiro's Paraiba basin, we opted to increase Scarborough's original minimum to 350 slaves (Salles and Muaze 2022). Based on this index, I found ten Agrarian Empires in the region of Vassouras, five of them belonging to the Werneck and Ribeiro de Avellar families, who were related to one another (Salles and Muaze 2022).

[8] The coffee complex comprises all existing production structure in a plantation, but also the adjacent farms owned by the same owner or his family (Muaze 2016).

In global terms, we must recognize the relationship among the creation of slave plantations in the Paraíba do Sul Valley, the expansion of industrial capitalist markets, and the rise of the second slavery. For Dale Tomich (2004), the second slavery constituted a new organization of slave economies around the world and was driven by multiple factors. On the one hand, population growth and the advent of the Industrial Revolution encouraged the increase in production and consumption of commodities on a large scale. On the other hand, the wars for independence in the Americas and the Haitian Revolution threw the Atlantic economy into disarray. As a result, production of its main commodities—sugar, cotton, and coffee—was restructured, as previously marginal regions of the Atlantic economy invested in these agricultural products and became central to their production and consumption on a large scale (Marquese and Tomich 2015). In this process of reconfiguring the world economy, newly independent states and their ruling classes supported the adaptation of slavery to the rising industrial capitalist order, the rationalization of work, and new technologies. Thus, the rising areas of the Americas—the Cuban sugar region, the cotton belt of the American South, and the coffee region of the Brazilian Paraíba Valley—gained prominence in the world order, guided by free competition, high productivity, and specialization of work. In all these areas, large numbers of enslaved people were working and living within plantation societies (Parron 2011: 27).

Although the household was a central space for the organization of production on coffee plantations, this theme has not been addressed in the historiography on the second slavery. This chapter focuses on enslaved men and women who provided domestic services, performing functions related to the maintenance of the house, the generation of wealth, and the care of the master's family. I want to demonstrate that the rationalization and specialization of work that took place on the plantations during the historical period of the second slavery were experienced not only by the so-called "field slaves" and free workers, but also by the "house slaves." Inside the big houses, the volume of wealth accumulated through the sale of coffee allowed large slaveholders and landowners to access sophisticated consumer products, valued by a new social *habitus*, which was inspired by the behavior of the European bourgeoisie. Thus, there was an exaltation of etiquette, social life, and refinement by members of the master class, which increased the demands on the work of male and female enslaved servants. They were now required to prepare refined dishes, serve according to the French style, coif fashionable hairstyles, take care of delicate clothes and objects, etc. As a consequence, domestic servitude became more specialized in plantations households and changed both the working conditions and the relationships among enslaved people and between them and their enslavers.

The Rationalization of Work, Spatial Division, and Occupations of Enslaved People on Coffee Plantations

> It is two o'clock in the afternoon, the workers are raking the coffee plantation; a mason works on the ground floor of the house, where I am making a deposit to store at least ten thousand kilos of coffee. Guilhermina and Guieta wash light clothing; Joana and the two twin mulatinhas are sewing; (...) the cook is preparing dinner; Camila, her youngest daughter, sleeps as one sleeps at age two; Rita, the washlady, is pounding heavy clothes in the river. (Alexandre Brethel, owner of São Joaquim farm, 1860)

Alexandre Brethel, a coffee grower in Minas Gerais, described with these words a daily scene on his farm during the golden age of coffee in the Paraíba Valley. His narrative reported a work situation, where enslaved men and women, some tied to one another through kinship, fulfilled different functions in the plantation community.[9] The exception was baby Camila, the cook's daughter, the only one of a non-productive age, who slept. When enumerating different occupations, Brethel pointed out the division of tasks and the specialization of work on his plantation. This rationalized configuration of slave labor relations became more common starting in 1845, when the productive structure of coffee was already set up and exports were in full swing. From then on, enslaved workers with specific occupations appeared more frequently in inventories (Salles 2008) and the more qualified their specialization, the more their prices went up. The same trend in terms of occupation can be seen in the comparative analysis of the ads in *Jornal do Commercio* of the 1840s and 1850s.

[9] In order to understand the structural asymmetry of master–slave relationships at the local level, I use the expression "plantation community" instead of "slave community" or "senzala community." In doing so, I contest the notion of a community as a harmonious group and conceive the slaves' agency as inevitably connected to their masters' dominion (Salles and Muaze 2022).

To define the categories of work and its output on the large plantations, and to analyze the specialization of domestic servants in the context of the second slavery, I used two different databases. The first contains advertisements for the sale of enslaved people in *Jornal do Commercio*,[10] the largest periodical in circulation in the Empire, and the second organizes information from 921 inventories, which list a total of 30,531 enslaved people from Vassouras.[11] In this way, the division based on workplace, such as "indoor slaves" and "outdoor slaves," already demonstrated by studies of urban slavery (Carvalho 2003; Graham 1998; Machado 2017; Silva 2011; Souza 2009), was also seen on plantations. However, this spatial division of labor was more fluid in rural areas and varied in accordance with coffee production cycles, which demanded more field laborers during the planting and harvesting periods.

Let's look at the definitions found in the sources consulted. In the advertisements for the purchase and sale of captives, or recovery of escapees, the terms "family house work," "domestic service," "house service," and "in-house services" are the most recurrent, whereas in inventories the expressions "house service," "every service," "housemaid," and "domestic service" stand out. As can be seen, in both cases housework was defined by its connection to the care of the house and the masters who lived there. Thus, among the 2,954 enslaved people whose occupations are listed in the Vassouras inventories from 1828 to 1888 (9.6% of the total), 22% were domestic, and they were distributed among different specialties: wet nurse, housekeeper, domestic servant, steward, presser, washwoman, maid, messenger boy, baker, page, butler, cook, servant, and confectioner.[12] Among them, 61% were women and

[10] The *Jornal do Commercio ads database* was built as part of the research project "Inside Big Houses: Domestic Slavery and Family Relationships in the Paraíba do Sul and Mississippi River Valleys (1820–1860)" financed by CNPq and is included in the cataloging of all slave advertisements (sale, rent, and escape) for the months of April, August, and December 1840 and December 1850, published in this periodical. The database "A year of the slave," Rio de Janeiro, Jornal do Commercio, 1840 (Keila Grinberg and Mariana Muaze) can be consulted on http://enslaved.org.

[11] The database of Vassouras inventories was produced by historian Ricardo Salles, who generously made it available to me (Salles 2008).

[12] Enslaved men fulfilled the last five specialties of household servants cited.

39% were men. There was thus a clear gender profile, with preference for women.[13]

The plantation household carried an intrinsic complexity because it was both a private and public space. It was the *locus* of the slaveholding family, of the activities of caregiving (feeding, maintaining hygiene, cleanliness) of its members, but it also functioned as the economic center of a productive structure which generated a enormous volume of wealth (Fox-Genovese 1988; Glymph 2008; Muaze 2008). Different from the urban residence, which people left to go to work, the household was the center of everything including family, socialization, and work (Fox-Genovese 1988). It also served to represent the family politically and socially, particularly through suppers, social and business-oriented parties, and meetings with other members of the ruling class. To support this complex institution, those with positions emimently related to the care of the house and the masters (domestic servants) were the most important enslaved workers who lived and worked in the household. However, enslaved people linked to production, under the direct command of the ladies (seamstresses, embroiderers, lacemakers, spinners, tailors) and masters (cashiers, clerks, peddler), or to the tasks eminently related to social ostentation (coachman, litter conductor, musician) made up 10.5% of the enslaved who worked within the big house. Gender played a role in organizing both the functions executed by the enslaved and in those who supervised their work.

Thus, in addition to domestic servants, other skilled enslaved workers performed their functions in the big houses. At Flores do Paraíso Plantation, for example, there was a sewing salon attached to the mansion (Andrade 1989, 255). At Fazenda Pau Grande, the seamstresses and spinners faced a heavy work routine, when they manufactured, under the supervision of the ladies, all the clothes that were distributed to the property's enslaved workers. The Viscountess of Ubá, who ruled the house, had a notebook with the monthly and annual quantity of pieces made. She recorded in it the names of the enslaved workers and the list of clothes distributed to each of them.[14] Her cousin, Viscountess of Arcozelo, wrote on July 22 in her diary: "all the black men of the Monte Alegre Plantation

[13] Research on urban slavery has confirmed that the majority of enslaved women were employed in domestic work.

[14] Mariana Velho de Avellar notebook, 1880–1884. Private collection of the Barros Franco family.

[their main farm] are going to wear wool sweaters and the black women, jackets made from soft wool (baeta)."[15] Their concern demonstrates a rationalization of the work of the seamstresses and the workday that lasted more than ten hours. The ladies' annotation of the production of clothes indicates their active participation in the administration of the house and interaction with the enslaved servants (Muaze 2008, 2022). The use of a large amount of female labor in the sewing of slave clothes on plantations is justified by the almost non-existant Brazilian textile industry, which made it more advantageous to use enslaved labor to sew than to purchase clothing from third parties (Stein 1979). Thus, the ladies were personally involved in the generation of wealth for their farms.

Another example of a craft exercised in the space of the house, without necessarily being a domestic function, was that of musicians. However, unlike the seamstresses' relation to production, the musicians were related to conspicuous consumption, which was valued within the new slavocratic *habitus* of the master class. Although they did not appear in large numbers in Vassouras inventories, this craft was frequent among the enslaved who appear in inventories elsewhere in the Paraíba Valley. The investment in musical bands went far beyond the simple labor destination for the function, involving the purchase of instruments, uniforms, musical score and even the hiring of conductors. José Procópio do Nascimento, a music teacher in the court, trained the enslaved musicians who were held by the Barons of Araruama, Muriaé, Pimentel, and Pilar. The Viscount of Rio Preto had a choir of 50 enslaved children singers and 45 enslaved instrumentalists, who performed in uniform during the festivities of the Fazenda Flores do Paraíso (Andrade 1989, 251). The couple José de Souza Breves and Rita Clara de Moraes Breves kept a separate music room and a "slave room" for their 9 enslaved musicians on Pinheiro Plantation. Masters also invested in other types of skilled labor in order to flaunt their wealth. An example is the woodworker Domingos, who made furniture in Louis XV and XVI style, who was purchased for 3,000$000 réis, and the esteemed artist, Justino, formerly apprenticed to the famous painter Jean-Baptiste Debret, who was valued at 4,500$000 réis, both of whom were workers on the Flores do Paraíso Plantation.

However, it is important to note that the architecture of most of the big houses erected during the rise of coffee separated the intimate (pantry,

[15] Diary of the Viscountess of Arcozelo, 1886. Archive of the Imperial Museum of Petrópolis.

kitchens), social (living room, dining room, games room, ballroom, music room), and commercial (office, office, alcoves) areas from the residence spaces. Thus, having access to the space of the house did not mean having access to the intimacy of the slaveholding family, a concession given only to domestic servants who were responsible for the direct service of the masters. To perform their heavy tasks, they lived in the big house, in rooms near the kitchens, service areas, or the gentlemen's dormitories, the latter being a common option for pages and maids (Almeida and Muaze 2020). More rarely, there were slave houses suitable for the servants behind the big houses or some of them were allowed to gather in the collective slave quarters to stay overnight with their spouses and families.

In regard to enslaved people who worked outside the big house, in crafts mostly linked to the production of wealth and the infrastructure of plantations, I found 58 different specializations that were mostly performed by enslaved men, without counting those who worked solely in the fields. The large plantations had several specialties ranging from nurses (male and female), midwives, and barber-bleeders, who took care of the health of the slaves to guarantee they were not absent from production. There was also a profusion of bricklayers, blacksmiths, woodworkers, engineers, ant-killers, and other skilled laborers needed to maintain the property's infrastructure. The specialization of functions related to the care of other enslaved people became more common after the end of the Atlantic traffic in 1850, when there was an increase in the labor force and masters began to invest both in the health of the slaves and in their natural reproduction by encouraging the formation of families.[16] Plantation management manuals of this period strongly recommended taking care of the slaves' health, food, and housing, encouraging the formation of families, allowing the cultivation of their own gardens, and authorizing festivities on Sundays as a way to improve the control of the slaves and the productivity of the farms (Marquese 2004).

[16] The slave family has been an important field of research in Brazil since the 1990s. Some historians argue that the slave family was the product of resistance, a hard-won achievement that allowed captive Africans and their descendants to maintain their social and cultural practices across generations, creating a slave identity that was molded in opposition to the master class (Slenes 1999). Others hold that the slave family was a concession, an instrument that allowed slave masters to guarantee peace in the slave quarters and exercise greater control over their captives (Florentino and Góes 1997). However, any approach that aims to produce a single, unitary view of the slave family's historical meaning may lead to false dichotomies, because the slave family could be both resistance and coercion (Salles 2008; Salles and Muaze 2022).

The degree of knowledge, specialization, and expertise required meant that prices were high for enslaved workers who performed skilled work. They were found mostly among men who, in addition to their skill, were listed with adjectives such as "master," "official," "expert," or "perfect." Among the most expensive slaves were blacksmiths. Adam, identified as a Creole [Brazilian-born] of the Ubá Plantation, was valued at 3,000$000 réis. Only one enslaved man among the 30,531 surveyed was appraised higher: a Blacksmith named was Aureliano, a Creole, 31 years old, worker of the São Pedro Plantation, valued at 3,500$000 réis. Such cases prove that, depending on the skill and expertise, a single enslaved worker could be valued two to three times higher than a "swidden" enslaved man of productive age, who would cost on average 1,200$000 réis in 1860 (Salles 2008: 164).

The enslaved workers who performed tasks directly aimed at planting, harvesting, processing, and bagging the coffee were listed as "roceiros," "roceiras," "de roça" (workers of the field) or simply did not have a specific occupation. They totaled 28,274 and made up more than 90% of all enslaved workers, around 70% of whom were male (Salles 2008). In terms of origin, from the time plantations were founded until the mid-1840s, the proportion of Africans was 70%. In 1850, with the end of the Atlantic trade, this rate began to decrease and, in the 1870s, those born in Brazil already comprised the vast majority of slaves (Salles 2008: 181–182). With regard to gender relations, the 1860s brought a greater balance between men and women and the incentive to form families. Even though only 9% of the slaves listed in the inventories are described as married or widowed, this does not mean that they did not live as a family, but rather that the union was not consecrated in the Catholic Church and/or that it was not recognized by the master.[17]

The increasing degree of specialization of slave labor during the second slavery was combined with the growth of families, the increase of enslaved people born in Brazil (creoles), and the greater supervision and control of workers. In the Paraíba Valley, the "senzalas" (slave quarters) were built in straight rows surrounding the courtyard, which enclosed the main production space, forming a rectangular area where the foremen watched

[17] The first record of a captive with specialization in the inventories of Vassouras was in 1848. The period coincides with the end of the installation phase of plantations in the region and demonstrates the importance that enslaved work has acquired in relation to previous decades (Salles 2008).

the work activities (Marquese 2006). With the same objective, in the hills where coffee was planted, the spacing between the trees increased, so that captives could be seen from a distance. Field workers were organized in groups of 20 to 25, under the supervision of foremen and overseers. To accelerate the pace, they promised workers small monetary or in-kind rewards if production targets were met (Marquese 2004). During the course of the agricultural cycle, skilled enslaved workers could be used for planting, harvesting, drying, processing, and bagging of coffee. Therefore, there was a fluidity of functions that changed the routine of workers and their families according to the season and production needs. Claudio Gomes Ribeiro de Avellar, Baron of Guaribu, recorded the dislocations—whether relating to space or occupation—of his captives:

> The following slaves are now present on the Fazenda Guaribú, although they belong to the Fazenda das Antas and are part of that place: Marçal, a carpenter, with his wife, children and brothers; Faustino Inhambane, a construction worker; Joaquim, a construction worker, Inhambane and his family; Albério Inhambane; Thomas Caseiro; Modesto Caseiro; Luiz Inhambane, a muleteer, with his family; Matheus, a muleteer, Messias, a muleteer, Antonio Moçambique, a muleteer; Simão Crioulo; Germano Inhambane, a cook; and Sabino, a muleteer.[18]

The same dislocation of enslaved people and their functions between different lands of the same owner was recorded in the diary of the Viscountess of Arcozelo: "Castro sent for help to come from Piedade to pick the coffee here" [at Monte Alegre Farm]. "I sent 6 girls and the 2 cooks to pick coffee."[19] Such examples demonstrate that, ultimately, the generation of the main wealth would speak louder, connecting the Empire and its ruling class to the international market and the so-called civilized world. To this end, dozens of skilled occupations were created in order to ensure the best quality and the shortest time in the services provided. However, skilled individuals were used for field work depending on the production cycle and the needs of each crop. In the end, there was an accumulation of functions and greater exploitation of the slave labor.

[18] All the farms mentioned in the source belonged to the same owner, the Baron of Guaribu. Will of Cláudio Gomes Ribeiro de Avellar,1863, Archive CDH-Vassouras.

[19] Diary of the Viscountess of Arcozelo. Collection of Museu Imperial de Petrópolis.

Domestic Slavery, Labor Specialization, and Slavocratic Habitus

The property depicted in the above photograph was one of the first erected in the Paraíba valley. By 1860, the Ubá Plantation had 30,000 coffee plants, being among the five largest agrarian empires of Vassouras. The selected photograph is rare in Brazilian visual culture. It was not common for masters and bondspeople to pose together in domestic environments or in photo studios (Mauad 2000). The image was made by award-winning photographer Revert Henrique Kumb, demonstrating the economic power of those who hired him. They wanted to show their

Fig. 7.2 Ubá Plantation, Vassouras, 1860, by Revert Henrique Klumb. José Pereira de Almeida, his wife, their relatives and two domestic servants (*Source* Instituto Moreira Salles Collection)

provincial farm in order to create an image not only of themselves, but also their plantation and servants (Fig. 7.2).

The scene photographed evokes an intimate situation. The master, at the center, emphasized his power as the patriarch of the family and in the management of the plantation. The ladies sitting around the table performed reading and sewing, reinforcing typically feminine activities within the contemporary gender order (Perrot 1991) inspired by European bourgeoisie social habitus. Young maids Martha and Lina appear standing, well dressed, in a position to serve, and they were the only ones to look at the camera. The image distinguished, with no subtlety, the world of the free and the enslaved, not only through the body position of the social agents in the scene, but also through its depiction of gender, race, and class relations. There is clear opposition between white women, who stage a domestic naturalness, and enslaved, uncomfortable black women on camera. Such differences and hierarchies—in the occupation of the photographic space, gestures, position of the gaze, clothing, objects—were not accidental. They reflected social cleavages that guided the daily life of big houses, formed a slavocratic *habitus* of domination, and sustained a broad culture of violence in the private sphere (Deetz 2017; Foz-Genovese 1988; Glymph 2008; Muaze 2017).

The place and angle of the photo were also not unintentional. They allow a view of the buildings of the coffee complex and the immensity of land belonging to its owners. The photographer has incorporated the areas of cultivation, processing, and coffee production within the big house space and the individuals who lived there and enjoyed a social *habitus* that combined refinement and slavery. Therefore, in addition to housing, the plantation household was a unit of economic-social production and reproduction. There, the family lived, engaged in politics, made deals, received people for social care, educated their children, sewed clothes for captives, and reproduced slave practices on a daily basis. In sum, it was a space where masters worked to maintain heritage, honor, and wealth. Within those walls, in the family space, intimacy and affection were combined with labor relations, production, political articulation, power and hierarchy (Muaze 2008, 2017, 2022). There, gender, race, and class relations played a fundamental role in strengthening slavery as a founding institution of Imperial society (Glymph 2008: 11–12).

The image also depicts the *habitus* valued by the master class of the Brazilian Empire, which, using the wealth generated by coffee, began to exalt European etiquette, refinement, and consumption practices, including photography, in order to consolidate new forms of behavior seen as civilized and sophisticated. Little by little, after 1840, the members of the dominant class resignified a European bourgeois habitus and reinvented it from the enslaving relations to which they were accustomed. In this process, a number of skilled crafts and services performed by enslaved people were introduced into the space of the house. They were oven and stove cooks, confectioners, and bakers who were responsible for the preparation of sophisticated dinners, tea parties, soirees, as well as daily meals on the farms. Each day, while the butlers served the table, the housekeepers, washwomen, and pressers performed the rest of the service. The maids and pages took care of the clothes, the preparation of the bath, and the personal needs of their masters and ladies. All this increasing variety of servants and social events contrasted with the low level of specialization and requirement for refinement in the houses of the former Brazilian colonial elite. In wealthy families, the rule became to have a maid or a page boy for each family member. Thus, even the children had their servants, who might be similar in age to themselves. Among the maids, the most desired were those who knew how to style hair, sew, embroider, etc. Among the pages, in addition to preparing the men's clothing and arranging them, they should know how to handle the horses and take care of the riding equipment. Social gatherings with other members of the master class became an opportunity to demonstrate refinement and to display the vast and well-trained enslaved workforce. In fact, the rationalization and specialization of the work envisioned in other spaces of the coffee plantation also took place inside the big house, even if for distinct purposes. Thus, the period of the second slavery was not only configured as a new political-economic order, but also as a new social and cultural order, which significantly changed the lives of its historical subjects.

According to the inventory of Elisa Constance, there were 9 enslaved domestic servants in the big house of the Ubá Plantation. Among the 483 captives of the property, only 83 were listed alongside their family members. In the case of the servants, only the maid Lina (19 years old) appeared alongside her daughter Guilhermina (5 months old).[20] However, by considering information obtained from the will of Elisa's

[20] Inventory of Elisa Constance de Almeida, 1860, Iphan-Vassouras Archive.

husband José Pereira de Almeida, it can be deduced that both the number of domestic servants and their families was higher:

> I leave [the following captives] free as though they had been born of free womb. First, my creole slave Leonidia, as compensation for having helped me with great affection to raise two children as a nanny. Second, my slave Bento, a creole of the Ubá Farm, son of Suzana who was a wet nurse to my son Joaquim and who is already free. Third, my slave Rachel, creole of the Ubá Farm and niece of the same Suzana. Fourth, Joana, [who is] brown, also from the Ubá Farm, and whose freedom is given because my wife raised her under her watch, and has a great feeling of friendship for her (Will of José Pereira de Almeida, 1874).

Analysis of other farm inventories also supports the hypothesis that Paraíba Valley plantations typically held a large number of servants. In 1851, Pinheiro Farm had 51 captives in the household out of 483 total. In 1872, 55 enslaved servants and 9 freedmen worked on the Pau Grande Farm and the house in Petropolis of the Ribeiro de Avellar family. These high numbers show that the masters invested heavily in domestic slavery to meet the luxury and social representation needs that arose from the new forms of behavior of the master class. In fact, by the middle of the nineteenth century, there was a significant increase in the number of household servants compared to colonial times to attend to the new *habitus* and the social and economic demands adopted by the master class members.

Analysis of Vassouras inventories (probate records) also allows us to view enslaved families and kinship relations. To understand them, it is important to include in the analysis affinal ties such as husband and wife, mother-in-law, sister-in-law, etc. From this perspective, the enslaved family (Florentino and Góes 1997; Salles 2008; Slenes 1999) appears with various compositions, and some reached the fourth generation of kinship, as demonstrated through the study of the farms of the Baron of Guaribu (Salles and Muaze 2022). Family life was also a reality for enslaved domestic servants. At Pau Grande Farm, for example, among the 55 servants, 30 maintained kinship ties involving one to 6 people "from domestic service" (Muaze 2017). On the Pinheiro Plantation, owned by José de Souza Breves, there were 12 family groups among the 51 domestic servants. In the first case, the largest family composition found was that of the presser Bernardina, who had three children:

enslaved domestic servants Martiniana and Ponciana (who was married to carpenter Ambrose and mother of Raul, Deolinda, and Florinda) and the page Leoncio (married to seamstress Laurentina). All of Bernardina's children were "indoor slaves," and their marriages brought skilled workers into the family. Leoncio's wife, Laurentina, besides being a seamstress, was the sister of the butler Firmino. Yet although Laurentina and Firmino managed to maintain positions within domestic slavery, their six siblings and their mother, the African woman Alda, worked in the fields.[21] At the Pinheiro Plantation, the largest family was that of the maid Emília, who was the mother of Luiza, also a maid, and the carpenters Emydio and Fernando.

The families of the presser Bernardina and the maid Emília involved more than one generation in the domestic work of the Pau Grande and Pinheiro Farms. However, not all of the members were incorporated into the services of the house. The existence of relatives performing tasks in different spaces of the plantation and the heavy daily toil made it very difficult to live among relatives. Even so, it is interesting to note that domestic servants tended to seek relationships with skilled bondspeople, as was the case of the carpenter José Sabirola and the maid Guilhermina from the Pinheiro Plantation, and the cook Daniel and the maid Aderandrina, from the Pau Grande Plantation. This can be seen as a strategy to ally with those who were more able to leave captivity, either by buying their emancipation through the sum of their savings, or by receiving freedom with the blessings of the slaveholding family (Slenes 1999).[22]

The number of enslaved men who worked in the kitchen was 55% of the total number of kitchen workers who appear in the inventories. Of the seven cooks who worked in the kitchen of the Pau Grande Plantation, six of them were bondsmen. At Pinheiro Plantation, there were seven enslaved people, five of whom were men. At the Ubá Farm, there were two female and one male cook. The services linked to the "dirty kitchen"—the handling of large and heavy iron pots, as well as killing, dressing, and loading animals—required great physical strength of

[21] Registration of slaves of Joaquim Ribeiro de Avellar, 1872. Pau Grande Farm. Barros Franco Family Private Collection.

[22] The group most frequently freed through wills were domestic workers, mainly wet and dry nurses, maids, and pages. However, when comparing the number of freed-slaves with the number of slaves in the squads, we will see that this concession reached a very small number of enslaved.

the men and women who executed them (Deetz 2017; Schwartz 2017; Sharpless 2010).[23] The tasks of the "clean kitchen" where pasta, sweets, refreshing drinks, and stews were prepared, were also performed by both genders and followed a more Bourgeois standard, as is illustrated by numerous advertisements in the *Jornal do Commercio.*

As this article sought to demonstrate, the period of the second slavery on coffee plantations was responsible for the rationalization of slave labor inside and outside the big house. After the initial phase of constructing the farms of the Paraíba Valley in the 1840s, the members of the master class began to divide their enslaved workers by skill, in order to organize the exploitation of the labor force and ensure the high productivity of coffee to supply world market demands. Thus, they created different occupations essentially linked to the care of the big house and the family (domestic service), to social representation, and to the maintenance of the plantation infrastructure and production. All these spheres of work implied different experiences, circulation spaces, places of residence, and division of tasks by gender and forms of family coexistence for the enslaved people.

In regards to the domestic servants, the rationalization of labor implied a high level of slave labor exploration with an increase in the number of people, volume of work, and specialization of tasks. In this process, the type of duties executed in the household became more sophisticated to attend the master class' slavocratic habitus inspired by European etiquette and forms of consumption. The gender division was strengthened in accordance with bourgeois gender norms, as domestic work was done mostly by women, with men concentrated in occupations such as cook, page, and waiter. Although the toil and the master's control were heavy for all the enslaved people who performed their functions there, servants formed families as a way to constitute small gaps for autonomy in a violent daily life of exhausting work. Being an enslaved domestic did not mean that one's relatives would follow the same path. It was common to see a family split with some relatives working inside the household and others in the plantation fields. Despite the increasing specialization of servants, in times of planting or harvesting, some of them could be relocated to the field to guarantee coffee production.

[23] The analysis of the advertisements of the *Jornal do Commercio* for the years 1840 and 1850 also points to the preference for male cooks.

The period of the second slavery also saw the ascent of the master class linked to the Rio de Janeiro coffee sector. As a way to build and reaffirm intra- and extra-class identities, its members adopted a slavocratic *habitus*, which was refined and inspired by the European bourgeoisie, without giving up slavery. Thus, in Brazil, those who prepared fine dinners, dressed the ladies or played the violin at receptions on the farms were enslaved men and women. Their daily lives underwent great transformations in order to perform with dexterity the new tasks required by the masters. In this process of intense economic, political, and cultural changes, the plantation household played multiple roles. On the one hand, it was fundamentally a productive space supervised by masters and mistresses, who controlled the coffee business from there. On the other hand, it was a space of coexistence and family intimacy, accessed by selected servants. In addition, it also presented itself as a *locus* of class representation, where the masters boasted prestigious elements consistent with a new social *habitus*, which combined the master class' idea of civilization and slavery.

References

Almeida, A. C. L. D. and Muaze, M. 2020. «Le dîner est servi!» La cuisine comme lieu de captivité à Rio de Janeiro au XIXe siècle. *Brésil (s). Sciences Humaines et Sociales*, 1–25.

Andrade, E. 1989. *O Vale do Paraíba*. Rio de Janeiro: Rio Gráfica e Editora.

Baptist, E. 2001. "Cuffy", "Fancy Maids", and "One-Eyed Men": Rape, Commodification, and the Domestic Slave Trade in the United States. *The American Historical Review* 106 (5): 1619–1650.

Baptist, E. 2014. *The Half Has Never Been Told: Slavery and the Making of American Capitalism*. New York: Basic Books.

Blackburn, R. 2017. Introduction: "Why the Second Slavery?". In *Slavery and Capitalism in the Nineteenth Century*, ed. D. Tomich, 1–38. Lanhan, MD, USA: Lexington Books.

Bourdieu, P. 2007. *O poder simbólico*. Rio de Janeiro: Bertrand Brasil.

Carvalho, M. F. M. 2003. De portas adentro e de portas afora: Trabalho doméstico e escravidão no Recife, 1822–1850. *Afro-Ásia* 29 (30): 41–78.

Cooper, F., T. Holt, and R. J. Scott. 2000. *Beyond Slavery: Explorations of Race, Labour, and Citizenship in Postemancipation Societies*. Chapel Hill: University of North Carolina Press.

Deetz, K. F. 2017. *Bound to the Fire: How Virginia's Enslaved Cooks Helped Invent American Cuisine*. Lexington: The University Press of Kentucky.

Elias, N. 1978. *The Civilizing Process*. New York: Urizen Books.
Elias, N., E. Jephcott, and S. Mennell. 2006. *The Court Society*. Dublin: University College Dublin Press.
Florentino, M. and J. R. P. de Goes. 1997. *A paz das senzalas. Famílias escravas e tráfico atlântico, Rio de Janeiro, 1790–1850*. Rio de Janeiro: Civilização Brasileira.
Fox-Genovese, E. 1988. *Within the Plantation Household:* Chapel Hill: The University of North Carolina Press.
Freyre, G. 1984. *O Escravo nos anúncios de jornais brasileiros do século XIX*. Recife: CBBA/Propeg.
Glymph, T. 2008. *Out of House of Bondage: The Transformation of the Plantation Household*. Cambridge: Cambridge University Press.
Graham, S. L. 1998. *House and Street: The Domestic World of Servants and Masters in Nineteenth-Centrury Rio de Janeiro*. Austin: University of Texas Press.
Grahan, S. L. 2002. *Caetana Says No: Women's Stories from a Brazilian Slave Society*. Cambridge: Cambridge University Press.
Machado, M. H. P. T. 2017. Between two Beneditos: Enslaved wetnurses amid slavery's decline in Southeast Brazil. *Slavery and Abolition* 38 (2): 320–336.
Marquese, R. B. 2006. "Revisitando casas-grandes e senzalas: a arquitetura das plantations escravistas americanas no século XIX". *An. mus. paul.* [online], 14 (1): 11–57.
Marquese, R. D. B. 2004. *Feitores do Corpo, missionários da mente: senhores, letrados e o controle dos escravos nas Américas, 1660–1860*, 479. São Paulo: Companhia das Letras.
Marquese, R. and D. Tomich. 2015. "O Vale do Paraíba escravista e a formação do mercado mundial do café no século XIX." In M. Muaze and R. Salles (eds.). *O Vale do Paraíba e o Império do Brasil nos quadros da segunda* escravidão, 21–56. Rio de Janeiro: 7 Letras.
Massa, F. 1977. *Alexandre Brethel: Pharmacien et planteur français au Carangola (1862–1901)*. Institut Armorican de Recherches Economiques et Humaine de Rennes: Universite de Haute-Bretagne.
Mattos, I. R. de. 1987. *O Tempo Saquarema*. São Paulo: Ed. Hucitec
Mauad, A. M. 2000. As fronteiras da cor: Imagem e representação fotográfica na sociedade escravista imperial. *Locus, Revista De História* 6 (2): 83–98.
Muaze, M. 2008. *As memórias da viscondessa: Família e poder no Império*. Rio de Janeiro: Zahar.
Muaze, M. 2022. Silenced Motherhood: Enslaved Wet Nurses in 19th Century Brazil. In *The Boundaries of Freedom: Slavery, Abolition and the Making of Modern Brazil*, vol. 1, 1 st ed, edited by B. Fisher and K. Grinberg, 108–127. Cambridge: Cambridge University Press.

Muaze, M. de A. F. 2016. "What Will These People Do When the Final Emancipation of Slaves is Decreted?"—Domestic Service and Slavery in the Paraiba Valley Coffee Plantations. *Almanack* 12: 65–87. https://doi.org/10.1590/2236-463320161205

Muaze, M. de A. F. 2017. Violence Appeased: Slavery and Coffee Raising in the Photograph of Marc Ferrez (1882–1885). *Rev. Bras. Hist.* 37: 33–62.

Muaze, M. and R. Salles. 2020. *A segunda escravidão e o Império do Brasil em perspectiva histórica*. São Leopoldo: Casa Leiria/ CNPq.

Parron, T. 2011. *A política da escravidão no Império do Brasil, 1826–1865*, 2011. Rio de Janeiro: Civilização Brasileira.

Perrot, M. (org.). 1991. *História da Vida Privada: Vol. 4: da Revolução Francesa à Primeira Guerra*. São Paulo: Companhia das Letras.

Rockman, S. 2018. Negro Cloth: Mastering the Market for Slave Clothing in Antebellum America. In *American Capitalism: New Histories*, edited by C. Desan and S. Beckert, 170 194. New York: Columbia University Press.

Salles, R. 2008. *E o vale era escravo. Vassouras, século XIX*. Rio de Janeiro: Civilização Brasileira.

Salles, R. and M. Muaze. 2022. "Agrarian Empires, Plantation Communities and Slave Families in a Nineteenth-Century Brazilian Coffee Zone". In *The Boundaries of Freedom: Slavery, Abolition and the Making of Modern* Brazil, edited by B. Fisher and K. Grinberg, 183–107. Cambridge: Cambridge University Press.

Scarborough, W. K. 2006. *Masters of the Big Houses*. Elite Slaveholders of the Mid-Nineteenth-Century South, Baton Rouge: Louisiana State University Press.

Schwastz, M. J. 2017. *Ties That Bound: Founding First Ladies and Slaves*. Chicago: University of Chicago Press.

Sharpless, R. 2010. *Cooking in Other Women's Kitchens: Domestic Workers in the South, 1865–1960*. North Carolina: University of North Carolina Press.

Silva, M. H. 2011. *Pretas de honra: vida e trabalho de domésticas e vendedoras no recife do século XIX (1840–1870)*. Recife: EDUPE.

Slenes, R. W. 1999. *Na Senzala uma Flor, esperanças e recordações na formação da família escrava: Brasil Sudeste, século XIX*. Campinas: Unicamp Editora.

Stein, S. J. 1957. *Vassouras, a Brazilian Coffee County 1850–1900*. Cambridge: Harvard University Press.

Stein, S. J. 1979. *Origens e evolução da indústria têxtil no Brasil, 1850–195*, edited by Rio de Janeiro. Campus.

Souza, F. F. 2009. *Para casa de família e mais serviços: O trabalho doméstico na cidade do Rio de Janeiro no final do século XIX. Master's Thesis*. São Gonçalo: FFP/UERJ.

Tomich, D. W. 2004. *Through the Prism of Slavery: Labor, Capital, and World Economy*. Lantham: Bowman & Littlefield Publishers Inc.

Tomich, D. W. 2018. The Second Slavery and World Capitalism: A Perspective for Historical Inquiry. *International Review of Social History* 63 (3): 477–501.
Zaluar, A. E. 1975. *Peregrinações pela província de São Paulo (1860–1861)*. São Paulo: Itatiaia/EDUSP.

CHAPTER 8

Plantation Colonialism in Late Nineteenth-Century Hawai‘i: The Case of Chinese Sugar Planters

Nicholas B. Miller

Introduction

A long-standing historiographical trope is that "King Cane" succeeded Hawai‘i's indigenous monarchy as its sovereign during the final decades of the nineteenth century. Present first in planter travelogs and periodicals, this formulation became a commonplace in histories of Hawai‘i after Vandercook chose "King Cane" as the title of his influential history of Hawai‘i's sugar industry (Boyce 1914; Carpenter 1925: 298; Vandercook 1939).[1] This account welded an implicit historical materialism to

N. B. Miller (✉)
Department of Humanities, Flagler College, St. Augustine, FL, USA
e-mail: nbmiller@flagler.edu

Historisches Institut, Universität zu Köln, Köln, Germany

[1] Research for this chapter began via a project that received funding from the European Research Council (ERC) under the European Union's Horizon 2020 research and innovation programme No. 695573, The Colour of Labour, PI Cristiana Bastos. Research was completed via a project that received funding from the European Union's Horizon 2020

C. Le Petitcorps et al. (eds.), *Global Plantations in the Modern World*, Cambridge Imperial and Post-Colonial Studies,
https://doi.org/10.1007/978-3-031-08537-6_8

how Hawai'i came to be a U.S. possession, suggesting that sugar plantations, in their status as a modern, industrial, capitalist, and Western form of production, inevitably eroded the archaic customary authority of Native Hawaiian elites. The demise of the Hawaiian monarchy in 1893 thereby was attributed to the islands' integration into the global capitalist economy, wherein the roles of individual historical actors—including insurgent white residents who violently strove toward U.S. annexation, including through illegal maneuvers—were minimized.

After a boon of plantation labor histories in the 1980s (Takaki 1983; Beechert 1985), a primary tendency of scholarship on Hawai'i around the turn of the century was to reprise individual political agency, particularly of Native Hawaiian actors contesting American overrule. Jonathan Osorio, Noelani Silva, and Tom Coffman advanced robust critiques of the neglected national and international politics that informed the overthrow of the Hawaiian Kingdom, joined by scholars working within the bourgeoning field of American empire studies, such as Eric Love, Daniel Immerwahr, and Christen T. Sasaki (Osorio 2002a; Silva 2004; Coffman 1998/2016; Love 2005; Immerwahr 2019; Sasaki 2022). Carol A. MacLennan's environmental history of "sovereign sugar" foregrounded the devastating transformations wrought by plantations upon Hawaiian natural and cultural ecologies, though likewise embraced an actor-focused account emphasizing the contingent character of the sugar industry that ultimately emerged in Hawai'i (MacLennan 2014).

During the past decade, the paradigm of settler colonialism has come to dominate the field, leading to a sustained inquiry of white settler ideological formations in Hawai'i (Chang 2016; Rohrer 2016; Schulz 2020; Lozano 2021). These works generally cast settler colonialism in Hawai'i as American in nature and take settler colonialism as a self-sufficient category for understanding historical developments in Hawai'i since the nineteenth century. As highlighted recently by Warrick Anderson, this has resulted in a tendency to leave unexamined "North American theoretical frameworks" that do not quite apply to the political, environmental, and contextual complexities of Hawai'i's place in the imperial mid-Pacific (Anderson 2021: 2). Nancy Shoemaker's explicitly non-exhaustive delineation of twelve forms of colonialism is here instructive, which includes settler colonialism as a subvariant along with planter, extractive,

research and innovation programme under the Marie Skłodowska-Curie Grant Agreement No. 889078.

trade, transport, legal, rogue, missionary, romantic, and even postcolonial forms (Shoemaker 2015). Pluralizing the forms of colonialism appraised as operative in nineteenth-century Hawai'i can yield new insights into its complex history, such as the spectrum of creative responses adopted by Native Hawaiian ruling elites, as Noelani Arista has recently examined in terms of law, writing, and authority during the 1820s (Arista 2018).

In view of the current state of scholarship on Hawai'i, this chapter suggests the utility of plantation colonialism as a prism to explicate the intertwined interactions between what this volume terms plantation ecologies and the sovereign-making power of plantation systems. I take my starting point from Lynn Hollen Lees' work on the relationship between plantations and the colonial state in nineteenth-century Malaya, drawing upon calls for applying transnational and Pacific World methodologies for the history of Hawai'i (Okihiro 2008; Chang 2016; Rosenthal 2018; Cook 2018; Dusinberre 2019). As defined by Lees, plantation colonialism was "a modern, global hybrid. Built with assumptions carried over from the Caribbean sugar growers, revised by colonial administrators who believed in an interventionist state, which for the most part neglected workers' needs, it brought together state and society in a harsh, hierarchical environment" (Lees 2017: 59).

Applying Lees' definition of plantation colonialism to Hawai'i requires certain caveats. The state administrators of nineteenth-century Hawai'i worked for an internationally-recognized independent Kingdom and a significant number were indigenous. Yet the effective outcome, as in other new sugar colonies across the nineteenth-century world, was the emergence of a plantation complex dependent upon global interconnections with pre-existing sugar-growing locations. Like Malaya, the incipient planter class was not merely European in character. Chinese sugar masters in both locales were in fact the first group to produce commercially viable sugar and maintained fluctuating and sophisticated relationships with indigenous and Western political elites throughout the century. Informed by the comparative example of colonial Malaya, this chapter recovers the experiences of three Chinese merchants turned sugar planters in late nineteenth-century Hawai'i.

Two persistently unexamined assumptions in much scholarship on Hawai'i are the notions that non-Westerners featured on plantations merely as laborers and were involved in sugar production as seeders rather than leaders. Native Hawaiians, or more precisely their seafaring ancestors, are credited with transplanting Southeast Asian cultivars prior to first European contact with James Cook in 1778. Chinese sugar masters in turn are noted as the first to attempt commercial processing during the early nineteenth century (Cushing 1985: 17–34). Some work has also considered the role played by Chinese sugar planters on the small Hawaiian sugar scene preceding the Reciprocity Treaty of 1874, which prompted a sugar boom by permitting the duty-free export of sugar to the United States (Char 1974: 3–10; Kai 1974: 39–75; MacLennan 1997: 97–125). Between 1874 and 1898, the year in which the United States took control of the islands, monocultures of sugar and rice had supplanted diversified small-scale crop cultivation, Asian and European indentured laborers replaced Native Hawaiians as the majority population, and the lands given over to sugar grew more than tenfold, from 12,283 to 125,000 acres, output surged by 1767%, and the number of laborers in the fields increased nearly eightfold, from 3,786 to 28,579 (Beechert 1985: 87; MacLennan 2014: 285).

What has gone less noticed is how dozens of Chinese merchants and Native Hawaiian elites participated in this boom with optimism, hoping to derive personal fortune from saccharine sources. While most generally failed, two planters, John Adams Kuakini Cummins at Waimānalo, Oʻahu and Chun Afong at Pepeʻekeo, Hawaiʻi Island, achieved considerable success during the 1880s. The pursuit of saccharine fortune ultimately undermined the position of Native ruling elites in Hawaiʻi, though in a nuanced way. The claims of *haole* settler nativists to racial, cultural, and political ascendancy after 1887 were hardly hegemonic.[2] Besides being bitterly contested by Native Hawaiian actors, certain *haole* sugar producers—notably Charles F. Hart in Kohala—loudly denounced what they perceived as an imperial power play by resident Americans up to the moment of U.S. annexation. Settler colonialism assuredly configured a set of social expectations in the islands, but the institutionalization of Christianity, common law, universal primary education, and bonded plantation labor in the islands was only gradual, and involved many actors not racialized as *haole*, White, Anglo-Saxon, European, or American. In providing the first substantial basis for local capital accumulation since the

[2] By *haole* or white settler nativists, I mean White American and European settlers and their descendants who staked undemocratic claims to political ascendancy through two interlocking prerogatives: racial superiority as Anglo-Saxons and, for those born in Hawaiʻi, status by birthplace as natives of the islands. I take my distinction between native and settler nativist claims to sovereignty from Sharma (2020).

demise of whaling, the rising plantation economy occasioned collisions between multiple projects of sovereignty—native (indigenous), nativist (*haole* settler), and integrative—and diverse forms of colonialism delineated by Shoemaker—extractive, trade, missionary, legal, planter, rogue, and settler.

The core complexity of plantation Hawai'i as a context is that processes of plantation colonialism intersected with older patterns of defensive elite modernization and extractive, trade, missionary, legal, and settler colonialism. The configuration of plantation colonialism in Hawai'i thus encompassed endogenous and exogenous factors. If we ignore the questions of why and how individual non-*haole* actors participated in the emerging sugar economy in the late nineteenth century, we silence those who lived complex, consequential, and perhaps, from our perspective, counter-intuitive intersections of ethnic identity, religious conviction, and economic aspiration. To rectify this, the chapter begins by providing the political, legal, demographic, and economic background to the Reciprocity Treaty of 1874, namely the rise of Anglo-American property and labor law, the distinctive biopolitical concerns of the Kingdom polity, and the formation of migrant Chinese urban and rural communities. The second and third sections go on to describe how three Chinese merchants turned to sugar after 1874: first, the powerful mogul Chun Afong (陳芳, 1825–1906) and second, the upstart duo of Goo Tet Chin Akina (GOO Tet-Tsin, 1838–1913) and Luke Aseu (CHANG Young Seu, 1841–1918). These three preliminary sections foreground an extended analysis of Hawai'i's largest labor rebellion prior to the overthrow of the monarchy, which occurred at Akina and Aseu's plantation at Kohala, Island of Hawai'i, in 1891 (Takaki 1983: 147).

State Formation Processes and Chinese Migration Before 1874

Sugar attained the dominant place in the Hawaiian economy only after a century of social, political, and economic interactions between Native Hawaiian governing elites and foreign merchants, missionaries, military officials, adventurers, and other sojourners. The formation of a plantation complex was facilitated by a court system based on Anglo-American common law that had become firmly entrenched by the mid-nineteenth century and served as a primary vehicle for the institutionalization of fee-title property and contract labor (Merry 2000). That is, plantation colonialism in Hawai'i began in earnest only decades after legal and missionary forms had become well established. Early Chinese migration to Hawai'i occurred in the backdrop of this state formation process. Among the effects of the distinctive social and political culture that emerged was greater space for Chinese settlement and economic activity than that found in classic settler colonies like Australia, Canada, and the United States, or in European-governed plantation colonies beyond Southeast Asia (McKeown 2001; MacLennan 2014: 103–144).

State building in early nineteenth-century Hawai'i was driven by the ambition of ruling elites to maintain political ascendancy in the face of increasingly asymmetric relations with Westerners. American Congregationalist missionaries first arrived in 1823, over forty years after Kamehameha I had begun integrating individual Westerners within chiefly power structures. Arista has stressed how early missionary settlement was conditioned on the acceptance of native chiefs, who sought to extract power from missionary knowledge, particularly writing (Arista 2018). Great social and cultural upheaval went hand in hand with the decimation of the Native Hawaiian population due to newly introduced diseases. The population of the islands plummeted from at least 300,000 in 1778 to 57,985 by 1878 (MacLennan 2014: 22; Swanson 2020: 345–355).[3] By the 1830s, Native Hawaiian elites, like those across the Asia-Pacific, faced an increasingly thornier sovereign challenge: Western powers' claims to extraterritoriality, or the right to intercede in matters of justice relating to their citizens abroad (Kayaoğlu 2010). At the heart of many of these disputes was the gulf between customary Hawaiian land tenure—distributed through kingly favor, revocable, and governed by the reciprocal sharing of produce—and emerging liberal notions of fee-simple title, or the full and irrevocable ownership of land by a fixed proprietor (Chinen 1966: 5–6). While the establishment by the government

[3] Population estimates for Hawai'i at the moment of encounter with James Cook (1778) vary considerably. Island-wide censuses were not carried out until 1823, decades after considerable population decline had been perceived. Estimates by nineteenth-century observers, including Native Hawaiian historian David Malo, ranged from 150,000 to 400,000. The long-standing consensus figure of 300,000 was challenged in an upward-direction by David Stannard in 1989 (1 million +) and more recently by David Swanson (ca. 683,000), both of whom relied principally on speculative population models based on date of original settlement of the islands by Polynesian seafarers in the first millennium C.E.

of Kamehameha I of a formal court system based largely on Anglo-American common law achieved international recognition of Hawaiian state sovereignty by major Western powers, it opened new vulnerabilities in the position of native elites.

A twin, revolutionary set of laws passed by the Kingdom's legislature in 1850 sowed the seeds of plantation labor and land relations by bringing both in conformity to Anglo-American forms. These laws intensified the effects of the comprehensive land redistribution known as the Great Māhele, which in 1848 legally dissolved customary relations between *aliʻi* (high chiefs) and *makaʻāinana* (commoners) by introducing fee-simple title and abolishing customary labor obligations (Coman 1903: 3–4; Chinen 1966: 15–24). Native Hawaiians were thereafter legally, if not immediately socially, subject to concepts of property and labor understood by contemporaries as doubly foreign (Anglo-Saxon) and modern (liberal) (Morgan 1948: 16–31, 205–206). Native elites and Westerners debated the merits of paternalist and pro-market responses to growing colonial intrusion. Over the opposition of two future kings, who were abroad on a political mission to the United States, the legislature of the Kingdom embraced a pointedly pro-market approach. The Masters and Servants Act of 21 Jun 1850, based on British and American precedents, formalized apprenticeship and indentured labor contracts, including provisions for their enforcement at the courts of the Kingdom (Hay and Craven 2014). While the Masters and Servants Act would constitute the legal basis of indentured labor migration after 1865, it was initially implemented with control of Native Hawaiian labor in mind (Rosenthal 2018). Less than a month later, the Alien Land Ownership Act of 10 July 1850 permitted property acquisition by foreigners. While some Native elites' position in the short term was enhanced through capital generated by land sales, the long-term effect was the alienation of most quality agricultural land to foreign ownership.

A legal structure capable of enforcing planter power thus preceded the transition of the Hawaiian economy to sugar by over two decades. After the exhaustion of sandalwood—a royal monopoly serving the Chinese market—through unsustainable extraction in the 1820s, Hawaiian exports of agricultural goods were modest, except when Hawaiʻi was geographically well placed to service fleeting market gaps at the Pacific borderlands of U.S. expansion, namely, the California Gold Rush of 1848 and the U.S. Civil War of 1861–1865 (MacLennan 2014: 23–25, 30–31). It was during this first boom that two nascent merchant communities—German and Chinese—grew considerably at the port of Honolulu. Presented with the aspirational property and labor reforms of 1848–1850, many of these migrants, who originally arrived as merchants, tried their hand at agricultural cultivation (Glick 1980: 45–65).

Socially, nineteenth-century Chinese migration to Hawai'i was defined by marriage with Native Hawaiians. The limit of social power exerted by Christian missionaries is reflected by the toleration of polygamous unions between Chinese men and Native Hawaiian women up to the end of the century. The overwhelming majority of Chinese migrants were young men from Guangdong (the Pearl River delta region), which included the ports of Hong Kong, Macau, and Guangzhou (Canton). Many were previously married through arranged unions in China. Once in Hawai'i, some took Native Hawaiian second wives, who sometimes possessed substantial land holdings. In the early twentieth century, Romanzo Adams estimated that between 1,200 and 1,500 Chinese men had established Chinese-Hawaiian families before 1900 (Glick 1980: 162–163). The children raised in these families, like the mixed children of Native Hawaiian women and Westerner fathers, were seen as intercultural brokers whose loyalty usually defaulted to Native Hawaiians.

Economically, Chinese settlement in Hawai'i was characterized by business collaboration with Native Hawaiians and Westerners. The nascent sugar industry preceding 1850 typically combined Chinese processing techniques with Hawaiian labor (MacLennan 2014: 84). Kamehameha III and other governing elites oversaw sharecropping endeavors between Hawaiian cane growers and Chinese millers in the late 1830s, regulating their business through contracts made in the Hawaiian language (Kai 1974: 55–57; MacLennan 2014: 112–113). Early Western planters likewise made use of Chinese expertise at all levels of production (Char 1974: 3–7). Unlike Westerners, Chinese merchant planters tended not to pursue land acquisition through purchase. Instead, they usually farmed land obtained through marriage or rented land owned by Native Hawaiians. They tended to practice economical forms of production requiring little capital investment (Glick 1980: 47–48). Given the turbulent market for Hawaiian agriculture prior to 1874, this provided a competitive advantage.

As MacLennan has studied at length, a model of sugar production emerged in the 1850s and 1860s focused around five regional plantation centers, featuring the dominance of the sugar industry by production units combining both cultivation and milling and the capital-intensive deployment of industrialized processing (MacLennan 2014: 123–145). The former aspect ran contrary to the general tendency of the industry in other global locations, such as Australia, Java, Cuba, and Puerto Rico, toward decentralized cane raising, ultimately pushing independent Chinese and Native Hawaiian planters out of the market (MacLennan 2014: 124–125). Despite this long-term tendency, exceptions are discernible, particularly on the Island of Hawai'i, where Chinese actors featured centrally in the emergence of the plantation centers at Hilo and Kohala.

Enduring elements of Hawaiian plantation life, such as the use of Hawaiian-language terms to refer to overseer (*luna*) or the end of work (*pau hana*), reflect how plantation agriculture in the islands first emerged with a dominant workforce of Native Hawaiians, and in a cultural sphere in which outsiders were expected to interact with Native Hawaiian commoners in their own language. Early Chinese planters hewed to this model and often utilized Native Hawaiians as their main source of labor (Merry 2000: 171). Native Hawaiian status hierarchies were reproduced through differentiated hiring of *lunas* and workers. While Native Hawaiian workers typically labored on one-year contracts, most Chinese workers left the contract labor system at their earliest possibility to pursue urban employment or to bond themselves to rural Chinese headmen, in a status often classified by governmental agencies as "day laborers" (Glick 1980: 39–41; MacLennan 2014: 133). This pattern was facilitated by the long-standing Chinese presence in the island, which was already firmly established in the 1830s (Morgan 1948: 189–190). As late as 1873, however, Hawaiian labor predominated. Seventy-nine percent of the 3,786 plantation laborers registered by the government that year were Native Hawaiian (Beechert 1985: 60).

The convergence of a declining Native Hawaiian population and hopes for increased agricultural production presented planters, whether Western, Chinese, or Hawaiian, with a challenge: to achieve any change of scale in Hawaiian agriculture, foreign labor migration was essential. During most of the second half of the nineteenth century, political discourse in Hawai'i featured a distinctive form of populationism, where planter preference had to contend with an electorate dominated by Native Hawaiians after the enactment of universal manhood suffrage in 1851 (Fuchs 1961: 26). Planter debate about the comparative merits of different races of laborers—a defining component of politics in Western-led plantation colonies since the eighteenth century—was modulated in Hawai'i through a concern over which groups would best "amalgamate" with Native Hawaiians (Miller 2020: 260–277; Rosenthal 2018). Combining biopolitics and proto-eugenics, these discussions grew tenser during the 1870s, as the Chinese population multiplied amidst the backdrop of growing Sinophobia across the settler Pacific (McKeown 2008: 119–184). Despite much heated discussion, China remained the main source of migrant labor to Hawai'i until the enactment of Chinese exclusion legislation in the mid-1880s, as discussed below. Between 1852 and 1878, Chinese migrants constituted 92.3% of all those whose mobility was recorded by the Hawaiian Board of Immigration (Schmitt 1977: 197).

Non-Western Planters and the Sugar Boom After 1874

The Reciprocity Treaty of 1874 fulfilled the long-standing ambition among aspiring island planters to gain advantageous entry to the closest market for Hawaiian produce: the West Coast of the United States. Similar treaties had been proposed and negotiated in 1855 and 1867 but failed to pass the U.S. Senate, in part due to the vociferous opposition of sugar-producing Louisiana (La Croix and Grandy 1997: 165–166). What had changed was the U.S.'s growing geopolitical aspirations, namely the prospect of a mid-Pacific coaling station at Pearl Harbor (Morgan 1948: 210–212). Kalākaua refused an early demand for its cession, but assented to a stipulation that Hawai'i could not grant it to any other power (Osorio 2002a: 210–224). Certain U.S. statesmen shared fears of resident Americans that British influence could rise in the absence of a treaty. Reciprocity ultimately tied Hawai'i's fortunes so closely to the United States that a disentanglement by century's end became economically unfathomable. Kalākaua, under pressure from militant White Honolulu businessmen and lawyers, conceded to American demands for the port's cession when the treaty came up for renewal in 1887 (Osorio 2002a: 210–224; MacLennan 2014: 233).

The highly integrated sugar oligopoly of early twentieth-century Hawai'i, dominated by the so called Big Five producers, contrasted markedly with the disaggregated plantation economy prevailing up to the time of the overthrow of the Hawaiian monarchy. Even after Reciprocity, in 1881, an English observer claimed that planters in Hawai'i were unable to co-operate with one another to promote their mutual interests, as done in other countries (Nicholson 1881: 158). This was due to the plurality of the aspirational planter class. In the wake of Reciprocity, a diverse set of Chinese merchants, Native Hawaiian small farmers, Part-Hawaiian elites, British judges, and German businessmen sought to enrich themselves through sugar planting, besides the well-known cases of American missionary descendants and the German-American Sugar-Baron Claus Spreckels (Fig. 8.1).

The principal non-European sugar producer, both before and after 1874, was Chun Fong (Afong), the most successful Chinese capitalist of nineteenth-century Hawai'i (Glick 1980: 3). Arriving in Hawai'i in 1849, he quickly rose to a position of great wealth by servicing the plantation trade. Like many Chinese merchants, he took a Native Hawaiian second wife after establishing himself in Hawai'i, with his first wife, Lee Hong, remaining in China. An unusual characteristic of his Hawai'i wife, Julia Fayerweather, was that she was of mixed Euro-American and Hawaiian descent. Estranged from her White American relatives, she was raised in the family of her *ali'i* kin. She provided Afong with familial and social

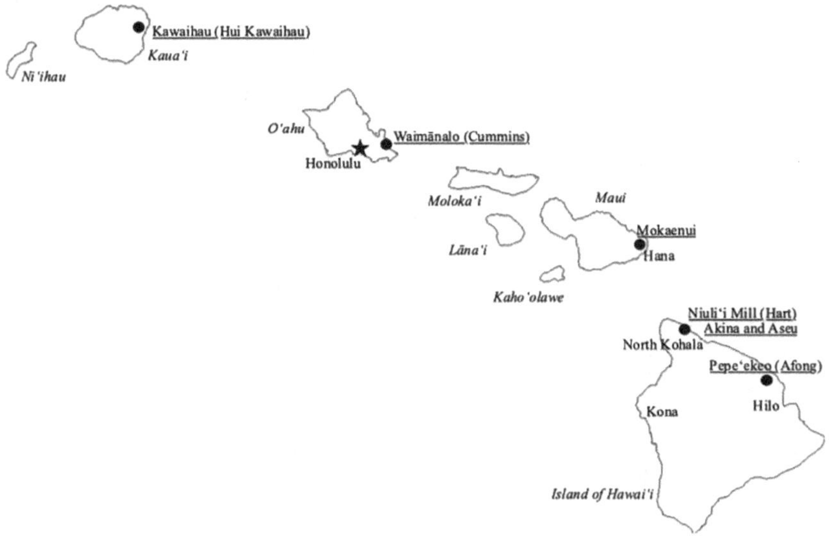

Fig. 8.1 Map of Hawai'i, with principal locations discussed indicated (Map by the author)

links to Hawaiian ruling elites. These ties helped Afong secure highly lucrative opium concessions in Hawai'i at various points in the 1860s and 1870s, which, like contexts across Southeast Asia, serviced the addiction of migrant Chinese laborers (Dye 1997: 93, 119–120). A vocal proponent of reciprocity for its potential to stimulate Hawaiian agriculture, he acquired a 1,500-acre plantation in the Hilo District of the Island of Hawai'i shortly before it took effect (Dye 1997: 126). In the 1880s, Pepe'ekeo plantation would become the most significant Chinese-owned plantation in the islands. During this period, it was overseen by his eldest son, Chan Lung (alias Alung). Alung's management served to connect Chinese-owned and-operated sugar production in Hawai'i with transnational projects by the Chinese imperial state to confront and adapt to Western encroachments of power. Alung graduated from Yale as part of the Chinese Educational Mission, a study-abroad program of Chinese elite youths sponsored by the Imperial government, and in 1874 served as a junior member of an Imperial commission into the abuse of Chinese indentured laborers in Cuba and Peru (Rimmer 2014: 344–364; Ng 2014: 39–62; Dye 1997: 107–109, 121, 144).

Through his ties by marriage to Julia Fayerweather, Afong was a close associate with the only Native Hawaiian owner of a major sugar plantation after 1880, John Adams Kuakini Cummins (1835–1913) at Waimānalo, on the Windward coast of O'ahu (Dye 1997: 152–154). Three years after Reciprocity in 1874, Cummins decided to try sugar cultivation on the immense holdings his English-born father had previously used for ranching, drawing on capital secured through the German-dominated merchant firm Hackfeld & Co. Raised as an *ali'i nui* (high chief) because of his mother's lineage, he had studied at the Royal School of Honolulu, also attended by all future Hawaiian monarchs after Kamehameha III. Like Afong, Cummins worked closely with Kalākaua to secure passage of the reciprocity treaty (Williams 1996: 160). Cummins has been praised for endorsing a type of paternalistic, royalist rule on his planation. The social building featured a reading room, a dance hall, Chinese and Japanese decorations on the ceiling, and prominent portraits of the Hawaiian royal family (Williams 1996: 154). Most higher-level positions, including those of *luna*, were staffed by Native Hawaiians, with a predominantly Chinese labor force. Unlike most other planters in Hawai'i at the time, Cummins did not practice penally enforced contract labor, instead employing individuals as day laborers. In 1887, 95.6% percent of the workforce was described as Chinese, with no workers subject to contract.[4] In 1892, the proportion of Japanese increased, but there were still no workers subject to contract. On the eve of the overthrow of the monarchy, it remained the third largest operation on the island of Oʻahu.[5]

As much as Afong was exceptional in his success, he reflected general social processes of interracial elite formation in the mid-nineteenth century that were imbricated with the transition to a sugar-based economy. An obscure case profiled by Sally Engle Merry is emblematic: George Washington Akao Hapai, district court judge for Hilo from 1878 until 1908. Son of a Chinese sugar master named Hapai (Lau Fai) and Iheu, an *aliʻi* from North Kohala, G.W. Hapai studied at an English-medium school run by Lucy Wetmore, wife of a missionary doctor. The school's student body in 1850 consisted of 17 children, 14 of whom had a Chinese father and a Hawaiian mother (Merry 2000: 175). He married Harriet Rebecca Kamakanoenoe Sniffen, a woman of mixed Hawaiian and *haole* ancestry, and his sisters married members of the *haole* Richardson family of planters as well as Native Hawaiian *aliʻi* (Merry 2000: 175). While Hapai was fluent in both English and Hawaiian, he wrote most of his cases down in Hawaiian (Merry 2000: 179). It is unclear if he could speak a Chinese language. Hapai rose to the court as replacement for two *haole* planters, S.L. Austin and D.H. Hitchcock, who had alternated as judges for the district in the 1870s. During his three decade-long tenure as district court judge, he enforced violations of labor contracts under Kingdom, Republic, and Territorial governments, and navigated the transition from predominantly Hawaiian to migrant labor.

Co-operative Production and the Case of Kohala, Island of Hawaiʻi

A neglected component of the story of sugar in Hawaiʻi were experiments with co-operative production, which constituted a primary means Chinese merchant planters other than Afong pursued sugar production after 1874. In this model, *haole*-owned sugar mills sourced their supply from small producers and practiced a form of profit sharing. An

[4] "Report of CN Spencer, Inspector General of Immigrants," *Pacific Commercial Advertiser*, 13 October 1887: 2.

[5] *Report of the President of the Bureau of Immigration to the Legislature of 1892* (Honolulu: Hawaiian Gazette, 1892): 10, 29.

overview was provided in 1883 in *Planter's Monthly*, the publication vehicle of the recently founded Planters' Labor and Supply Company of Honolulu. It began by reassuring its planter readership that co-operation was opposed to "communism, socialism, and agrarianism."[6] It instead "fully recognized private or individual ownership" and aimed merely at "joint operation, laboring together to one end [...] for mutual profit in the purchase and distribution of commodities for consumption, or in the borrowing and lending of capital among workmen."[7] While claiming that the approach was absent from the United States, the piece pointed to its success in France and ongoing implementation in Hawai'i. Native Hawaiian-led efforts included cane planting at Mokaenui, Maui; a co-operative store on O'ahu (the Kalihi and Moanalua Trading Association); the Hui Kawaihau on the island of Kaua'i, which featured the involvement of King Kalākaua; and the sugar plantation of John Adams Kuakini Cummins at Waimānalo, O'ahu (Dole 1929: 8–15). The example discussed as greatest length was however Niuli'i Mill at Kohala, Island of Hawai'i, which "due to the patient kindness of its chief manager and projector, Judge Hart," had successfully enabled a number of small Hawaiian and Chinese producers to emerge in the surrounding area. In that year, Niuli'i Mill was the largest sugar producer in North Kohala, processing 1,600 of a total 7,300 tons of cane (Hansen 1963: 6).

Reflecting Eurocentric blinders, the *Monthly* noted in passing that the co-operative model adopted at Charles F. Hart's mill closely resembled capital pooling practices amongst Chinese migrants in rice growing, business, and retail.[8] Hart was no doubt aware of this. He served as judge for the Hawai'i Island districts of Kona and later North Kohala from the 1860s until 1887, a period witnessing heavy Chinese merchant-planter activity in both areas (MacLennan 2014: 128–129). After the overthrow of the Hawaiian monarchy, editorials written for English-language newspapers reveal a pointedly anti-American stance and deep familiarity with the role of Chinese migration in British colonialism in Singapore and

6 "Co-Operation," *Planters Monthly* 1:11 (1883): 273–276.

7 "Co-Operation": 273–276.

8 "Co-Operation": 273–276.

Malaya.[9] While not challenging the basic rubrics of Western Civilization as the yardstick for progress, he took aim at annexationist ideologue William Alexander's claim that Chinese migrants were "unassimilable."[10] Contesting the rise of American imperialism and segregationist thinking, Hart remained wedded to mid-nineteenth-century social and business practices based on inter-ethnic collaboration and the local enrooting of migrant men—both Western and Chinese—through marriage to Native Hawaiian women.[11]

Complicating the common notion of American commercial ascendancy throughout Hawai'i after 1874, British interests prevailed in Kohala up to the end of the nineteenth century (MacLennan 2014: 128–129). H.S. Restarick, President of the Hawaiian Historical Society during the 1920s, recalled that "in the eighties of the last century, Kohala, Hawai'i, was sometimes called 'Little Britain' because many Britishers resided there, most of them engaged in planting cane."[12] Cane cultivation in Kohala during this time featured British collaboration with Chinese and Hawaiian small planters, within a policing and judicial apparatus staffed almost entirely by Native Hawaiians. British socialization centered at the Kohala Club, which emerged as a hotbed of royalist sentiment after the overthrow of the monarchy (Hall 1927: 13–14). In 1880, Hart co-owned Niuli'i Mill with Godfrey Rhodes, a prominent British merchant and member of government under Kalākaua, and used T.H. Davies & Co., the leading British firm in the islands, as his agent (MacLennan 2014: 72).[13] The region was transformed during the 1880s, becoming site to the first railway on the Island of Hawai'i in 1882.

With a distinctively complementary set of identity-crossing networks, Goo Tet Chin Akina and Luke Aseu were the most successful of the Chinese planters associated with Hart. Akina practiced the older model

[9] Charles F. Hart, Letter to the Editor, "British Rule at Singapore," *Pacific Commercial Advertiser*, 27 June 1895: 5. Also see: Charles F. Hart, Letter to the Editor, *Hawaiian Star*, 7 December 1896, p. 1; *Pacific Commercial Advertiser*, 14 January 1897: 3.

[10] *Pacific Commercial Advertiser*, 27 June 1895: 5.

[11] Hart's wife was an *ali'i* named Rebecca. "Ua haalele mai ikei ola ana o Mrs. Rebecca Hart," *Ka Nupepa Kuokoa*, 1 December 1916: 3.

[12] H.S. Restarick, "Elections in Old Hawaii; Kohala Club and Other Reminiscences," *Honolulu Star-Bulletin*, 28 April 1928: 6.

[13] Bowser, *The Hawaiian Kingdom, Statistical and Commercial Directory and Tourists' Guide, 1880–1881* (1880): 419.

of local integration and land accumulation via marriage with a Native Hawaiian woman, Harriet Maiaka Kalua Akina (1856–1893). Arriving in Kohala around 1870, he turned to cultivating rice and sugarcane in his wife's lands in the Waipio and Pololū valleys (Lothian 1983: 151). His later business partner Aseu by contrast was a fervent Christian convert who in 1882 married a Chinese woman educated at the Basel mission school in Guangdong.[14] While Akina and Harriet Maiaka Kalua were both Christians, they never held church leadership positions. Building on their prior collaboration as co-proprietors of general stores in North Kohala and Hilo, they established a joint sugar enterprise during the late 1870s. Akina was already referring to his "sugar plantation" at Kohala to a Chinese business partner in San Francisco in October 1880.[15] Expanding on the lands he had acquired through marriage, Akina would be formally granted a lease of 1,300 acres of crown lands on 7 January 1882 by King Kalākaua at Pololū, a valley at the eastern fringe of the district of North Kohala.[16] The size of this concession allowed Akina and Aseu to produce at a scale beyond those of other Chinese sugar planters in the region, such as Chulan Kee (Glick 1980: 57). By 1885, their plantation was the largest source of cane for Niuli'i Mill, cultivating a sixth of the 1,200 acres processed at Hart's mill.[17]

Aseu's Christian commitments lay on one side of an emerging fault line in the Chinese community in Hawai'i, which added religious difference to long-standing ethnic tensions between Punti and Hakka people carried over from Guangdong.[18] Chinese converts to Christianity in

[14] *Hawaiian Star*, 31 December 1904: 6.

[15] Hawai'i State Archives, Records of the Judiciary, First Circuit and Supreme Court Series, Law Case Files of the First Circuit Court, Series 6, Box 35, Case File 1392, *Ging Kee & Co. vs. L. Aseu* (1882).

[16] "E na Lede a me na Keonimana! O ka makani apaapaa o Kohala," *Ka Nupepa Kuokoa*, 22 May 1879: 3. *Annual Report of the Department of the Interior, Miscellaneous Reports, Part III, Governor of Hawai'i* (Washington: Government Printing Office, 1904): 219.

[17] *Saturday Press*, 4 April 1885: 3.

[18] The two primary Han Chinese ethnic subgroups amongst migrants to Hawai'i were the Punti, a Cantonese people who staked indigenous claims to Guangdong, and the Hakka, who were viewed as foreign settlers. Clan wars between the two groups from 1855 to 1868 occasioned around a million deaths, the destruction of thousands of villages, and the mass migration of Hakka people outside the region, including Guangxi province, Southeast Asia, and to a much smaller extent, Hawai'i.

Hawai'i were predominantly Hakka, though a large proportion of Hakka sought community instead through Taoist clan-based brotherhoods, or "secret societies," whose "evils" were decried by Frank Damon in 1882 (Glick 1980: 192).[19] In 1886, the third brotherhood to be established in the archipelago, the Tung Wo Kung Si (Company of Harmonious Peace), was founded in Kohala, with a membership mainly of non-Christian Hakka (Chong 1983: 157). Conversely, Aseu contributed to efforts to found a distinctly Christian Chinese community in North Kohala, working together with influential American Congregationalists, including Frank Damon in Honolulu and Elias Bond, proprietor of the Kohala Plantation, the first *haole*-run sugar plantation in the region (Glick 1980: 159–160; MacLennan 2014: 128–129; Beechert 1985: 71–72). In 1878, Elias Bond had pursued the labor migration of around 100 Hakka converts from Guangdong, working with contacts to the Basel mission, including Rev. Rudolph Lechler (Char 1983: 99–100). Landing alongside the migrants was Rev. Kong Tet Yin, who had trained at the Basel Mission in Guangdong and served previously as a missionary in Australia (Soong 1997: 151–178; Glick 1980: 87). Furthering these earlier efforts, Aseu and his wife played key parts in missionary efforts in North Kohala during the 1880s, including the establishment of St. Paul's Episcopal Church in 1882 and a Chinese Christian private school in 1887 (Kastens 1978: 64; Lutz 2009: 145; Opsahl 1969).

Evidence relating to worker conditions on Akina and Aseu's plantations is scarce, limited to snippets from oral histories, scattered incidents involving the police force and court system, and occasional interactions with the government board of immigration. Two disturbances from the 1880s reveal that Akina and Aseu worked closely with the local police force, staffed entirely by Native Hawaiians. In July 1881, angry workers caused Akina to flee the plantation after a *luna* punished them for eating seed cane.[20] Later, on 24 November 1886, a riot followed an attempted opium bust by four Native Hawaiian policemen. After two unnamed officers deserted, Constables I.K. Kaohi and Nakanelua fought off 30 Chinese workers armed with "hoes and other weapons."[21] Kaohi was left

[19] F.W. Damon, "Tours among the Chinese, No. 2: The Island of Kauai," *The Friend*, Chinese Supplement, 7 July 1882: 80.

[20] *Saturday Press*, 30 July 1881: 3.

[21] *Daily Bulletin*, 29 November 1886: 3.

in a critical state with a skull wound, while Nakanelua broke his right arm. The police responded with greater force the following day, with Deputy Sheriff Charles H. Pulaa venturing out with the entire North Kohala police force and arresting six people. Pulaa and his crew stayed for two days, equipped with "two repeating rifles and a supply of ammunition."[22]

Akina and Aseu, like other non-Western plantation owners, continued to exclusively use Chinese and Native Hawaiian laborers throughout the 1880s. After the initiation of subsidized contract labor migration from Portugal in 1878, the Kingdom began including queries about preferred races of laborers in island-wide biannual inspections of plantations. The putative purpose was to provide data about planter demand for the consideration of legislators and the Board of Immigration. Akina and Aseu, Cummins at Waimānalo, and Afong at Pepe'ekeo all expressed preference for Chinese and Native Hawaiians during the late 1880s.[23] The only Europeans employed by Afong at Pepe'ekeo were British engineers and boilers.[24] In this sense, non-Western sugar operations did not participate in the transient Europeanization of Hawai'i's labor force from 1878–1886, nor its Nipponization thereafter (Miller 2020).

Amidst the turbulent three-year period preceding the overthrow of Queen Lili'uokalani, all major Chinese sugar producers exited from the market. Political and economic factors were intertwined. A market crisis for Hawaiian sugar was set off in 1890 by the McKinley Tariff, which eradicated Hawai'i's competitive advantage by permitting all foreign sugar duty-free access to the United States. Hawaiian exports plummeted nearly 40%, from \$13 million in 1890 to \$8 million in 1892 (Schmitt 1977: 540). Further, incipient anti-Chinese legislation intensified in what has become known in the literature as the "Bayonet Constitution," promulgated in 1887 after a *haole*-led coup stripped King Kalākaua of most of his effective power. Suffrage thereafter was limited to a racially circumscribed "special electorate" of wealthy property owners of Hawaiian, European, or American descent, and business owners were prohibited from maintaining records in any non-European language besides Hawaiian (Dye

[22] *Daily Bulletin*, 29 November 1886: 3.

[23] "Report of CN Spencer, Inspector General of Immigrants," *Pacific Commercial Advertiser*, 13 October 1887: 2. *Hoike a ka Peresidena o ka Papa Hoopae Limahana i ka Ahaolelo Kau Kanawai o 1888* (Honolulu: Gazette Publishing Co., 1888): 16.

[24] *Planters Monthly* 7, no. 7 (July 1888): 308.

1997: 217–218; MacLennan 2014: 74–75). The logic of both policies was distinctly anti-Chinese. Sensing that the winds of prejudice were to intensify, Afong sold Pepe'ekeo and returned to China in 1890 following the suspicious death of his son Alung in August 1889, while sailing between the plantation and Honolulu (Dye 1997: 220). His long-time friend Cummins hosted a farewell party in Waimānalo on 16 October 1890, and Afong reached the passenger steamer that would bring him back to China, on which he had booked first-class accommodation, aboard Waimānalo plantation's transporter (Dye 1997: 221–222). Once under *haole* management, the labor profile at Pepe'ekeo changed markedly, with all managers and *lunas* registered as European or American, and most workers described as Japanese. In Kohala, Chulan Kee, Aseu and Akina's main Chinese competitor, sold their small sugar plantation to an American firm (Glick 1980: 57; Chinese in Hawaii 1913: 27; 1929: 2). Aseu and Akina went on to sell their sugar business in late 1892 to Hart, though Akina retained his rice land.[25] This followed a fascinating incident whereby Aseu attempted in 1890 to mimic the successful labor brokering of Afong as well as Chulan Kee between the 1860s and 1880s (Dye 1997: 140). Aseu's experience reveals much about the fraught relationship between Chinese sugar planters and Chinese indentured laborers on the eve of American ascendancy in Hawai'i, wherein different status positions in relation to plantation sovereignty yielded co-ethnic antagonism and inter-ethnic elite solidarity.

The Kohala Rebellion of 1891

In 1891, just a year before selling his and Akina's plantation, Luke Aseu took on the unenviable role as public face of the Kingdom of Hawai'i's Chinese restriction acts. Inspired by motives of profit and proselytization, Aseu was the first person to attempt a return to labor brokering activities following the enactment of exclusion in 1884. The effort proved a disaster, occasioning the biggest worker rebellion prior to the overthrow of the monarchy. This complicated case has yet to be studied in depth. Here, I recast the Kohala Rebellion as a trial of contested and overlapping claims to sovereignty. At the heart of the revolt was laborers' frustration with the restrictive nature of their contracts, which mandated

[25] *Hawaiian Gazette*, 3 January 1893: 4.

the retention of one-fourth of their earned wages to be used as a bond to incentivize their departure from Hawai'i at the end of their contracts. Also imbricated in the uprising were Aseu's practice as labor broker, questions of citizenship and extraterritorial representation, a contest for political supremacy between the Legislature and Supreme Court of the Kingdom of Hawai'i, and above all, the question of just whose interests the punitive exercise of state sovereignty in Hawai'i actually served.

Bowing to the vociferous anti-Chinese sentiment of certain resident *haole* in Hawai'i, Kalākaua begrudgingly assented to the passage of the Kingdom's rendition of Chinese exclusion acts in 1884 (Osorio 2002a: 209). Occurring during the apex of nativist rule during the ministry of American adventurer Walter Murray Gibson, the policy was a compromise to long-standing opponents of Chinese migration. Kalākaua, like most Hawaiian ruling elites before him, was positively disposed to Chinese migrants, pointing to their willingness to live together with Hawaiians and, indirectly, serving as a reliable source of state revenue through opium and gambling tax farms (Glick 1980: 146). Earlier efforts by the government to blunt the demographic impact of Chinese migration included the apportionment of over $1 million to subsidize the indentured migration of other laboring populations, namely Portuguese, Japanese, Germans, Norwegians, and South Sea Islanders from 1878 to 1893 (Miller 2020: 260–277). Hawai'i's initial exclusion laws in 1884 were comparatively light, banning only the new migration of laborers (Lydon 1974). Kalākaua and Gibson's compromises ultimately did not placate the violent cohort of *haole* residents in Hawai'i stridently opposed to Chinese migration, who were obsessed with Yellow Peril anxieties of demographic and commercial eclipse (Glick 1980: 202).

Following the coup in 1887 by the Honolulu Rifles, a White American settler-dominated militia, Gibson's ministry was ended, Kalākaua was deprived of most of his constitutional power, and the Legislative Assembly attempted to institute stricter forms of Chinese exclusion legislation. These efforts were however blunted by Hawai'i's legal system. After 1887, the Supreme Court repeatedly intervened to overrule legislative attempts to ban all Chinese migrants regardless of class (Beechert 1985: 92). A system emerged wherein all Chinese migrants were required to obtain entry visas issued under the purview of the Kingdom's recently created Chinese Bureau. The central institution in this system was Hawai'i's consulate in Hong Kong, which throughout the second half of the nineteenth century was headed by British representatives of the powerful firm

Jardine, Matheson, and Co. (Miller 2020: 268, 273). Originally based in the tea and opium trade, the firm was a key factor in the British colonization of Hong Kong, becoming one of the colony's largest landowners and employers (Bennett 2021: 34). Laws requiring official licensing of Chinese brotherhoods were also passed during this period, taking as their basis the Dangerous Societies Suppression Ordinance in British Malaya in 1869 (Glick 1980: 193).

Since Japanese contract labor migration to Hawai'i initiated at this same time, it was expected that planters would not suffer for new laborers. However, patterns of racialized preference remained. This was particularly true for Chinese planters, who preferred the employ of co-ethnic migrants and Native Hawaiians with whom they had previously forged personal relationships. In view of the expressed preference by several planters for additional Chinese laborers, the legislature in 1890 amended the Chinese exclusion laws of 1887. This permitted the resumption of Chinese labor migration with a punitive twist, under a regime of "special residence permits." Laborers emigrating with these permits were bound to a contract of indenture of maximum five years in duration, at the expiration of which they were required to return to China. One-fourth of monthly earnings up to $75 were to be retained and paid out upon the migrant's departure from Hawai'i. Breaking the provisions of the contracts was deemed a criminal offense, subject to immediate deportation to China at the migrant's own expense (Kuykendall 1979: 183–184). This policy was modeled after practice across the British colonial world, where it often occasioned great resent amongst laborers (Stanziani 2013: 1218–1251). Hawai'i would prove no exception.

In early 1891, Luke Aseu would be the first broker to attempt labor migration through the remits of the amendment of 1890.[26] Aseu fielded inquires across plantations in North Kohala for Chinese labor migrants, in addition to calculating the number of labor migrants needed for his and Akina's plantation. He submitted an application to the Board of Immigration for 350 laborers, receiving approval on 24 Dec 1890.[27] Drawing on his missionary connections, he also intended to include a proportion

[26] Besides a small exception, he would be the only one.

[27] *Report of the President of the Bureau of Immigration to the Legislature of 1892* (Honolulu: Hawaiian Gazette, 1892): 66.

of converts among his recruits, thus placating a plank of *haole* opposition to Chinese migration on religious grounds. During the virulent anti-Chinese politics prevailing after the Bayonet Constitution of 1887, Christian missionaries constituted a major plank of pro-Chinese support, heartened by examples of seemingly authentic converts like Aseu. In early 1891, Aseu ventured to Hong Kong and spent several months leading recruitment efforts.[28] An American ship, the *Pactolus*, was chartered in Hong Kong under Captain Beadle, and 436 migrants were engaged from the Guangdong region (290 men, 60 women, 86 children). The share of women and children among these migrants was higher than normally observed with Chinese migration to Hawai'i, reflecting a significant proportion of Christian converts among the cohort. One of the migrants, Ling Shee, in an interview with her son, recalled that she and her husband had agreed to the terms of indenture as "It was the only way out," given they held neither land nor work in their home village in Bao'an County, Guangdong (Zane and Soong 1983: 133–134). After sixty days in a barracoon in Macao with other Hakka migrants, they set sail in May 1891 for Hawai'i, arriving off the coast of Kohala on 15 July 1891.[29]

It is at this point in the story that the historical testimony, sourced through court records, immigration board reports, and newspaper articles, begins to diverge. Aseu had returned to Hawai'i aboard a different ship, awaiting arrival of the *Pactolus* in North Kohala together with a team of three set by the Board of Immigration.[30] Most importantly from a legal perspective, the migrants claimed to have only been informed about the withholding clause in their prospective contracts while docked off Māhukona, which served as the harbor for North Kohala. This violated the legal premise of indenture as a voluntary and consensual act of temporary bondage. As Aseu was overseeing the signing of 3-year labor contracts to individual plantations aboard the ship on 16 July 1891, a Native Hawaiian boatman brought a secret letter aboard the ship given to him by Pan Fong, *luna* at the American-owned Pūehuehu Plantation

[28] *Daily Bulletin*, 18 May 1891: 3.

[29] *Report of the President of the Bureau of Immigration to the Legislature of 1892* (Honolulu: Hawaiian Gazette, 1892): 32, 66–68.

[30] *Report of the President of the Bureau of Immigration to the Legislature of 1892* (Honolulu: Hawaiian Gazette, 1892): 68.

and, according to Aseu, headman at the local Taoist Chinese brotherhood, the Tung Wo Kung Si.[31] Undermining Aseu's authority, the letter promised those aboard that they were not required to accept his assignments or contract conditions, but rather could land freely and work as day laborers for better rates of pay and living conditions.[32] Indeed, in 1892, 83% of all Chinese male plantation workers were "day laborers," where, in the words of the Kingdom's Inspector General of Immigrants, they worked "under the control of Chinese contractors who work for a stipulated amount [...] In some instances this proves satisfactory labor, but as a rule [sic] is expensive."[33] Further, there appear to have been some migrants aboard who had previously worked in Hawai'i, and who, in view of their prior experience as day laborers, advised their fellow passengers against committing to Aseu's terms, presumably unaware of the new restrictive legislation.[34]

Aseu struggled for days to convince the migrants to sign the contracts. After about 48 hours of resistance, Sheriff Hitchcock and Deputy Sheriff Charles H. Pulaa came aboard the ship with five policemen on the morning of 17 July 1891.[35] To those who refused to sign their indenture, Aseu threatened transshipment back to China without food or water supplies, thus facing a miserable death.[36] Aseu also sent several Chinese men aboard who the passengers later alleged applied further pressure upon them to sign.[37] It took four days to convince all the migrants to

[31] *Report of the President of the Bureau of Immigration to the Legislature of 1892* (Honolulu: Hawaiian Gazette, 1892): 71.

[32] *Daily Bulletin*, 5 September 1891: 3.

[33] *Report of the President of the Bureau of Immigration to the Legislature of 1892* (Honolulu: Hawaiian Gazette, 1892): 39.

[34] Hawai'i State Archives, Records of the Judiciary, First Circuit and Supreme Court Series, Law Case Files of the First Circuit Court, Series 6, Box 80, Case File 3068, *L. Aseu vs. C. Alee* (1892), Testimony of W.S. Akana (12 February 1892).

[35] *Daily Bulletin*, 8 September 1891: 2.

[36] *Chong Chum vs. Kohala Sugar Co.*, in *Reports of Decisions Rendered by the Supreme Court of the Hawaiian Islands, Volume 8* (Honolulu: Hawaiian Gazette, 1893): 426.

[37] Hawai'i State Archives, Records of the Judiciary, First Circuit and Supreme Court Series, Law Case Files of the First Circuit Court, Series 6, Box 80, Case File 3068, *L. Aseu vs. C. Alee* (1892).

sign the contracts.[38] Migrants did not merely oppose the contractual provisions; they also "objected strongly" to having their thumb marks taken as part of the Immigration Board's new registry system for Chinese laborers.[39]

Scarcely a month later, on the evening of 23 August 1891, hundreds of the contracted workers assembled in front of Luke Aseu's plantation home at Pololū. Aseu had met earlier in the day with the workers but had not resolved their grievances to their satisfaction.[40] Returning in the afternoon from church, he locked himself and his family inside their home, beset with terror.[41] Aseu once again turned to Deputy Sheriff Pulaa.[42] Arriving around midnight, Deputy Sheriff Pulaa found a group of more than 20 Native Hawaiians guarding the dwelling, with Aseu's family sheltered in one room, lights-off, "in a terrible fright."[43] Pulaa decided to wait until the morning to investigate. In the meantime, the protesting workers took control of Aseu's house and installed themselves on the verandas. They were joined by additional protesters overnight, raising their total number to at least 200. Speaking through interpreters, who were longer-resident Chinese workers fluent in Hawaiian, Pulaa identified two core grievances. First, the workers objected to the practice of wage withholding, which they found unjust, and which they maintained Aseu had not explained prior to their migration. Second, they claimed to be "deceived" in having to labor at *haole*-led plantations. As Pulaa rendered it, "they don't want to work for the haoles but to go and work for Aseu,

[38] Hawai'i State Archives, Records of the Chinese Bureau, MFL 123, *SS Pactolus* Travel Bonds and Rejected Chinese Arrivals. *Report of the President of the Bureau of Immigration to the Legislature of 1892* (Honolulu: Hawaiian Gazette, 1892): 72.

[39] *Report of the President of the Bureau of Immigration to the Legislature of 1892* (Honolulu: Hawaiian Gazette, 1892): 73.

[40] *Daily Bulletin*, 5 September 1891: 3.

[41] Statement of Charles H. Pulaa, Deputy Sheriff of North Kohala, 14 September 1891, in *Report of the President of the Bureau of Immigration to the Legislature of 1892* (Honolulu: Hawaiian Gazette, 1892): 75.

[42] Statement of Charles H. Pulaa, Deputy Sheriff of North Kohala, 14 September 1891, in *Report of the President of the Bureau of Immigration to the Legislature of 1892* (Honolulu: Hawaiian Gazette, 1892): 75.

[43] Statement of Charles H. Pulaa, Deputy Sheriff of North Kohala, 14 September 1891, in *Report of the President of the Bureau of Immigration to the Legislature of 1892* (Honolulu: Hawaiian Gazette, 1892): 75.

they don't know the haoles."[44] Pulaa subsequently received rumors of a plan to murder Aseu aboard the newly established Kohala train line. Violence ensued, with shots fired from both Aseu's and Pulaa's pistols.[45] Overpowered, Pulaa agreed to arrest Aseu, but redirected the protesters' attention to the local courthouse.

Proceeding to Kapa'au that afternoon, the total number of Chinese protesting laborers grew to over 300.[46] Pulaa had instructed the aggrieved workers to formally state their complaints to the responsible judge for North Kohala. Their case was not formally heard, but they were met by representatives of their respective employers as well as the Deputy Sheriff of the Island of Hawai'i, George H. Williams. Aseu was not present. They were promised that the Chinese commercial agent would be called.[47] After being ordered back to their plantations, a riot broke out. A blanket order was "given to natives to arrest the Chinese." While some proceeded peacefully, others resisted. This was met with violent reprisals by the deputized officers, "a large number of plantation natives [...] armed with bullock whips" who entered several laborer houses, where they "demolished every window, strewed the premises inside and out with stones, seized every Chinaman they came across, and yanked forty or more by their queues to the leper cells," where they imprisoned them.[48] At least 55 protesters were taken to the local jail and imprisoned overnight, charged with "battery on Government officials." Convictions ultimately were not pursued and they were returned to their plantations the next day.[49]

[44] Statement of Charles H. Pulaa, Deputy Sheriff of North Kohala, 14 September 1891, in *Report of the President of the Bureau of Immigration to the Legislature of 1892* (Honolulu: Hawaiian Gazette, 1892): 76–77.

[45] *Daily Bulletin*, 27 August 1891: 3.

[46] Statement of Charles H. Pulaa, Deputy Sheriff of North Kohala, 14 September 1891, in *Report of the President of the Bureau of Immigration to the Legislature of 1892* (Honolulu: Hawaiian Gazette, 1892): 77.

[47] *Daily Bulletin*, 5 September 1891: 3.

[48] *Pacific Commercial Advertiser*, 7 September 1891: 2.

[49] Statement of Charles H. Pulaa, Deputy Sheriff of North Kohala, 14 September 1891, in *Report of the President of the Bureau of Immigration to the Legislature of 1892* (Honolulu: Hawaiian Gazette, 1892): 78.

The mood remained tense for another week, and news of the incident reached the Honolulu press in less than 48 hours.[50] The Sinophobic *Daily Bulletin* used it to highlight the imperative of "restrictions for the protection of Caucasian and Hawaiian labor against Mongolian aggression."[51] Aseu, feeling misrepresented, fled back to his home in Honolulu's Chinatown on 5 September 1891 to provide his rendering of events.[52] Robert Wallace, manager of Pūehuehu Plantation in Kohala, interceded to defend Pan Fong, his *luna*.[53] A little more than three weeks later, Aseu was served with a warrant for his arrest ordered by the Chinese commercial agent in Hawai'i, Ching King Chun Alee, who had succeeded Afong in this capacity in 1882 (Dye 1997: 187–188; Glick 1980: 204–225, 296).[54] As the case proceeded through the courts of the Kingdom, Afong's advice from 1881 to Chen Lanbin, the Chinese Ambassador to the United States, Peru, and Spain, proved prescient: "The interests of all the Judges of the Islands are in Sugar Plantations; consequently, there is no possibility of [any] case being decided impartially" (Glick 1980: 225).

Charged with providing consular protection to Chinese subjects in Hawai'i, Alee accepted the protecting workers' accusations that Aseu misrepresented contractual conditions and engaging in labor trafficking. To learn more about the complaints of the *Pactolus* passengers, Alee had sent an agent, W.S. Akana, to North Kohala to conduct interviews. Meeting with over 60 contracted workers between 12–16 September 1891, Akana heard the constant complaint that the contractual statements made by Aseu in China were "very different to those made here."[55] The interviews were conducted at the small Chinese sugar plantation owned by Chulan and Company, Akina and Aseu's primary Chinese rivals. Revealing somewhat compromised interests, Alee was a partial investor. Chulan and Company were aligned with American business factors in the region and were also active in the Honolulu commercial circuit. They had

[50] *Daily Bulletin*, 26 August 1891: 2.

[51] *Daily Bulletin*, 16 September 1891: 2.

[52] *Daily Bulletin*, 8 September 1891: 2.

[53] *Daily Bulletin*, 16 September 1891: 2.

[54] *Pacific Commercial Advertiser*, 30 September 1891. "Hopuia o L. Aseu", *Ka Nupepa Kuokoa*, 3 October 1891: 2.

[55] Hawai'i State Archives, Records of the Judiciary, First Circuit and Supreme Court Series, Law Case Files of the First Circuit Court, Series 6, Box 80, Case File 3068, *L. Aseu vs. C. Alee* (1892), Testimony of W.S. Akana (12 February 1892).

been active in Chinese labor migration during the 1870s. It is likely that Chulan and Company resented that the Board had had only granted Aseu permission to bring migrants within the provisions of the Amendment of 1890 (Dye 1997: 132; Glick 1980: 205). The resulting lawsuit thus cast two Chinese merchant actors against each other, drawing on competing sources of state sovereignty to buttress their case.

Aseu's labor brokering debacle was quickly politicized, with its sovereign implications brilliantly articulated in an English-language editorial in *Ka Leo o ka Lahui*, the organ for the opposition Hawaiian National Liberal Party, and the most widely circulating Hawaiian-language newspaper of the 1890s. It was likely written by John E. Bush (1842–1906), a Native Hawaiian politician who had attained prominence during the Gibson Ministry and a vocal opponent to the political order prevailing after the Bayonet Constitution. The piece argued that it was "Very natural" that the "Pactolus coolie slaves" should "have revolted and have entered a suit against "the A.B.C.F.M.'s Church protege, the Christian Aseu."[56] "Our satisfaction lies in the unearthing of the diabolical system practiced by the immigrant agents of the Sugar-Barons, and the part taken by a weak and imbecile [sic] government, representing the Hawaiian People. We have always claimed that the whole system is rotten." Queen Lili'uokalani's cabinet, in permitting "such a practice to be committed unrebuked, is likely to bring this teapot of a government into a typhoon of a tempest that will cause the wreck of sovereign and people." To blame were not "the people"—Native Hawaiian and other workingmen—who through "their representatives" during the 1880s—such as himself—had done "all they could to help the country in its labor difficulties." However, "the unscrupulous sugar planters and the capitalist [sic], assisted by a pair of sycophantic administrations [...] have gone to work, and, with its [sic] usual custom, tried to obtain cheap labor by trying to deceive those whom they have engaged." Both "the planter and capitalist are smiling under their sleeves, and are even hoping to see the country involved in trouble, and in that way obtain a change of government better suited to their aristocratic tastes."

The incidents at Kohala gave rise to two cases at the Supreme Court of the Kingdom of Hawai'i with divergent outcomes. The first, heard between 9–14 October 1891, was decided in Aseu's favor. The plaintiffs

[56] "Suit by Chinese Laborers," *Ka Leo o ka Lahui*, 30 September 1891: 4.

were four of the contract laborers, with Aseu as individual defendant. On 16 October 1891, Supreme Court Justice Sanford Dole ruled that Aseu's conduct, though perhaps "wicked," could not "be made the foundation of a criminal prosecution under our statute of gross cheats."[57] "It does not seem to me that mere silence in regard to the restrictive conditions of the laws here would amount to a false pretense."[58] Alee's protests were rejected on grounds that Hawai'i had no formal treaty with China.

Merely a fortnight later, the Court, in *Chong Chum v. Kohala Sugar*, ruled in favor of one of the contract laborers. Crucially, Aseu had been replaced as defendant by the sugar plantation owned by his friend Reverend Bond (Beechert 1985: 92–93).[59] Now featured merely as an agent of Kohala Sugar, Aseu was absolved of potential criminal prosecution and public opprobrium, with his leading role in the disastrous contract labor migration shunted to the margins of history. In the majority decision read 26 Feb 1892, Dole struck down the withholding clause of the Amendment of 1890 as unconstitutional. He argued that the contractual wage retention was tantamount to an individual waiving, by contract, the "inalienable rights recognized by the Constitution as belong to "all men" (Art. 1)" and tending thus to "class legislation."[60] The junior Supreme Court justice, Charles J. Judd, contended that at issue was not "the right to impose such conditions and restrictions upon the entry of aliens (with whose nation this Kingdom has no treaty to the contrary) into the territory of this Kingdom as the Legislature deems essential to the welfare, peace, and safety of the state." The Legislature was entitled to "impose conditions as to length of residence and character of the employment in which the immigrant can engage." Rather, the unconstitutionality of the law lay in the wage retention, which was used to pay the cost of the laborer's deportation to China.[61] Through this decision, Chong Chum was released from his contract and free to pursue the occupation of his choice. The Amendment of 1890 was overturned,

[57] *Daily Bulletin*, 16 October 1891: 3.

[58] *Daily Bulletin*, 16 October 1891: 3.

[59] *Chong Chum vs. Kohala Sugar Co.*, in *Reports of Decisions Rendered by the Supreme Court of the Hawaiian Islands, Volume 8* (Honolulu: Hawaiian Gazette, 1893): 425–433.

[60] *Chong Chum vs. Kohala Sugar Co.*, in *Reports of Decisions Rendered by the Supreme Court of the Hawaiian Islands, Volume 8* (Honolulu: Hawaiian Gazette, 1893): 429–430.

[61] *Chong Chum vs. Kohala Sugar Co.*, in *Reports of Decisions Rendered by the Supreme Court of the Hawaiian Islands, Volume 8* (Honolulu: Hawaiian Gazette, 1893): 432–433.

and no further migration from China occurred until the overthrow of the monarchy.

The implications of the Kohala Rebellion and the court decisions that followed are plural. Co-ethnic rivalry was mediated by inter-ethnic collaboration committed to the legal preservation and perpetuation of planter power. In serial fashion, a Chinese sugar planter turned labor broker was defended by his Native Hawaiian employees, a Native Hawaiian Sheriff, and a *haole* missionary Supreme Court judge against challenges posed by his co-ethnic contracted laborers and the acting representative of the Chinese government. At Pololū as well as the Kohala courthouse, state and planter control was maintained only through the informal deputization of Native Hawaiians as a disciplinary force against rebellious Chinese laborers, who challenged terms of labor they found unjust. A Chinese face to restriction law did not reduce the extent to which laborers found its provisions repugnant; indeed, it may have only inflamed it.

Conclusion

In highlighting the role of Chinese merchants turned sugar planters in the formation of a sugar plantation complex in Hawai‘i, this chapter indicates the need for further study of plantation colonialism as a transnational force in nineteenth-century Hawai‘i. That individual Chinese and Native Hawaiians owned and directed sugar plantations up to the 1890s is a story almost entirely lost from local memory and at the margins of the voluminous archive of plantation Hawai‘i, reflecting in part the persisting legacy of early twentieth-century scholarship to racialize the figure of the planter as much as that of the laborer (Coman 1903: 1–61; Adams 1925; Adams 1937). As this chapter has shown, countervailing traces remain recoverable through scattered testimony—including government statistics, court depositions, contemporary newspapers, planter periodicals, and early twentieth-century oral histories. The analysis of these materials highlights historical developments that figure only awkwardly within settler colonial frameworks, including the concept of “Asian settler colonialism” (Fujikane and Okamura 2008). The agency of Chinese actors invested in Hawai‘i’s emergent sugar plantation complex cannot be reduced to a fixed embrace of white settler cultural ascendency, particularly prior to the twentieth century. In their attempts to derive profit through plantation production, nineteenth-century Chinese sugar planters navigated collision points between competing state claims of sovereignty, including the Hawaiian government over the people and territory of Hawai'i, the Chinese Empire over its migrant subjects, and the British and U.S. governments over overseas migration in an age of imperial anti-trafficking regulation and Chinese exclusion legislation (McKeown 2008; Sharma 2020). Within Hawai'i, they likewise had to balance interlayered sources of power, including a government headed by an indigenous monarch, a firmly established court system of Anglo-American common law, a religious scene dominated by American Congregationalists, a plantation world increasingly directed by British, German, and American agents, and a financial and economic sector more and more tethered to San Francisco.

Amidst the political ascendancy of *haole* nativists during the 1880s and 1890s, the Chinese sugar planters studied in this chapter—Afong, Aseu, and Akina—faced an institutionalization of forms of exclusion that curtailed their scope for maneuver. Each reacted differently. Afong, the most successful of the three as an extractor of sweet fortune, voted with his feet shortly before the overthrow of the monarchy, retreating to Macau, where he pursued new business opportunities to greatly profitable effect. Conversely, Akina and Aseu remained in Hawai'i amidst the turbulent sovereign contests of the 1890s, obtaining sovereign privileges as old-timer migrants upon U.S. annexation in 1898. By dint of their prior naturalization as Hawaiian citizens, they were conferred U.S. citizenship, a status otherwise proscribed by the U.S. Congress from persons racialized as Chinese and of non-American birth since 1882. Akina, Aseu, and their descendants thereafter shaped life trajectories empowered by this fortuitous exceptionalism. Aseu returned with his wife, U.S. passports in hand, to China in the first decade of the twentieth century to advance renewed Christian missioning, this time in Shanghai; their children would settle on either coast of the U.S. mainland.[62] Surviving his wife Harriet Maiaka Kalua by almost two decades, Akina remained on his plantation in Kohala until his death in 1913. Their eldest son, Ernest A.K. Akina (1884–1956), born during the sugar days in Pololū, worked in office positions for *haole*-run sugar plantations across the Island of Hawai'i as a young man, before winning election as a Republican Senator for Kohala in the Territorial Legislature during the 1920s and the 1930s (Rosa 2014: 49; Tamura 1994: 135). Attaining a public prominence unthinkable for his father during the late nineteenth century, he continued his father's

[62] *The Hawaiian Star*, 31 December 1904: 6.

interactions with sugar production, now under a regime of American sovereignty. He was most assuredly not the type of future politician envisioned by many *haole* nativists of the 1880s and 1890s in their reveries of a future White Hawai'i. In the Territorial Hawai'i of the early twentieth century, what Ernest provided was a genealogical link between older projects of sovereignty and the continued economic primacy of sugar, embodying the continued localization of foreign sources of power integral to the configuration of sovereignty in modern Hawai'i.

Further study of plantation Hawai'i should recover additional experiences in the spectrum of actor responses to the intersection of state and carceral power, ethnic and national identity, religious conviction, and sugar-derived capital prior to American overrule. As suggested by the plurality of social and religious commitments held by the three Chinese sugar planters studied in this chapter, national and ethnic identities need not be the inevitable basis of this analysis. While racially based affinities certainly grew in importance during this period, they were not the only prism through which actors in fin-de-siècle Hawai'i co-operated with one another, as evidenced by Afong's alliance with John Adam Cummins, Akina and Aseu's partnership with the anti-American judge turned sugar mill operator Charles F. Hart, or Aseu's close ties with Congregationalist actors. The conjoined factors of exploitation and collaboration in the emergent Hawaiian sugar economy had long-term effects on mediating the character of plantations, colonialism, and sovereignty in the islands, cutting across the temporality which Josep A. Fradera has termed imperial transition (2018). During the 1870s and 1880s, there were hopes by many actors that a multicultural planter class might emerge in Hawai'i. There was also increasing criticism by an interracial coalition of observers of the fundamentally exploitative character of plantation colonialism in the islands. It was only during the 1890s, when militant *haole* nativists found common cause with a rising faction of U.S. imperialists, that the stakes of sovereignty in the islands became fundamentally reframed. The monarchy's embrace of plantation colonialism no longer served to invite inter-ethnic elite collaboration and to occasion political fissures among Native Hawaiian nationalist radicals like Robert William Wilcox and John E. Bush. Instead, support for the restoration of the monarchy came to represent the rejection of *haole* nativists' assertion of cultural and political primacy over Native Hawaiians. The violent seizing of state power by white settler nativists in the late 1880s acted to racialize Hawaiian politics in a newly acute way; contemporary scholars might exert more caution in uncritically reproducing the frameworks and assumptions that followed in their wake.

References

Primary

Bowser, G. 1880. *The Hawaiian Kingdom, Statistical and Commercial Directory and Tourists' Guide, 1880–1881.* Honolulu and San Francisco: George Bowser and Co.

Chinese in Hawaii. 1913. *A Resume of the Social, Industrial, and Economic Progress of the Chinese in the Hawaiian Islands.* Honolulu: Honolulu Star-Bulletin Press.

Chinese of Hawaii. 1929. Honolulu: Overseas Chinese Penman's Club.

Dole, C.S. 1929. "The Hui Kawaihau." *Papers of the Hawaiian Historical Society* 16: 8–15.

Kingdom of Hawai'i, Board of Immigration. 1888. *Hoike a ka Peresidena o ka Papa Hoopae Limahana i ka Ahaolelo Kau Kanawai o 1888.* Honolulu: Gazette Publishing Co.

Kingdom of Hawai'i, Bureau of Immigration. 1892. *Report of the President of the Bureau of Immigration to the Legislature of 1892.* Honolulu: Hawaiian Gazette.

Kingdom of Hawai'i, Supreme Court. 1893. *Reports of Decisions Rendered by the Supreme Court of the Hawaiian Islands, Volume 8.* Honolulu: Hawaiian Gazette.

Nicholson, H.W. 1881. *From Sword to Share: Or a Fortune in Five Years in Hawaii.* London: W.H. Allen.

United States of America, Department of the Interior. 1904. *Annual Report of the Department of the Interior, Miscellaneous Reports, Part III, Governor of Hawai'i.* Washington: Government Printing Office.

Secondary

Adams, R. 1925. *The Peoples of Hawaii: A Statistical Study.* Honolulu: Institute of Pacific Relations.

Adams, R. 1937. *Interracial Marriage in Hawaii: A Study of the Mutually Conditional Process of Acculturation and Amalgamation.* New York: MacMillan.

Anderson, W. 2021. "Review Essay of Possessing Polynesians: The Science of Settler Colonial Whiteness in Hawai'i and Oceania by Maile Arvin and Staking Claim: Settler Colonialism and Racialization in Hawai'i by Judy Rohrer." *The Journal of Pacific History* 56 (3): 365–367.

Arista, N. 2018. *The Kingdom and the Republic: Sovereign Hawaiʻi and the Early United States*. Philadelphia: University of Pennsylvania Press.
Arvin, M. 2019. *Possessing Polynesians: The Science of Settler Colonial Whiteness in Hawaiʻi and Oceania*. Durham: Duke University Press.
Bastos, C. 2018. "Portuguese in the Cane: The Racialization of Labour in Hawaiian Plantations." In *Changing Societies: Legacies and Challenges, Vol. 1, Ambiguous Inclusions: Inside Out, Inside In*, ed. S. Aboim, P. Granjo, and A. Ramos, 65–96. Lisbon: Imprensa de Ciências Sociais.
Beechert, E.D. 1985. *Working in Hawaiʻi: A Labor History*. Honolulu: University of Hawaiʻi Press.
Bennett, M.M. 2021. "Whose Offshore? Rescaling Hong Kong from Asia's World City to China's Greater Bay Area." *Area Development and Policy* 6 (1): 31–41.
Bonk, W.J. 1974. *Chinese Fraternal Society Sites: Island of Hawaii*. Hilo: University of Hawaiʻi at Hilo Press.
Boyce, W.D. 1914. *United States Colonies and Dependencies, Illustrated*. Chicago and New York: Rand McNally.
Carpenter, F.G. 1925. *Throughout the Philippines and Hawaii*. New York: Doubleday.
Chang, D.A. 2016. *The World and All the Things Upon It: Native Hawaiian Geographies of Exploration*. Minneapolis: University of Minnesota Press.
Char, T.-Y. 1983. "Chinese Christians Among Early Immigrants Here." In *Chinese Historic Sites and Pioneer Families of the Island of Hawaii*, ed. T.-Y. Char and W.J. Char, 99–100. Honolulu: University of Hawaiʻi Press.
Char, W.-J. 1974. "Chinese Merchant-Adventurers and Sugar Masters in Hawaii: 1802–1852: General Background." *Hawaiian Journal of History* 8: 3–10.
Chinen, J.J. 1966. *The Great Mahele: Hawaii's Land Division of 1848*. Honolulu: University of Hawaiʻi Press.
Chong, D.D.L. 1983. "Tong Wo Society Turns Back Clock 70 Years." In *Chinese Historic Sites and Pioneer Families of the Island of Hawaii*, ed. T.-Y. Char and W.J. Char, 157–160. Honolulu: University of Hawaiʻi Press.
Coffman, T. 1998/2016. *Nation Within: The History of the American Occupation of Hawaiʻi*. Durham: Duke University Press.
Coman, K. 1903. "The History of Contract Labor in the Hawaiian Islands." *Publications of the American Economic Association* 4 (3rd Series): 1–61.
Cook, K. 2018. *Return to Kahiki: Native Hawaiians in Oceania*. Cambridge: Cambridge University Press.
Cushing, R.L. 1985. "The Beginnings of Sugar Production in Hawaiʻi." *Hawaiian Journal of History* 19: 17–34.
Dusinberre, M. 2019. "The Changing Face of Labour between Hawaiʻi, Japan and Colonial Taiwan." *Historische Anthropologie* 27 (3): 336–360.

Dye, B. 1997. *Merchant Prince of the Sandalwood Mountains: Afong and the Chinese in Hawai'i*. Honolulu: University of Hawai'i Press.

Fradera, J.M. 2018. *The Imperial Nation: Citizens and Subjects in the British, French, Spanish, and American Empires*. Princeton: Princeton University Press.

Fuchs, L.H. 1961. *Hawai'i Pono: A Social History*. San Diego: HBJ.

Fujikane, C., and J.Y. Okamura. 2008. *Asian Settler Colonialism: From Local Governance to Habits of Everday Life in Hawai'i*. Honolulu: University of Hawai'i Press.

Glick, C.E. 1980. *Sojourners and Settlers: Chinese Migrants in Hawai'i*. Honolulu: University Press of Hawai'i.

Hall, J. 1927. *Kohala's "Gay Nineties," or the Log of a Luna*. Honolulu: Honolulu Advertiser.

Hansen, A.R. 1963. *Kohala Sugar Company, 1863–1963*. Honolulu: n.p.

Hay, D., and P. Craven, eds. 2014. *Masters, Servants, and Magistrates in Britain and the Empire, 1562–1955*. Chapel Hill: University of North Carolina Press.

Immerwahr, D. 2019. *How to Hide an Empire: A History of the Greater United States*. New York: Frrar, Straus and Giroux.

Kai, P. 1974. "Chinese Settlers in the Village of Hilo Before 1825." *Hawaiian Journal of History* 8: 39–75.

Kastens, D.A. 1978. "Nineteenth-Century Chinese Christian Missions in Hawaii." *Hawaiian Journal of History* 12: 61–67.

Kayaoğlu, T. 2010. *Legal Imperialism: Sovereignty and Extraterritoriality in Japan, the Ottoman Empire, and China*. Cambridge: Cambridge University Press.

Kuykendall, R. 1979. *The Hawaiian Kingdom, Vol. 3: The Kalakaua Dynasty, 1874–1893*. Honolulu: University of Hawai'i Press.

La Croix, S.J., and C. Grandy. 1997. "The Political Instability of Reciprocal Trade and the Overthrow of the Hawaiian Kingdom." *Journal of Economic History* 57 (1): 161–189.

Lees, L.H. 2017. *Planting Empire, Cultivating Subjects: British Malaya, 1786–1941*. Cambridge: Cambridge University Press.

Lothian, C.R.N. 1983. "Pololu Rice." In *Chinese Historic Sites and Pioneer Families of the Island of Hawaii*, ed. T.-Y. Char and W.J. Char, 151–153. Honolulu: University of Hawai'i Press.

Love, E.T. 2005. *Race over Empire: Racism & U.S. Imperialism, 1865–1900*. Chapel Hill: UNC Press.

Lozano, H.K. 2021. *California and Hawai'i Bound: U. S. Settler Colonialism and the Pacific West, 1848–1959*. Lincoln: University of Nebraska Press.

Lutz, J.G. 2009. "Chinese Emigrants, Indentured Workers, and Christianity in the West Indies, British Guiana, and Hawaii." *Caribbean Studies* 37 (2): 133–154.

Lydon, E.C. 1974. *The Anti-Chinese Movement in the Hawaiian Kingdom, 1852–1886*. San Francisco: R&E Research Associates.
MacLennan, C.A. 1997. "Hawai'i Turns to Sugar: The Rise of Plantation Centers, 1860–1880." *Hawaiian Journal of History* 31: 97–125.
MacLennan, C.A. 2014. *Sovereign Sugar: Industry and Environment in Hawai'i*. Honolulu: University of Hawai'i Press.
McKeown, A. 2001. *Chinese Migrant Networks and Cultural Change: Peru, Chicago, and Hawaii 1900–1936*. Chicago: University of Chicago Press.
McKeown, A. 2008. *Melancholy Order: Asian Migration and the Globalization of Borders*. New York: Columbia University Press.
Merry, S.E. 2000. *Colonizing Hawai'i: The Cultural Power of Law*. Princeton: Princeton University Press.
Miller, N.B. 2020. "Trading Sovereignty and Labour: The Consular Network of Nineteenth-Century Hawai'i." *International History Review* 42 (2): 260–277.
Mintz, S.W. 1986. *Sweetness and Power: The Place of Sugar in Modern History*. New York: Penguin.
Morgan, T. 1948. *Hawaii: A Century of Economic Change, 1778–1876*. Cambridge: Harvard University Press.
Ng, R. 2014. "The Chinese Commission to Cuba (1874): Reexamining International Relations in the Nineteenth Century from a Transcultural Perspective." *Journal of Transcultural Studies* 5 (2): 39–62.
Okihiro, G.Y. 2008. *Island World: A History of Hawai'i and the United States*. Berkeley: University of California Press.
Opsahl, C. 1969. "From a Mustard Seed-Chinese Christians Commemorate 90th Anniversary in the Islands." *Honolulu Star-Bulletin and Advertiser*, May 25.
Osorio, J.K. 2002. *Dismembering Lāhui: A History of the Hawaiian Nation to 1887*. Honolulu: University of Hawai'i Press.
Rimmer, S. 2014. "Chinese Abolitionism: The Chinese Educational Mission in Connecticut, Cuba, and Peru." *Journal of Global History* 11 (3): 344–364.
Rohrer, J. 2016. *Staking Claim: Settler Colonialism and Racialization in Hawai'i*. Tucson: University of Arizona Press.
Rosa, J.P. 2014. *Local Story: The Massie-Kahahawai Case and the Culture of History*. Honolulu: University of Hawai'i Press.
Rosenthal, G.S. 2018. *Beyond Hawai'i: Native Labor in the Pacific World*. Oakland: University of California Press.
Sasaki, C.T. 2022. *Pacific Confluence: Fighting over the Nation in 19th Century*. Oakland: University of California Press.
Schmitt, R.C. 1977. *Historical Statistics of Hawaii*. Honolulu: University of Hawai'i Press.
Schulz, J. 2020. *Hawaiian by Birth: Missionary Children, Bicultural Identity, and U.S. Colonialism in the Pacific*. Lincoln: University of Nebraska Press.

Sharma, N. 2020. *Home Rule: National Sovereignty and the Separation of Natives and Migrants*. Durham, NC: Duke University Press.

Shoemaker, N. 2015. "A Typology of Colonialism." *Perspectives on History: The Newsmagazine of the American Historical Association* 53 (7): 29–30.

Silva, N.K. 2004. *Aloha Betrayed: Native Hawaiian Resistance to American Colonialism*. Honolulu: University of Hawai'i Press.

Soong, I.T. 1997. "Sun Yat-sen's Christian Schooling in Hawai'i." *Hawaiian Journal of History* 31: 151–178.

Stanziani, A. 2013. "Local Bondage in Global Economies: Servants, Wage Earners, and Indentured Migrants in Nineteenth-Century France, Great Britain, and the Mascarene Islands." *Modern Asian Studies* 47 (4): 1218–1251.

Swanson, D. 2020. "The Number of Native Hawaiians and Part-Hawaiians in Hawai'i, 1778 to 1900: Demographic Estimates by Age." In *Population Change and Public Policy*, ed. B. Jivetti and M.N. Hoque, 345–355. Cham: Springer.

Takaki, R. 1983. *Pau Hana: Plantation and Labor in Hawai'i*. Honolulu: University of Hawai'i Press.

Tamura, E. 1994. *Americanization, Acculturation, and Ethnic Identity: The Nisei Generation in Hawaii*. Urbana: University of Illinois Press.

Vandercook, J.W. 1939. *King Cane: The Story of Sugar in Hawaii*. New York: Harper & Bros.

Williams, R.M. 1996. "John Adam Cummins: Prince of Entertainers." *Hawaiian Journal of History* 30: 153–168.

Zane, K.F., and I. T. Soong. 1983. "Duck Soup and Salt Fish: A Kohala Story." In *Chinese Historic Sites and Pioneer Families of the Island of Hawaii*, ed. T.-Y. Char and W.J. Char, 133–138. Honolulu: University of Hawai'i Press.

PART III

West Africa and Its Diasporas: Excavating Forgotten Pasts and Haunted Presents

CHAPTER 9

The Materialities of Danish Plantation Agriculture at Dodowa, Ghana: An Archaeological Perspective

David Akwasi Mensah Abrampah

Introduction

Historical and archaeological research has shown that between 1788 and 1850 the Danes established plantations along the foothills of the Akuapem Mountains and the estuary of the Volta River, in south-eastern Gold Coast/Ghana, and used the labour of enslaved Africans to cultivate them. The establishment of these plantations was meant to replace the trans-Atlantic slave trade, in which Denmark had been deeply involved. In 1803, Denmark and Norway abolished the trans-Atlantic slave trade; however, this did not end slavery itself, either in Africa or in the Americas, and neither did it end the trade itself, which continued illegally. The Danish colonists' intensification of cash-crop agriculture on the

D. Akwasi Mensah Abrampah (✉)
Department of Archaeology and Heritage Studies, University of Ghana, Accra, Ghana
e-mail: damensahabrampah@ug.edu.gh

C. Le Petitcorps et al. (eds.), *Global Plantations in the Modern World*, Cambridge Imperial and Post-Colonial Studies,
https://doi.org/10.1007/978-3-031-08537-6_9

West-African coast provoked an upsurge in the local slave trade: as the plantation economy solidified in Ghana, increasing numbers of enslaved people were engaged to labour in these plantations. This chapter mainly examines the historical and archaeological materials associated with one of the earliest Danish plantations (Frederikssted plantation) established in 1794 in Dodowa by a Danish slave trader, Jens Neilsen Flindt. Flindt was a former assistant of Paul Erdman Isert (Danish surgeon and botanist in the Gold Coast) and was in charge of Frederiksnopel plantation after the death of Isert. Data for the present research were obtained mainly through archaeological excavations in and around the eighteenth-century plantation house at Frederikssted. The excavation team comprised two lecturers, three postgraduate students, three undergraduate students, one technician (all from the Department of Archaeology and Heritage studies, University of Ghana) and two local research assistants from Dodowa town. While previous archaeological works were concerned mainly with the Danish period, this study explores how material culture can illuminate the period and the aftermath of Frederikssted plantation.

Danish Plantation System in Ghana

Denmark was one of the several European nations that came to the Gold Coast/Ghana and scrambled for West-African material and human resources, carting away both forest products and enslaved Africans. It is clear that the primary interest of the Danes in West Africa was trade, which the monarchy had intended to use revivify the national treasury in the face of a looming economic downturn at the time. Even though the Danes established a long-term contact with the Gold Coast from 1658 (when they negotiated for Swedish forts in cape Coast), initial trade contacts with Africa began close to the mid-seventeenth century. This is because the first successful voyage by a Danish ship to Guinea is reported to have taken place around 1649 (Norregard 1966: 12). However, the Danes established a more sustained contact in 1671, when Denmark founded the West India and Guinea Company—tasked with the responsibilities of trading and colonisation, and to administer the Gold Coast colony on behalf of the Danish crown. The Danes stayed in the Gold Coast continuously until 1850, when they sold all their possessions to the British and left.

In fact, the practical idea of establishing plantations in the Gold Coast was mooted by Paul Erdman Isert. He was a Danish botanist and was also appointed as chief surgeon to the Danish establishments on the Guinea Coast between 1783 and 1786 (Norregard 1966: 173). In 1788 Paul Isert, representing the Danish Crown, established the first Danish plantation in the hilltop hinterland of Akropong. However, this plantation collapsed after the sudden death of Isert on February 21, 1789. The then assistant to Isert, Jens Neilsen Flindt did not continue with the Frederiksnopel plantation (because of its inaccessible location), he instead came down to Dodowa and established his own plantation and named it Frederikssted (meaning Frederick's settlement) after the Danish Crown Prince Frederick, regent to the Danish monarchy. In 1792, Flindt was granted a sum from the fund *"Ad usus publicos"* for new plantations, and he started laying out Frederikssted. The crops cultivated on this plantation were mainly cotton and maize. There were fifteen slaves, ten men and five women who had been brought from the then defunct Frederiksnopel plantation at Akropong. They were among the 19 slaves who were poorly fed and lived under pitiable conditions at Frederiksnopel. The remaining four were said to be aged and infirm and therefore could not work (Hernæs 2013: 177). There are no accounts as to what happened to these "left over" slaves when Frederiksnopel was closed in 1793. They most probably got integrated into the Akropong community. The 15 slaves who were re-engaged in servitude on Frederikssted plantation provided the labour that cultivated the plantation. Flindt erected three buildings, a grain store and a barn as well as a larger dwelling, 70 × 18 feet, on this plantation. Flindt was recalled to Denmark in 1795, a time that he should have been greatly involved in the plantation work and as a result, about 4,730 cotton plants that should have been planted were discarded. Frederikssted thus fell into disrepair and was abandoned in 1802 which was to be reoccupied afterwards.

This study is a significant sequel to earlier archaeological works in Ghana—such as Bredwa—Mensah's (1996; 2002) on Frederiksgave plantation and Bibiase plantation, respectively, Boachie-Ansah's (2007) on Brockman plantation and DeCorse's (1993) on Daccubie plantation, all located in the Akuapem Mountains area in Ghana. These earlier studies, particularly Bredwa-Mensah (2002; 1996), seek to examine both planter and slave living sites and have used the material and non-material culture to analyse social class on the plantations. The studies have also addressed the ways in which the archaeological study of slavery illuminates plantations' social structures, and their works have influenced and will continue to influence research directions of all subsequent plantation archaeology in Ghana.

The Frederikssted plantation settlement site was inhabited by diverse residents, including the Danish plantation owners, enslaved African fieldworkers and free local elite inhabitants in later periods. The material culture excavated at Frederikssted is very significant, representing different occupational episodes by different categories of people. The various excavations, the finds and their distribution within the excavated units indicate that the plantation landscape is a place of settlement, abandonment and reoccupation. The material remains belong to varied epochs, spanning the eighteenth to the twentieth centuries. They do not represent continuous, seamless occupation but show resettlement at the site. This suggests that the assertion made by earlier scholars (Jeppssen 1966) that Frederikssted plantation abruptly fell into disuse in 1802 cannot be accepted uncritically.

The Study Area

Dodowa is located in, and is the capital of, Shai Osudoku District in the Greater Accra Region of Ghana, covering an area of about 5 km^2. About 30 km northeast of the city of Accra, the town is situated at the foothills of the Akuapem Mountains that are characterised by sandstone rock formations and rise about 450 m above sea level (Kesse 1985: 10). Dodowa lies between two contrasting local reliefs to the south and to the north. The immediate southern stretch falls within the Accra plains characterised by low-lying landscape and coastal savannah ecology, while the northern section is circumscribed by the undulating topography of the Akuapem ranges with a relatively lusher tropical rainforest vegetation, which supports agricultural activities. Frederikssted plantation is located about a kilometre (from Lower Dodowa) north of the forest ecosystem of the Dodowa valley, where the historic footpath and the Dodowa River can also be found.

The majority of the people of Dodowa today belong to the Shai/Sɛ ethnolinguistic group, part of the larger Dangme language family. The history of this group in Dodowa dates back to 1892, when the British colonial authorities accused them of non-payment of tax, and thus expelled them from their original settlement area in Shai Hills about 20 km from present day Dodowa (Anquandah 1993: 646). They eventually formed communities in their various farm lands located on the

Accra plains, which stretch north of the base of the Akuapem Mountains, including Dodowa. Before the arrival of Shai people in 1892, the Dodowa settlement was limited to Lower Dodowa where some Akuapem people were already living. The population of the new arrivals thus overwhelmed the original Akuapem inhabitants. However, much of the contemporary area of Lower Dodowa is occupied by people of Akuapem descent. This suggests that between 1802 and 1892 Dodowa was intensively populated by Akuapem people, some of whom established merchandise outlets in Lower Dodowa. Some reoccupied the Frederikssted plantation site during the post-plantation period after.

Lower Dodowa is a suburb of Dodowa town, which became the central business district of the town during the nineteenth century. The uniqueness of Lower Dodowa stems from contact situations, settlement patterns, exchange (trade) and the desire to control it (Cusick 1998: 4). The encounter between different groups of Europeans and Africans, who settled there for trading purposes, began with the establishment of Frederikssted plantation in 1794. The Lower Dodowa suburb is still characterised by numerous extant European/colonial merchandise outlets, comprising buildings used by Danish, British and Swiss companies such as Joseph Wulff, United Africa Company (UAC) and Union Trading Company (UTC). All these trading entities jostled for the opportunities that abounded in Dodowa. They sold European produced alcoholic beverages, different types of clothing, European ceramics, canned food items and other personal and household items and exported palm oil, indigo, pepper and other spices from Dodowa to Europe. These companies were private enterprises that characterised the mercantilist era during the twentieth century and did not have defined public sovereign roles from the British colonial administration. They however, improved manufacturing in Europe since the Gold Coast served as a big market centre for so many kinds of goods manufactured in Europe.

Frederikssted Plantation

The ruins of the plantation are located in the broad valley of the Dodowa River. The site map (Fig. 9.1) has been sectioned into two: *Locus 1* and *Locus 2* to indicate the nature of the plantation landscape. The archaeological data discussed here were excavated at the main plantation building area (*Locus 1*) and in the area immediately north (*Locus 2*).

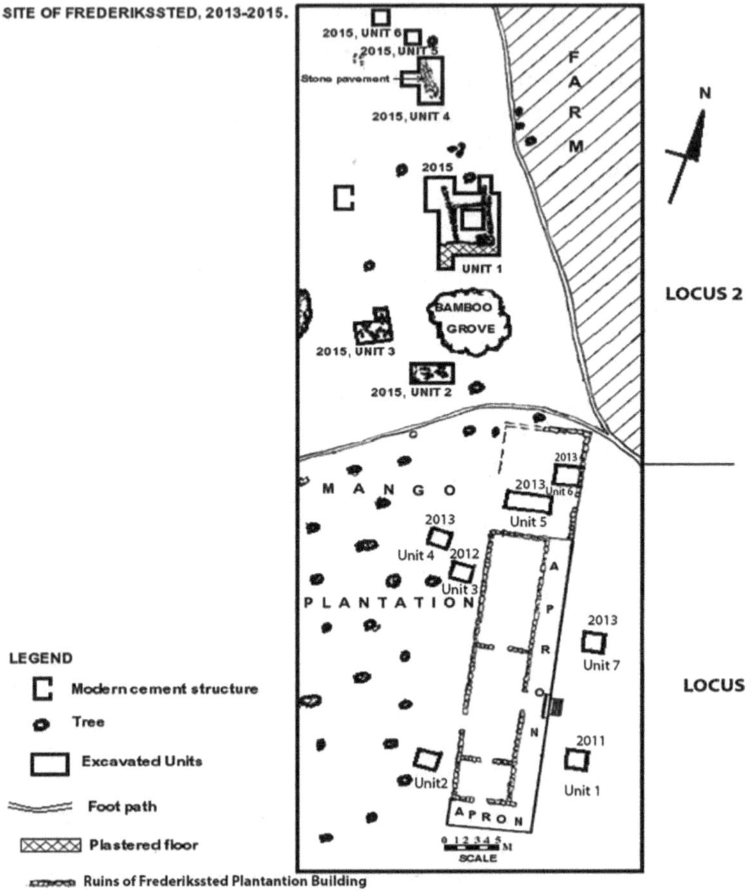

Fig. 9.1 Site map of Frederikssted plantation excavations (Map by the author)

The plantation house, built with cut stone from the nearby mountain, is believed to have been inhabited by the European planters from 1794 to 1802 and later (from 1803 onwards) by a local elite family from Dodowa who used the site mainly as residence and trading centre. Reoccupation or later occupation emerges unequivocally from evidence at Locus 2, where nineteenth-century house trash was found located under a building foundation. The stone foundation, which was laid on top of the refuse dump (belonging to the nineteenth century, post-plantation era), is believed to have been built and occupied at a later stage in the mid-twentieth century. Evidence of education- and entertainment-related artefacts, kitchenware materials, foreign beads and evidence of sewing throw more light on the elite lifestyle of the occupants during the post-plantation period. Since these nineteenth- and twentieth-century artefacts were found in the same archaeological context as the local materials, it seems likely that elite indigenous people reoccupied Frederikssted during the post-plantation period.

The main Frederikssted plantation building comprises a sequence of single rooms, laid out south to north. The building is accessed by a stair-step (about 1 m high) that connects an apron (verandah) at the eastern (main) entrance. The apron was made of red earth with the upper surface paved with stone slabs. However, the entire upper surface has deteriorated, exposing only the red earth on most parts of the surface. The apron, which is about 1 m high, stretches about 40 m south-north. Archaeological investigations have revealed four rooms of varied sizes. This was the residence of the planters or the plantation managers and was also the centre of authority and supervision during the plantation period.

Plantations have been described as the planter's "power domain" (Orser 1990: 115; Mills 1956). The plantation's main house usually has more physical and ideological visibility than other structures associated with the plantation, for it was a place where the planters exercised their power and authority. Furthermore, such buildings are often the best preserved and thus often become the first sites to be studied by archaeologists.

The archaeological excavations at Frederikssted plantation and the resultant items of material culture reveal that Frederikssted plantation site lived on (but mainly as residence) after it was shut by the Danes in 1802 (Figs. 9.2, 9.3, and 9.4).

Material Artefacts

Frederikssted's material culture can be categorised according to items' utilitarian functions (see Table 9.1). In each category, some of the materials are dated to be contemporaneous with the period the plantation existed, while others date after the plantation phase. Table 9.1 shows the materials and the dates they existed on the plantation landscape. Table 9.2 on the other hand shows materials according to their utilitarian functions.

Fig. 9.2 Ruins of Frederikssted plantation house

Fig. 9.3 Excavations under way in Unit 1, Locus 2

Drinking and Eating at the Plantation

The eating and drinking category of materials comprises tableware and other receptacles used for food, alcoholic and non-alcoholic beverages.

Fig. 9.4 Students from Ghanata Senior High School in Dodowa touring the site

Barrel Hoops

The metal hoops have been identified as bands that were used to fasten wooden barrels/casks used to transport both liquid and non-liquid items from Europe to Dodowa, most likely alcoholic products, especially wine and whisky (Fig. 9.5).

Royal Copenhagen Porcelain

Royal Copenhagen is a pottery company founded in Denmark in 1772 and still in operation today. The company produced relatively expensive porcelain materials comprising smooth bodied ceramics as well as the popular "fluted lace" patterns in Denmark from ca. 1770 (Armstrong et al. 2013: 282–283; Eschen 2003: 158). The artefact illustrated below is a smooth bodied Royal Copenhagen porcelain teacup exhibiting a blue, hand-decorated floral pattern on the entire body, and a single circular blue line at both the inner and the outer surface of the rim.

Table 9.1 Materials and the period they existed at the Frederikssted plantation site

Materials dated to the plantation period (1794–1802)	*Materials dated to the post-plantation period (between 1803 and late 20thC)*
Wines glasses	Whieldonware vase
Tumblers	Sponge stamped bowls
Decanter	Willow pattern on pearlware
Barrel hoops	Ceramic dolls
Royal Copenhagen teacup	Malkin Bell semi-porcelain
Stoneware bottles	Telegraph wire insulators
Windmill decorated porcelain	Mineral water bottles
Brick hammer	Sauce and pickle bottles/stoppers
Splitting maul (axe)	Square bottles: gin/schnapps
Cast-heart padlock and keys	Beer/Wine/champagne bottles
Machete blade	Victorian poison bottles
Strap hinges	Perfume bottles
	Local beads/moulds
	European/imported beads
	European/imported smoking pipes
	Locally made smoking pipes
	Steel nails and washers
	Bedknobs
	Steel reeds of Harmonica
	Bed shaft of Singer sewing machine
	Blade of scissors
	Canned fish/beef keys
	Cutlery
	Pig jaw
	Local pottery
	Cowry shells
	Slate and slate pencils

Stoneware

In the latter part of the seventeenth century the English started producing a salt-glazed type of stoneware, which was traded in Europe and other British colonies including Gold Coast/Ghana. Stoneware bottles had been important utilitarian vessels from the beginning of the fifteenth century up to the twentieth century. Between the eighteenth and the twentieth centuries stoneware vessels were used to bottle beer, spirits/liquor, non-alcoholic beverages as well as a host of liquid-based products.

Table 9.2 Material inventory according to their utilitarian functions

Item category	*Components*
Drinking and eating	Wine glasses and tumblers, Fragments of wine decanter, Barrel hoops, Royal Copenhagen porcelain Stoneware bottle, Windmill decorated plates, Creamware deep bowl vessels, Willow decorated plate, Malkin Bell semi-porcelain Saucer, Corned beef and sardine tin keys, Mineral water bottles, sauce bottles, case bottles and cylindrical bottles
Building implements	Screws and washers, nails, strap hinges, Brick hammer, splitting maul and Cast-heart Padlock and keys
Farm tools	Machete blade
Ornamentation	Whieldonware vase, Bedknobs and Perfume bottles
Entertainment	Ceramic doll, Steel reeds of Harmonica
Rural telephony	Telegraph wire insulators
Domestic/industrial chemicals	Victorian poison bottles
Cottage industry	Local beads, Local bead moulds, European/imported beads, sewing machine part and scissors blade
Smoking at the plantation site	European/imported smoking pipes and local smoking pipes
Household tools/items	Cutlery and local pottery materials
Currency	Cowrie shells
Faunal remains	Jaw of a pig
Accounting/bookkeeping/writing	Slate pencil and a piece of slate

Windmill Decorations

Windmills have played crucial roles in the manufacture of pottery products in Europe, most especially England, Holland and France. During the eighteenth century, most European pottery manufacturers either owned or shared the use of water or windmill for grinding materials. Holland therefore became famous for windmills, decorating its pottery with native Dutch scenes with windmills, fishing boats or sailing ships, hunting scenes, landscapes and seascapes. Even though windmills were widespread across Europe and America, they were readily identified with the Netherlands as part of Dutch pottery decorations. However, the English adopted printed decorations featuring windmills in the twentieth century, circa the 1930s (Denker 1996: 66). The sherds illustrated exhibit typical Dutch

Fig. 9.5 Drinking and Eating (1: Wine glasses (a) and tumblers (b); 2: Fragments of wine decanter; 3: Barrel hoops exposed in-situ in Unit 1, Locus 2)

scenes of coastal windmill landscapes, comprising windmills, water, a sailing boat, a chalet printed beneath scroll foliate cartouche in brown and blue. The windmill-decorated pottery is likely part of the material culture brought and used by the Danish planters during the latter part of the eighteenth century (Fig. 9.6).

Fig. 9.6 Drinking and Eating (1: Royal Copenhagen porcelain (teacup); 2: Fragments of Stoneware bottles; 3: Windmill printed pattern on creamwares; 4: Creamware deep bowl vessels)

Willow Pattern

Willow motifs are found on blue-on-white ceramic materials, with depictions of landscapes that were imported into England from China in the eighteenth century. The Oriental pattern "Willow" first appeared hand painted on eighteenth-century Chinese porcelain, then on English porcelain and earthenware after 1813. Quite a number of potteries in the United Kingdom still produce the "Willow" pattern, a good case in point being Churchill (Snodin 2006: 84; Snodin and Howard 1996: 203). The fragment (half) of a pearlware soup plate recovered from Frederiksted has a decoration of a typical "Willow pattern" printed in underglaze blue, used by the local elites in the nineteenth century as it dates to the post-plantation period.

Semi-Porcelain

The trans-Atlantic trade led to the introduction of variants of porcelain materials to West Africa. Semi-porcelain is refined earthenware usually fired at around 1,200 degrees Celsius. This makes semi-porcelain products appear heavier and thicker than their porcelain counterpart. Semi-porcelain materials were part of the archaeological inventory recovered from the Frederikssted excavations at Dodowa. One of the semi-porcelain fragments, which is the base of a plain saucer, has a scallop rim and floral scroll at the border area with a single black circular line below the border. It has a design on the circular panel, a crown above a circle containing in the centre an eight-pointed star surrounded by writing: *Royal Semi Porcelain. Fred Malkin Belle Works Burslem* written on the border. *England* and inscription likely to be serial number *3375DSsi* are also written outside the circle.

Corned Beef and Sardine Keys

Other metal artefacts related to food items, recovered from Frederikssted's main house (Locus 1) and Locus 2, have been identified as key-winds that were used to open canned fish and corned beef. The sardine keys that were recovered numbered 21, while the corned beef keys were 10 in number. These types of keys were used to open cans by rolling or tearing away a metal strip from the top or side of the can. The use of these cans and the associated keys began in the nineteenth century, around 1866, and continues to the present (Waechter 2007), indicating they were used by the nineteenth-century local occupants of the plantation house (Fig. 9.7).

Mineral Water Bottles and Tumbler

These are short necked cylindrical bottles with flat bottoms, capped with ceramic closures and fastened with copper wire to flip open. The whole bottle (A) and one closure (C) bear the inscription Wasser Steinike and Weinlig. The other closure (D) bears the inscription J. FERD. NAGEL SÖHNE HAMBURG, all of which are of German origin. Since the manufacturing of these bottles dates to the 1860s (Vermeulen 2013: 1), they are likely to have been used by the post-plantation local occupants.

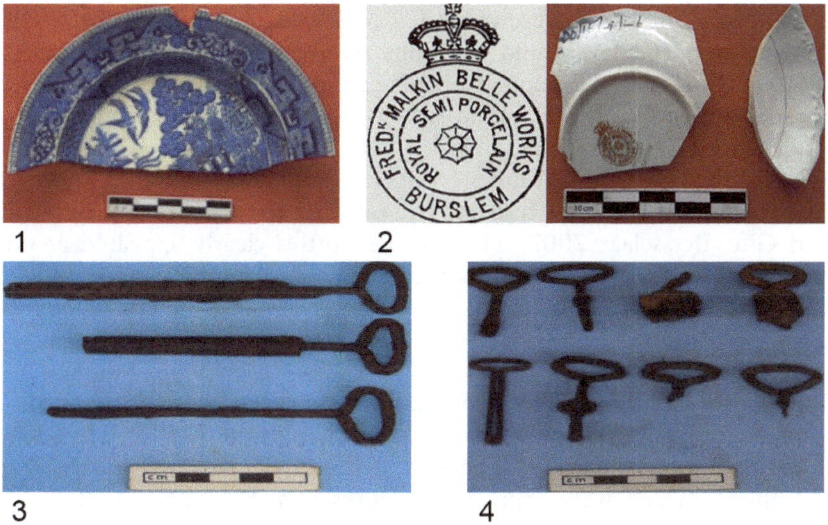

Fig. 9.7 Drinking and Eating (1: Willow pattern on pearlware; 2: Malkin Bell semi-porcelain saucer; 3: Sardine tin keys; 4: Corned beef keys)

Food-Related Bottles (Sauce and Pickle Bottles)

In most archaeological sites in Ghana, these types of bottles usually make up one of the largest categories of the food-related bottles. They are characterised by a wide mouth and square or cylindrical shape. Apart from their unique shape and design, sauce and pickle bottles also are almost exclusively aqua colour. The fragments recovered from Frederikssted comprise largemouth aqua colour cylindrical bottles with round bases, and most likely capped with round glass stoppers as some of the glass stoppers were found in association with them (food bottles).

Square Bottles (Gin/Schnapps Bottles)

Square bottles containing gin or schnapps are generally known as case bottles. Bottles of this nature are known to have been produced in Europe at least as early as the mid-seventeenth century and appeared in the New World around the 1750s and 1770s (Jones and Smith 1985: 15). Dutch gin and schnapps were imported into West Africa by a variety of makers (with a variety of marks) throughout the nineteenth century. It is known that Dutch spirit breweries J. J MELCHERS and J.H HENKES exported gin (Genever) and schnapps to West Africa beginning circa 1850, and some of the popular brands at the time were the Stork brand of gin (Genever) and Star brand which represented Aromatic Schnapps produced by J.H HENKES while J. J MELCHERS exported its popular Elephant brand of gin (Vander-Sloot 1975; Bersselaar 2007: 112). In West Africa, these were, respectively, referred to as Elephant Gin and Bird Gin (Bersselaar 2007: 112). These bottles clearly appeared at the Frederikssted plantation site during the nineteenth century.

Cylindrical Bottles (Wine/champagne)

These bottle neck fragments display a flattened string collar below the lip, a characteristic feature of both wine and champagne bottles. However, champagne bottles have exaggerated patterns. These have square ring lip applied, which were capped with corks. They are believed to have originated from England and are still in production today. These Champagne shaped bottles were produced circa 1810 and used to bottle cider, champagne or beer (Fig. 9.8).

Building Implements

Screws with Washers

Some of the screws were excavated with washers attached to them while others had no washers. The washers, which are always attached to screws, are able to distribute pressure of the screw evenly over the surface of the material it fastens so that the surface is protected from damaging. The presence of machine-made iron nails manufactured in the early 1830s clearly shows that the roofing of Frederikssted's main building had gone through modification and alteration. The nineteenth century, post-plantation African occupants most likely re-roofed the entire house, perhaps due to deterioration, at which time inexpensive, machine-cut iron nails were readily available.

Strap Hinges

The two strap hinges obtained from Frederikssted excavations were tough hand-forged iron with each having a single knuckle. Their surfaces are

Fig. 9.8 Drinking and Eating (1: Mineral water bottles and a tumbler; 2: Sauce bottles (A&D) and pickle bottle (B) while (C) is a stopper; 3: Club sauce stopper; 4: Square bottles: gin/schnapps; 5: Wine/champagne bottles)

corroded but about four nail/screw holes can still be observed on them. They have a single dummy arrow head, probably the appropriate hinge type for the Frederikssted plantation doors, gates or shutters which were used to secure rooms stocked with farm produce and other.

The Brick Hammer

The brick hammer is also known as Stoneman's hammer and generally has a sharp, square and flat face which is shaped like a chisel blade. The other end is square and flat and is used as a hammer. The brick hammer was designed for the purpose of hammering nails and for splitting blocks or bricks. The sharp chisel-end can be used to chip off edges or small pieces of stone or to cut bricks and concrete. It delivers light blows or sharp blows to give sudden impact on the brick and can either split the brick/block into different parts or remove chips for fine-trimming to shape. The brick hammer retrieved from Frederikssted excavations shows the chisel-like shank, square slot in which a wooden handle was hafted and the hammer end which was modified into an ovoid shape due to impact from usage.

Axe (Splitting Maul)

The type of axe recovered from Frederikssted excavations has been identified as splitting maul, also known as sledge axe. This splitting maul may have been used to split firewood for domestic purposes or it was used to process lumber at the sawmill which was attached to the Frederikssted plantation described by Jeppesen (1966).

Padlock and Keys

A single padlock among the metal assemblage recovered from Locus 1 has been identified as a cast-heart iron padlock, which was made in the nineteenth century. The cast heart is a nineteenth-century version of Scandinavian style locks which were originally invented by Christopher Polhem in the early eighteenth century (Pulford 2007: 224). The *Cast-heart* padlock became the preferred padlock for industrial businesses as well as railroads mainly because of the drop mechanism which protected the lock from moisture and dust. It also functioned well in both tropical, hot climate and temperate icy environments. Two iron keys that were found in association with the *cast-heart iron* padlock, however, have diverging features. They have different bows but similar blades, and one slightly longer than the other. This may suggest they belong to two different padlocks (Fig. 9.9).

Farming Tools

Machete Blade

The farm implements recovered comprised two fragments of machete blades, one complete machete blade and two fragments of a hoe blade. The two machete pieces and the two hoe blade fragments were retrieved

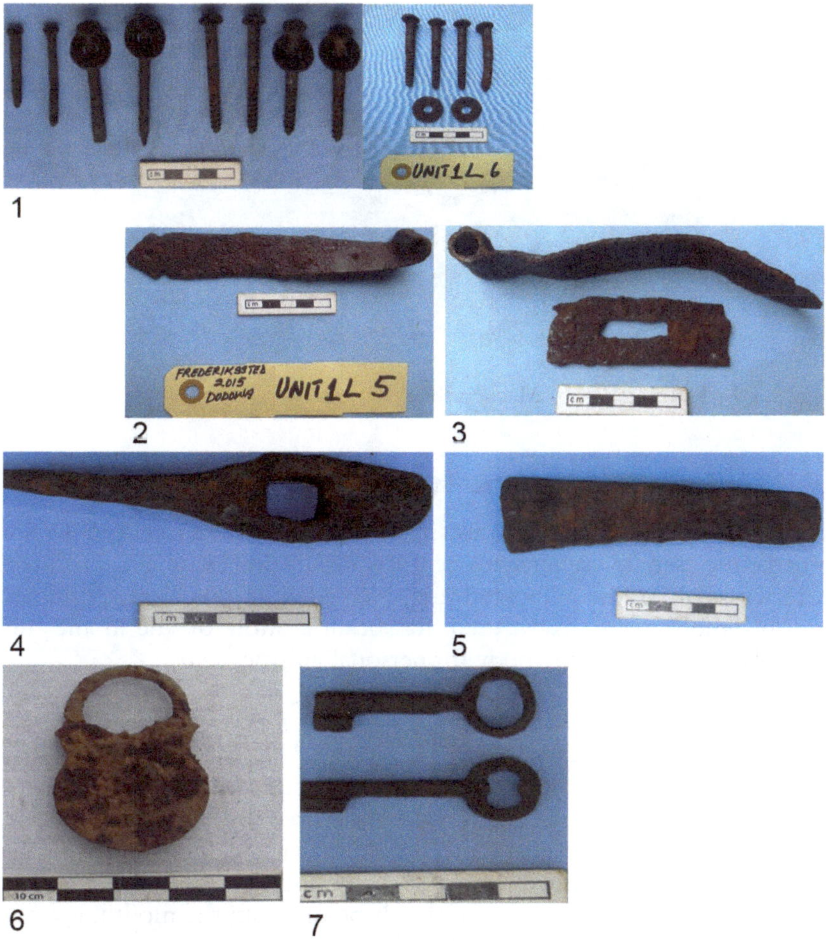

Fig. 9.9 Building Implements (1: Machine-cut iron nails and screws with washers; 2: Strap hinge; 3: strap hinge and lock plate; 4: Brick hammer; 5: Splitting maul; 6: Cast-heart Padlock; 7: Keys)

from Locus 1, and they were likely part of the implements used to clear the bush to make way for farming and also to clear weeds that grew among crops. These implements were fashioned by local iron smelters and smiths as local blacksmiths still forge them today (Fig. 9.10).

Fig. 9.10 Farming Tools: Machete blade

Ornamentation

The archaeological data has also provided information related to the ornaments used by nineteenth-century local families at Frederiksted. Artefacts such as the Whieldonware, pierced-edge porcelain, perfumes, and bedknobs were likely used for beautification of the home and symbolic purposes on the body for personal enhancement.

Whieldonware

Whieldonware (sometimes referred to as *Tortoise shell ware*) is a generic name for cream-coloured pottery, characterised by a variegated polychrome surface as a result of metal oxides that are fired under a clear lead glaze. The fragments, decorated with clouded glazes in green and splotches of brown, composed of the shape of a fish; the mouth, eye and scales of the fish can be identified in them.

Pierced-Edge Porcelain

The Frederiksted excavations yielded 15 fragments of a pierced white porcelain plate. It has a fluted rim and the border is repeatedly pierced in such a way that the holes formed a pattern indicative of the shape of the fern plant. Pierced wares were in most cases not utilitarian vessels; they were, rather, symbolic (commemorative) objects. Their inner surfaces were flat and unperforated and usually bore motifs in floral, avian and human designs. In most colonial sites, the human motif could be that of a reigning monarch, which in the case of Frederikssted could be the Danish monarch but could as well be the British monarch. As the inner surface and other marks of the manufacturers were not found it is difficult to tell which part of Europe the pierced porcelain originated from.

Perfume Bottles

Since perfumes are always expensive to produce, bottle manufacturers have also made special bottles to contain them. The nineteenth century, in particular, was a period of experimentation by bottle manufacturers. Numerous bottle-makers made decorative bottles in various shapes, sizes and colours. Bottles identified as perfume bottles from Frederikssted are of three types. Figure 28A is a cylindrical bottle with collar, but the mouth area is broken. It bears the inscription *Parfumerie*, probably of French origin. *B* is a cathedral-shaped aqua-marine coloured glass with two rings along its elongated neck.

Bedknobs

Other domestic items showing ornamentation also recovered have been described as bedknobs. These hollow metal objects are oval in shape with short necks, probably an indication of ostentation. They have been observed as decorating materials used mainly for aesthetic functions since the nineteenth and the twentieth centuries (Fig. 9.11).

Entertainment

Two types of materials that are believed to have been associated with entertainment have been identified as ceramic doll and reeds of harmonica (musical instrument).

Ceramic Dolls

Two parts of ceramic dolls, identified as China dolls, were recovered from Frederikssted excavations at Dodowa. The doll parts (which could be from the same doll) comprise shoulder-head and one leg. They are believed to have been made during the mid-nineteenth century (Pearson 1992: 11, 41, 179). The shoulder-head is characterised by plain white

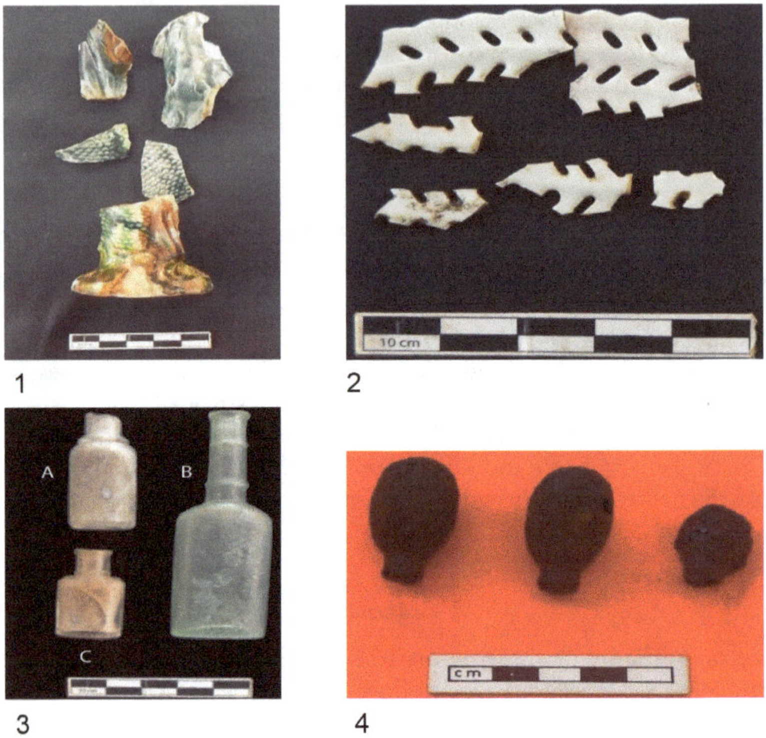

Fig. 9.11 Ornamentation (1: Whieldonware vase; 2: Pierced-edge porcelain; 3: Perfume bottles; 4: Bedknobs)

colour, black hair, pinkish cheeks and sloping shoulders. It shows evidence of attachment (glued) to cloth or leather torso. The leg shows a single circular groove above the calf with the foot/boot painted in brown colour. In spite of the fact that there is no documentary or historical evidence suggesting the presence of children on the Frederiksted plantation, dolls recovered from many archaeological site have been attributed to the presence of children (Davies and Ellis 2005: 15; Prichett and Pastron 1983: 326). If this is tenable, then the recovery of dolls indicates that child rearing was an important aspect of the nineteenth-century post-plantation life at Frederiksted plantation site by the local occupants.

The examination of the material culture and life experiences of childhood on Frederikssted plantation landscape shows how the occupants on the plantation understood the concept of childhood as a distinctive phase of life different from adulthood. As materials made for the enjoyment and socialisation of children, dolls/toys also have an essential role to play in understanding childhood and family life, as well as site-dating and exchange patterns (Davies and Ellis 2005: 15).

Harmonica

The harmonica is said to have been invented in Germany in the early nineteenth century. Two corroded pieces of metal that were excavated have been identified as steel reed plates of a harmonica or mouth organ. The recovery of the reeds as evidence of musical instrument indicates another aspect of entertainment which involved music. The harmonica may have been used as source of entertainment by adults or children of families who occupied the Frederikssted plantation landscape after the plantation was shut (Fig. 9.12).

Rural Telephony

The occupants of the Frederikssted plantation landscape appeared to have enjoyed the benefits of telephone communication services due to the recovery of two pieces of telegraph-wire insulators.

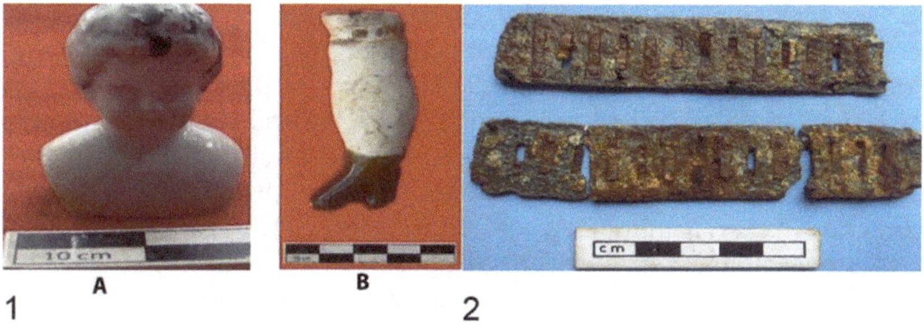

Fig. 9.12 Entertainment (1: Ceramic dolls. Shoulder-head (A) and leg (B); 2: Steel reeds of mouth organ: Harmonica, musical instrument)

Telegraph Wire Insulators

The two pieces of telegraph-wire insulators that were found on the surface of *Locus 2* appear heavier and thicker than imported ceramics found in the excavations. They are believed to be part of the telegraph infrastructure constructed by the African Direct Telegraph Company established in 1885 by John Pender, of British origin. The company was one of the several cable companies John Pender established in different parts of the world. In the Gold Coast, the African Direct Telegraph Company provided cable and wireless services to a number of coastal and immediate hinterlands at the beginning of the twentieth century (Headrick 1991; Huurdeman 2003: 137). Some of the telegraph poles can still be seen standing in the Dodowa valley along the historic path to the Akuapem Mountains. The Dodowa elite family who reoccupied the Frederikssted plantation site may have used the telephone facility during the nineteenth and the twentieth centuries (Fig. 9.13).

Domestic/Industrial Chemicals (Poison Bottles)

Poison bottles, by the very nature of their contents, are of a very distinctive type. Most of the poison bottles that were manufactured in England and America during the mid-nineteenth century were made in dark shades of blue, brown and green in order to serve as another form of identification aid. Griffenhagen and Bogard (1999: 91–92) have also noted that specially shaped containers for poisons were in use in Europe and America as early as the eighteenth century. They were specially designed, to prevent accidental dispensing of poisonous substances in pharmacies and accidental ingestion of poisons by humans at home. Two bottle fragments from Frederikssted have been identified as Victorian poison bottles as they are characterised by a dark green colour with vertical striations. Some of the initial Victorian bottles were manufactured in attractive cobalt blue glass bottles as a warning, and the dark glass also protected the content from the effects of sunlight. According to Dale (2012: 12), because many people were illiterate in the 1800s, English bottles containing poisonous substances were made with ridges and grooves on them in addition to the words such as "poison" or "poisonous" or "NOT TO BE TAKEN" engraved on the other side of the bottle (Hedges 2002: 16). This makes it possible that even in dim light they could still be identified by touch and by an illiterate person. The Frederikssted poison bottles could have

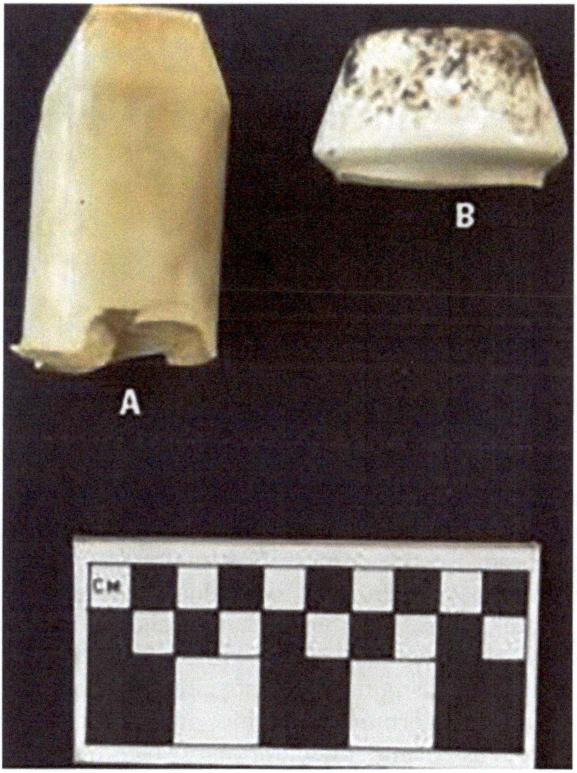

Fig. 9.13 Domestic/industrial chemicals (Victorian poison bottles)

been used to control plants (weeds) and vermin, and as surface cleaners (Fig. 9.14).

Cottage Industry (Beads and Sewing)

Local Beads

The local beads recovered from Frederikssted excavations were mainly glass beads. Glass beads in Ghana are generally made from discarded glass materials or older beads, crushed into smaller chips or pounded into powder. The bead makers pour the crushed or powdered glass into a mould made of fired clay with cylindrical cavities. Normally, the stem of

Fig. 9.14 Rural telephony (Telegraph wire insulators)

a cassava leaf is placed in the middle of the glass powder already poured into the mould; this stick will burn away leaving a vertical hole in the middle of the bead, for the purpose of stringing. In Ghana, both local and foreign beads have been used for bodily decoration, and may also symbolise political status, religious affiliation and be used in particular ceremonies (Kumekpor et al. 1995: 16; Wilson 2003: 1).

Even though Ghana originally did not produce glass, glass materials have been found in enormous quantities in both coastal and inland areas due to the trans-Atlantic trade, through which European merchants brought many glass vessels containing different types of liquid. The glass used to make the beads may have come from Dodowa town, where people made use of and discarded different types of glass materials. It is also possible that the glass was obtained from the Frederikssted plantation site—either discarded by Danish planters (during the plantation period) or the local elite (during the post-plantation period). The presence of local beads and their manufacturing accoutrements (bead moulds) shows evidence of a cottage industry at the Frederikssted plantation. The distribution of the local beads and the bead moulds among mid-nineteenth-century materials suggests that the production of the beads could have been carried out by the free people who reoccupied the site after the collapse of the plantation. They probably took advantage of Dodowa as an existing bead-production and trading centre to sell the beads manufactured at the plantation site.

European/Imported Beads

Beginning from the 1600 s a number of European traders arrived in West Africa and dominated the West-African maritime trade. Some of the trade items included beads. European-imported beads traded in West Africa eventually suffocated the indigenous bead industry. Imported beads found in Frederikssted excavations numbered 102. These foreign beads are believed to have been imported from Europe and Asia. Most of the imported beads have been dated to the mid-nineteenth century, originating from Venice, India and Bohemia.

Sewing Machine Part

The part of the sewing machine recovered from the excavations has been identified as a bed shaft located at the base of the sewing machine. The component illustrated below is from a hand-operated Singer sewing machine. The Singer sewing machine was invented and patented in America by Isaac Merritt Singer in 1851 (Bishop et al. 1864: 606). Singer machines became popular and efficient sewing machines in Ghana during the nineteenth and the twentieth centuries, and Frederikssted local inhabitants may have used them for either domestic/private or commercial sewing during the nineteenth century (Fig. 9.15).

Smoking at the Plantation Site

Other consumable items obtained from the Frederikssted excavations which have also been ascribed to the occupants of the plantation site are smoking pipes, comprising both local and European types.

European/Imported Smoking Pipes

Based on the presence of pipe fragments, it appears that smoking was a common activity at the Frederikssted plantation site. The excavations recovered 32 European tobacco-pipe fragments. They comprise 29 pieces of stem, 1 whole bowl with a short stem attached and 2 bowl fragments.

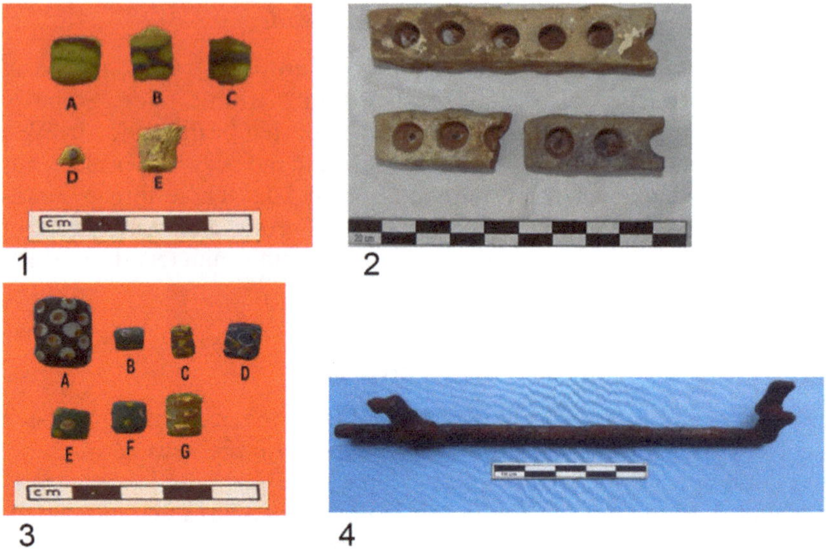

Fig. 9.15 Cottage industry (beads and sewing) (1: Local beads; 2: Vertical bead moulds; 3: Imported beads: Wound beads with polka dots; 4: Bed shaft of Singer sewing machine)

Local Smoking Pipes

Two bowl fragments of local red-clay smoking pipes were found at Locus 1. One (A) has a flat ring close to the mouth of the bowl with the middle hole clearly visible. The other local clay pipe (B) also has oblique roulette impressions covering the entire surface of the fragment. These clay smoking pipes were likely made by the Africans in an attempt to imitate the European types. Ozanne (1966) indicates that the local Shai people in nearby Accra plains were in the habit of using local clay in making smoking pipes for smoking tobacco (Fig. 9.16).

Household Tools/Items

It seems the occupants who lived on the plantation site during the nineteenth century and beyond made use of local pottery as well as adopting European cooking and eating practices through the use of European-made aluminium cooking materials and cutlery.

Fig. 9.16 Smoking at the plantation site (1: European-imported smoking pipes; 2: Locally made smoking pipes_A and B)

Cutlery

Items in this category were all excavated from Unit 1 of Locus 2; they include one fork and two different knives. The tines of the fork (A) had broken off probably due to corrosion, leaving only the handle in the archaeological record. One of the knives recovered from Frederikssted (B) has a handle made of horn core; it shows three corroded spots denoting the points where three rivets were inserted to fasten the metallic tang and the horn core together. Though a major part of the blade is missing due to extensive corrosion, the bolster area and the entire tang can still be seen. The other knife (C), which is highly corroded, has been identified as a folded knife. One section of the handle and a short fragile blade remain.

Local Pottery Materials

Local pottery material constitutes the dominant find from the excavations at Frederikssted. The profile reconstruction of the sherds shows jars and bowls as the two main types of pottery obtained from the site. The rim sherds were used to identify two main functions, namely *bowls* and *jars.*

Most of the jars had flaring everted rims, hemispherical in shape and gradually becoming narrower at the neck. The outward curvature of the rims makes them separate from the necks. These are normally used for cooking food, medicine and storing of water and other items (Fig. 9.17).

Fig. 9.17 Household tools/items (1: A: Fork B: Knife with horn core handle, C: Folding knife; 2: Local pottery: bowl with everted rim and carinated shoulder; 3: Local pottery: Jar with flaring everted rim)

Faunal Remains

Our understanding of faunal resources at the Frederiksted plantation site is derived largely from an analysis of the animal bones that were excavated. Zoo-archaeological analyses of the faunal materials have revealed a mixed consumption culture of wild and domesticated animals on the site. The identifiable faunal assemblage was dominated by mammals, the majority of which were identified as bovid. The domesticated taxa that were recovered were cattle, goat/sheep and domestic pig. All the faunal materials came from Unit 1 of Locus 2. This is refuse only associated with African inhabitants of the site. The supposition, therefore, is that the faunal materials were associated with the African inhabitants during the post-European/plantation occupation period in the nineteenth and the twentieth centuries (Fig. 9.18).

Currency (Cowrie Shells)

Cowries became highly valued items in West Africa and were widely used as currency long before the colonial period. Two types of cowry shells

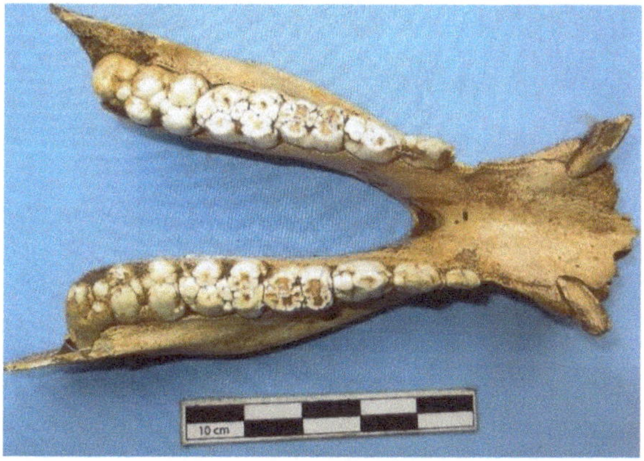

Fig. 9.18 Faunal remains (Lower jaw of a pig)

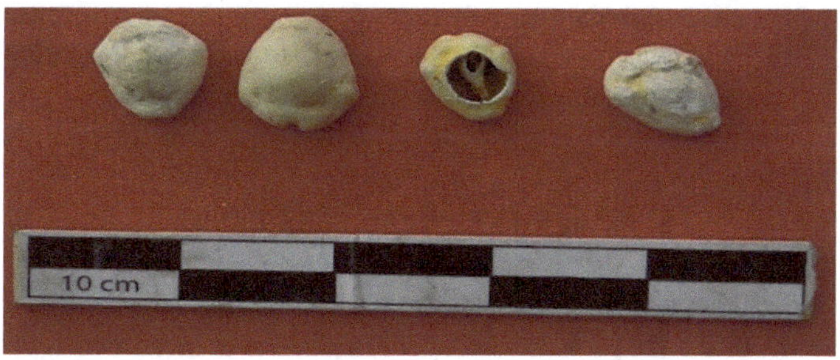

Fig. 9.19 Currency (Cowrie shells)

(*Cypraea moneta* and *Cypraea annulus)* have been identified as the types that were brought by Europeans from the Indian ocean to West Africa to serve as currency (shell money). Later, the locals used them as divination objects (Bascom 1993). Cowry shells retrieved from Frederiksted plantation site were 23 in number and they were all located in Unit 1 of Locus 2. The cowry shells may have played a dual role of serving as currency (as part of the trading activities on the site) or as ritual paraphernalia (Fig. 9.19).

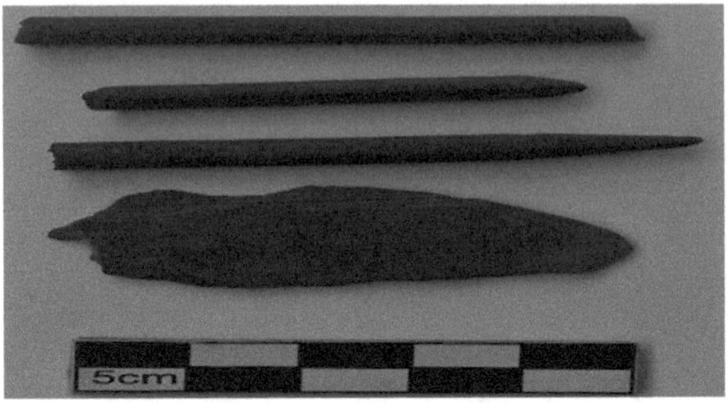

Fig. 9.20 Accounting/bookkeeping/writing (Slate pencil and a piece of slate)

Accounting/Bookkeeping/Writing

Writing-related items from Frederikssted excavations are few but significant. They include 20 slate pencils and 5 writing slate fragments. These materials provide evidence of the presence of a literate population at the site. The items could be used for keeping business records by the nineteenth-century local occupants, as paper was uncommon and expensive (Fig. 9.20).

Conclusion

The Frederikssted material remains, comprising the plantation ruins and the excavated materials (both local and foreign), and extant European merchandise outlets in Lower Dodowa can be described as the preserved witnesses of the Danish slave plantation system in Dodowa. This chapter has therefore shown how archaeological research at Frederikssted plantation can be used to provide an understanding of the many issues embedded in the wider sweep of the entire Danish plantation system in Ghana.

Firstly, the chapter explores how the material culture can be used to examine the presence of elite Africans on the Frederikssted plantation landscape. Previous plantation archaeological researches in Ghana have often produced copious material culture relating to European occupation, and always portrayed the African occupants as slaves who lived in perpetual indigence. More so, plantation archaeologists in different parts of the world have often overlooked the third category (free people) of plantation occupants, and in doing so, scholars' perception of slaves and their masters remains the dominant research theme in plantation research. As part of the efforts to decolonise plantation archaeology in Ghana, much efforts must be made to explore how Africans became part and lived on Danish plantation landscape under different circumstances during and after the plantation period. The African elements at Frederikssted plantation comprise two categories, thus, the enslaved Africans and free local people who lived on the plantation landscape after the collapse of the plantation. The Frederikssted material culture discussed in this chapter largely focuses on the presence of the free local elite who were not enslaved but considered the plantation site as a comfortable place to live and trade after the plantation had shut.

The material pattern during the post-plantation period shows high economic status of the local occupants who had been acculturated to the use of various types of European materials to define their status. They were part of the elite local merchants, majority of whom resided in Lower Dodowa during the nineteenth century. These Dodowa indigenes or merchants reoccupied the plantation site and utilised nineteenth-century materials which formed the majority of the artefact that were excavated. The integration of the nineteenth-century materials (local and European materials) suggests that the local occupants who reoccupied the plantation site built a way of life dictated by the acculturative effects of the European contacts in Dodowa. This acculturation in Dodowa was as a result of the Danish plantation economy, slave trading and trading in material goods between the eighteenth and the twentieth centuries. They used distinct material culture such as European ceramics, canned fish, European alcoholic drinks, dolls and other foreign quotidian materials. The changing consumption patterns of these indigenes towards a preference for European-imported materials reflected greater local participation of "elites" in a global consumer culture. This represents culture change propelled by material innovation in Dodowa which became a frontier zone as well as one of the epicentres of European trading activities in the Gold Coast.

The second focus of this chapter is to use the archaeological data from Frederikssted to highlight the issue of reuse or reoccupation of plantation sites. The Frederikssted findings contain many artefacts that can be dated from later in time (after the plantation shut in 1802) and indicate the reuse of the plantation landscape during the nineteenth and the twentieth centuries. This therefore suggests a significant degree of continuity encompassing the plantation and post-plantation periods. The period after the collapse of the plantation saw a different category of people reoccupying the site.

The Frederikssted archaeological data seem to support the hypothesis of a distinguishable artefact pattern belonging to the plantation as well as to the post-plantation context. Orser (1990: 121) alluded to the fact that many of the slave plantation houses continued to be occupied or reoccupied as residences or venerated because of their association with notable events and personalities. Boachie-Ansah (2007: 558) has also observed from his work at Brockman plantation that the excavated materials neither relate to Governor Brock (the plantation owner) nor the period that the plantation existed (1833). If the interpretation is correct, then, the excavated materials do not belong to the Danish plantation period and may best be ascribed to the post-1850 phase, when some indigenous family reoccupied the Brockman plantation site. This presents a challenge when we describe all plantation finds as belonging to only slaves and their masters. The Brockman material culture throws light on the trend I have observed with the Frederikssted artefacts which belong to slaves, masters and free local people who reoccupied the plantations sites at later times.

The excavations at Frederikssted plantation, comprising Locus 1 and Locus 2, the finds and their distribution within the excavated units, demonstrate that the plantation landscape is a place of occupation, abandonment and reoccupation. The material remains belong to varied periods, spanning the eighteenth to the twentieth centuries. The bulk of materials indicate reoccupation at the site. This contradicts the claim made by Jeppesen (1966: 53) that Frederikssted plantation abruptly shut down and the site was simply abandoned in 1802.

It is apparent that the people who lived on the Frederikssted plantation site comprised European planters, African slaves and local free people who together created and shaped the Frederikssted archaeological landscape. The main reason of this continuous occupation is likely the contact created by the Danish plantation economy and the attractiveness of the Dodowa valley environment. Indeed, it can be convincingly argued that most former Danish slave plantations have served as housing units for free people who occupied them after the plantations collapsed. For this reason, when plantation archaeologists limit the interpretation of plantation finds to plantation owners and their enslaved workers, we may either miss or misinterpret some of the material culture from the excavations. The materials may come from the same archaeological context but may not necessarily come from the same historical context. The archaeological data presented here suggest that the interpretation of plantation finds must go beyond the dichotomy between slaves and their masters. It is my expectation that archaeological research at Frederikssted will arouse new research questions (and provide answers) regarding what happened to the Danish plantations in Ghana and other plantations elsewhere after they were abandoned. It is hoped that the article will spur future archaeological researches about slave plantation system in Ghana to be formulated outside the currently held views.

References

Adler, B. 2005. *Early Stoneware Steins from the Les Paul Collection: A Survey of All German Stoneware Centers from 1500 to 1850*. München: Verlag.

Anquandah, JK. 1993. 'Urbanization and State Formation in Ghana during the Iron Age', In T. Shaw, et al. (eds), The Archaeology of Africa: Food, Metals and Towns, Routledge, London.

Armstrong, D. V., C. Williamson and A. D. Armstrong. 2013. "Networked Interaction: Archaeological Exploration of Walled and Terraced House Compounds in the Danish Colonial Port Town of Charlotte Amalie, St. Thomas." In Magdalena Naum and Jonas M Nordin (eds.), *Scandinavian Colonialism and the Rise of Modernity*. New York: Springer Science.

Bascom, W.R. 1993. *Sixteen Cowries: Yoruba Divination from Africa to the New World*. Bloomington: Indiana University Press.

Bersselaar, D. van den. 2007. *The King of Drinks: Schnapps Gin from Modernity to Tradition*. Leiden: Brill.

Bishop, J.L., E.T. Freedley, and E. Young. 1864. *A History of American Manufactures from 1608 to 1860*, vol. 2. Philadelphia: Edward Young and Co.

Boachie-Ansah, J. 2007. Excavations at a Danish Plantation Site at Brockman, Ghana. *EAZ Heft* 48: 537–562.

Bredwa-Mensah, Y. 2002. "Historical-archaeological Investigations at the Frederiksgave Plantation, Ghana: A Case Study of Slavery and Plantation Life on A Nineteenth Century Danish Plantation on the Gold Coast." *Unpublished PhD Dissertation*

Bredwa-Mensah, Y. 1996. Slavery and Plantation Life at the Danish Plantation Site of Bibease, Gold Coast, Ghana. *EAZ Heft* 4: 445–458.

Crossland, L.B. 1998. *Pottery from the Begho B2 Site, Ghana*. Calgary: University of Calgary Press.

Cusick, J.G. 1998. Perspectives on the Study of Culture Contact in Archaeology: Concepts and Critiques. In *Studies in Culture Contact: Interaction, Culture*

Change, and Archaeology, ed. J.G. Cusick, 1–22. Illinois: Southern Illinois University.

Dale, R. 2012. *Digging for Treasure: A Guide to Finding Valuable Victorian Rubbish Dumps*. Bloomington: Xlibris Corporation.

Davies, P. and A. Ellis. 2005." The Archaeology of Childhood: Toys from Henry's Mill." *The Artefact: the Journal of the Archaeological and Anthropological Society of Victoria, 28*: 15–22.

DeCorse, C. 1993. The Danes on the Gold Coast: Culture Change and the European Presence. *The African Archaeological Review* 11: 149–173.

Denker, B. 1996. *Substance of Style: Perspectives on the American Arts and Crafts Movement*. Delaware: Henry Francis du Pont Winterthur Museum.

Eschen, A. 2003. *Collectible Mice*. Maryland: Hobby House Press.

Griffenhagen, G. B. and M. Bogard. 1999. *History of Drug Containers and their Labels*. Madison: American Institute of the History of Pharmacy.

Headrick, D.R. 1991. *The Invisible Weapon: Telecommunications and International Politics, 1851–1945*. New York: Oxford University Press.

Hedges, A.A.C. 2002. *Bottles and Bottles Collecting*. Buckinghamshire: Shire Publications.

Hernæs, P. 2013. "A Danish Experiment in Commercial Agriculture on the Gold Coast, 1788–93." In S. Schwarz, R. Law and S. Strickrodt (eds.), *Commercial Agriculture, the Slave Trade and Slavery in Atlantic Africa*. 158–179. Woodbridge, Suffolk: James Currey.

Huurdeman, A.A. 2003. *The Worldwide History of Telecommunications*. New Jersey: John Wiley & Sons.

Jeppesen, H.A.F. 1966. Danish Plantations on the Gold Coast 1788–1850. *Geografisk Tidsskrift* 65: 73–98.

Jones, O. R. and C. Sullivan. 1985. *Glass Glossary*. Ottawa, Canada: Canadian Parks Service.

Jones, O. R., and E. A. Smith. 1985. *Glass of the British Military ca. 1755–1820*. Ottawa: Parks Canada.

Kesse, G. O. 1985. The Mineral and Rock Resources of Ghana. Rotterdam, Netherlands: A.A Balkema Publishers.

Kumekpor, ML, Bredwa-Mensah, Y., and Landewijk, JEJM. 1995. The Ghanaian Bead Tradition, Wilco Publicity, Accra.

Lynch, G. 2007. *The History of Gauged Brickwork*. Burlington: Elsevier Ltd.

Mills, C.W. 1956. *The Power Elite*. New York: Oxford University Press.

Norregard, G. 1966. *Danish Settlements in West Africa, 1658–1850*. Boston: Boston University Press.

Orser, C.E. 1990. Archaeological Approaches to New World Plantation Slavery. *Archaeological Method and Theory* 2: 111–154.

Ozanne, P. 1960. *Tobacco-Pipes of Accra and Shai*. Accra: Institute of African Studies, University of Ghana.

Pearson, S. 1992. *Dolls and Teddy Bears (Miller's Antiques Checklist)*. Thirsk: Miller's Publications.
Prichett, J., & Pastron, A. 1983. 'Ceramic Dolls as Chronological Indicators: Implications from San Francisco Dump Site', in AE Ward (ed.), Forgotten Places and Things: Archaeological Perspectives on American History, Center for Anthropological Studies, Albuquerque, New Mexico.
Pulford, G. 2007. *High-Security Mechanical Locks: An Encyclopedic Reference*. Burlington, Massachusetts: Elsevier Academic Press.
Snodin, M. 2006. *The V&A Book of Western Ornament*. New York: Harry N. Abrams.
Snodin, M., and M. Howard. 1996. *Ornament: A Social History since 1450*. New Haven: Yale University Press.
Van der Sloot, H. 1975. *150 Jaar Henkes: A look at the Distilling Industry in Holland's Delfshaven Area over 150 years*. Rotterdam: Historic Museum Voorheven-Delftshaven.
Waechter, S. A. 2007. *How Old is "Old"? Recognizing Historical Sites and Artifacts*. Sacramento: California Department of Forestry and Fire Protection.
Walker, A. 1987. *Scent Bottles*. Buckinghamshire: Shire Publications.
Wilson, A. 2003. The Bead is Constant, Ghana Universities Press, Accra.

CHAPTER 10

"Sweet Mother": The Neoliberal Plantation in Sierra Leone

Nile Davies

Introduction

Plantation assemblages are by their very nature externally imposed forms of ordering life, land and labor with capital. Notoriously harmful to ecologies and workers themselves, the plantation operates on the basic premise that industrial rationality and efficiency are an improvement on locally existing modes of social and ecological reproduction (Murray Li and Semedi 2021). Sugar is a famously potent symbol of the colonial world, epitomizing the racialized labor regimes and systems of extraction that fueled the political economy of modern capitalism (Mintz 1985; Scott 2004). In the twenty-first century, sugar plantations remain an enduring concept-metaphor for relations of labor defined by asymmetrical relations of power, "an accumulated repertoire of forms for creating and controlling work," paralleled with narratives of repression as the grounds of a

N. Davies (✉)
Department of Anthropology, Columbia University, New York, USA
e-mail: n.davies@columbia.edu

C. Le Petitcorps et al. (eds.), *Global Plantations in the Modern World*, Cambridge Imperial and Post-Colonial Studies,
https://doi.org/10.1007/978-3-031-08537-6_10

more ambiguous modernity constituted by forms of colonial encounter (Taylor 2014).

This chapter considers the histories of productive life at Chinese sugar plantation in Sierra Leone, established as part of China's aid program in the 1970s and revived after the civil war (1991–2002) by a Chinese engineering contractor, COMPLANT (China National Complete Plant Import Export Corporation). Since the turn of the millennium, following the entry of China into the WTO in 2001, extraterritorial agribusiness enterprises continue to be part of a wider strategic policy for Chinese companies *Going Global*.[1] While narratives of enduring loyalty between Sierra Leone and the PRC have been heralded by official Chinese sources as the ideal structure of bilateral relations inscribed by the ethos of "friendship," "cooperation" and "mutual benefit" between states, public signs of development fix the spectacular presence of Chinese investment, framing national leaders breaking new ground in Sierra Leone as brokers of the future in their collaborative assemblage with foreign partners.

While the term "China–Africa relations" often euphemizes Chinese extractive rationales in Africa, offering moral condemnation of the seemingly unequal partnership in these exchanges, it also tends to overlook African agency, or how China's economic transformations mirror more generic forms of global capitalist expansion. Descriptions emphasizing the strategic aims of Chinese territorial expansion are less clear about the day-to-day or granular accounts of these relationships or their actors, or how infrastructures of development can be understood as an enduring material archive. The plantation at Magbass indexes the long and intricate history of economic cooperation between Sierra Leone and the PRC, beginning in 1971, when China received a decisive vote from Sierra Leone at the 26th United Nations General Assembly, restoring its "legitimate seat" at the UN.[2] In the rendering of social goods without explicit conditions, critics of corporate giving have understood elite benefaction as a fundamentally hierarchical and unilateral practice which fosters social ties and

[1] "COMPLANT Launched Ukraine Agriculture Package Project," Sinomach, 14 May 2013.

[2] By contrast, Taiwanese agricultural training projects in Africa (particularly Taiwanese rice techniques) have been understood as an embattled medium of recognition in the context of long-term effacement owing to the PRC's One China policy in which Taiwan is increasingly a geopolitical proxy. See "Building on Past Achievements and Joining Hands to Make an Even Brighter Future of China-Sierra Leone Friendship," Chinese Ambassador Zhao Yanbo (Ministry of Foreign Affairs of the People's Republic of China), 1 Aug 2016.

obligations. Like the famous accounts of prestation in Mauss's 1925 study *Essai Sur Le Don,* classical anthropological theories of the gift understand such relations as suffused with meaning, but also generative of social effects. Indebtedness creates social bonds between individuals, formatting them in relation to each other. Yet in contexts where fantasies of development and its localized effects are elaborated through the enthusiastic uptake of schemes for investment, the generosity of investment and its implications of a primary, inaugural or originary *giving*—rather than, for example, originary accumulation—remains an undertheorized notion in our understanding of corporate responsibility. Inscribed with fraternal idioms of nation building and mutually beneficial economic relations, anthropologists have contributed to a long-term understanding of industrial experts as agents for postcolonial development (Englund 2008; Schmitz 2021).[3]

This chapter situates such gestures within a broader field of ambivalence concerning the relationship between corporations and "communities," one that thickens our understanding of Chinese entrepreneurship in Africa. Scenes of structured loss invite us to dwell on the form and intention of investment in the post/de-colonial state within a longer narrative of development and rural productivity. Conspicuously "Chinese" in its official renderings, the public form of state-sponsored collaboration increasingly shifts from itineraries of *aid* without conditions to regimes of long-term collective *profit*, with its speculative temporality and ethical calculus: crucial terms in the moral economy of investment. This shift, and the increasing solicitation of local workers as agents in their own development, is also central to local narratives of dependency, toxicity and accelerated death. Attentive to the language of investment as an ethical alibi for accumulation, this chapter calls for an understanding of such capital as a figure of both life and death, both poison and cure. Paying attention to historical itineraries of plantation labor as a vehicle for growth offers insights into the shifting forms of Chinese state enterprise in Sierra

[3] While collaborative projects of development have shaped both urban skylines and rural landscapes in Sierra Leone, these spectacular infrastructures have served ambivalent purposes if they are to be understood beyond the act of giving as an end in itself. As Mariane Ferme and Cheryl Schmitz (2014) have written, a focus that extends beyond the more obvious monumental projects instantiated by the PRC in Sierra Leone may enrich our understanding of Chinese–African engagements over time.

Leone within the context of anthropological debates of globalization and neoliberal development.

Idioms of corporate benevolence signify the double bind endured by rural communities like those in Magbass, solicited by the magic of power of foreign investment in narratives of future prosperity, increasingly indivisible from accounts of attritional degradation for workers (Nixon 2013). I understand that impasse through Lauren Berlant's analysis of "slow death" (2012) in which precarity is managed and reproduced as the generative condition of possibility under late capitalism. Like colonial forms of extraction, these assemblages of labor are structured by relations of paternalistic control (of bosses over workers) and dependence (of workers on wages). At stake here is an understanding of the plantation form as a structure of affective binding: a future-oriented attachment to the profits of productive life, and the promise of the foreign as an ambivalent vector of futurity. In this chapter I hope to show how such projects are also sites of cyclical ruination, abandonment and long-term precarity within a longer genealogy of the plantation as a repertoire of forms for racial capitalism.

"Bold Experiments"

Sierra Leone became a member of the Food and Agriculture Organization of the United Nations (FAO) in 1962, a year after independence, embarking on an expansive range of technical and communications projects across the country.[4] Faced with the debilitating effects of structural adjustment and the encroaching collapse of the economy, by the end of his tenure in 1985, President Siaka Stevens spoke of the collective determination "to eradicate the scourge of hunger from our land" through closer collaboration with the FAO. The same year, in conjunction with the 40th anniversary of the FAO, the Director General pledged his organization's unyielding commitment to Sierra Leone. Mass sensitization promoted the widespread use of fertilizers for improved rice yields alongside informational films on rural credit, workshops on the virtues

[4] "Sierra Leone—FAO Cooperation and Development," October 1985, FAO and Ministry of Agriculture and Natural Resources.

of the mechanized plough, produce prices, hog castration and the vaccination of livestock against rinderpest.[5] In the claim of the "common endeavor" to eradicate hunger and poverty was an argument for global agricultural cooperation as a moral imperative which claimed "food and freedom from want" as a basic human right, the natural privileges of personhood:

> The poorer countries of the world are so beset by climatological and ecological restraints, so crushed by the staggering burden of debt, so frustrated by the consequences of recession and the growing meshes of protectionism, that only a total lack of realism and human solidarity could lead to some degree that a solution to their problems may be found merely through their own efforts and without cooperation from the outside.

If deepening the material entanglements between the "poorer countries" and "the outside" was presented by some as the road to self-sufficiency, aspirations for economic prosperity in Sierra Leone highlighted the pernicious global distribution of rural poverty, and the continual interpellation of rural communities by technical fixes that mirrored the classical histories of colonial improvement. Fused with the moral tenets of universal human rights, which understands the alleviation of poverty as an ethical imperative, global cooperation has long been framed as the natural engine for the development of impoverished lives. Such a story corresponds with the parallel history of neoliberal intervention in the second half of the twentieth century in which decolonizing nations, increasingly fitted with Western solutions to remedy their poverty, were solicited by spectacular projects for improvement that often yielded destructive consequences for those same societies (Tsing 2000).

By contrast, official narratives of China's own national development have self-consciously articulated an enduring spirit and ethic of labor as a repudiation of Western imperialism. To the extent that collaborative nation-building through forms of Chinese expertise has been understood as an *alternative* to Western aid programmes, both models hold that improving outcomes for the world's poor means offering a way for countries to "grow" themselves out of poverty: a means of harnessing human

[5] Once a net exporter of the crop, by 1980 Sierra Leone was a net importer of rice, accentuated by a severe imbalance of payments. Persistent failures to meet obligations to the International Monetary Fund caused the devaluation of the Leone from its near 1:1 parity with the US Dollar in 1980 to a state of massive inflation by the end of the decade.

value and natural resources in neglected markets. Of late, Chinese narratives have referred to a decades' long history of bilateralism between China and Sierra Leone to suggest lofty ideological claims about the capacities for *mutual* benefit through corporate assemblages that marry the technological mastery of Chinese experts with local bodies.[6] As one recent press release reads:

> China relied on the solid and unremitting efforts of generations of Chinese people, which is represented in the typical case of "800 million shirts in exchange for a Boeing airplane". [...] China relied on a pioneering spirit, like crossing the river by feeling for stones, neither retracing the steps of imperialism and colonialism, nor copying the development model of Western countries, but blazing its own path with bold experiments, based on its own conditions, experience and lessons as well as the achievements of other civilizations.[7]

Here one cannot help but be reminded of the critique offered by Walter Rodney, who, already in 1972, had vociferously argued that postcolonial development models were fatally compromised by the promise of the foreign, ensuring only "that the natural resources and the labor of Africa produce economic value which is lost to the continent." As Rodney argued, if investment seemed to hold out the prospect of riches in freedom, it also served to sustain the entrenchment of "international capitalist experts" in the delivery of "so-called aid" (2018 [1972]: 27–28). Philanthropic rationales explicitly drive the colonization of national development regimes through ever-increasing partnership between the private and public (Brautigam 2011).While critics of large-scale Chinese projects like the Tanzam Railway have long argued that the accumulation of Chinese debt and infrastructure restage the dependent relations of a century earlier between colonized nations and European powers (Graham 1974; Carmody 2011), less is known about how narratives of growth have been instrumentalized by Chinese actors and experienced by those solicited by Chinese expertise as a modality of "amicable capitalism."

[6] Daily Report: People's Republic of China, United States Foreign Broadcast Information Service, 20 December 1978.

[7] "China and the World in the New Era," The State Council Information Office of the People's Republic of China, September 2019.

In December 2013, when a Chinese medical corps arrived at Magbass offering free treatments to hundreds of employees and their families, the head doctor was called upon to recount a time-honored tale about the history of collaboration that joined the two countries in relations of care and the sharing of expertise. For the past 40 years, Chinese medics had been deployed in government hospitals all over Sierra Leone, he said, working to supplement nationwide shortcomings in public health and medical services, training nurses in traditional Chinese medicine, treating malaria and syphilis and conducting minor surgeries, "helping to save the lives of Sierra Leoneans." In the words of the plantation's Chinese manager, the company's presence was characterized by a sense of mutual affection and cooperation, indicative of the company's future intentions "*to do more for the people and the community as a way of giving back to Sierra Leone...*".

While healing the sick and other signs of "giving back" can be understood in relation to their anticipated effects within the imagined community at Magbass, nowhere mentioned in the press coverage is how the medical event coincided with a memorandum of understanding (MOU) signed earlier that month between COMPLANT and the Government of Sierra Leone, outlining plans for the expansion of the plantation's acreage. Citing the terms of the original lease signed 10 years earlier, the text of the MOU recites the pivotal role played by Chinese entrepreneurship in the narrative of Sierra Leone's post-conflict reconstruction as the first foreign agribusiness investor to return to Sierra Leone "after the turbulence," stressing the capacity of productive life at Magbass to generate new jobs, education and infrastructure for "an impoverished rural population."[8] Indeed, in recognition of the assumption that the very presence of the plantation would attract other foreign investors to Sierra Leone, the terms of the contract offer generous tax exemptions and legal rights over the leased territory of the plantation, "free and clear of all encumbrances, hypothecation and power limitation."[9]

Locals who considered the presence of large-scale land deals as a general social good for their ambient benefits to communities also understood these corporate transformations in reference to a logic of reciprocity

[8] Complant Magbass Sugar Complex Co. Ltd., Memorandum of Understanding, 2013.

[9] Lease Contract on Magbass Sugar Complex of Sierra Leone. 23 January 2003. Freetown, Sierra Leone.

that seemed, ostensibly, to asymmetrically favor these foreign benefactors. When I spoke to Michael, a long-term COMPLANT employee who worked in Human Resources at Magbass, his account of the plantation's history was underscored by the interests of "the Chinese" in profit as evocative of a more general regard toward African countries:

> With China, they see that the more they come to Africa, the more they get benefits. It's like what the Bible says: "The more you give, the more you receive". That's why the Chinese go the extra mile. When they pour money, they know that they will get something that is more than what they give.

While certain investments can transform a landscape over a short period of time, remaking the worlds in which they are situated, they are also guided by their own temporality of long-term profit; that is, that operations remain conditional on financial liquidity. Michael's biblical homily underscored a familiar ethic of redistribution implicit in the principles of a profitable investment: that to give generously is to enter into a social relation through which the donor ultimately recoups their losses, exceeding their initial outlay. To his mind, the idea of Chinese generosity in Africa presupposed a calculus that future profits would negate past expenditure: a guarantee that anything given would be regained *in excess*.

Foreign agribusiness enterprises are today framed as a part of a wider strategy for Chinese companies which emerged on the eve of the Millenium as official policy of the Chinese Communist Party, urging firms to "go out" and seize advantage of booming global markets in the 1990s. Chinese firms increasingly engaged in new forms of economic and technological "cooperation" across the Global South and further afield, accelerated by the dawn of unprecedented transcontinental free trade with the fall of the Soviet Union. G*oing Global* draws on the poetics of collectivity, service and duty characteristic of the Cultural Revolution, when young Communists were sent "up to the mountains, down to the countryside" in service of the Chinese people. In a self-conscious orientation toward an increasingly globalized future world, China's leaders today encourage their companies to go "down to the African countryside" to further the strategic interests of the PRC (Brautigam and Xiaoyang 2009).

As mainstream accounts of China's own development have emphasized the success of economic reforms, such rhetorical echoes—pastoral symbols of Chinese nation building projected onto African landscapes—recall the longer history of Chinese technical interventions as part of the developmentalist promise, characterized by ideals of capitalist modernization as a means of alleviating poverty and suffering. On the ground such interventions are less shaped by rigid national policy but increasingly characterized as Chinese *entrepreneurship*, even though they slot neatly into national itineraries for *development*. Indeed, it is important to underscore that many Chinese operations in Sierra Leone do not have direct oversight from Beijing, nor is "China" a unitary actor. At the same time, as scholars have turned attention to the systems of obligation and dependence that Chinese welfare has occasioned for its own citizens (see Pan 2020), idioms of corporate responsibility in foreign enterprise reflect the diminishing role of the state as an agent of social security in Sierra Leone in place of increasing client–patron relations which solicit the community as self-interested collaborators[10] (Figs. 10.1 and 10.2).

Sweet Times at Magbass

This photo, taken around 1990, is the earliest image I have of workers at the Magbass Sugar Complex, a vast sugar cane plantation in Tonkolili District, Sierra Leone. Faded and bearing the signs of water damage accrued over the intervening years, I encountered it long after its capture among the personal belongings of a man called Hassan.[11] As we sat through a heavy rainstorm on the veranda of his home in the neighboring village of Magbass, Hassan recounted for me the story of employment in one of the few technical jobs available to Sierra Leoneans at the processing plant of the complex, where he began as an apprentice plumber. The photograph depicts Hassan among a handful of young Sierra Leonean men known locally as *industrialists*, distinguished from seasonal field workers by their full-time technical roles at the factory site, working closely alongside Chinese experts. Though it served no official purpose, the print was kept alongside other official objects and documentation in a small black belt-bag, with voter ID cards and others, long expired, issued by the management at the plantation over the years. Other photos showed

[10] For the contentious rendering of idioms for social elevation in Chinese-language sources, see Rob Schmitz, "Who's Lifting Chinese People Out Of Poverty?," *NPR*, January 17, 2017.

[11] All names used are pseudonyms.

Fig. 10.1 Billboard highlighting Chinese cooperation in the SLPP government's "Presidential Infrastructure Initiative," Freetown, Sierra Leone (Photo by author)

him with other industrialists observing the thick pipes and valves in the water treatment room where millions of gallons of water were withdrawn from the River Rokel for washing and boiling the cut cane stalks.

Buoyed by structures of feeling that located revolutionary capacity in the rhetoric of proletarian internationalism, projects of economic experimentation between China and Third World countries found material form in corporate assemblages between Chinese experts and indigenous workers, united by the axioms of Maoist political economy ("*to take agriculture as the foundation and industry as the leading factor*").[12] Staged as a collaborative monument to national development and an ethic of mutuality by China's aid program, the Magbass project was conceived

[12] "Build a Prosperous Country Energetically, Diligently, and Thriftily." *People's Daily*. Peking New China News Agency, 1 Oct, 1963.

Fig. 10.2 Workers at the Magbass Sugar Complex circa 1990 (Photographer unknown)

in cooperation with the Sierra Leonean Government in the late-1970s just as demonstration farms established by experts from the "People's China" staged a vision of the brighter future available to Sierra Leoneans through rural modernization as a long-term investment, transforming the lives of hungry subsistence farmers increasingly solicited as subjects for international development at the dawn of the neoliberal age (*APC* 1978).

At Magbass, by the time of the first trial production in 1981, a thousand hectares of rural land had been demarcated into rows and sections, permanently reshaping local fluvial systems through an intricate grid of gates and channels. Walled compounds housing segregated quarters for Chinese managers were constructed on site alongside the Magbass plant, which processed cane from the surrounding fields into white sugar and bioethanol using grinding machines from Communist Cuba. In its heyday, more than 2,000 permanent and seasonal workers were engaged at the complex. When I went there in 2018 to interview workers and local residents, those old enough to remember Magbass in the 80s recalled for me a golden era. Older men told me how the Chinese liked to pay wages promptly in the morning, before lunch time. The late J.P. Kamara—an esteemed local employee at Magbass before the war—could even *speak* Chinese along with several other men of the earlier generation sent to the PRC for training, beyond living memory of many of the young farmers. As one man wistfully described the prosperity that accompanied the years before the civil war (1991–2002): "If you had been there, you wouldn't even have wanted to go to Freetown…".

Memories of agricultural prosperity at Magbass described an unthinkable inversion of a rural exodus in Sierra Leone. As early as 1950, colonial officials observed the swell of *useless mouths* in the labor market: "a considerable urban population more or less divorced from the land" (Annual Report of the Labour Department of Sierra Leone 1950: 3; also see Harvey 1966). But the rhythms of industry at Magbass hold a mirror up to disaster. Since the first cane entered the rollers, two significant interruptions have marked its history: the first in 1995 when the Chinese agricultural experts, along with other foreign nationals in the country, fled en-masse from the spread of insurgent conflict that would later be historicized as the Sierra Leone Civil War (1991–2002).[13] Rebel militias who claimed the cause of the rural peasantry as their guiding ideation destroyed and looted the grounds of the Magbass factory after unsuccessful attempts to run the site to fund their military campaign. Many like Hassan went as refugees to neighboring Guinea and Ivory Coast, where they waited out the war in camps, returning as subjects of a tentative reconstruction of an already precarious economy.[14]

[13] Distinguished in the popular imagination for the willful destruction of the built environment and an exceptional brutality toward the civilian population, at least 70 thousand people were killed in the conflict. This violence remained visible in the landscape of burned villages and abandoned farms. Over half the total population—at least two million people—were displaced from their homes. In Koidu, the capital of Kono District, 90 percent of the buildings were damaged or destroyed following the retreat of AFRC and RUF fighters from the diamond-rich East of the country. "IRIN Update 999 of events in West Africa," United Nations (OCHA) Network for West Africa. 19 June 2001. Online: https://reliefweb.int/report/chad/irin-update-999-events-west-africa.

[14] "Case Study: Sierra Leone, Evaluation of Assistance to Conflict-Affected Countries." New York: United Nations Development Program, 2006. 4. Online: http://web.undp.org/evaluation/documents/thematic/conflict/SierraLeone.pdf.

For Hassan, these ID cards and the damaged photograph served as evidence of his formal association with the plantation and a cordial working relationship with the Chinese managers. They were the first things that he grabbed as he fled, in hope and expectation that he would one day return to reclaim his former position. "I didn't mess around with my documents!" he told me, grinning. In my role as anthropologist, I too am tempted to view the photograph as a form of documentation, however partial and contingent, even if its contents necessarily resist authoritative interpretation (Buckley 2014).[15] All tenses collide in the image, and its referents exist in a kind of perpetual stasis, a melancholic stillness, destined to be defeated by time. When I asked Hassan to tell me something more about the other pictured figures, he explained that the war had "*scattered*" the subjects of the image. He knew that "the Chinese returned to China" but that the others had died: "all died." Of all the others pictured, only Hassan returned to work at the factory after the war, under new management. I pressed him, asking if he knew about the specifics. Their deaths, he explained, were the cause of working poverty, labor and hardship, both generalized and embodied, but could not be attributed to any specific ailment or event.

While damage to the photograph obscures certain details, others prick the eye. The idle car with its burgundy paintwork was a rare symbol of the status that accrued to the management of the plantation in this remote rural part of Sierra Leone, a day's travel from the capital even now, with smoother roads and wide intercity highways built after the war by China's Seventh Railway Group, a construction conglomerate from Zhengzhou. The evidence of these working relationships between the two nations would accrue an even greater value in later years, after the end of war, when the Government of Sierra Leone began the task of initiating national recovery, attracting the return of foreign investment to a country characterized by narratives of humanitarian catastrophe and state failure. In 2003, the Ministry of Agriculture signed a contract with the Chinese engineering contractor COMPLANT for the rehabilitation of the Magbass complex, awarding the company a 30-year lease to resume the large-scale cultivation of sugar on the ruined site as a strictly corporate

[15] Compelled by the evidentiary power of the camera image as a mode of natural representation, scholars have argued that photography can function as an archive or appendage to ethnography, but with reservations about its efficacy as a tool for gleaning historical information.

entity. The contract stressed that workers at the old complex—many of whom had assiduously kept hold of their ID cards and papers throughout a decade of upheaval—would be afforded no special privileges.

Still, for those who had anticipated the return of productive life at Magbass for nearly a decade, such news could not have come soon enough, even if the signatories agreed that workers' salaries would be set at "the lowest wage standard in the region."[16] Indeed, many saw the very presence of large-scale agribusiness in the region—a former rebel stronghold—as a recuperative gesture toward a population disarrayed by a decade of war. As one of the largest employers for miles, the promise of new investment to absorb ex-combatants and struggling subsistence farmers into a waged labor force had been repeatedly recalled as an augur of reconstruction at a national scale—a vital means for social restoration (Miller 2015). But local voices had been far more circumspect in their appraisals of the revived foreign presence in the area. Villagers told me that the large fish which once filled the river could no longer be found, poisoned by work which eradicated a vital source of protein in the local diet. Business operations had been mired in disputes between COMPLANT and landowners over a gamut of issues: from complaints regarding the non-payment of surface rents, to reports about the habitual dumping of toxic runoff from the processing plant, poisoning local water sources and blighting the soil. A decade after the jubilant return of the Chinese operations, demands from COMPLANT to further expand the plantation's acreage emerged amidst a history of bitter labor actions and complaints over pay and conditions. There were accusations of sabotage and claims that sections of the cane had been purposefully set ablaze by local workers. In 2012, the newspaper *Awoko* had heard from a man in one of the seven villages comprising the plantation's eminent domain that the Chinese were "killing them slowly on a daily basis…".[17]

The claim of slow death here, recalled in visceral accounts of relations with the plantation at Magbass, appeared to name what scholars have variously articulated as the attenuating effects of precarious life. Its distinctive temporality is one of managed and quotidian violence, ordinary subjection that does not propose the possibility of an end-point but, on the

[16] Lease Contract on Magbass Sugar Complex of Sierra Leone. 23 January 2003. Freetown, Sierra Leone.

[17] "SiLNORF & PS North Mediate in Magbass land dispute," *Awoko,* 8 August 2012.

contrary, gives name to "the destruction of life, bodies, imaginaries, and environments by and under contemporary regimes of capital" (Berlant 2012: 104). Workers who conveyed the resonance of the ephemeral presence of the Chinese spoke to the fractious temporality of prosperity and its promised arrival in the form of waged employment which has characterized the idea of the modern in Sierra Leone (as elsewhere). By contrast, the "traditional" nature of village life in Sierra Leone has come to stand as a vague euphemism for the suffering of rural poverty, disingenuously dehistoricized and coded as an expression of primordial culture. In 2013, one Minister of Agriculture went so far to describe the predicament of the country's rural poor as one of "sub-existing," with local nutrition and livelihoods even falling short of what could be called *subsistence*.[18] Who, in such circumstances, would not welcome the arrival of a wealthy investor, even if this gift horse presented its own precarities?

And yet, a deep ambivalence remains regarding the speculative premise of foreign investment (which purports that labor improves the lives of workers, and posits extraction as a generative, life-giving gesture) and the experiences of workers themselves, who are solicited as subjects and agents of their own development (Kish and Leroy 2015). As scholars who have sought to underscore the relation between agricultural indebtedness and crisis accumulation have shown, agribusiness drives land and property reforms in service to commodity exports, leading to the increasing intermediation of rural populations by financial logics and neoliberal ideologies of growth, particularly when projects of national development are congealed with the private and the corporate (Mendonça and Pitta 2018; Elsheikh 2013).

Just as China's rise as a global power is increasingly subject to claims of its role in a "new scramble for Africa" in which putatively benevolent interventions are made on the back of material enticements such as trade and investment, little has been made of how such narratives of exceptional growth have been mobilized as a pedagogical reference in countries desiring development.[19] In Sierra Leone (but also Jamaica,

[18] Minister of Agriculture, Forestry and Food Security; FAO representative in Sierra Leone, direct communication, 11 October 2010. Quoted in "Understanding Land Investment Deals in Africa—Country Report: Sierra Leone," Oakland, CA: *Oakland Institute*.

[19] In 2018, a story broke in French newspaper *Le Monde* accusing China of systematically hacking the African Union headquarters in Addis Ababa, a building funded by

Togo and Ukraine), turnkey agribusiness and the rehabilitation of defunct operations have become a stage for the capacities of Chinese technical intervention as a crucial "engine" for accelerating national growth.[20] At root in accompanying narratives of the neoliberal plantation is also a sense of the happy affect of development, in which the promise of productive life purports to produce "new and beautiful" things for local communities. At the same time that scholars have turned attention to the political idealism inscribed in the wake of Bandung and its political afterlives as a diagnostic for the promise and failures of internationalism, this chapter asks that we consider such histories with reference to the parallel history of transnational intervention, one in which new concentrations of capital and itineraries of improvement yielded depressingly familiar cycles of domination and harm (Eslava, Fakhri and Nesiah 2017; Tull 2010)[21] (Fig. 10.3).

The Promise of Productive Life

Between the ruined photograph and the ruined site, stories of ruined bodies greeted me when I arrived in Magbass. Speaking to lawyers from a legal empowerment network at their office in Freetown, I learned that COMPLANT's operation at Magbass had achieved its own infamy for the alleged use of banned chemicals: most notably, *Furadan*, the brand name for Carbofuran, a broad-spectrum chemical insecticide with devastating effects on the human nervous system. In perhaps the most spectacular display of its hazards, a group of about twenty field workers at Magbass had suffered severe physical effects after inhaling fumes from a shipment of the chemical in the process of unloading it from the back of a vehicle. Several of these workers had collapsed and fallen into a coma and were rushed to the nearest hospital. In 2009, the Environmental Protection

Beijing and constructed by state-owned contractors. Ghalia Kadiri and Joan Tilouine, "A Addis-Abeba, le siège de l'Union africaine espionné par Pékin," *Le Monde Afrique,* 26 January 2018. Richard Poplak, "The new scramble for Africa: how China became the partner of choice," *The Guardian,* 22 December 2016, Alexis Okeowo, "China in Africa: The New Imperialists?," *New Yorker,* June 12 2013.

[20] "COMPLANT wasting no time," *The Gleaner*, August 16 2011.

[21] Thanks to Rosalind C. Morris for the observation that war between India and China broke out soon after Bandung, and China's anti-Indian stance is not unrelated to its "pro-Africanism."

Fig. 10.3 View from the factory grounds at Magbass (Photo by author)

Agency (EPA) ruled to comprehensively restrict the use of carbofuran products, effectively banning the use of Furadan in the United States. It cited that effects of aggregate exposure to the chemical throughout the population—in the trace doses present in food and drinking water—posed "acute" and "unacceptable risks," particularly to children, and revoked previously defined levels of "tolerance." The EPA's toxicology report provides a long enumeration of the physical signs and symptoms of carbofuran in the human body, citing that: "Acute exposure is defined as an exposure of short duration, usually characterized as lasting no longer than a day."[22]

[22] Synthesized and manufactured by the Philadelphia company, FMC Corporation, since 1967, the widespread use and attendant harms of Furadan first drew wide attention in 1985, when the U.S. Fish and Wildlife Service noted the acute toxicity posed by the chemical to aquatic life and birds. It reported on the prevalence of bird deaths and the contamination of drinking water near farmlands where it had been applied extensively on food crops destined for the domestic market. Reports claimed the kills of egrets in

The chemical tolerances defined by the EPA might be understood as one representation of human value: a sense of social knowledge in which the biological capacity of bodies for toxic endurance meet their agreed-upon limits.[23] The extent to which physical burdens are deemed "tolerable" by human bodies rests on an implicit rationalization of hazard by judging the highest degree of harm a body can take. It is a reasoning that derives vindication from an imagination of injury within bearable limits—of life at the threshold of death. Three decades after the environmental impact of Furadan and the effects of its use were widely publicized, carbofuran products continue to be consumed in FMC's international markets under a variety of names and analog formulations. At Magbass, "in the time of Chinese," women and men wore sprayers filled with Furadan strapped around the body, with perhaps a rag around the face or a pair of sunglasses above the nose—methods of the meagerest protection.

In Mamuntha, I stood and listened as workers described the effects of Furadan on their bodies in terms of rashes, aches and pains. The chemicals had soaked into the soil and groundwater around the complex for many years, maybe decades: "Some of our brothers get *bad bad* sicknesses. Because we have no protective gear... no directions to say this is what you should use, or how you should protect yourself." Alpha, who sprayed pesticides and fertilizers for COMPLANT told me about his experiences with another chemical which he knew as *DVD*: "especially dangerous when mixed in the open air," when a strong breeze might carry the fumes into the path of a flying bird, killing it instantly. As he described how these chemicals were prepared, Alpha indicated with his hands: "If you poured it *over here*, they would go and stand *over there* and tell the blacks to go and mix it. They knew that it was a dangerous something." The Chinese "did not care," he said.

As he spoke, my thoughts ran to *DDT,* the chemical compound whose "indiscriminate" use in the United States throughout the 1960s led to the coalescence of a popular ecological consciousness around the human harms of pesticides and their toxic accumulation in the food chain (Carson 2000 [1962]). Like Furadan, DVD is an infamous poison at Magbass,

Louisiana and the extensive poisoning of river fish. See Carbofuran; Proposed Tolerance Revocations, Environmental Protection Agency, Jul 31, 2008.

[23] According to regulatory systems in the European Union, notions of chemical tolerance are measured by "maximum residue levels"—the highest possible amount that can be present in trace amounts.

but one whose substance remains somehow inaccessible, encrypted in this reference to a new but increasingly outmoded media technology. The repetitious insistence of accounts suggesting an acute awareness of the dangers posed by these chemicals was corroborated by farm workers whose relative proximities to the toxic threat seemed to underscore the deliberate and differential distribution of harm at the plantation under the direction of Chinese overseers.

> "If you use it all day, if you use it *all day,* it affects you. You collapse..."
> "*Did you tell them?* I asked.
> "We told them and we told them and we told them," he said. "Those chemicals are not good for *mortal man*."

Mortal man is a term in the Krio language which you could translate as "human being," but carries with it the sense of vulnerability to death that is the human condition. Owing to the industrial efficacy of these chemicals in plantation ecologies—where the killing of non-human animals with pesticides remains a crucial procedure in the making of agricultural modernity—their long-term effects in specific communities are less known than their advertised effects (Murphy 2017). Such workers are wary, both of their usefulness and the carelessness through which they are subjected to harm, where the stability of a term like "tolerance" is coded in a complex symbolic repertoire of work as a means for transcending the living death of rural poverty (from *sub-existence* to surplus) even as that path is laden with risk. Plantation workers at Magbass who attribute their poisoning to foreign sources also rely on their proximity to these poisons as signs and sources of life. Parallel to these accounts describing the cumulative effects of plantation toxicity from local workers whose habitual exposure to these chemicals marks the differential distribution of harm. Chinese managerial narratives are embedded in the logics of collectivity and service to the corporate body, celebrating the affordances of tolerance as subordinate to the logic of profit.

In October 2007, the management of the Magbass Sugar Complex responded to the threat of strike action and resistance to their plans for expansion with a two-page message addressed to workers. Written in English, the letter was printed and pasted in numerous locations on the factory's walls, to be read and shared by employees of the plantation. Detailing the terms of the company's lease in an introductory section ("*1.*

Why We Are Here"), the address goes on to describe the socially stabilizing effect of the rehabilitation four years earlier, mobilizing the image of a new consumerism made possible to local women and men with the wages of their work.

> 2. "What We Have Done"
> Thanks to all the efforts and endeavors from the relevant sectors, to date the Company could have embraced three productions with the first one as trial. No one could deny the great changes brought along for the local areas since the establishment of the Company, in addition to vast job opportunities created so far. We are happy to know that the local women many now afford to buy new and beautiful clothes. We are happy to hear that local man could now drive their motorcycles around; we are more than happy to see the children waving aloft their little hands and saying hello to us, as they realize their new and beautiful schoolbags would never come too reality without the presence of Chinese here. Now, one primary school is there as our donation to local society. Such contribution, as one of our ways for returning to the people of Sierra Leone, will be continuing.

Local hopes had been fueled with COMPLANT's commitments to the villages who had relinquished their lands to the plantation, including assurances to develop a "social infrastructure," attending to fundamental deficiencies in schools and health facilities in the local area. Crucially, these calls appeared to locate the inherent value of employment and the affordances of a sympathetic community, geared toward a common set of aspirations and endeavors (Fennell 2012):

> Let's work together and push the Company forward so that we may achieve your aim and also realise our goal. As our GM said in the meeting on Oct. 22, we are brothers, as we are working in the same place; we are colleagues, as we are employees of the same company. So, why couldn't we join together, hand in hand? But now we are facing another urgent difficulty: our plan of land expansion was stopped, and it is one of the important issues the Management embarked upon. The earlier we expand the land for growing more sugar cane, the sooner the Company could get rid of the deficit and the earlier you receive more payment. From this point of view, your benefits and ours are actually mutual-linked. We appreciate and are grateful if anyone of you could try to persuade the local people and allow us to continue our job on land expansion.

In spite of the heavy initial outlay, the letter told workers that the factory continued to operate at a loss, and that more capital and land were necessary in order to recoup their investment. As administrators invoked the financial struggles of the company, the letter reiterated the nebulous promise of better days ahead, calling on the workers of Magbass to redouble their efforts in the expansion of the plantation grounds. But the tone of the letter takes a shift in the closing Sect. (*4. Our Good Will*) in reference to an illegal strike the previous month:

> .... recently we are told that some of you will hold another strike on Nov. 1 if their salaries are not satisfied. We hope it is merely a rumor. We sincerely hope that no one of you will resort to extreme action because your job is not a matter for kidding. At least, as one of our commitments, the Company pays you each month, so that each month you can physically receive your income which might be the only source for supporting your family. And if there is anyone who still feels unhappy, please do not hesitate to come to the management's office to talk, to discuss, or even to negotiate with us. Anyone who is clear-minded and reasonable would like to settle a matter by means of friendly discussion rather than laying down tools. Agree? Hope so. Please do keep it your mind: we are here not only for purpose of profit, but also for a close relationship with Sierra Leone people, for the development of local economy, and for the improvement of living standard for local inhabitants.
>
> Let's pray for a better-off Complex to come!
> Let's share the weal and woe, the rise and fall of the Company!
> Let's join together, hand in hand to embrace a more bright future!
>
> God bless you!
> Management of the Company
>
> Management of the Company

In its appeal to "hard-working, reasonable and self-disciplined" employees in the future profitability of the company, the letter evokes the history of developmentalist rationales which summoned Sierra Leoneans in the years after decolonization. Continuous drives toward agrarian prosperity hailed the country's citizens as lapsed farmers, enjoining their return to the "bush" as a means of alleviating their own poverty through a collective struggle to gain self-sufficiency in the nation's staple crop—*rice*. Like this acrostic published in a Department of Agriculture newsletter in 1986, industrial plantations signified the arrival of a certain kind of agricultural modernity in Sierra Leone, embodying the idioms of progress and development articulated by the postcolonial state, particularly the All People's Congress government.

> —**G**o now and —**R**estore —**E**very available land to —**E**nsure —**N**ational food self-sufficiency —**R**evolutionize production in —**E**very —**V**alley —**O**r —**L**and to —**U**rgently —**I**mprove —**T**he living conditions of the people and —**O**ur **N**ation.[24]

When I visited Magbass in 2018, it was possible to still hear many people tell stories that President Stevens had personally traveled out to the swampy *boli* nearly 40 years earlier, driving over dirt roads to strongarm the Paramount Chiefs and landholding families into signing the contract which enshrined the plantation into law, conjoining seven villages (Mamuntha, Rochain, Maforba, Makapr, Rothongbai, Mathinka and Magbass). In my interviews with Sierra Leoneans old enough to remember, many vividly alluded to a "call" to the fields throughout the 1970s and 1980s as a palliative to the nation's hunger against the backdrop of a "Green Revolution" which paradoxically saw an increasing dependency on rice imports in West African countries (Davidson 2016). Mahmoud, a schoolteacher who once worked at Magbass for a stint in the 1980s, recalled how the disembodied voice of President Stevens was broadcast over the country's airwaves, urging urbanite government workers to return to their villages rather than complain about the exorbitant prices of rice or the meagre size of their salaries, which would

[24] This was under President Momoh who ruled from 1985–1991, the terminal years of what is termed in the literature of the period as a "shadow state." Also observable in the discourse of Sierra Leone's Green Revolution is a brand of anti-elite sentiment that would be echoed in the discourse of economic populism during the rebel war, particularly in the imagery of the peasant masses conjured by the ideology of the Revolutionary United Front (RUF), and for whom a "revolutionary" critique of foreign exploitation appeared fully embedded in resource nationalism. As the newsletter notes: "For the urban privileged sitting in the comfort of their homes or place of work, the Green Revolution may not have started…".

routinely arrive one, two and often three months late. Stevens' rationale went as follows: for every three months spent grumbling in the city without pay, a hard-up civil servant could have returned to the fields to plant and harvest a crop of "three-month rice." Money was waiting to be unearthed *in the bush*, he told listeners on the radio, through the diligence and tenacity of a people with a long and rich history of rice cultivation. Reprising the traditional roles of their ancestors, "it would be impossible," said Mahmoud, quoting Stevens, "to work in the field for three months and not harvest!".

Consider then, by contrast, the scenes of abject poverty at Magbass described by Michael (the administrator) after the plantation's closure, when the work ceased overnight. He moved to Freetown to oversee the maintenance of the complex and the sourcing of new investment, becoming one of the few remaining Sierra Leoneans still on the company's payroll. When the Chinese managers left him with the office and flew home, he told me:

> I couldn't just think of myself. I said to myself: "Without the Chinese being here, I'll be able to get a job elsewhere." But there are people there who lived there... wholly and solely, who would say: "After Magbass, unless I die, I'm not going anywhere" or "I won't be able to get a job anywhere." So when the work closed down, some died, some deteriorated. You might see a boy of 18 or 20, you'd think he was 30 or 35. Because of poverty. People are suffering in that place.

Fallow fields coincided with accounts of accelerated biological aging for locals, some of whom appeared to embody their abandonment. For many, the absence of productive life at the plantation meant a regressive turn to the traditional lifeways of "hoe and cutlass" farmers in the country, tilling familial lands under customary tenure with rudimentary tools. The narrative of death and deterioration as a consequence of their unemployment posited "the Chinese" (and the mode of production for which their presence was a metonym) as a life-giving presence. During its years of operation, even small farmers had grown accustomed to the affordances of the plantation. Signs on the factory wall spoke of punishments and offered rewards for information leading to the culprits of thefts of ethanol. Cheap gasoline and fertilizer, acquired from unlocked storerooms and backs of company trucks and sold on the black market had become hallmarks of the company's presence, supplementing familial farms outside the plantation. Not only did these unofficial "subsidies" increase yields, mitigating the need for manual farm work; they also allowed for subsistence farmers to sell their excess crops in ways unforeseen by the Chinese. In the wake of their departure, that transformative power was all the more apparent as people in the region reconciled themselves to an altogether different kind of displacement: the migration of young men from their homes in the provinces to the city to find waged work (Fig. 10.4).

Moving around the plantation grounds, I heard stories from those who had tried and failed to abandon their own farms for Freetown, only to return in a matter of days or weeks, unable to survive without networks of kin and the means of subsistence (like rice farms or poultry) taken for granted in the provinces. Some had been in the process of taking their senior school exams, only to end their studies abruptly with the departure of the Chinese in 2015, when "Ebola wrecked the last of the white man jobs." Such narratives of wreckage compounded the magnetism of the city, which drew these men to join its precarious class of rural migrants, subsisting from the land in other ways (as wood cutters and stone-breakers) or by joining the ranks of commercial motorbike riders. After the epidemic was declared over, most of the former employees of the complex had returned to tending small farms of rice and groundnuts

Fig. 10.4 Satellite imagery of the grid at Magbass (Google Earth)

in familial smallholdings at the edges of the plantation, taken over by tall grass in place of the towering cane. In the village of Mabure, many of those who received wages at Magbass had mobilized what little they had been able to accrue toward vocational training and education. They traced for me the itinerance of men who had left the region in search of work in Freetown as manual laborers: carrying sand on their backs for construction, or digging for gold near Bo, before returning "upline" in the months before the rains to help with the harvest. Another young man who had trained to use heavy machinery during the operation of the plantation told me he had no money to apply for his license, so he stayed in Mabure to be with his family: "People here don't have money to help us go forward in life."

But other locals expressed deeper attachments to rural livelihoods that exceeded dependency on the plantation, asserting their own relationships to the land as its own kind of sovereignty. They were more cynical about the claims of worklessness offered by local men in the absence of the Chinese: "They are parasites!" one older man exclaimed. "Look at the bush! Why can't you go and make cassava farms?" he asked. "There are hoes around here, cutlasses!" In the meantime, the plant's machines had remained in a state of complete inactivity, its precious stores of fuel and fertilizer attended day and night by a rotation of no fewer than 60 security guards, who remained on the company's payroll. In our conversations, a few of these guards told me that prostitution had been rife after the war, with children fathered by Chinese contractors who had "kept girlfriends" among local women. They told me a story that I heard many times at Magbass: that during the earliest iterations of the plantation—at the time of the Chinese aid project in the 1970s—Chinese workers who arrived in Sierra Leone had been injected and temporarily sterilized "so they didn't use the women too much." I could hardly believe it, but the accounts were too numerous to ignore. That notion of sexual restraint had changed with the arrival of COMPLANT in 2003, a guard explained: "With these new ones who are just investors, they're *free*...".

What to make of such a story? If Sierra Leone's government was involved in a mass-sterilization scheme of Chinese expatriate workers in the 1970s, there was no trace of it in the archives at the Ministry of Agriculture. It's tempting to read into that gendered and racialized account of penetrability (both of the Chinese and of local women) the anxieties of sovereignty at Magbass. In his juxtaposition of the libidinal freedom

Fig. 10.5 View from the factory grounds at Magbass (Photo by author)

of investment with the respect and restraint of mutual economic "cooperation," the guard's account literalized the relations of bodily use on the plantation. It named the nature of entrepreneurship without conditions: the freedom of the free market in which local women could also sell their labor. Young men I knew in Freetown called home, hoping to *draw* their girlfriends from the villages. But if they followed and went to work in the city where would they sleep? They had been visited in the past as subjects of sympathy, fed rumors and promises "in the media" about the impending development in their community. Many farmers who had begun to resume work on the abandoned fields for their own crops had been ordered to stop. They heard that the Chinese were returning imminently, *this year*, *very soon*.

Conclusion

If the 1980s in Sierra Leone are recalled doubly—both as a traumatic decade of structural adjustment and as the peaceful antebellum before the slide into state failure—they also track with the broader collapse of the Bandung project, constituting a wholesale reorientation, if not ruin, of postcolonial politics (Scott 1999: 196). Chinese presences in Sierra Leone have long been heralded as a sign of productive futures, part of the nation's flagship infrastructures of development, perhaps nowhere more so that at Magbass over the decades since its construction. Like the ontology of the photograph, one must also contend with the ambivalence of the ruin, which insists on its being in multiple times at once. In the narration of Chinese investment as an ethical gesture, corporate occupation (notoriously harmful to local ecologies and workers themselves) is steeped in narratives of promise and development which operate within a future-oriented trajectory of labor and reward. As inhabitants and former workers at the plantation complex described the unreliable temporality of prosperity at Magbass, they did so in reference to a discourse of developmentalism that has long derived its rhetorical power from narratives of large-scale, mechanized production in agricultural communities. The history of that labor, marked by lingering ailments of remaining inhabitants who live on the plantation site, must be understood through the lens in which individuals are called upon to transcend their poverty through work (Fig. 10.5).

As plantation infrastructures leave behind traces of past history, chemical accretions and affective resonances of past development (Agard-Jones 2013) this text calls for a greater attunement to how such repertoires are deeply relational, reliant on the rehearsal of useful idioms of commonality, fraternity and friendship. The *xeno*-figure of foreign intervention symbolizes both the ends and means of that development alongside more and less spectacular forms of long-term material transformation.[25] New highways and offices cannot be thought of without their counterparts: 99-year leases, ruined ecosystems and chemical accretions whose origins remain elusive. The double bind is endured by rural communities like those in Magbass, solicited as subjects of development by narratives of

[25] I borrow this term from Christopher Pinney (2002) whose argument about the material traces of cultural forms is particularly germane here.

growth and instrumentalized as part of Sierra Leone's push toward "self-sufficiency." And yet, as workless employees at Magbass await the return of "the Chinese" they reveal the contradictions inherent in the anticipation of a *return* to productive life, marking the radical foreclosure of alternatives to a possible future held in abeyance.

References

Agard-Jones, V. 2013. "Bodies in the System". *Small Axe*, 17 (3 [42]): 182–192.

Annual Report of the Labour Department of Sierra Leone. 1950. Freetown: Government Printer.

APC: A Decade of Development and Progress. 1978. Freetown: Government Printer.

Berlant, L. 2012. *Cruel Optimism*. Durham: Duke University Press.

Brautigam, D. 2011. *The Dragon's Gift: The Real Story of China in Africa*. Oxford: Oxford University Press.

Bräutigam, D., and X. Tang. 2009. China's Engagement in African Agriculture: 'Down to the Countryside.' *The China Quarterly* 199: 686–706.

Buckley, L. 2014. Photography and Photo-Elicitation after Colonialism. *Cultural Anthropology* 29 (4): 720–743.

Carson, R. 2000 [1962]. *Silent Spring*. London: Penguin.

Carmody, P. 2011. *The New Scramble for Africa*. Malden: Polity Press.

Davidson, J. 2016. Rice and Revolution: Agrarian Life and Global Food Policy on the Upper Guinea Coast. In *The Upper Guinea Coast in global perspective*, ed. J. Knorr and C. Kohl, 174–196. New York: Berghahn Books.

Eisler, R. 1985. "Carbofuran hazards to fish, wildlife, and invertebrates: a synoptic review". *U.S. Fish and Wildlife Service Biological Report* 85 (1.3).

Elsheikh, E. 2013, October 22. Notes on Global Structural Inequality: Land and Neoliberal Politics in Africa, *Oakland Institute*.

Englund, H. 2008. Extreme Poverty and Existential Obligations: Beyond Morality in the Anthropology of Africa? *Social Analysis: THe International Journal of Anthropology* 52 (3): 33–50.

Eslava, L., M. Fakhri, and V. Nesiah, eds. 2017. *Bandung, Global History, and International Law: Critical Pasts and Pending Futures*. Cambridge: Cambridge University Press.

Ferme, M.C., and C.M. Schmitz. 2014. Writings on the Wall: Chinese Material Traces in an African Landscape. *Journal of Material Culture* 19 (4): 375–399.

Fennell, C. 2012. The Museum of Resilience: Raising a Sympathetic Public in Postwelfare Chicago. *Cultural Anthropology* 27 (4): 641–666.

Graham, J.D. 1974. The Tanzam Railway: Consolidating the People's Development and Building the Internal Economy. *Africa Today* 21 (3): 27–42.

Harvey, M. 1966. "A geographical study of the pattern, processes and consequences of urban growth in Sierra Leone in the twentieth century." Ph.D. dissertation Durham University.
Kish, Z., and J. Leroy. 2015. Bonded Life. *Cultural Studies*, 29 (5-6): 630–651.
Mauss, M. 2011. *[1925], The Gift*. London: Routledge.
Mendonça, M.L., and F.T. Pitta. 2018. International Financial Capital and the Brazilian Land Market. *Latin American Perspectives* 45 (5): 88–101.
Millar, G. 2015. Investing in peace: Foreign direct investment as economic restoration in Sierra Leone? *Third World Quarterly* 36 (9): 1700–1716.
Mintz, S. 1985. *Sweetness and Power*. New York: Penguin.
Mintz, S., and E. Wolf. 1989. Reply to Michael Taussig. *Critique of Anthropology* 9 (1): 25–31.
Murray Li, T., and P. Semedi. 2021. *Plantation Life: Corporate Occupation in Indonesia's Oil Palm Zone*. Durham: Duke University Press.
Murphy, M. 2017. Alterlife And Decolonial Chemical Relations. *Cultural Anthropology* 32: 494–503.
Nixon, R. 2013. *Slow Violence and the Environmentalism of the Poor*. Cambridge: Harvard University Press.
Pan, J. 2020. *Welfare for Autocrats: How Social Assistance in China Cares for its Rulers*. New York: Oxford University Press.
Pinney, C. 2002. Creole Europe: The Reflection of a Reflection. *Journal of New Zealand Literature: JNZL* 20: 125–161.
Rodney, W. 2018. *How Europe Underdeveloped Africa*. London: Verso Books.
Schmitz, C. Mei-ting. 2021. Making Friends, Building Roads: Chinese Entrepreneurship and the Search for Reliability in Angola. *American Anthropologist* 123 (2): 343–354.
Scott, D. 1999. *Refashioning Futures*. Princeton: Princeton University Press.
Scott, D. 2004. Modernity That Predated the Modern: Sidney Mintz's Caribbean. *History Workshop Journal* 58: 191–210.
Stoler, A.L. 2016. *Duress: Imperial Durabilities in Our Times*. Durham: Duke University Press.
Stoler, A.L., ed. 2013. *Imperial Debris: On Ruins and Ruination*. Durham: Duke University Press.
Taussig, M. 2018. *Palma Africana*. Chicago: University of Chicago Press.
Taylor, C. 2014. "Plantation Neoliberalism." *New Inquiry*. July 8.
Tsing, A. 2000. The Global Situation. *Cultural Anthropology* 15 (3): 327–360.
Tull, D. 2010. "China's Engagement with Africa: Scope, Significance, and Consequences." In C.r J. Lee (ed.), *Making a World after Empire: The Bandung Moment and its Political Afterlives*, 459–479. Athens: Ohio University Press.

CHAPTER 11

"New Slavery", Modern Marronage and the Multiple Afterlives of Plantations in Contemporary Italy

Irene Peano

The condition of migrant laborers in the Italian farming sector has received increasing (though erratic) attention in the last two decades, both nationally and internationally. Across different fora, it is often glossed in terms of "a new form of slavery". Such definition is not the prerogative of the media alone, whether local, national or international—albeit certainly they employ the image very frequently when

Most of the research and analysis for this piece was carried out between 2017 and 2020, within the ERC Advanced Grant project "The Color of Labor: The racialized lives of migrants" (grant no. 695573, PI Cristiana Bastos). Subsequent work has been supported by a grant from the Portuguese Foundation for Science and Technology (FCT), grant no. 2020.01002.CEECIND/CP1615/CT0009.

I. Peano (✉)
Institute of Social Sciences, Univeristy of Lisbon, Lisbon, Portugal
e-mail: irene.peano@ics.ulisboa.pt

C. Le Petitcorps et al. (eds.), *Global Plantations in the Modern World*, Cambridge Imperial and Post-Colonial Studies,
https://doi.org/10.1007/978-3-031-08537-6_11

dealing with the highly precarious working and living conditions of (especially West African) farm laborers. Politicians from across the spectrum, as well as international organizations, NGOs, trade unionists, activists and academics have relayed these depictions, if with different emphases. Workers themselves are among the least likely to identify with the label—although this does happen occasionally. Such representations may be ascribed to what critical appraisals have dubbed as the "new abolitionist" discourse on slavery (O'Connell Davidson 2015): global in sweep, it resurfaced onto the international public arena in the 1990s, concomitantly with growing policy preoccupations with the control of transnational crime and its presumed connections with cross-border migration.

Such endless summoning of "slavery" in descriptions of migrant workers' living and labor conditions in Italian agro-industrial districts, as I have recorded them in ten years of research and engagement, prompted the questions I address here. Recurrent evocations of slavery, and their critiques, are always also preoccupations with a past (or rather a multiplicity of pasts) whose weighty, but partially disavowed or displaced, specters haunt the present. If, as Julia O'Connell Davidson reasons, "'Modern slavery' names not a thing, but a set of claims about what is (and what is not) morally and politically obscene" (2015: 26), then just what these claims might be; how they are articulated, responded to or occluded; what in turn they themselves work to occlude and, most poignantly, through what deployments of historical narratives deserve further attention in the context at hand. In particular, it is to the specters of "the plantation" as the (ob)scene of "modern slavery" that I turn, in order to trace alternative genealogies of the current organization and representation of migrant farm labor in Italian agro-industrial districts.

Multiple, geographically and temporally heterogeneous plantation pasts haunt contemporary agribusiness districts, the slums and labor camps which punctuate them, and their patterns of labor management, in different and even contradictory ways. My reflections are based on ten years of engaged, participatory research among migrant farm workers across several agro-industrial enclaves in Italy (mostly the Apulian Tavoliere, the Plain of Gioia Tauro in Calabria and the district surrounding the town of Saluzzo in Piedmont), supplemented by historical, archival and other secondary material, as well as by interactions with farmers, third-sector and state employees, and other actors who have engaged with such representations in different ways.

Speaking of Slavery Today

While contemporary forms of "slavery" (often labelled as "modern" or "new") have been identified across many economic sectors, in Italy the complex discursive assemblage that coalesced around the notion now invests farming more than any other activity except that of prostitution, where the latter is equated with sexual exploitation. (Indeed, this is the domain in which the discourse was first articulated, both in public debate and through legal dispositifs[1]). In some cases the two spheres are juxtaposed, as when the plight of female farm workers and the sexual harassment and violence to which they are subjected is exposed,[2] or when describing the slum-like spaces in which African laborers live, where (mostly Nigerian) prostitutes also work.[3] Narratives produced by the media, by politicians, NGOs, researchers, activists and unionists, but also legal dispositifs and their offshoots into corporate-management regulations and trade certificates have somehow internalized and relayed the notion that hyper-exploitation in the agri-business sector is to be identified with enslavement.

In their discourses, different actors have of course emphasized different aspects in relation to such imageries, stemming from a range of positionings, dispositions, assumptions and intentions. However, slavery is invariably associated with migrant, most often black (African) laborers, and the isolated, precarious camp- or slum-like housing patterns which have been the cipher of their condition and its representation in the last decade. Just what the term of comparison might be—the "old" slavery against which this "new" form is pitted—often remains unacknowledged, but several clues point to New-World plantations as its paragon. Clearly,

[1] Critical literature examining the emergence and significance of discourses on slavery related to sex trafficking and prostitution in the contemporary period is vast. For specific references to the Italian context, see for example Andrijasevic (2010) and my own work (Peano 2011).

[2] See for example Tondo, L. and A. Kelley 2017. "Raped, Beaten, Exploited: The 21st-century Slavery Propping up Sicilian Farming. Thousands of Female Romanian Farm Workers Are Suffering Horrendous Abuse". *The Guardian*, 12th March - https://www.theguardian.com/global-development/2017/mar/12/slavery-sicily-farming-raped-beaten-exploited-romanian-women, retrieved 31st January 2022.

[3] Barbaro, E. 2019. "Metà donne, metà schiave. Le vie della prostituzione sono infinite". *Terre di Frontiera*, 30th October—https://www.terredifrontiera.info/le-vie-della-prostituzione-sono-infinite/, retrieved 31st January 2022.

the analogy with trans-Atlantic triangulations is lent particular power when applied to capitalist agriculture and racialized (black or brown) workers, reactivating plantation imaginaries that may be triggered by a spectrum of affective investments—from indignation and even repugnance to cruel detachment, manipulation and hypocrisy or sheer, perverse enjoyment derived from a feeling of omnipotence and the power to subjugate.

Several politicians, including former Minister for Internal Affairs, Matteo Salvini, have related "new slavery" to undocumented migration. Commenting on the news of seven speedboats, which carried 187 Tunisian citizens, landing at Lampedusa harbor on 15th September 2018, during a meeting with his colleagues from across the EU, he confidently declared: "We don't feel the need to have new slaves to replace the children we no longer have".[4] The instrumental use of humanitarian sentiment to criminalize migration (here equated to a biopolitical conspiracy towards "ethnic substitution") has indeed been a common feature in the repertoire of the notoriously anti-immigrant politician, as well as of many others. Before and after taking office, Salvini repeatedly justified inhumane policies of border closure and refoulment with the need to combat the trafficking, enslavement, torture and death of African migrants in Libya and across the Mediterranean (cf. De Genova 2017 on similar claims being made in 2015 by the previous legislature's social-democratic prime minister, Matteo Renzi). In the media, images of makeshift boats and dinghies stuffed with black human cargo are sometimes juxtaposed with the plight of African farm workers, implying a direct and even exclusive connection between the (chronic, if policy-crafted and yet naturalized) "migration emergency" along the central Mediterranean route with the issue of migrant farm-labor exploitation.

While the "border spectacles" (Cuttitta 2012; De Genova 2013) of Mediterranean crossings have been seen to evoke the Middle Passage (Stierl 2019), their association to farm labor under hyper-exploitative conditions works to reinforce the analogy between the historic plantation complex and contemporary agribusiness.

[4] Grignetti, F. 2018. Migranti, Salvini contro tutti: "Non ci servono nuovi schiavi", *La Stampa* 15th September—https://www.lastampa.it/politica/2018/09/15/news/migranti-salvini-contro-tutti-non-ci-servono-nuovi-schiavi-1.34045228, retrieved 31st January 2022.

Visual artists have also produced portraits of disarticulated, reified and racialized body parts (such as chained black wrists and ankles, for example) that act as metonyms of migrant laborers and symbolize their exploitation in the farms (see Figs. 11.1 and 11.2). The same visual trope is found on countless book and magazine covers, on flyers, photographs and posters promoting discussions and analyses on the subject of migrant farm labor. In summoning, and even exploiting, the specter of extreme forms of alienation, carceral discipline and racial terror that have in American plantations their most recognizable, even primal, stage, these depictions at the same time deny workers' very subjectivity, reproducing that fungibility (King 2016) that lay at the core of the enslaved condition on historic plantations.

In some instances, it is employers' attitudes against workers that have prompted such analogies, as in the case of a farmer in the Pontine area, part of the district of Latina, south of Rome. News of his arrest, which took place in October 2019, reached international media outlets, including British daily *The Times*, whose correspondent wrote: "An Italian farmer has been accused of terrorizing his migrant workers with a shotgun and a knife and forcing them to work in the fields like slaves". The reporter quotes sociologist Marco Omizzolo, who has been conducting research among the Indian Sikh workers in the area, declaring "It's a new form of the slavery once seen in the American south".[5] Another article relating the incident, this time from a local newspaper, describes it as "an occurrence which seems to come straight out of the 2013 film masterpiece, directed by Londoner Steve McQueen, '12 years a Slave'".[6] Farmers themselves, or those in their close circles, have even been caught employing the term "slaves" to describe workers. Such is for example the case with one of the three men arrested in the district of Foggia (Apulia) in February 2020, following an investigation from which it emerged that dozens of workers (from West Africa, Morocco and Albania) were severely exploited, and even beaten, in two large and wealthy farms. In a phone call intercepted by the judiciary and published in the local press, a friend

[5] "Italian Farmer Used Shotgun to Keep Migrant 'Slaves' in Line", 15th October 2019, https://www.thetimes.co.uk/article/italian-farmer-used-shotgun-to-keep-migrant-slaves-in-line-vt5f62v68, retrieved 27th January 2022.

[6] https://latinatu.it/larresto-dellagricoltore-schiavista-fa-il-giro-del-mondo-e-finisce-sul-times/?fbclid=IwAR0zeUkXB-yqNTPkTVPBAG-a4XqChJ7L6QOQEmuEGUBpmBcrm7CgujSJX98, retrieved 30th January 2022. All translations are mine.

Fig. 11.1 "Solo braccia" (arms only), an installation by visual artist Alessandro Tricarico, commissioned by medical NGO InterSOS in 2020 to commemorate the death of 16 West African farm workers returning from a day's work in tomato farms, in two separate road accidents that took place in the district of Foggia in the summer of 2018. The 32-m-high paper print was glued upon the dismissed wheat silos that tower over the railway line at Foggia's northeastern end (Photograph by Marta Selleri)

Fig. 11.2 "No slaves"—Unknown author, mural painting spotted outside the train station in Rosarno, Plain of Gioia Tauro, 2018 (Photograph by the author)

of one of the defendants casually remarks "I went by [your farm] and I saw *the slaves* working".[7] Farmers' and gangmasters' use of weapons and of other forms of physical violence, as well as of verbal abuse and threats—as a means of disciplining workers and more generally asserting authority and inculcating terror—has been witnessed by several African farm laborers whom I encountered in the district of Foggia, and again may suggest analogies with the original scene of capitalist, colonial export agriculture. In my experience, migrant farm workers often equate the conditions of dire exploitation, vulnerability and existential precarity to which they are subjected to a process of animalization (cf. Peano 2020), clearly identifying the dehumanizing nature of structural racism and thus arguably also evoking American plantation enslavement as the context in which such racism was first, and to some extent most thoroughly and overtly, experimented and elaborated.

As anticipated, the new-slavery gloss inflects not only media rhetoric, political discourse, research, trade-union activism, artistic productions

[7] https://www.immediato.net/2020/02/12/caporale-foggiano-arrestato-le-intercettazioni-ho-visto-gli-schiavi-lavorare-il-reclutatore-se-padrone-non-risponde-cerco-altro-padrone/, retrieved 27th January 2022.

and labor relations themselves, but also legal provisions against what is deemed to be the major *cause*, or instrument, of migrant farm workers' subjection: illicit labor brokering, known in jargon as "*caporalato*" (gangmastership), a term denoting a quasi-military form of work discipline (cf. Ravano and Sacchi, this volume). New laws punishing such misconduct were introduced into the Italian criminal code following a two-week long, 400-strong wildcat strike staged by African migrants, that took place in the summer of 2011 and was heavily mediatized (Brigate di Solidarietà Attiva et al. 2012; Perrotta 2015). The workers had been employed in the harvest of tomato and watermelon in the countryside surrounding Nardò, a municipality in the district of Lecce, southern Apulia, and recruited by several migrant brokers. The bill, which was first drafted years before but had never made it to parliamentary debate until then, turned unlicensed labor intermediation (previously an administrative breach) into a criminal offense, initially punishing gangmasters only. In 2016 it was amended to include employers' joint liability, thus redressing, at least on paper, a classist and racialist bias—for, in the majority of cases, gangmasters happen to be themselves migrants, and are certainly represented as such by mainstream descriptions, although a considerable "market" for Italian farm workers exists. Especially in the southern regions, local workers (the majority of whom are women) are recruited by Italian intermediaries. It was the death, in the summer of 2015, of one such workers on the job, 49-year-old mother-of-three Paola Clemente, that prompted the further tightening of repressive measures. It is as if Italian farmers could only be thought accountable if their behavior affected "one of their kind".

The legal dispositif criminalizing labor intermediation was inserted into the section of the penal code that punishes crimes against individual personality (such as reduction into or maintenance in a condition of slavery or servitude, child pornography and trafficking), as a subspecies of the crime of duress ("*plagio*"). Unsanctioned labor intermediation, therefore, oddly shifted from being considered by the law as a mere administrative breach to being rated among the most severe crime typologies contemplated by the code, so-called "natural crimes" (Di Martino 2015). Significantly, critical legal interpretations have pointed to the fact that the newly established offense, especially in its previous formulation, did not appear to display any conspicuous qualitative difference from that of enslavement, for both refer to situations of "violence, threat, intimidation, deception or the profiting from conditions of vulnerability, physical or psychic inferiority, and need" (Ibid.: 79–81 *passim*, my translation). In general, and given the bill's slippery definition of the nature of the crime, few trials and even fewer sentences have applied it so far (Torre 2019).[8]

Even before the 2011 reform, in judicial cases such as that which followed the strike in Nardò, enslavement and trafficking also featured among the charges leveled against the 16 defendants—who included both farmers and brokers—once again operating a slippage and an implicit, partial equivalence between them and the exploitation of waged farm labor (cf. Carlini 2016 for an analysis of the first-degree trial). While initially confirmed by the court, who convicted the defendants to several years' prison terms, the appeal trial overturned the ruling on the ground that not enough evidence supported the conviction. In March 2022, the Supreme Court of Appeal (*Corte di Cassazione*, or Cassation Court) in turn annulled the appeal sentence, intimating that the trial start afresh.

To this day, despite the difficulties in elaborating reliable statistics and notwithstanding the extension of liability to employers, based on my interaction with African farm workers and with those accused of unlawful intermediation, it is evident that racialized migrants are generally the most heavily penalized by the law.[9] In the implementation of controls, ostensibly against gangmastership, migrants are routinely stopped at roadside checkpoints, usually at the end of the harvesting season, and may be incarcerated for various unrelated charges, most often for the purchase of stolen vehicles and for driving without the necessary licenses and insurance—conducts to which they may be forced by a mix of factors, from undocumented status to scarce or no literacy and financial constraints. Further, when employers are held accountable alongside migrant labor brokers, the latter are often subjected to heavier precautionary measures

[8] *Altro Diritto*, an interuniversity legal-research center that set up a lab focusing on labor exploitation and the protection of its victims, reports having found notice of 220 judicial inquiries initiated under such crime hypothesis in the agricultural sector, which led to 208 trials, between 2011 and 2021, predominantly concerning the southern regions (Santoro and Stoppioni 2022: 11). No data is provided on the number and nature of convictions resulting from such trials.

[9] The figures reported by the study cited above (see fn. 8) point to a higher number of trials (154) involving farmers (alone or alongside intermediaries) than those involving only or also intermediaries (118; cf. Santoro and Stoppioni 2022: 17). However, no indication is given as to the actual number of defendants and their role, nor of sentences and their terms. Often, intermediaries are more numerous than farmers in trials of this kind, and they are dealt heavier sentences.

(most commonly imprisonment itself, sometimes on the grounds of a supposedly higher risk of flight, or of the lack of a valid address where to serve house arrest or at which to be reached by law enforcement, as many such defendants live in slums or abandoned, formally uninhabitable buildings). Moreover, companies with a clean record in relation to labor offenses are automatically exempted from any future check by the labor inspectorate after voluntarily adhering to the so-called "quality farm-labor network" (*Rete Lavoro Agricolo di Qualità*). Instituted in 2014 as part of a package of measures to contrast exploitation and illegal brokering in agriculture, it was then broadened and inserted into the bill that modified the criminalization of gangmastership in 2016.

Finally, besides the Italian criminal code, the notion of slavery in the legal domain concerns also multinational companies' corporate social responsibility. Princes LTD, a Liverpool-based subsidiary of the Mitsubishi group that commercializes processed foods, has since 2011 run the largest tomato-processing plant in Europe, located in the Industrial Complex of Incoronata, just outside the city of Foggia. The surrounding flatland (known as *Tavoliere*) is home, in turn, to the second most extensive and productive district in Italy for the farming of industrial tomato. Like all UK-registered companies with an annual turnover of 36 million sterling pounds or higher, since the approval in 2015 of the *Modern Slavery Act*, Princes is legally bound to provide a "slavery and human trafficking statement for each financial year" listing "the steps the organization has taken to ensure that slavery and human trafficking is not taking place (i) in any of its supply chains, and (ii) in any part of its own business" (Part 6, Transparency in Supply Chains Etc.). As it is often the case, to comply with such requirements, in its annual statements the company demonstrates its goodwill by declaring conformity to GlobalGAP international safety certification standards—which, as several studies have demonstrated (Bain 2013; Busch 2000; Busch and Bain 2004; Caruso 2018), rely entirely on privatized assessment, performed mostly through self-administered forms and checklists.[10] UK daily *The Guardian* revealed how in 2016 and 2017 Princes had sourced part of

[10] In their 2019–2020 business report, the company claimed that the totality of the tomatoes processed at their Italian facility "came from farms with independent ethical accreditations (Global GAP/GRASP or SA 8000)"; cf. Princes Group 2020, *2019–2020 Business Report*: 60—https://issuu.com/princes6/docs/princess_-_business_report-feb_19_v15_single_p, retrieved 31st January 2022.

its raw produce from a farm in the district of Lecce, where in 2015 47-year-old Sudanese worker Abdullah Muhammed had died of exhaustion on the job.[11] This was the same farm whose owner, among others, from 2013 till March 2022 stood at the bar in the trial that followed the 2011 strike in Nardò, was convicted in the first degree and acquitted by the appeal sentence, and is now awaiting retrial.

In the summer of 2016, the Princes plant was blockaded by hundreds of West African (and some Bulgarian) farm workers, who identified in the processing and commercialization giant one of the main players in the industrial-tomato supply chain, for which tens of thousands of migrant workers are employed during harvest in the district of Foggia alone. Demonstrators demanded respect of labor agreements, with a commitment by companies across the supply chain to contribute to fairer conditions, and legal recognition as migrant workers. They saw in the interruption of the chain itself their most effective weapon. Some Italian lorry drivers delivering fresh tomato to the plant also joined in, exasperated by the drawn-out, days-long waiting times they are forced to endure outside the factory's premises before they can offload their freight—delays which they attribute to a deliberate strategy on the part of Princes' management to make the tomato dry up under the summer sun and thus reduce its weight and price. In 2020, three high-ranking members of Foggia's main criminal cartels were finally sentenced to several years' imprisonment, following a judicial inquiry that had begun in 2016, for the extortion of the same lorry drivers, to whom the cartels granted "protection" while stationed outside the factory, in exchange for cash payments.[12] Furthermore, Princes plant workers whom I was able to intercept between 2015 and 2018, both in the district of Foggia and in their native villages in south-western Romania, spoke of a fee they were forced to pay to be able to secure the job.

[11] Hunter, I. and L. Di Pietro 2018. "Food firm Princes linked to inquiry into worker abuses in Italy's tomato fields. British company uses supplier currently under investigation for exploiting migrant workers who pick fruit sold in UK and European supermarkets", *The Guardian,* 12th January—https://www.theguardian.com/global-development/2018/jan/12/italian-tomatoes-food-firm-princes-linked-to-labour-abuses-inquiry, retrieved 31st January 2022.

[12] https://www.foggiatoday.it/cronaca/foggia-ordini-carcerazione-processo-rodolfo-pellegrino-capuano-ruggiero.html, retrieved 1st February 2022.

Besides its flagged commitment to anti-slavery standards, Princes also established an agreement with Catholic third-sector giant, Caritas, to employ 9 West African migrants within a project titled "*Lavoro senza frontiere*" (work without borders), for which initiative in September 2021 the company was awarded a prize (bearing the motto "fighting inequality, it's possible") by transnational human-right NGO, Oxfam, and later, in June 2022, by the UN's High Commission for Refugees (UNHCR), at the presence of Italy's Minister of Labor.[13] According to Princes' CEO, interviewed in 2020 by national daily *Il Messaggero,* the merger of the company—established and previously owned by an Italian entrepreneur long under trial for mafia-related crimes, from which he was finally acquitted—was not

> a predatory one, but a virtuous example that favored the import of both English and Japanese labor philosophy, that sees the employee at the center, a sort of managerial humanism. By virtue of such approach, all processes and strategies are aimed at empowerment because each person working within the company possesses their own degree of responsibility and autonomy that must be safeguarded and fostered with a view to welfare and professional valorization.[14]

While the company can claim compliance with anti-slavery standards and human-right protection, other forms of violence, exploitation and injustice, which fall outside the script of "modern slavery", have continued to take place unabated within and around the Princes plant in Foggia, for which they could simply shrug off (or ignore) accountability, aided by their adherence to corporate social responsibility and fair-trade standards that say next to nothing about actual labor conditions.

In view of the sensationalism, shallowness and even active mystifications of abolitionist apparatuses' representations, critics have highlighted how their definitions of what would count as slavery and exploitation are skewed, selective and racism-blind (cf. Howard 2017; Howard and Forin 2019 for specific reference to the industrial-tomato supply

[13] https://www.avvenire.it/attualita/pagine/lavoro-agli-sfruttati-dei-campi-premio, retrieved 1st February 2022; https://www.foggiatoday.it/attualita/princes-premio-alto-commissariato-nazioni-unite-inserimento-lavorativo-rifugiati.html, retrieved 11th July 2022.

[14] https://www.ilmessaggero.it/home/pia_princes_industrie_alimentari_senza_welfare_non_ce_futuro_per_lazienda-5197306.html, retrieved 31st January 2022.

chain that has the district of Foggia at its core). In such discursive assemblages, "new slavery" amounts to an exception-making mechanism treating extreme forms of exploitation as the remnants of a distant past, which has in the new-world plantation its most recognizable, if often implicit referent. New abolitionist discourse transposes and replicates such distant chronotopes into the present of some backward "other" place (such as Southern Italy, especially in its connections with "Africa") where equally backward subjects (southern farmers or migrant gangmasters) are held responsible for the crime of enslavement. The continuities between different forms of labor exploitation and management, that are foundational to current, global political-economic arrangements, are thereby eclipsed. Ultimately, new-abolitionist ideology and its transposition into law and governance tools do not address the structural root causes of exploitation in global neoliberal capitalism. Rather, they criminalize subjects made into passive, infantilized and objectified "Others" or adopt cosmetic accountability measures aimed at staving off bad press more than at concretely improving labor conditions. Furthermore, these discursive operations rely on a selective and recursive summoning of history that occludes other potential connections with alternative space-times, in turn preventing any reckoning with their durable character into the present.

Before, Against and Beyond Echoes of the Middle Passage

The instrumental nature of discourses on "new slavery" has egregious antecedents in the past two centuries, when the denunciation of practices of enslavement was expedient in justifying racist and sexist, imperial and extractive projects in the name of a dubious, paternalistic and self-serving humanitarianism (cf. e.g. Doezema 1999 on the moral panic over "white slavery" and its echoes in contemporary anti-trafficking discourses). In the Italian context, a possible genealogy of this rhetorical strategy can be traced through the 1935 colonial campaign of Mussolini's Fascist government for the conquest of Ethiopia, when the abolition of "Abyssinian slavery" was employed to justify Italian troops' invasion through the mobilization of a powerful set of propaganda tools, which also enlisted intellectuals (Satta 2014, 2016; cf. Trevisani 1937).

More generally, Italy's colonial endeavor, which began in the late nineteenth century with alternating fortunes, could rely on the arguments and findings of the Italian Antislavery Society, established in 1888 under the auspices of Pope Leo XIII, as well as on the parallel and somewhat converging institutional consolidation of the discipline of criminal anthropology and its "scientific racism" (Epstein 2001). The Society was at pains to demonstrate that whatever forms of slavery had existed on "Italian" soil in previous centuries, they were clearly less abominable than those practiced in the New World. Concomitantly, it sought to push the agenda of Italian imperialism in Eastern Africa by citing the example of freed black slave-turned-saint, Benedetto of Palermo, a Franciscan monk known also as "*il moro*" (the moor). Allegedly from "Ethiopia" (which in the sixteenth century could stand for any African provenance), he was made into an exemplar of how all Christian, black Africans had to be freed of their bondage and could (and thus *should*) become "Italian"—yet of course barred from most of the privileges afforded to white citizens. The specter of the American plantation was here a paragon of supreme evil, in ways that are not entirely dissipated today, and served to reinforce the colonialist myth of "*italiani brava gente*" (Del Boca 2005), of a "proletarian" and humane form of colonialism favorably compared to its British and French counterparts.

At the same time, the notion of slavery has deeper and equally consequential ramifications in Western political philosophy. Several scholars have pointed to the genealogy of discourses against slavery, common in European political fora since at least early modernity, as reflections upon political freedom that drew on and reinterpreted Classical, Greek and Roman thought. These were rallies against tyranny that only applied to those who were already deemed as "free men". Their references to slavery had nothing to do with, and actively worked to erase, the systematically silenced or ignored predicament of actually enslaved human beings in both the Old World and in the plantation system of the New (Buck-Morss 2009; Lowe 2015; Nyquist 2013; O'Connell Davidson 2015; cf. Epstein 2001: 50, 150, for specific instantiations of such deployments of the term in the Italian context).[15] In this sense, "slavery" works as a trope of injustice with high currency even today, regardless of the particular object to which it is applied.

[15] Angela Davis (1981) made the same point in discussing early nineteenth-century white feminists' association of marriage to slavery in the US context. At the same time, historical linkages between the abolitionist cause in the US and Romantic nationalist movements in nineteenth-century Italy (Dal Lago 2015) point also to the possibility of convergence between different types of anti-slavery discourse.

It is thus possible to read in this vein the ramblings of S., a farmer from the Gioia Tauro plain, Calabria—one of the most important districts for the production of citrus fruit in Italy, located at the southernmost tip of the peninsula. A man with a history of emigration to the United States, now in his late 70s, divorced from the woman for whose sake he had decided to return to his homeland, and with a strong penchant for verbosity and monologues, for several years he sought to organize his fellow farmers against the strangling of the sector by what he identified as "masonic powers". His target were not only politicians, but also the powerful lobbies that work to concentrate land and trade in the hands of few well connected actors, misuse public money destined for farmers and allow for ruthless competition and the consequent depreciation of produce—to the point where, as he was very keen to show anyone who would have the patience to listen to his endless lamentations and follow him in his roamings across the countryside, many had decided to eradicate the trees they had so carefully tended to for decades, in the "gardens" (*giardini*) inherited from their fathers.

Of course, like most farmers in the area and in the rest of the country, S. routinely employed migrant day laborers for harvest and other work on his gardens, at the usual conditions (half the minimum wage, no social security or other benefits). In the presence of one of them, during a meal when he systematically ignored the young African man, at the peak of his rhetorical fervor he exclaimed: "*We* are the real slaves!". This was also the slogan he had printed on the fliers with which he had littered the villages and towns of the citrus district. Like other farmers, he was embittered by what he regarded as the exclusive, obsessive attention reserved by politicians to the issue of *caporalato* and the plight of migrant workers whom, many claimed, were actually better off than farmers. The latter, at the same time, often justified the breach of labor laws on account of the low prices they received from the sale of their produce. The erasures and reversals that this type of discourse on slavery operates are significant and shot through by racist logics.

Furthermore, besides liberal attachments to slavery as the abstract, spectral double of a freedom that is always already barred from racialized subjects, and beyond evocations of New-World plantations, other, deeper and more complex genealogies can be traced from current preoccupations with slavery and its pasts. Steven Epstein (2001), pondering over the (especially linguistic) remnants of the semi-forgotten Medieval and Early Modern slavery that existed across different parts of Italy, has argued that this history "affects the way in which Italians are thinking about race today". He notes how "By the Fascist period the rediscovery of Medieval slavery and the development of modern thinking about race, antislavery and the colonies formed the milieu in which Italians conceived slavery's past" (13). The alleged persistence of "African blood" in what during the course of the nineteenth century were progressively identified as southern Italian "races" (and their consequent, enduring stigmatization) was based on the understanding that African slaves had been bought and sold in great numbers in the ports of Mezzogiorno. Arab and Slavic captives were also added to the mix. At Lucera, now in the district of Foggia, a "Saracen slave colony" (made up of Muslim rebels from Sicily at the time of Christian re-conquest) was established by King Frederick II during the thirteenth century (Taylor 2003), and historians have speculated that it was through the Adriatic trade that the first "slaves", as indeed the term itself, arrived on Italian territory.

The work of several historians further shows how different polities across what is now Italy played a significant role in shaping the European-derived history of slavery in the modern period, and the transatlantic trade itself (Blackburn 1997; Davis 2000, 2003; cf. Lombardi-Diop 2008, 2021). Indeed, it was in the context of Genoese and Venetian mercantilism that *both* the plantation model *and* the term "slave" (or *sclavus*, in Medieval Latin) were forged and diffused, if only partly in the same contexts (Craton 1984; Curtin 1998, 2015). Venetian and Genoese merchant-controlled Cyprus, Crete and then Sicily were the first locations for experiments in capitalist sugar plantations, before these moved to southern Spain, Portugal, the Atlantic islands and then the so-called New World. A mixture of slave and nominally free labor was employed in such establishments, with slaves imported from Africa (among whom were the parents of San Benedetto of Palermo), the Middle East and the Balkans. David Brion Davis (2003) further argued that the imbrication of race and enslaveability, which characterized the plantation system's ideological apparatus well into the nineteenth century, originated in the Genoese and Venetian slave trade between the eleventh and the fifteenth centuries, especially along the Dalmatian coast (hence the term "*sclavus*", from "Slavic"). This trade, Davis argues, "foreshadowed almost every aspect of the soon-to-appear African slave trade" (Ibid.: 18).

When the transatlantic trade did emerge, also thanks to Italian merchants' financial support, it linked the term "slave", and the stigma that attached to it, to people "with supposedly visible African ancestry". Gradually, "somatic or physical characteristics came to signify a new kind of social and psychological boundary" (Ibid.: 30). But the tendency to justify slavery in terms of innate characteristics and dispositions—the emergence of a relation between skin color, other bodily and genealogical features and enslavement—was already identifiable in the Mediterranean trade during the Middle Ages and the Early Modern period, first among the Arabs and then in the Italian context, where slaves were called by terms such as "Turks", "moors" or "negroes" (Bono 2010; Epstein 2001). Besides plantations, slaves in Italy were employed in high numbers as domestic servants and, above all, as rowers in the Genoese galleys. Just as for new-world plantations, a (literally) carceral regime of racialized labor discipline was implemented through slavery in many contexts in the Mediterranean.

How exactly the elaboration and deployment of these technologies of sorting, discipline, containment and extraction were to become part of the global circulation of knowledge and matter in the following centuries is a story yet to be fully written. What is clear is that a planetary regime of carceral containment and labor discipline represents one of the afterlives of slavery—whose ensemble Saidya Hartman (2007: 6) has described as "skewed life chances, limited access to health and education, premature death, incarceration and impoverishment"—all conditions which apply equally well to the current predicament of migrant farm laborers in Italy as elsewhere, and which a certain "anti-slavery" discourse actively fosters. Overall, according to the official records almost a third of migrant farm workers in Italy are EU citizens (and more than a third are European, when non-EU citizens are factored in), with Romanians as the most represented nationality in absolute terms (i.e. including non-EU citizens). Among them, a significant proportion of those I met, especially in the district of Foggia, identify as Roma or "gypsy". And yet, the association of European workers' own plight with "slavery" is less common. The same holds for Moroccans (who rank second in terms of absolute numbers), Albanians (fourth) and Tunisians (sixth)[16]—another instance in which more localized genealogies of enslavement, that in fact featured "Slavs", "tartars" and "moors" are covered over.

[16] For official statistics on the numbers of migrant farm workers in Italy, see Magrini (2022).

At the same time, current regimes of migration governance—a key aspect of the institutional racism oppressing such subjects and fostering forms of hyper-exploitation and vulnerability (Peano 2021)—have also been seen as emerging from the rise and then the breakdown of the transatlantic system of racial slavery, and the consequent need to create new mechanisms for the control of labor mobility. The introduction of "coolie" indentured labor, and the concomitant adoption of the passport on a larger scale (after having been initially envisaged to control slaves' movements in the North American plantation system—cf. Browne 2015; Parenti 2003), are often cited as the key mechanisms in this process (Mongia 2018; O'Connell Davidson 2015; cf. Ravano and Sacchi, this volume). And yet, even in this case, Mediterranean antecedents can be dug to the surface: prohibitions against transporting slaves without owners' written permissions, and against slaves leaving the city of Genoa without the proper papers, were in place "as early as 1300 [when] Genoa had a pass system for slaves outside the city and suburbs" (Epstein 2001: 119).

Finally, what is depicted as contemporary Italian farmers' adherence to New-World planters' ethos and comportment might as well be genealogically traced to farm-labor discipline in nineteenth and early twentieth-century large estates, where landowners' stewards, overseers and rent collectors were regularly armed (for the case of Tavoliere, see e.g. Snowden 1986; Rinaldi and Sobrero 2004). Indeed, labor discipline in the capitalist farm estates of early twentieth-century Tavoliere has been defined as nothing short of "carceral" (Cioffi 1984: 377; Mercurio 1989: 162). As noted, references to military-like labor discipline have survived in the now proliferating term, *caporalato*, with which gangmastership—especially when associated with farming—has been indicated in some parts of Italy at least since the nineteenth century.

Thus, not only are instrumental forms of abolitionism and humanitarianism, as well as selective, race- and class-blind conjurings of the idea of enslavement, integral to modern European thought and its colonial offshoots, and clearly identifiable in the Italian context. The casual evocation of the transatlantic trade and the new-world plantation as the scene against and in relation to which the contemporary ("new" or "modern") "slavery" of migrant farm laborers is pitted, through spectacularized images of objectified black and brown bodies, as well as too narrow a focus on the North American context as the original and unique scene of capitalist plantation slavery, occlude other genealogies and trajectories which impinge upon our present. The American plantation and the trans-Atlantic trade that supplied it pervade mainstream imaginaries in ways which reproduce the plantation complex's race-making operations, even when representations are meant to distance themselves from its workings. Allewaert and Moore have coined the notion of the "plantation-obscene" to foreground such plantation spectacles' reifying effects. Drawing on Hartman's work, they note how

> plantations and the social forms that followed in their wake—the ghetto, social work, the reformatory, the prison, the police—have produced, as the title of her first book puts it, scenes of subjection that feed the appetites of white onlookers. This mode of looking perpetuates a pornography of black suffering, which the plantation obscene marks as an ethical problem tied to the everyday violence of extractive racial capitalism. (n.d.: 3)

Furthermore, in the context of contemporary Italy and by reference to agro-capitalist extraction, references to a past that is actively made to feel spatially and temporally distant through several erasures occlude both alternative, and perhaps more poignant genealogies, as well as structural patterns within the current political economic regime, individualizing relations of exploitation and silencing racialized subjects' power to speak and act, both individually and collectively.

Against these erasures, Allewaert and Moore urge for the development of "critical methods that attend to the ways of knowing and living that produced outsides to the plantation" (Ibid.: 4). Similarly, other authors have proposed to counter neo-abolitionist dogmas by paying attention to practices of "modern marronage" (O'Connell Davidson 2021; cf. Stierl 2019) in relation to histories of fugitivity, thereby foregrounding, rather than erasing, the crucial role that dispositifs of mobility control play in fostering extractive operations, but also acknowledging the subjectivity of those who are their targets. More than in enslavement, the echoes of the New-World plantation today may materialize in the desires of migrants for escape. Some scholars have located such emerging practices of knowledge production, resistance and flight within what they conceptualize as the "Black Mediterranean" (Danewid 2017; Hawthorne 2017; Proglio et al. 2021; Smythe 2018; cf. Gilroy 1993; Robinson 1983). In the concluding section, I seek to take up such insights and intuitions, weaving them together to trace alternative genealogies in the margins and "in the wake" (Sharpe 2016) of plantations past.

Coda: The Black Mediterranean, Modern Marronage and Their Shadows

Transatlantic history and its Euro-Mediterranean antecedents certainly play a part in explaining not only current regimes of racialized violence, terror and exploitation in Italy, but also idioms of resistance to them, which may also employ the notion of slavery in oppositional terms. I have frequently heard West African migrants complain about their fellow farm workers and slum dwellers, saying they have "a slave mentality"—meaning they accept oppressing conditions. Others, commenting on their predicament in Europe, also remark how "slavery never finished; they just *modernized* it" by making people pay for their own journeys, for example. When talking about their origins, Gambian migrants are especially proud of the iconic figure of national(ized), semi-fictional enslaved hero, Kunta Kinte, and sometimes recall how the first known European to sail up the Gambia river was in fact Venetian explorer and slave trader Alvise Ca' da Mosto.

The self-assigned toponyms of the shantytowns where West African migrants live, and from which many are recruited for farm labor, are also significant in this respect. Many are known as "ghettos"—a term drawn from Jamaican English via its Ghanaian assimilation, according to my interlocutors, indicating a space on the margins of or outside the law, where alcohol, drugs and sexual services may be purchased in dedicated *joints* or *connection houses*. Yet, the term also exceeds Black Atlantic imaginaries and their Afro-Mediterranean readaptations. While it clearly bears North American, Black geographical referents as well, dating back to the early twentieth century, its genealogies lead, once more, all the way back to fourteenth-century Venice, where the original Jewish *geto* was established (cf. Hutchinson and Haynes 2012), again summoning the (mostly eclipsed) Mediterranean prehistories of modern, racialized containment. Besides acting as recruitment hubs and devices of spatial segregation, these slums are also knots along migratory routes that originate on the southern end of the Sahara Desert and extend, along tortuous and ever-changing trajectories, to the far northern shores of continental Europe—what Harney and Moten (2013) would call "undercommons", spaces of black fugitivity (cf. Peano 2021) (Fig. 11.3).

Black-Atlantic, Caribbean and North American connections also manifest in references to some or other version of Rastafarianism and more

Fig. 11.3 Layers of drawings and writings on a shack in the slum of "Mexico", district of Foggia, 2018. The shack has since gone through several alterations, and the inscriptions are no longer visible (Photographs by the author)

generally to Jamaican culture (linked to the awareness of living in "Babylon"; see Fig. 11.3), or in the scathingly and bitterly ironic nicknames some such ghettoes or squatted buildings are given ("Washington"'; "the White House"; "Guantánamo"; "Mexico"). Appeals to Rastafarianism interestingly produce a reverse narrative to those discourses in which Ethiopian (and thus by extension, in the present, "African") forms of enslavement justified oppression cloaked in the rhetoric of humanitarianism and the civilizing mission. Ras Tafari Makkonen (Emperor Haile Selassie, Rastafarianism's Messiah) had been depicted by Fascist imperial propaganda as a megalomaniac and despotic leader who tolerated the endurance of slavery in Ethiopia, ignoring his efforts to eradicate it (Bekele 2008; Forgacs 2014: 76; Sbacchi 1985). Even the Chicanx and Latinx experience surfaces in this constellation of images: the now largest African farm-worker shantytown in the district of Foggia is known by its inhabitants (at least the older ones) as "Mexico", by virtue of having been cut off from the asylum-seeker reception center of which its initial nucleus was a part—"we didn't cross the border, the border crossed us": echoes of other occlusions, in the truly global time of plantation afterlives.

Even when workers do make recourse to the language of slavery, they might evoke alternative genealogies to those of the American plantation, and only to detach themselves from them. During a field trip to Sliven, the Bulgarian city with the highest Roma population, many of whose members migrate seasonally to be employed in large numbers in farming work in the districts of Foggia and Caserta, an elderly man strolling down the street of the tellingly named Nadezdha (*hope*) neighborhood inquired about the reason for the presence of myself and my travel companions. Upon learning that we were interested in talking to people about the conditions of life and labor of the town's migrant workers in Italy, the man invited us to his house, enlisting also his brother to support his story. He had been employed for several years as a daily farm laborer in Calabria, he explained. In excited and emphatic speech, when wishing us goodbye after an engaged conversation over tea and sweets, he recommended: "Go and tell your leaders that the Roma are not slaves!" He obviously referred to the centuries-long, much-forgotten bondage of their ancestors (Achim 1998; Beck 1989; Marushiakova and Popov 2021).

Contemporary racial and labor politics in Italy certainly developed in dialogue with, and were influenced by, what occurred across the Atlantic and with reference to imperial projects. And yet, local specificities and their durabilities, to borrow Ann Stoler's (2016) concept, also matter—as do the reverse movements whereby forms of enslavement and the ideological apparatuses support them, like early experiments with the plantation mode of production more generally, traveled from the Mediterranean to the "New World" in the early modern period. The history of the transatlantic trade and the New-World plantation doubtlessly have a prominent, spectral presence—evoked not only by selective references to slavery, but also through images of boats stuffed with black human cargo, by portraying disarticulated, objectified and racialized body parts, and in the coinage of the notion of a "Black Mediterranean" as a redemptive parallel to the "Black Atlantic". Yet, the tracing of alternative genealogies and the identification of recursive patterns, through which the histories of plantations and slavery are wielded for instrumental purposes, are irrenounceable tools for truly abolitionist struggles.

References

Achim, V. 1998. *The Roma in Romanian History*. Budapest: Central European University Press.

Allewaert, M., and S. S. Moore (n.d.). *Plantationocene - Plantationobscene - Plantationoscenes* [Virtual Symposium Presentation]. Global Plantation Symposium, Princeton University, United States, 15 October 2020.

Andrijasevic, R. 2010. *Migration, Agency and Citizenship in Sex Trafficking*. Basingstoke: Palgrave MacMillan.

Bain, C. 2013. "Chilean Temporeras and Corporate Construction of Gender Inequalities in Global Food Standards." In *Gendered Commodity Chains: Seeing Women's Work and Households in Global Production*, ed. W. Dunaway, 119–134. Stanford: Stanford University Press.

Beck, S. 1989. "The Origins of Gypsy Slavery in Romania." *Dialectical Anthropology* 14 (1): 53–61.

Bekele, S. 2008. "La modernizzazione dell'Etiopia prima e dopo i cinque anni d'occupazione: Da una società tradizionale a un paese che si sviluppa." In *L'impero fascista. Italia ed Etiopia (1935–1941)*, ed. R. Bottoni, 63–85. Bologna: Il Mulino.

Blackburn, R. 1997. "The Old World Background to European Colonial Slavery." *William and Mary Quarterly* 54 (1): 65–102.

Bono, S. 2010. "Schiavi in Italia: maghrebini, neri, slavi, ebrei e altri (secc. XVI-XIX)." *Mediterranea* 7 (19): 235–252.

Brigate di Solidarietà Attiva, Nigro G., M. Perrotta, D. Sacchetto, and Y. Sagnet. 2012. *Sulla pelle viva. Nardò: la lotta autorganizzata dei braccianti agricoli*. Rome: DerivEApprodi.

Browne, S. 2015. *Dark Matters: On the Surveillance of Blackness*. Durham: Duke University Press.

Buck-Morss, S. 2009. *Hegel, Haiti, and Universal History*. Pittsburgh: University of Pittsburgh Press.

Busch, L. 2000. "The Moral Economy of Grades and Standards." *Journal of Rural Studies* 16: 273–283.

Busch, L., and C. Bain. 2004. "New! Improved? The Transformation of the Global Agrifood System." *Rural Sociology* 69 (3): 321–346.

Carlini, G. 2016. "Le voci dei migranti in un'aula di tribunale: Analisi etnografica del processo Sabr (Lecce)." *Antropologia* 3 (2): 101–124.

Caruso, F. 2018. "Certificazioni e lavoro nelle filiere agroalimentari: Il caso GlobalGap in Italia." *Meridiana* 93: 231–250.

Cioffi, L. 1984. "Capitalismo agrario e fascismo nelle campagne di Capitanata: L'azienda Pavoncelli di Cerignola nella crisi degli anni venti-trenta." In *Produzione, mercato e classi sociali nella Capitanata moderna e contemporanea*, ed. A. Massafra, 321–401. Foggia: Amministrazione Provinciale di Foggia.

Craton, M. 1984. "The Historical Roots of the Plantation Model." *Slavery & Abolition: A Journal of Slave and Post-Slave Studies* 5 (3): 189–221.

Curtin, P. 1998. *The Rise and Fall of the Plantation Complex: Essays in Atlantic History*, 2nd ed., Studies in Comparative World History. Cambridge: Cambridge University Press.

Cuttitta, P. 2012. *Lo spettacolo del confine: Lampedusa tra produzione e messa in scena della frontiera*. Milan: Mimesis.

Dal Lago, E. 2015. *The Age of Lincoln and Cavour: Comparative Perspectives on Nineteenth-Century American and Italian Nation-Building*. New York: Palgrave MacMillan.

Danewid, I. 2017. "White Innocence in the Black Mediterranean: Hospitality and the Erasure of History." *Third World Quarterly* 38 (7): 1674–1689.

Davis, A. 1981. *Women, Race & Class*. New York: Vintage.

Davis, D. 2000." Looking at Slavery from Broader Perspectives." *The American Historical Review* 105 (2): 452–466.

Davis, D. 2003. *Challenging the Boundaries of Slavery*. Cambridge: Harvard University Press.

De Genova, N. 2013. "Spectacles of Migrant 'Illegality': The Scene of Exclusion, the Obscene of Inclusion." *Ethnic and Racial Studies* 36 (7): 1180–1198.

De Genova, N. 2017. "Introduction: The Borders of 'Europe' and the European Question." In *The Borders of "Europe": Autonomy of migration, Tactics of Bordering*, ed. N. De Genova, 1–36. Durham: Duke University Press.

Del Boca, A. 2005. *Italiani, brava gente? Un mito duro a morire*. Vicenza: Neri Pozza Editore.

Di Martino, A. 2015. "'Caporalato' e repressione penale. Appunti su una correlazione (troppo) scontata." In *Leggi, migranti e caporali. Prospettive critiche e di ricerca sullo sfruttamento del lavoro in agricoltura*, ed. E. Rigo. Pisa: Pacini.

Doezema, J. 1999. "Loose Women or Lost Women? The Re-emergence of the Myth of WHITE Slavery in Contemporary Discourses of Trafficking in Women." *Gender Issues* 18: 23–50.

Epstein, S. 2001. *Speaking of Slavery: Color, Ethnicity, and Human Bondage in Italy*. Ithaca: Cornell University Press.

Forgacs, D. 2014. *Italy's Margins: Social Exclusion and Nation Formation Since 1861* (Cambridge Social and Cultural Histories). Cambridge: Cambridge University Press.

Gilroy, P. 1993. *The Black Atlantic: Modernity and Double Consciousness*. Cambridge: Harvard University Press.

Harney, S., and F. Moten. 2013. *The Undercommons: Fugitive Planning and Black Study*. Wivenhoe: Minor Compositions.

Hartman, S. 2007. *Lose Your Mother: A Journey Along the Atlantic Slave Route*. New York: Farrar, Straus and Giroux.

Hawthorne, C. 2017. "In Search of Black Italia: Notes on Race, Belonging, and Activism in the Black Mediterranean." *Transition* 123: 152–174.

Howard, N. 2017. "Of Coyotes and Caporali: How Anti-trafficking Discourses of Criminality Depoliticise Mobility and Exploitation." In *Routledge Handbook of Human Trafficking*, ed. R. Piotrowicz, C. Rijken, B. H. Uhl. London: Routledge.

Howard, N., and R. Forin. 2019. "Migrant Workers, 'Modern Slavery' and the Politics of Representation in Italian Tomato Production." *Economy and Society* 48 (4): 579–601.

Hutchison, R., and B. Haynes. 2012. *The Ghetto: Contemporary Global Issues and Controversies*. New York: Westview Press.

King, T. 2016. "The Labor of (Re)reading Plantation Landscapes Fungible(ly)." *Antipode* 48 (4): 1022–1039.

Lombardi-Diop, C. 2008. "Ghosts of Memories, Spirits of Ancestors: Slavery, the Mediterranean, and the Atlantic." In *Recharting the Black Atlantic: Modern Cultures, Local Communities, Global Connections*, ed. A. Oboe and A. Scacchi, 162–180. London: Routledge.

Lombardi-Diop, C. 2021. "Preface." In *The Black Mediterranean: Bodies, Borders and Citizenship*, ed. G. Proglio, C. Hawthorne, I. Danewid, P. K. Saucier, G. Grimaldi, A. Pesarini, T. Raeymaekers, G. Grechi, and V. Gerrand. Cham: Springer Nature.

Lowe, L. 2015. *The Intimacies of Four Continents*. Durham: Duke University Press.

Magrini, R. (2022). "I lavoratori stranieri nel settore agricolo." In *Dossier Statistico Immigrazione 2022*, ed. Centro Studi e Ricerche IDOS. Rome: Centro Studi e Ricerche IDOS.

Marushiakova, E., and V. Popov, ed. 2021. *Roma Voices in History: A Sourcebook. Roma Civic Emancipation in Central, South-Eastern and Eastern Europe from the 19th Century until World War II*. Leiden: Brill.

Mercurio, F. 1989. "Agricolture senza casa: Il sistema del lavoro migrante nelle maremme e nel latifondo." In *Storia dell'agricoltura italiana in età contemporanea, vol. I: Spazi e paesaggi*, ed. P. Bevilacqua. Venice: Marsilio.

Mongia, R. 2018. *Indian Migration and Empire: A Colonial Genealogy of the Modern State*. Durham: Duke University Press.

Nyquist, M. 2013. *Arbitrary Rule: Slavery, Tyranny and the Power of Life and Death*. Chicago: University of Chicago Press.

O'Connell Davidson, J. 2015. *Modern Slavery: The Margins of Freedom*. London: Palgrave MacMillan.

O'Connell Davidson, J. 2021. "Slavery Versus Marronage as an Analytic Lens on 'Trafficking.'" In *The Palgrave Handbook of Gender and Migration*, ed. C. Mora and N. Piper, 425–439. London: Palgrave Macmillan.

Parenti, C. 2003. *The Soft Cage: Surveillance in America from Slavery to the War on Terror*. New York: Basic Books.

Peano, I. 2011. *Ambiguous Bonds: A Contextual Study of Nigerian Sex Labour in Italy*. PhD dissertation, Department of Social Anthropology, University of Cambridge.

Peano, I. 2020. "Ways of Making a Human Otherwise: After-ethnography with Migrant Laborers in Italian Agro-Industrial Enclaves." In *Modos de Fazer/Ways of Making*, ed. V. O. Jorge, 219–230. Porto: CITCEM.

Peano, I. 2021. "Turbulences in the Encampment Archipelago: Conflicting Mobilities Between Migration, Labour and Logistics in Italian Agri-Food Enclaves." *Mobilities* 16 (2): 212–223.

Perrotta, D. 2015. "Agricultural Day Laborers in Southern Italy: Forms of Mobility and Resistance." *South Atlantic Quarterly* 114 (1): 195–203.

Proglio, G., C. Hawthorne, I. Danewid, P. K. Saucier, G. Grimaldi, A. Pesarini, T. Raeymaekers, G. Grechi, and V. Gerrand, ed. 2021. *The Black Mediterranean: Bodies, Borders and Citizenship*. Cham: Springer Nature.

Rinaldi, G., and P. Sobrero, ed. 2004. *La memoria che resta: Vita quotidiana, mito e storia dei braccianti nel Tavoliere di Puglia*. Lecce: Edizioni Aramirè.

Robinson, C. 1983. *Black Marxism: The Making of the Black Radical Tradition*. Chapel Hill: University of North Carolina Press.

Santoro, E., and C. Stoppioni. 2022. *IV Rapporto del laboratorio "Altro Diritto"/FLAI-CGIL sullo sfruttamento lavorativo e sulla protezione delle sue vittime*. Available online at http://www.adir.unifi.it/laboratorio/quarto-rapporto-sfruttamento-lavorativo.pdf. Retrieved 11th July 2022.

Satta, G. 2014. "L'ultimo baluardo della schiavitù: La "barbarie abissina" nella propaganda per la guerra d'Etiopia." In *Variazioni africane: Saggi di antropologia e storia*, ed. F. Viti, 67–93. Modena: Il Fiorino.

Satta, G. 2016. "Civiltà di Roma e barbarie abissina: La propaganda antischiavista e la guerra d'Etiopia." *Parolechiave* 1: 67–76.

Sbacchi, A. 1985. *Ethiopia Under Mussolini: Fascism and the Colonial Experience*. London: Zed Books.

Sharpe, C. 2016. *In the Wake: On Blackness and Being*. Durham: Duke University Press.

Smythe, S. 2018. "Suffering and the Limits of Relief." *Middle Eastern Report* 286: 3–9.

Snowden, F.M. 1986. *Violence and the Great Estates in the South of Italy: Apulia, 1900–1922*. Cambridge: Cambridge University Press.

Stierl, M. 2019. "Of Migrant Slaves and Underground Railroads: Movement, Containment, Freedom." *American Behavioral Scientist* 64 (4): 456–479.

Stoler, A. 2016. *Duress: Imperial Durabilities in Our Times*. Durham: Duke University Press.

Taylor, J. 2003. *Muslims in Medieval Italy: The Colony at Lucera*. Lanham: Lexington Books.

Torre, V. 2019. "Lo sfruttamento del lavoro: La tipicità dell'art. 603-*bis* cp tra diritto sostanziale e prassi giurisprudenziale." *Questione Giustizia* 4: 90–97.

Trevisani, R. 1937. *L'affrancamento degli schiavi nell'impero fascista*. Rome: Edizioni di Politica Sociale.

PART IV

South and South-East Asia: Indigenous Labor, More-Than-Human Entanglements and the Afterlives of Multiple Crises

CHAPTER 12

The Multispecies World of Oil Palm: Indigenous Marind Perspectives on Plantation Ecologies in West Papua

Sophie Chao

In October 2019, I traveled through an oil palm plantation with Gerfacius, an Indigenous Marind man from the district of Merauke in the Indonesian-controlled region of West Papua.[1] As we walked down the rows of oil palms, Kosmas pointed out the dents in the crown of one of the trees. He explained that rats had nested there and fed their

[1] Pseudonyms are used for persons and places except for major provinces and districts. Terms in Marind are underlined and terms in Indonesian or *logat Papua* (the Papuan creole version of Indonesian) are italicized.

This chapter is a revised version of an article published in *American Anthropologist*, copyright Taylor & Francis, available online: https://anthrosource.onlinelibrary.wiley.com/doi/abs/10.1111/aman.13592.

S. Chao (✉)
University of Sydney, Sydney, NSW, Australia
e-mail: sophie.chao@sydney.edu.au

C. Le Petitcorps et al. (eds.), *Global Plantations in the Modern World*, Cambridge Imperial and Post-Colonial Studies,
https://doi.org/10.1007/978-3-031-08537-6_12

offspring on the developing fruit bunches. Rats, Gerfacius continued, are one of many animals that prey on oil palm's fruit, flowers, and fronds. They reproduce rapidly and can bring down hundreds of trees within a few weeks. Later in our journey, my companion identified the traces of other parasites of oil palm—the rotting stems of trees where rhinoceros beetles laid their eggs and incubated, the powdery bases of tottering trunks ravaged by a Ganoderma fungus, and the half-eaten fruit bunches devoured by possums and pigs.

When we arrived at the concession boundary, Gerfacius pointed to a nearby pile of oil palm fronds, cleared by workers to allow sunlight to reach the undergrowth. Atop the dark, rotting mulch, white mushrooms flourished in dense clusters, their pale contours translucent in the late afternoon light. "This mushroom we call abaduk," Gerfacius said. "In some ways, abaduk is like *Ganoderma*. It's just trying to survive. But abaduk is also different. For *Ganoderma* to live, oil palm must die. But abaduk? Abaduk has made a friend of oil palm. It knows how to live with oil palm. Friends and enemies (*lawan kawan*)—there are plenty in the plantation. It's not easy—but everyone learns to survive in different ways."

Large-scale monocrops, such as the one Gerfacius and I traveled through in late October 2019, are classic emblems of the Anthropocene. Indeed, the unprecedented scale and impacts of industrial plantations have brought environmental humanities scholars to describe the current era as the "Plantationocene" (Haraway 2015: 162, footnote 5).[2] Within the agribusiness nexus, the palm oil sector is particularly notorious for its adverse environmental effects. Oil palm plantations radically reduce biodiversity, threaten endangered species, and undermine critical ecosystem services such as nutrient cycling and soil stability. Research suggests that oil palm concessions support less than half of primary forest biodiversity levels in the tropical areas where they tend to be established. Recent findings in ecological science, however, point to diverse communities of

[2] Haraway et al. define the "Plantationocene" as an era characterized by "the devastating transformation of diverse kinds of human-tended farms, pastures, and forests into extractive and enclosed plantations, relying on slave labor and other forms of exploited, alienated, and usually spatially transported labor" (2015, 162, footnote 5). Prior to the articulation of the "Plantationocene," the plantation as spatio-temporal formation was extensively theorized by scholars in critical race and literary studies and has since become the object of renewed interdisciplinary inquiry (see Chao 2022a; Davis et al. 2019; Jegathesan 2021; McKittrick 2013; Wolford 2021).

flora and fauna that are finding ways to live in symbiosis with oil palm. In contrast to the charismatic mega-fauna often mobilized by environmental activists in anti-palm oil campaigns, these critters are labeled as "background," "generalist," or "tramp" species in conservation biology. They include microbes, ants, lichens, wasps, and caterpillars—some native, others introduced. While larger mammals struggle to survive in monocrop ecologies, modest yet resilient ménages of squirming arthropods, crawling invertebrates, and flourishing fungi, are discovering new fodder and futures in the company of oil palm.

This essay examines the divergent meanings attributed to oil palm ecologies by Indigenous Marind in the Upper Bian region of Merauke District, West Papua.[3] Since the launch of a mega-development scheme known as the Merauke Integrated Food and Energy Estate in 2010, agribusiness projects in this area have multiplied at an unprecedented rate. These projects are routinely implemented by the Indonesian government and corporations without the free, prior, and informed consent of Marind. At the time of writing, the majority of Upper Bian community members were involved in grassroots campaigns to secure their land rights and curb oil palm expansion, with the support of local and international non-governmental organizations as well as humanitarian branches of the Catholic Church. Meanwhile, a small but growing number of villagers had ceded their territories to agribusiness corporations in exchange for employment as plantation harvesters and pesticide-sprayers. Fearing retributions from their activist kin, these plantation workers tended to leave their home villages and relocate with their families to plantation lodgings, or to Merauke City. Pro- and anti-oil palm factions were far from static. Over the course of my fieldwork, individuals once actively involved in land rights advocacy joined the plantation industry as seasonal workers. Other individuals resigned from their employment in the agribusiness sector after just a few weeks or months. Neither fixed nor bounded,

[3] I undertook eighteen months of fieldwork in the Upper Bian villages of Khalaoyam, Mirav, and Bayau as a doctoral candidate between August and December 2015, March and July 2016, and August and November 2017, and as a human rights advocate between March and June 2013. This research explored how agribusiness developments reconfigure the multispecies lifeworld of Upper Bian Marind. In addition to participant-observation, interviews, ethnobotanical research, and sensory attunement to the everyday interactions and discourses of Marind and other-than-human lifeforms in the villages, forests, and plantations, I undertook fieldwork in an oil palm plantation to acquire further insights into oil palm ecosystems and management specifically (see Chao 2018b).

internal factions and their constituents in the Upper Bian were malleable, contingent, and shifting.

Of particular interest to this essay are the *more-than-human* actors whom Marind invoke in their divergent assessments of the oil palm sector, and how these other-than-human entities' relationships to oil palm speak in turn to Marind's own conflictual stance toward agribusiness, capitalism, and the Indonesian state. Villagers both for and against oil palm identify with the fate of native species that, like Marind, have been displaced to make way for oil palm monocrops and their primarily non-Papuan labor force and operators.[4] On the other hand, parasites of oil palm that undermine the plant's growth become figures of hope for villagers who conceive resistance to capitalist projects as the only legitimate course of action and path to justice. Meanwhile, species that succeed in establishing mutualistic relations with oil palm point to collaboration and cooperation as alternative strategies of survival under hegemonic political and capitalist regimes. Species that flail or flourish in oil palm's company thus become potent, if ambivalent, trigger points for reflection among Marind over what their *own* stance toward oil palm and the state should be, and the more-than-human implications of endorsing or eschewing agribusiness and colonial-capitalist architectures that undergird it.

Marind engage materially and imaginatively with plantation science and ecologies—or what Arturo Escobar (1999) calls "capitalist natures"—in ways that both draw from and counter the epistemic imperialism of the monocrop model and its colonial undergirdings. In particular, two kinds of interspecies relations in monocrop ecologies—those where one party lives at the other's expense, or parasitism, and those where both parties live better from living together, or mutualism—generate indexical relations of trans-species significance for Marind that are at once material, political, affective, and moral, and historically situated. Parasites and mutualists of oil palm constitute active participants in the production of these shifting metonymic relations through their contrasting bodily and

[4] Plantation workers in the Papuan oil palm sector originate primarily from Java and Sumatra. The operators of these plantations include Indonesian corporations, as well as foreign conglomerates based in Singapore, Malaysia, and Korea.

symbolic modes of symbiosis, or what Donna Haraway calls "material-semiotic actors" (1992: 298).[5] Alternately conceptualized by Marind as friends or enemies, paragons of resistance or models of collaboration, these organisms become "excessive things with a force of their own" (Hetherington 2013: 66) whose multiple identities both enable and preempt the possibility of justice in both human *and* multispecies terms (Chao et al. 2022).

Indeed, Marind characterizations of oil palm's multispecies lifeworld complicate the prevailing critique of monocrops as ecologically impoverished landscapes of "out-and-out exterminism" (Haraway, cited in Mitman 2019: 6, 10) that negate the possibility of interspecies care and love (e.g. Marder 2013; Shiva 1993). Rather, plantation ecologies emerge as complex realms of interspecies negotiation, collaboration, and friction, where the sovereignty exercised by other-than-human beings speaks in politically charged ways to the sovereignties denied, yet always still possible, of Indigenous Marind themselves in the settler-colonized region of West Papua. In plantations, plants and their symbiotes exist as either allies or foes—or "friends" and "enemies," to borrow Gerfacius' words. These organisms form meaningful bodily and semiotic relationships with the humans who alternately care for or kill them. Their moral valences, I demonstrate, are defined less by their specieshood than by the particular *kind* of relationship—material and metonymic—they entertain with other, equally morally meaningful, human and non-human others. Alternately threatened *by*, threatening *to*, or thriving *with* oil palm, other-than-human subjects act as conflicting exemplars of the fates and futures of Marind themselves as they seek to reconcile aspirations for sovereignty and self-determination under entrenched and emergent regimes of color (race) and capital.

[5] Haraway deploys the concept of "material-semiotic actors" to counter the notion that organisms and entities are passive, raw materials that matter only in terms of their functional uses and meanings for humans. Rather, Haraway contends that organisms and entities are endowed with diverse symbolic and bodily attributes that they *themselves* produce in their situated and often asymmetric interactions with other actors, including humans (1991, 200; 1992, 298).

Destruction

The villages of Khalaoyam, Mirav, and Bayau are three of seven villages in the Upper Bian, a region covering some 8,593 km^2 and sitting 300 kilometers north of Merauke District's capital and main urban center, Merauke City. The villages are home to 600 households who, like other Indigenous Upper Bian inhabitants, self-identify as Marind of the forest (Marind-deg). Upper Bian Marind derive their subsistence from hunting, fishing, and gathering in the forest—a realm they describe as "enlivened" (*hidup*) by the growths, movements, and stories of diverse plant and animal lifeforms (Chao 2017, 2022b). These organisms, whom my interlocutors call "grandparents" (amai) or "siblings" (namek), share common descent with different Marind clans (bawan) from ancestral spirits, or dema. Interspecies clan affiliations play a central role in determining local land tenure arrangements, hunting rights, intermarriage, and trade relations among Marind and with neighboring Mandobo, Auyu, and Jair tribes. They are also reflected in the nomenclature of Marind clans, which often includes the name of the clan's kindred species followed by -ze, meaning "children of" (van Baal 1966; Verschueren 1970).

The interactions of amai and humans (anim) are anchored in principles of mutual and restrained care. Amai grow to support their human kin by providing them food and other resources. In return, anim must exercise respect and perform rituals as they encounter amai in the forest, recall their stories, hunt, gather, and consume them. These transcorporeal encounters enable Marind and their forest kin to "share skin (igid) and wetness (dubadub)," an expression that refers to life-sustaining exchanges of bodily fluids including sweat, blood, sap, grease, and water (Chao 2018a: 6–7). Marind persons thus emerge from their ancestral and present relations to other-than-human beings within the eco-cosmology of the forest, in what might be described as a literal form of anim-ism.

Central to the more-than-human ontology of Marind personhood is a respect for the wildness of plants and animals as free and autonomous beings, or what I describe elsewhere as an ethos of restrained care (Chao 2019a). To this end, Marind actively refrain from overly influencing or controlling the movements, growth, and reproduction of forest species. Instead, community members seek to enhance the *environment* of plants and animals in ways that support their autonomous thriving. For instance, villagers clear pathways for pigs and deer to travel to water catchments, leave fruit and nuts behind when foraging for cassowaries to feed on, and avoid disturbing the canopy during birds' mating season. These minimal manipulations produce the forest as a realm of multispecies abundance achieved through a range of indirect human actions that are situated within a wider web of past and other-than-human activities. The material intimacies of human–animal relatedness thus go hand in hand with a need to respect their different *modalities* of being. In this light, being wild means being able to live autonomously yet in relation to others as part of multispecies social and ecological networks. Amai may punish anim who fail to respect the principle of restrained care, or who fail to share skin and wetness with the forest and its living organisms, by turning their skin taut, dry, grey, or hard (Chao 2019b). Such transgressions include neglecting rituals prior to hunting or sago processing, polluting or diverting watercourses, killing female game or their young, or failing to share one's catch with the broader community. Illnesses that provoke dry skin, such as dysentery, malaria, dengue, and more recently, AIDS, as well as climactic conditions such as droughts and floods, are also frequently interpreted by Marind as the consequence of a wrongdoing on the part of the diseased toward fellow anim or amai.

Interspecies relations in the Upper Bian underwent notable transformations during West Papua's colonization by the Dutch Empire and then the Republic of Indonesia. Forced sedentarization, missionization, and the abolishment of rituals during Dutch rule restricted Marind's capacity to maintain life-giving exchanges of skin and wetness with their forest kin and to transmit their embodied forest knowledge to their children, who were instead educated in mission schools (see Chao 2021; Derksen 2016; Pouwer 1999). The plume trade of 1910–1924 led to an influx of foreign hunters into Merauke, who exploited the forest without restraint and radically depleted local bird of paradise populations (Swadling 1996). Marind themselves were brought to the verge of disappearance following devastating epidemics of introduced viral influenza and bacterial donovanosis in 1919 and 1937 (Richens 2021). Transformations in the more-than-human landscape intensified after the forceful incorporation of West Papua into the Republic of Indonesia in 1969, which was accompanied by a dramatic expansion in extractive industries across the region, including logging, oil, coal, and gas mining, paddy cultivation, and pulp and paper plantations (Down to Earth 2011). The proliferation of these capitalist ventures went hand in hand with intensive militarization and settler inmigration and was facilitated by the lack of recognition of customary land tenure under national law (Kusumaryati 2019).

For most Upper Marind, however, it is the introduction of oil palm by the Indonesian government in 2010 that has most radically jeopardized the forest and its other-than-human dwellers. Prior to oil palm, Marind explained, agribusiness projects in rice, peanut, and corn cultivation initiated by the Dutch and by Indonesia were located near the coast and urban centers, rather than in the hinterland inhabited by Upper Bian Marind. These projects were relatively small in both numbers and scale. In contrast, oil palm plantations have expanded across some 1.7 million hectares in Merauke District over the last decade and now occupy over 20% of the Upper Bian. Operated by thirty-six national and international corporations, their boundaries creep right up to the edge of the villages, encroaching on sago groves, hunting zones, and sacred graveyards and ceremonial sites. With dozens more companies applying for operational permits at the time of writing, agribusiness continues to expand relentlessly across the region.

While my interlocutors are aware of the government and corporate forces driving agro-industrial expansion in Merauke, the vast majority attribute the destructive effects of the industry to the voracious and self-interested disposition of oil palm itself (see Chao 2018a, 2020). For instance, many Upper Bian Marind describe oil palm as an "enemy of the forest" (*musuh hutan*), "murderer" (*pembunuh*), and "colonizer" (*penjajah*) that "devours" (*makan habis*) the land and rivers to the point of annihilation. Like the state, settlers, and soldiers occupying West Papua, oil palm is an introduced and parasitic entity that dispossesses Indigenous peoples of their sovereignty over territories and natural resources. Many villagers also associate the cash crop with non-Papuan settlers who are drawn to Merauke by labor opportunities in the agribusiness sector and represent over 60% of the District's population (Ananta et al. 2016).

Unlike neighboring Papuan peoples, with whom Upper Bian Marind historically entertained mutualistic relations of trade, intermarriage, and ritual cooperation, settlers are said to differ radically from Papuans in their behavior, appearance, and habits. They do not entertain kinship relations with the forest ecology, share skin and wetness with the environment, nor recognize plant and animal beings as sentient, consequential beings that merit respect and care. Non-Papuans are also widely resented by Marind because they monopolize employment positions, occupy lands granted to them by the government without Indigenous consent, and treat Papuans in racially discriminating ways because of their black skin and forest-based way of life. Other villagers situate the ecological destruction wrought by oil palm within an ongoing process of cultural genocide in West Papua—one that has come to constitute a critical denominator in the formation of Papuans' collective identity (Giay and Ballard 2003: 12; see also Mote and Rutherford 2001). This slow genocide manifests in the form of systemic torture, extra-judicial killings, and the forced sterilization of Papuan women. Alien and invasive, oil palm thus perpetuates in a vegetal guise the historical subjugation of West Papuan bodies and landscapes to the hegemonic domination of the Indonesian state and its corporate allies.

But Marind are not the only beings whose lives and futures are jeopardized by oil palm. Their plant and animal kin, too, struggle to survive, in oil palm ecologies that are characterized by low canopies, sparse undergrowth, high temperatures, low humidity, highly variable micro-climactic conditions, and a toxic mélange of chemical fertilizers and pesticides. Monocrops also create impervious barriers to species migration and reproduction. As oil palm replaces complex components of forest vegetation such as lianas and epiphytic orchids, herbivore diversity, above-ground structural complexity, and canopy height are reduced, with cascading effects down the food chain. Meanwhile, conserved forest fragments within plantations and along their boundaries are susceptible to edge effects whereby forest quality continues to deteriorate over time, causing species communities to shift toward a simpler composition dominated by a few common types. Bamboo clusters and sago groves collapse as the soil is depleted of its minerals and nutrients. Plants and animals that once thrived in the forest, wilt and starve. Life-sustaining exchanges of skin and wetness across species are subverted as oil palm saps the waters of the rivers and occupies ever-growing swaths of land. The terrains and tributaries of the landscape, once fertile and flowing, turn dry and murky. Human and other-than-human bodies, once glossy and strong, become dry and wizened. Each organismic death provoked by deforestation and monocrop expansion thwarts the affectively and morally imbued material interdependencies that enable Marind and their other-than-human kin to survive and thrive.

Parasitism

The multispecies destruction provoked by oil palm today thus sits within a layered history of Indigenous subjection to parasitic "others" who have systematically occupied, exploited, or contaminated Marind bodies and environments, to the detriment of their mutualistic relations with forest organisms, with each other, and with neighboring Papuan peoples. These parasitic "others" include colonial bird-hunters, deadly viruses and bacteria, the Indonesian state, settlers, and corporations, and now introduced oil palm. In the last few years, however, parasitism has taken on new meanings in light of Marind's growing understanding of the biotic affordances of oil palm's diverse symbiotes—meanings that speak in turn to Marind's own uncertainty over whether to endorse or oppose agribusiness expansion, and the political implications of these positions.

Since 2010, many Marind in the Upper Bian have attended plantation management and agronomic science trainings facilitated by oil palm corporations and government bodies as part of their promotional and recruitment campaigns. Those who have taken up employment within the agribusiness sector now spend most of their time in oil palm plantations, where they interact on a daily basis with oil palm and its symbiotes as pesticide and fertilizer sprayers. One such individual, a pesticide-sprayer from Bayau called Geronimo, once told me, "Oil palm kills the forest. But oil palm is not invincible. It, too, can become sick and die. It, too, can be destroyed." In a similar vein, Karolus, a plantation herbicide sprayer from Khalaoyam, noted, "When people look at plantations, they think there is only oil palm and nothing else. But that is not so. For every oil palm tree, there are a dozen more pests. Oil palm is the enemy of the forest. But oil palm, too, has enemies (*sawit de juga pu lawan*)."

Oil palm parasites, or "enemies," in Gerfacius' words, abound in the monocrop plantation. Culprits identified in the plantation by Geronimo and other laborers include the chartreuse-green coconut nettle caterpillar that devours the leaves of young and mature palm leaves and wounds the hands that seek to remove it with the venom of its urticating spines. The larvae of furry *Mahasena corbetti* bagworms gestate on the undersurface of oil palm fronds, scraping away at the epidermis of leaflets and eventually causing palm necrosis. The Rhinoceros beetle is the most destructive of oil palm's insect parasites, according to Pius, a young Marind pesticide-sprayer from Bayau. Under the cover of the night, the armored creature burrows through the petioles of young palms and developing spears of the crown into the soft tissues of unopened leaves, mining labyrinthine galleries through the terminal bud, thriving in the rotting stems of felled palms, and laying its eggs in empty fresh fruit bunches. The Rhinoceros beetle is also one of many parasites that recruits—or "makes friends" (*jadi kawan*), in Pius' words, with other species to further their mutual proliferation. The damage inflicted by the Rhinoceros beetle, for instance, becomes a fertile spreading ground for the spotted red palm weevil. In return, red palm weevil infections provide the conditions necessary for the development of the beetle's larvae.

Fungal parasites of the palm, too, can trigger epidemics of dramatic proportions. Stem, root, bud, spear, and leaf diseases caused by fungal epidemics include Fusarium wilt, white stripe disease, brown germ, and Curvularia leafspot and blast. In the plantation, Geronimo pointed to me the patchy discolorations and sooty molds that had developed along the fronds of trees afflicted by these diseases. Their leaves had begun to fracture and desiccate. Eventually, the palms would suffer generalized chlorosis and die as fungi appropriate the water, minerals, and light necessary for their growth. Most resistant to chemical and biological controls among oil palm's fungal "enemies" is *Ganoderma*, the fungus that had decimated a third of the palms in the plantation near Geronimo's home village and for which no long-term cure has yet been identified. Known among plantation workers as "cancer," *Ganoderma* spreads through the root systems of host and neighboring palms, where it can remain dormant for several years before bursting into action. Fructifications of *Ganoderma* in the form of hard, orange mushrooms then appear along the oil palm trunk. The root cortex beings to rot while fungal sporophores multiply without bounds. The base of the palm stem blackens and exudes a viscous gum. Eventually, the crown of the tree falls off and the trunk collapses.

The lethal entanglements of palms and parasites within monocrop ecologies suggest to many community members that oil palm, while indubitably harmful in its effects on forest lifeforms, is not itself immune to more-than-human violence. Rather, different necrobiopolitical assemblages alternately enable or undermine the cash crop's proliferation. As Karolus noted, "Oil palm, too, has enemies." For Marind activists, oil palm's disease and death at the hands of parasites constitutes a form of retributive justice. As Laurenzius, a young activist from Mirav, explained, "Oil palm kills our forest. Now, insects, animals, and mushrooms kill oil palm because oil palm doesn't belong here. It's like the Indonesian government. The settlers. They don't belong in Papua. So, now, the forest is fighting back. Quietly and secretly, the forest is fighting back This is a kind of justice. We have much to learn from oil palm's enemies."

Individuals like Laurenzius conceptualize parasitism as an expression of more-than-human sovereignty and resistance, with potent indexical implications *for humans themselves*. Parasitic action undermines the growth of oil palm as a biological entity. In doing so, parasites and their "feral ecologies" (Tsing 2018) sabotage the productivist ethos of technocapitalism and its putatively totalizing control over a homogeneous and instrumentalized nature. Microparasites, as such, do not always collude or comply with the agendas of the state and corporations, or what Brown (1987) calls "macroparasites." Rather, microparasites can end up parasitizing the very same entities that unwittingly *create* the ecological conditions conducive to their thriving.

The particular ways in which oil palm parasites operate are relevant here. Parasites, Laurenzius described, operate "secretly" and "quietly." In rhizomatic manner, these resilient organisms ceaselessly resprout, multiply, and spread across, above, and underground. They form multispecies composites—insects, fungi, mammals—that, like the West Papuan independence movement, have no fixed center or origin, and are therefore difficult to control (Kirksey 2012: 51–78). Unlike the organized and spectacular violence of the Indonesian state, the slow violence of parasitism is often invisible to the human eye. It occurs in the hidden depths of subterranean root systems and the inner core of trunks and fronds. Working away silently but stubbornly at the heart of the agroindustrial nexus, parasites thus become hopeful paragons for Marind like Laurenzius, who read in their surreptitious lives and labors a call for collective human resistance to oil palm and its colonial-capitalist undergirdings, and in doing so, reframe the plantation itself as a more-than-human "ecology of resistance" (Allewaert 2008).

But if activists find in parasites useful allies and indexical archetypes in their struggle against capitalism, plantation workers are more conflicted about their relationship to these organisms. Much like the moral economy of Darjeeling plantations described by Sarah Besky (2013), plantation ecologies are sustained through selective forms of violence and care on the part of human workers, whose labors enable some organisms to live while requiring that others perish. Pesticide-sprayers eradicate organisms like the Rhinoceros beetle to sustain the wellbeing of oil palm—the plant their livelihoods depend on. But this also means destroying organisms that incarnate the power of resistance to a plant that embodies the top-down control of a colonizing state and its capitalist agendas. Siding *with* oil palm by killing its parasites thus means siding *against* entities (human and non-human) who undermine oil palm's proliferation and the broader political forces this proliferation represents.

These conflicting metonymic relations are further complicated by pesticide-sprayers and parasites' shared exposure to chemicals intentionally deployed by the one in order to destroy the other. Workers spend over eight hours a day in the plantations and are particularly vulnerable to the adverse effects of pesticides including the highly toxic herbicides glyphosate and paraquat, as well as glufosinate ammonium, triclopyr, deltamethrin, and trichlorfon. Absorbed through inhalation and epidermal contact, exposure to these chemicals can cause dizziness, nausea, and skin rashes, and cancer, infertility, and heart attacks in the long term.

With alternative employment opportunities difficult to come by in rural Merauke and protective gear too expensive to purchase, many plantation workers voice resignation and powerlessness in the face of the potentially deadly effects of plantation labor on their bodies and health—a powerlessness that, as Agard-Jones (2013) notes, speaks to the loss of bodily sovereignty of peoples subjected to the visceral violence of global capitalist-colonialist systems. But just as disquieting to laborers are the uncanny similarities they identify between their own vulnerability to chemical exposure and that of its intended targets—the parasites themselves. Workers and parasites stand in an oppositional relation of killer to killed, and yet both ultimately inhabit the same toxic atmospheric milieu. Troubling "chemo-socialities" (Shapiro and Kirksey 2017) arise as chemically induced vulnerabilities simultaneously index and challenge relations of sameness and difference, and of life and death, across parasites, plants, and people. But parasitism is not the only relation at play in the multispecies politics of plantation ecologies. Just as important as oil palm's "enemies" are its "friends," whose mutualistic relations to oil palm I turn to next.

Mutualism

The abaduk mushroom that Gerfacius and I encountered in the oil palm plantation is one of several organisms that have developed mutualistic relations with oil palm. Gerfacius pointed out several other such species to me during our trip, often comparing them to pictures in the dog-eared Ecosystem Services Manual given to him by the plantation managers. They included an auburn grasshopper perched atop a mature fresh fruit bunch. A delicate fern lodged between the ridges of an oil palm trunk in circinate vernation. A barking owl nesting amidst mature oil palm fronds.

Other oil palm symbiotes include various species of arthropods, butterflies, dragonflies, dung beetles, bees, and snakes. Unlike larger primates, mammals, and birds of specialized frugivorous or insectivorous diets, as well as monocotyledons and pteridophytes, that fare poorly in monocrop ecologies, these organisms have learned to survive, in Gerfacius' words, by "becoming friends" (*jadi kawan*) with oil palm.

Mutualistic alliances in the plantation embody what Stengers calls "reciprocal capture," or relations in which each species has an interest in seeing the other maintain its existence (2010: 35–36). Some alliances revolve around pollination, facilitated by oil palm's shallow flowers which blossom in conspicuous aggregations throughout the year. The slender flower thrips, for instance, pollinates oil palm while making its home in female inflorescences. At nightfall, delicate Momphid moths take on the pollinating relay, while their larvae are nourished by the palm's developing seed-heads. Chemical molecules emitted by oil palm flowers attract insects of the *Elaeidobius* genus such as the long-snouted pollinating weevil. The slightly stronger anise-scented estragol of male flowers compared to female flowers attracts the weevil to the former and then the latter, in a crafty vegetal strategy of olfactory deception.

Some mutualistic relations, as plantation worker Paulinus explained, are leveraged by agribusiness companies as part of Integrated Pest Management programs. These programs of "planned biodiversity" harness the biotic capacities of beneficial species to control and contain pest populations. Rat infestations, for instance, are controlled by predators such as leopard cats, Asian palm civets, snakes, and diurnal birds such as the Yellow-bellied prinia, Lesser coucal, Ashy tailorbird, Great tit, Oriental magpie-robin, and barn owls, that are bred in rearing centers and then released into the plantation. Yellow assassin bugs, Tachinid flies, and Chalcidoid wasps act as parasitoids of the Rhinoceros beetle's eggs, while entomopathogenic microorganisms including fungi, bacteria, and non-occluded RNA viruses attack the epidermal cells of the beetle's larvae.

Other "friends" of oil palm include an array of fast-growing and abundantly leaf-shedding plants including *Cassia cobenensis, Cassia tora*, and *Euphorbia heterophylla*. These species aid in soil nitrogen fixation and moisture retention, prevent soil erosion and weed growth, and provide nourishing humus to support oil palm's maturation. Leguminous ground cover plants prevent the chippings of felled palms from becoming breeding grounds for the rapacious Rhinoceros beetle. An array of bacterial communities is also harnessed by plantation operators as biofungicides and biofertilizers that inhibit the growth of pathogenic fungi on oil palm trees. These include bacteria from the genus *Trichoderma, Aspergillus, Fusarium*, and *Burkholderia*. Alongside other "multispecies entrepreneurs" (Kirksey 2015), oil palm mutualists support the plant's healthy growth while furthering their own proliferation.

If parasitism reveals oil palm's vulnerability to *lethal* interspecies relations, mutualistic entanglements under planned and associated biodiversity systems reveal that *lively* interspecies relations with oil palm are also possible. Furthermore, the capacity of mutualistic species to share—rather than lose—their space and resources with oil palm points to interspecies community-building and cooperation as alternative strategies of more-than-human survival. Striving toward what Stacey Langwick (2018: 436) describes in the context of Tanzanian gardens as an emergent "politics of interspecies habitability," mutualists co-exist with oil palm as a tentative companion species. Unlike parasites, that thrive at the expense of oil palm and disrupt the productionist ethos of the plantation system, mutualists work *within* the logic of agro-industrial capitalism by repurposing oil palm as ally rather than foe.

Mutualists offer ambivalent solace to Marind workers engaged in the difficult yet daily labor of deciding who gets to live or die in oil palm's company. As Gerfacius explained:

> The Rhinoceros beetle is an enemy of oil palm. The Yellow Assassin bug is a friend of oil palm. Some days, my job is to kill pests – like the Rhinoceros beetle. I do this so oil palm can grow well, and I can feed my family and children. But these creatures are just like us – they are just fighting to live. Other days, I help spread Yellow Assassin bugs in the plantation so oil palm can grow well, and I can feed my family and children. The Yellow Assassin bug and oil palm, they don't fight. They live together. Maybe that's the way forward. Yes, it means the companies can produce more palm oil and the government continues to control our land. But who would you rather be? The beetle or the bug?

Plantation workers like Gerfacius are widely criticized by their activist kin and friends because they endorse the destruction of the forest lifeworld through their collaboration with the agribusiness sector. In doing so, they forget the sounds and species of the forest, undermine the skin and wetness of their plant and animal kin, and instead become "slaves" (*budak*) of the oil palm. The fiercest criticism is invariably directed at pesticide-sprayers like Gerfacius, who are said to make a living from "killing the resistance" (*bunuh perlawanan*).

Yet like organisms that must forge mutualistic relations with oil palm in order to survive, Gerfacius and others see their involvement with the agribusiness sector less as a choice than as a necessity. Employment opportunities outside the plantation—for instance, in primary and secondary schools, the police force, and clinics—are limited and tend to be occupied by non-Papuan settlers. Marind who do not work in oil palm plantations receive cash income from state support programs and from the occasional sale of non-timber forest products and home-grown vegetables in Merauke City. Such income, however, is scarce and sporadic, as government funds only occasionally reach the villages and community members' access to urban markets is impeded by distance and transport costs. With the forest disappearing and oil palm proliferating relentlessly, working with corporations and the state thus becomes a necessary strategy of survival—one that depends less upon sustaining pre-existing interspecies relations than on forging new relations with entities like oil palm, the state, and corporations that are alien and invasive, but ultimately here to stay.

Other villagers, meanwhile, describe working within the capitalist system less as a necessity than a *desired* pathway to a different, and potentially better, future—one characterized by a stable and decent income, access to higher education, heightened social and physical mobility, and the promise of improved material wellbeing. Scholarships offered by agribusiness corporations to employees' children in particular were deemed critical to overcoming low literacy rates in the Upper Bian, where less than half the population finish high school and only 1% attend university. For some community members, the modern way of life promised by plantation labor also offers potential emancipation from the racial stigma they routinely suffer from due to their pathologized association on the part of the Indonesian government, corporations, and settlers with a forest-based and primitive past.

In these future-oriented imaginations, the lives and labors of mutualists themselves come to represent the potential of negotiation and accommodation (rather than resistance and opposition) in the crafting of livable shared worlds with oil palm—an introduced plant with whom Marind might not entertain intimate and ancestral kinships but may potentially develop mutually beneficial friendships. As Viktor, a young plantation worker put it, "Oil palm's friends have learned to share space with oil palm. The forest is gone so they must find ways to survive. They have learned to live together. Some Marind say we should learn from oil palm's enemies. Perhaps we also have something to learn from oil palm's friends."

How, then, do Marind's moral assessments of plantation ecologies shape their everyday actions and decisions? On the one hand, the ethos of co-existence undergirding mutualist's lifeways increasingly figures in the rationale given by some Marind activists for their decision to join the agribusiness sector as laborers and harvesters. On the other hand, a small number of Marind plantation workers who had resigned from their positions and returned to the village explained to me that they could no longer bear making a living from "killing the resistance." Some had begun this exiting process long before their formal resignation—by spraying far less pesticide than their bosses ordered them to, for instance, or purposefully neglecting to inform management of budding fungal diseases and pest populations. These acts of strategic passivity were described as a form of redemption for the many lives the workers had killed for oil palm to thrive. But such actions could not be sustained indefinitely. The bosses would find out. Decisions had to be made. For many Marind workers, these decisions remain in-the-making, informed on a daily basis by the ongoingly lively and lethal dynamics of the industrial ecologies that these individuals are paid to sustain, but occasionally also choose to subvert.

Conclusions

In grounding its analysis in Indigenous theories, concepts, and discourses, this essay has given precedence to Marind's *own* understandings of agribusiness-driven transformations, as marginalized peoples most deeply and directly mired in the fraught predicament of interspecies care and violence. These grounded discourses and experiences shed important insights into a number of conceptual framings that have recently been developed to characterize the current era. For instance, they offer a multispecies angle on the "Capitalocene" (Moore 2015) by highlighting the lively agency of cash crops *themselves* as consequential, animate beings—rather than passive, material commodities—that forge alternately lethal and benign relations with other lifeforms. They foreground the uneven distribution of living and dying (well) in the "Anthropocene," and particularly in settler-colonial contexts, where racial and ethnic discrimination continue to position Indigenous peoples as sub-human before the law (see Caluya 2014; Yusoff 2019). Perhaps most importantly, Marind understandings of plantation lifeworlds offer important empirical and theoretical insights into the more-than-human dynamics of the Plantationocene and its conflictual horizons of justice for both humans and non-humans.

In these ostensibly homogeneous and ecologically impoverished zones, diverse organisms are pursuing tentative "arts of living" (Tsing et al. 2017) that rely alternately on interspecies domination, subordination, or collaboration. If capitalism undermines some multispecies relations, it also enables others. And capitalist natures themselves are not immune to multispecies violence. The plantation, to borrow Kristina Lyons' (2016) terms, thus constitutes a realm of transformative potentiality distributed across diverse human and other-than-human actors, that materializes through these actors' indexical yet often asymmetric labors of making or letting live, and making or letting die. Oil palm and its symbiotes themselves partake in shaping plantation ecologies in ways that can evade human control or be repurposed in politically imbued forms. Replete with creative patterns of multispecies survival and resistance, monocrop landscapes represent fertile spaces for the crafting of shifting trans-species indexicalities, possibilities, and positionalities, in which parasitism and mutualism are themselves bound in a mutual (or parasitic) relationship.

The concomitantly lively *and* lethal multispecies relations that together produce the plantation as a material-semiotic ecology thus bring us to interrogate what species benefit or suffer from agribusiness expansion, which lives and deaths matter within capitalist natures, and to whom. They invite us to consider who must die in order for whom to live in plantation landscapes, and what part Marind themselves play in shaping plantation ecologies through their material and hermeneutic labors, both within and against the agribusiness model. Importantly, analyzing oil palm through its parasitic and mutualistic relations with other species, and through Marind's politically charged interpretations *of* these relations, disrupts the representation of monocrops as realms devoid of biotic diversity and semiotic meaning. Instead, plantations reveal themselves complex multispecies assemblages produced by situated interactions between people, between people and organisms, and the technologies, labors, knowledges, infrastructures, institutions, chemicals, meanings, and bodies, that mediate these relationships. Within these affective ecologies, humans and other-than-humans become materially and symbolically involved in one another's lives through ethically fraught weaves of living, dying, and killing, that promise or disable different futures for different multispecies collectives—even as they continue to perpetuate the extractivist logic of colonial-capitalism.

My aim is not to celebrate capitalist natures or suggest that the thriving of some organisms in plantation lifeworlds justifies or counterbalances the loss of others. Rather, I have sought to offer a more nuanced perspective on the possibilities of justice afforded or subverted by plantation formations for their human and more-than-human dwellers. A multispecies analysis of capitalist ecologies foregrounds the incommensurability of lives at play, the hopeful congruence of some interspecies relations, and the incompatibility of others. It reveals how parasites and mutualists come to matter less as fixed categories than as situated and metonymic *relations*, whose moral significance is defined as much by their own subjectivity as by that of their object. It also sheds light on the shifting indexicalities Upper Bian Marind establish with parasites and mutualists as they negotiate the changing social and ecological fabrics of their more-than-human world. Such an approach invites critical attention to the particular *kinds* of interspecies dynamics that shape the multispecies ecologies of industrial plantations, or what Franklin Ginn et al. (2014) might call "awkward flourishings." Awkward flourishings work with and against situated multispecies communities—some of which prosper and some of which flail. Such flourishings invite us to reflect on who lives and dies well under existing ecological regimes, and how these regimes might be better configured (2014: 17). And they draw attention to the ecological itself as always at once biological, affective, political, and moral.

Just as plantations may not be as "mono" as they appear, so too Marind are divided over the implications of oil palm's symbiotic relations for their own (dis)engagement with agribusiness and the state, and for the possibility of justice within the "uneven conditions of more-than-human livability" (Tsing et al. 2019: S186) that characterize agroindustrial landscapes. When it comes to destroying (or living with) oil palm, plantation organisms and Marind are not only "much like" one another—they are on the same opposing teams and bound in metonymic relation. The multispecies dynamics of monocrop formations—destructive parasites on the one hand and accommodating mutualists on the other—thus speak in politically and morally charged ways to Marinds' own conflicting orientations toward agricultural industrialization and its human actors as potential "friends" or "foes." These contrasting types of interspecies relations also provide potent, if ambivalent, material-semiotic idioms for

Marind to critique their present condition and the theft of sovereignty over more-than-human lands and bodies that contemporary agribusiness expansion both perpetuates and intensifies.

Indigenous Marind idioms recognize that human and other-than-human lives and futures are always mutually implicated, if not always aligned. They defy singular and anthropocentric narratives of dominance and victimhood. Instead, they highlight how more-than-human forms of personhood, desire, and survivance partake in the forging of multispecies resilience—a resilience that starts with the material and imaginative labor of becoming-with plants, humans, and their alternately friendly or antagonistic companions. In thinking and theorizing *with* these interspecies relations, Marind unearth imaginative ways of transcending conditions of suffering and subjection under settler-colonial rule. This imaginative labor is at once speculative and counter-hegemonic. It operates with, within, and against the sovereignty of the plantation model and its anthropocentric, extractive logic. It offers tentative—and contested—visions of what equitable human and multispecies justice might look and feel like amidst the toxic ecologies of agroindustrial capitalism.

CODA

The multispecies politics of Merauke's plantations took an unanticipated turn in early 2018. A rumor had spread that the conglomerate managing the concession Gerfacius and I had traveled through had gone bankrupt. In a notice published in a local newspaper, the company attributed the closure of its operations to a "suboptimal labor force" and "unfavorable climactic conditions." But the real problem, plantation laborer Viktor told me, was neither the workers nor the weather. The problem was *Mucuna bracteata,* a leguminous cover plant introduced by the company for its soil moisture retention capacities. In the absence of natural predators, however, *Mucuna* had multiplied uncontrollably and been reclassified by plantation management as an invasive species. Efforts to eliminate it chemically and replace it with less tenacious plant varieties had failed. Hundreds of oil palms had died from lack of water, including many that had barely survived the recent *Ganoderma* epidemic.

The transformation of species from beneficial allies to unruly invasives reveals that strategies of biological control in plantation ecologies can backfire dramatically when organisms turn the tables on their human counterparts. Indeed, Upper Bian activists were quick to repurpose

Mucuna—a former "friend" of oil palm—as unequivocal evidence of the triumph of resistance over "oil palm bosses" (*bos sawit*) who erroneously believed they were "in control of nature" (*mampu mengatur alam*). Gerfacius, meanwhile, read a different meaning in *Mucuna*'s unexpected proliferation. "Today I am the Yellow Assassin bug—working with oil palm," he said. "But tomorrow, I might become the Rhinoceros beetle—fighting against oil palm. *Mucuna* knows how to work the system because it is part of the system. Maybe *Mucuna* is who we should learn from."

As Gerfacius suggests, "friends" and "enemies" in the plantation assemblage are neither fixed or bounded entities, but rather malleable and dynamic relationalities. Organisms like *Mucuna* act as potent exemplars of the unpredictable and shifting forms that multispecies resilience can take in capitalist natures. Neither beetle nor bug yet both, *Mucuna* challenges anthropogenic classifications of species as pests or beneficials. It embeds itself as an ally within technocapitalist agendas, only to then subvert them. In doing so, mutualists that unexpectedly repurpose *themselves* as parasites suggest that collaboration and compliance are not necessarily ends in themselves. Rather, befriending oil palm in the here and now may enable more radical forms of multispecies resistance and justice in the future, from *within* the architectures of agroindustrial capitalism—a formation that, while indubitably destructive and dispossessory, has never fully succeeded in dominating either plants or people.

References

Agard-Jones, V. 2013. "Bodies in the System." *Small Axe* 42: 182–192.

Allewaert, M. 2008. "Swamp Sublime: Ecologies of Resistance in the American Plantation Zone." *PMLA* 123 (2): 340–357.

Ananta, A., D.R.W.W. Utami, and N.B. Handayani. 2016. "Statistics on Ethnic Diversity in the Land of Papua, Indonesia." *Asia & the Pacific Policy Studies* 3 (3): 458–474.

Baal, J.V. 1966. *Dema: Description and Analysis of Marind-Anim Culture (South New Guinea)*. The Hague: Martinus Nijhoff.

Besky, S. 2013. *The Darjeeling Distinction: Labor and Justice on Fair-Trade Tea Plantations in India*. Berkeley: University of California Press.

Brown, Peter J. 1987. "Microparasites and Macroparasites." *Cultural Anthropology* 2 (1): 155–71.

Caluya, G. 2014. "Fragments for a Postcolonial Critique of the Anthropocene: Invasion Biology and Environmental Security." In *Rethinking Invasion Ecologies from the Environmental Humanities*, ed. J. Frawley and I. McCalman, 31–44. London: Routledge.

Chao, S. 2017. "There Are No Straight Lines in Nature: Making Living Maps in West Papua." *Anthropology Now* 9 (1): 16–33.

Chao, S. 2018a. "In the Shadow of the Palm: Dispersed Ontologies Among Marind, West Papua." *Cultural Anthropology* 33 (4): 621–649.

Chao, S. 2018b. "Seed Care in the Palm Oil Sector." *Environmental Humanities* 10 (2): 421–446.

Chao, S. 2019a. "The Plastic Cassowary: Problematic 'Pets' in West Papua." *Ethnos* 84 (5): 828–848.

Chao, S. 2019b. "Wrathful Ancestors, Corporate Sorcerers: Rituals Gone Rogue in Merauke, West Papua." *Oceania* 89 (3): 266–283.

Chao, S. 2020. "A Tree of Many Lives: Vegetal Teleontologies in West Papua." *HAU: Journal of Ethnographic Theory* 10 (2): 514–529.

Chao, S. 2021. "Children of the Palms: Growing Plants and Growing People in Merauke, West Papua." *Journal of the Royal Anthropological Institute* 27 (2): 245–264.

Chao, S. 2022a. "Extraction, Extinction, Emergence: (Un)Worlding the Plantationocene." *ETropic: Electronic Journal of Studies in the Tropics* 21 (1): 165–191.

Chao, S. 2022b. *In the Shadow of the Palms: More-Than-Human Becomings in West Papua*. Durham: Duke University Press.

Chao, S., K. Bolender, and E. Kirksey, eds. 2022. *The Promise of Multispecies Justice*. Durham: Duke University Press.

Davis, J., A.A. Moulton, L.V. Sant, and B. Williams. 2019. "Anthropocene, Capitalocene, … Plantationocene?: A Manifesto for Ecological Justice in an Age of Global Crises." *Geography Compass* 13 (5): 1–15.

Derksen, M. 2016. "Local Intermediaries? The Missionising and Governing of Colonial Subjects in South Dutch New Guinea, 1920–42." *The Journal of Pacific History* 51 (2): 111–142.

Down to Earth. 2011. "Twenty-Two Years of Top-Down Resource Exploitation in Papua. Down to Earth." http://www.downtoearth-indonesia.org/story/twenty-two-years-top-down-resource-exploitation-papua.

Escobar, A. 1999. "After Nature: Steps to an Antiessentialist Political Ecology." *Current Anthropology* 40 (1): 1–30.

Giay, B., and C. Ballard. 2003. "Becoming Papuans: Notes Towards a History of Racism in Tanah Papua." Paper Presented at the Annual Meeting of the American Anthropological Association. Chicago, United States.

Ginn, F., U. Beisel, and M. Barua. 2014. "Flourishing with Awkward Creatures: Togetherness, Vulnerability, Killing." *Environmental Humanities* 4: 113–124.

Haraway, D.J. 1991. *Simians, Cyborgs, and Women: The Reinvention of Nature*. London: Free Association.
Haraway, D.J. 1992. "The Promises of Monsters: A Regenerative Politics for Inappropriate/d Others." In *Cultural Studies*, ed. L. Grossberg, C. Nelson, and P.A. Treichler, 295–337. New York: Routledge.
Haraway, D.J. 2015. "Anthropocene, Capitalocene, Plantationocene, Chthulucene: Making Kin." *Environmental Humanities* 6: 159–165.
Hetherington, K. 2013. "Beans Before the Law: Knowledge Practices, Responsibility, and the Paraguayan Soy Boom." *Cultural Anthropology* 28 (1): 65–85.
Jegathesan, M. 2021. "Black Feminist Plots before the Plantationocene and Anthropology's 'Regional Closets.'" *Feminist Anthropology* 2 (1): 78–93.
Kirksey, E.S. 2012. *Freedom in Entangled Worlds: West Papua and the Architecture of Global Power*. Durham: Duke University Press.
Kirksey, E.S. 2015. *Emergent Ecologies*. Durham: Duke University Press.
Kusumaryati, V. 2019. "Adat Institutionalisation, the State and the Quest for Self-Determination in West Papua." *The Asia Pacific Journal of Anthropology* 21 (1): 1–16.
Langwick, S.A. 2018. "A Politics of Habitability: Plants, Healing, and Sovereignty in a Toxic World." *Cultural Anthropology* 33 (3): 415–443.
Lyons, K. 2016. "Decomposition as Life Politics: Soils, Selva, and Small Farmers under the Gun of the U.S.-Colombia War on Drugs." *Cultural Anthropology* 31 (1): 58–81.
Marder, M. 2013. *Plant-Thinking: A Philosophy of Vegetal Life*. New York: Columbia University Press.
McKittrick, K. 2013. "Plantation Futures." *Small Axe* 17 (3): 1–15.
Mitman, G. 2019. "Reflections on the Plantationocene: A Conversation with Donna Haraway and Anna Tsing." Edge Effects. http://edgeeffects.net/wp-content/uploads/2019/06/PlantationoceneReflections_Haraway_Tsing.pdf.
Moore, J.W. 2015. *Capitalism in the Web of Life: Ecology and the Accumulation of Capital*. Brooklyn: Verso.
Mote, O., and D. Rutherford. 2001. "From Irian Jaya to Papua: The Limits of Primordialism in Indonesia's Troubled East." *Indonesia* 72: 115–140.
Pouwer, J. 1999. "The Colonisation, Decolonisation and Recolonisation of West New Guinea." *The Journal of Pacific History* 34 (2): 157–179.
Richens, J. 2021. *Tik Merauke: An Epidemic Like No Other*. Melbourne: Melbourne University Press.
Shapiro, N., and E.S. Kirksey. 2017. "Chemo-Ethnography: An Introduction." *Cultural Anthropology* 32 (4): 481–493.
Shiva, V. 1993. *Monocultures of the Mind: Perspectives on Biodiversity and Biotechnology*. London: Zed Books.
Stengers, I. 2010. *Cosmopolitics I*. Minneapolis: University of Minnesota Press.

Swadling, P. 1996. *Plumes from Paradise: Trade Cycles in Outer Southeast Asia and Their Impact on New Guinea and Nearby Islands Until 1920*. Boroko and Queensland: Papua New Guinea National Museum and Robert Brown.

Tsing, A.L. 2018. "Getting by in Terrifying Times." *Dialogues in Human Geography* 8 (1): 73–76.

Tsing, A.L., N. Bubandt, E. Gan, and H.A. Swanson. 2017. *Arts of Living on a Damaged Planet: Ghosts and Monsters of the Anthropocene*. Minneapolis: University of Minnesota Press.

Tsing, A.L., A.S. Mathews, and N. Bubandt. 2019. "Patchy Anthropocene: Landscape Structure, Multispecies History, and the Retooling of Anthropology." *Current Anthropology* 60: S186–S197.

Verschueren, J. 1970. "Marind-Anim Land Tenure." *New Guinea Research Bulletin*. 38 (December): 42–59.

Wolford, W. 2021. "The Plantationocene: A Lusotropical Contribution to the Theory." *Annals of the American Association of Geographers* 111 (6): 1622–1639.

Yusoff, K. 2019. *A Billion Black Anthropocenes Or None*. Minneapolis: University of Minnesota Press.

CHAPTER 13

Colonial Plantations and Their Afterlives: Legal Disciplines, Indian Historiographies and Their Lessons. An Interview with Rana Behal

Marta Macedo, Irene Peano, and Colette Le Petitcorps

M. Macedo · I. Peano (✉) · C. Le Petitcorps
Institute of Social Sciences, University of Lisbon, Lisbon, Portugal
e-mail: irene.peano@ics.ulisboa.pt

M. Macedo
e-mail: martamacedo@fcsh.unl.pt; marta.macedo@ics.ulisboa.pt

C. Le Petitcorps
e-mail: lepetit.colette@wanadoo.fr

I. Peano
Institute of Contemporary History, NOVA School of Social Sciences and Humanities, Lisbon, Portugal

C. Le Petitcorps et al. (eds.), *Global Plantations in the Modern World*, Cambridge Imperial and Post-Colonial Studies,
https://doi.org/10.1007/978-3-031-08537-6_13

Rana Behal taught history at Deshbandhu College, University of Delhi between 1972 and 2014 and at Cornell and Syracuse Universities and Oberlin College in the USA. He held numerous positions as a visiting researcher, both in Europe and India. He conducted research on tea plantations and their labour force in Assam during colonial rule. His publications include *One Hundred Years of Servitude: Political Economy of Tea Plantations in Colonial Assam* (New Delhi: Tulika Books, 2014).

1. In your book "*One hundred years of servitude. Political Economy of Tea Plantations in Colonial Assam*" (Tulika Books 2014), you insist on the fact that Assam tea plantations, which use the workforce of migrant agrarian communities that are transformed into "coolies", are different from slavery-based plantations. Could you explain this important distinction?

Assam did not have a slave-based production system in place in tea plantations before the advent of indenture. From the very inception tea planters in Assam adopted labor-intensive methods of production. Assam tea planters were unable to persuade/coerce local agrarian communities to take up employment. A majority among the labor force, therefore, was recruited and transported from among agrarian communities from Chotanagpur, Santhal Parganas and other parts of the Bengal Presidency. These communities were subdued and marginalized through "pacification campaigns" launched by the British colonial army and alienated from their land in a big way by the introduction of colonial land tenures. Many hill villagers, nobles, chiefs and headmen were dispossessed. Such conditions of distress provided a fertile hunting ground for the native *arkattis* and *sirdars* to recruit and transport these communities to work in Assam tea plantations. *Arkattis* were local recruiters in the catchment areas, the lowest in the recruitment structure hierarchy. *Sirdars* were tea garden laborers sent by the planters to recruit labor from their native areas.

Here workers were employed to produce tea for a growing global market. They were contracted for a period of five years under the indenture law at minimum wage, and were called 'coolies', a pejorative term for migrant labor in vogue in the colonial world. Non-compliance with the contract was criminalized: planters were given powers to arrest laborers who 'absconded' without warrant, and imprisonment was the penalty for refusal to work. Thus, formally they were contract laborers under the indenture law passed by the colonial state in 1865. It was not a system of slavery such as that which was in practice in the Antebellum era in the American South and Caribbean. The laboring body was not owned by the planter. However, for most workers the five-year contract got extended into generational servitude, as I have shown in my book. Despite the veneer of formal wage-contract employment, in reality the workers did not have freedom of movement. A very effective system of surveillance was placed enforced both at the place of their work and in living quarters. The minimum wage was below subsistence and had to be supplemented by a wage in kind. Work and living conditions in these plantations were appalling and resulted in very high mortality rates. Equally unpleasant and fatal were workers' travel experiences from their homes to the plantations, a long distance they traversed walking, by train and river transportation, over several weeks. It is not surprising that many contemporaries, including those in the highest echelons of the colonial hierarchy, Indian nationalists and some Christian missionary activists often referred to the indenture regime in Assam tea plantations as a form of slavery. I do not interpret indenture as slavery, but any analogy between slavery and indenture is nearer the truth than the attempt by revisionist scholarship to equate it with the free emigration of Europeans to America in the nineteenth century.

2. Moving beyond local processes, what are the connections between the indenture system that supplied labor for Assam plantations and broader patterns of global labor recruitment in the post-abolition phase, both within the British empire and beyond it?

Responding to growing demands by World markets, British capitalists opened plantations producing tea, coffee, sugar and rubber, in India as well as in several overseas colonies of the British Empire—in the Caribbean, Fiji, Mauritius, Ceylon and Malaya, from the 1830s onwards. Sugar plantations already existed in the Caribbean and operated under local slave labor. Emancipation ended slavery in the British Empire in 1834. The slave-owning planters were compensated by the British to the tune of 20 million pounds sterling. In most of these colonies planters' inability to 'persuade' local communities to accept employment led them to bring in migrants from British India to work under indenture laws enacted by the colonial government. The vast majority of these migrants were mobilized and transported with the support of the colonial state, from among the increasingly marginalized agrarian communities in different parts of British India. While the Imperial Government was more actively involved with labor recruitment from India for overseas British capitalist plantation enterprises, it was the Indian colonial state that played a predominant role in Assam plantation-labor recruitment. Most of the small islands overseas were plantation-dominated, production-based colonies where the local colonial administration and the planters often negotiated directly through the Imperial Government in London.

Once mobilized, these migrants were immobilized under the indenture system on arrival in the plantations. The pejorative term 'coolie' became synonymous with indenture-contract migrant laborers in all these plantations. With the growing requirement of labor towards the end of the nineteenth century, Ceylon and Malaya opted out of the indenture system and began recruiting Indian migrants through *kanganies*, who were headmen among labor communities. With the massive expansion of tea cultivation in Ceylon, the *Kangani* system of recruitment became the dominant feature of mobilization of immigrant labor from South India to Ceylon plantations, and went through several incarnations. It was considered free migration as the laborer had the legal right to quit his employer's service at a month's notice. The *Kangani* system involved a short-term (usually 30 days) contract, generally verbal rather than written. Workers were free to leave whenever they wished. However, unlike the Assam recruitment system, under this system laborers had to bear the cost of their transportation and recruitment. *Kanganies* received 'coastal advances' from the planters for recruitment. Out of the 'coastal advances' the *kanganies* spent on food, clothing and transit of the recruits during the trip to Ceylon. These expenses were charged by the planters as 'debt' against the *kanganies* and their recruits which, in reality, were recovered from the laborers. This put them in debt—a debt that they found hard to repay, and which effectively tied them to their *kanganies* and the planters. In reality both these plantation regimes were characterized by physical and sexual coercion, low wages, debt traps and exploitation. Not many could return to their native places and got into generational servitude. In due course, those who could get out of the contract settled in these plantation colonies. Today the descendants of these 'coolies' constitute the bulk of the Indian diaspora in the former British overseas colonies.

3. Where would you situate your own research and academic trajectory vis-à-vis that of Subaltern and Postcolonial Studies' scholars? For example, Chakrabarty's *Rethinking Working Class History* is not referenced in your book. How do you position yourself in regard to that scholarly tradition, which critiqued the universalizing logics of a Marxian historical-materialist approach and stressed the explanatory power of cultural aspects and local realities?

Chakrabarty articulated a powerful critique of reductionist frameworks. He carried on a sharp polemic against the dominant assumptions in labor history in India. He argued that even those more sensitive to issues of culture tended to reduce culture to certain economic variables. Chakrabarty's radical culturalism disturbed the certainties of conventional Marxist approaches and presaged some of the later shifts in the historiography of labor. In opposition to Marxist writings that see working-class history in terms of a continuous unfolding of class identities, Chakrabarty's account valorizes certain fixed notions of caste and community identities. While Chakrabarty critiques frameworks which reduce culture to economic determinants, he tends to reify culture by seeing identities in terms of fixed cultural meanings. Chakrabarty's work brought about a shift in the labor studies scholarship in South Asia. Not referring his work in my book is not exceptional. I have refrained from citing a large number of works on industrial labor in my book. There is a large sample of published, high-quality scholarship on industrial labor in South Asia. Somewhere else I have written about those works on the historiography of South Asian labor. As far as your question about the Subaltern Studies, please note that most of the celebrated Subaltern Studies' volumes are silent on the issue of labor. With the exception of Dipesh Chakrabarty's work, the dominant concern of the historians of the Subaltern Studies group was with peasant movements. I am not sure why the Subaltern group ignored labor history after Chakrabarty's seminal article. I see my own contribution within the Marxist framework but away from orthodox Marxism, more compatible with the works of Marcel van der Linden.

4. In your work you never address the issue of race straightforwardly, but racialization practices and discourses are present in your analysis of both the migrant workers that were taken to Assam plantations

and the local communities that refused to work for these same plantations. Other scholars working on Indian tea plantations, such as Piya Chatterjee, have explicitly referred to the ways in which racial categories were grafted onto earlier distinctions based on caste and religion, and how these categories keep being revitalized across the colonial-postcolonial transition. Did you believe the concept was not pertinent? And why?

The racial attitude of White Managers towards the labor force is clearly revealed right through my work though I did not bring in any theoretical discussion on this category. My study of labor relations is framed in the larger canvass of modern capitalism that includes features like racialism, economic and sexual coercion, dehumanizing labor, violence, surveillance and the denial of the freedom of movement. I have not shied away from using the category of caste, though religion as such was not a major issue in the everyday production relations. Piya Chatterjee's fine work deals with post-colonial Bengal tea plantations that were owned and managed by Indians, several owned by her family. The New Independent Indian State modified some of the provisions of existing labor laws formally permitting the formation of labor unions. Despite perceiving themselves in the frame of Burra Sahibs, including their life styles, there were changes in the attitude of Indian Managers towards the labor force. During colonial times white managers were called Burra Sahibs (Big Master). They indulged in physical coercion, like flogging workers, and used racial epithets as means of taming labor, as it was the norm in colonial-state coercion of labor and convicts. In contemporary Indian tea plantations, managerial positions are held by Indian personnel. While the kind of omnipresent authority and the lifestyle of the Burra Sahib still exist, racialism is replaced by the power of class hierarchy. With the emergence of worker agency in the form of labor unions, Indian managers are in no position to display the kind of racialism and violence that were regular features of plantations during the colonial regime. This distinction needs to be recognized while comparing colonial and contemporary plantation-labor relations in south Asia. This is not to suggest that economic exploitation and dependency relationships ceased to exist. Workers still get paid part of their wage in kind. Tea-plantation workers' life in India remains grossly impoverished, underfed, unhealthy and devoid of education even after nearly two centuries of continued operations to produce tea for national and global markets.

5. Many of the contributions to this volume analyze the complex entanglements between sovereignty and plantation systems. In some of these cases, plantations act as the kernels, so to speak, for the development of full-blown state control, both by developing institutional arrangements (police, the judiciary, the sanctioned use of force) and by fostering subjective dispositions and the habitus of modern possessive individualism. The case of Assam you describe in your work, however, is perhaps more complex. Here, colonial sovereignty clearly precedes and favours the establishment of tea plantations, whilst also being transformed and maybe strengthened in the process. It figures as the outcome of processes of economic investment and management (East India Company, Assam Company) which straddle the border between legality and illegality—there seems to be a constant feedback between the imperial state and private business, where one provides the other with sovereign powers (e.g. planters' and their representatives' power to arrest coolies for the breach of their contracts). Do you agree with this reading, and can you elaborate on what you think are the most significant relations between these plantations and processes of imperial sovereign development?

Modern capitalist plantations opened in the colonial tropical geographies were integral to imperial sovereign European states like the UK, the Netherlands and France during the nineteenth century. The European metropolis became the centre of powerful business associations/institutions that successfully lobbied with their respective Imperial States to support their colonial investments and enterprises in the colonies. Tea plantations in Assam were the first and largest capitalist enterprise that was originally set up by the colonial state and then transferred to private British capital free of cost. For their further growth and development, the colonial states facilitated the acquisition of vast amounts of waste and forested lands cheaply, the mobilization of migrant labor on a huge scale and the building of infrastructure for the transportation of tea and labor.

While formally enacting a legal framework to control and regulate labor relations, the colonial state itself introduced the element of extra-legality by sanctioning the planters' power, as pointed out above, to privately arrest runaway laborers and hold them on the tea estate for a week before producing them in front of the Magistrate. I have argued in my book that in the public domain the colonial state formally announced to be playing a mediatory role between capital and labor. This was asserted by colonial officials. However, in reality the state was not averse to overlook illegal and extra-legal coercion and the use of violence by the planters against their labor force. Racial and cultural affinities between the white planters and colonial officials were an important factor. They shared the twin vision of promoting capital for the 'development' of a 'backward' colonial world for their own benefit, as well as a 'Civilizing Mission' to salvage the heathen marginalized 'tribal', 'semi-tribal' and 'aboriginal' agrarian communities by transforming them into wage-earning 'coolies'. Here I would like to point out that colonial bureaucracy was not a monolith entity. There were instances of bureaucrats who disapproved of planters' extra-legal violence and produced critical information about labor conditions. I have referred to Viceroy Curzon in my work, who privately expressed contempt of planters and considered the indenture system to be like slavery. Chief commissioner Henry Cotton got on the wrong side of the planters when he ordered a very small rise in the wages of workers in the plantations. However, this did not transform into empathy towards the labor force and their sufferings. The interests of Capital and Imperial Sovereignty were mutually entwined in the colonies and had to be promoted irrespective of the officially reported sufferings and high rate of mortality of the labor force.

6. In this volume we seek to think through the *durabilities* of plantation systems beyond their demise, or at any rate through their transformations. Whilst your work has focused more prominently on British colonial plantations in Assam, can you reflect upon the imprints they have left in post-independence India—economically, politically, culturally and socially? Do you see a role for such durabilities in current political and economic developments, particularly in Assam but also in relation to farmers' protests?

Many modern capitalist plantation systems, apart from Assam, have been very durable and survived after the demise of Empires and are now regulated under the laws enacted by post-colonial States. A significant part of their commodity production is still for the global markets. Tea plantations in contemporary India employ more than a million permanent workers, and perhaps more than twice as many seasonal laborers. This makes the industry the largest private-sector employer in the country. But workers depend upon plantations for more than just employment: millions of workers and their families still live on the plantations, and rely on them for basic services, including food supplies, healthcare and education. These services were provided for under the Plantation Labor Act (PLA), the most significant labor legislation passed immediately after Independence by the Indian Parliament, in 1951. Workers are politically more aware and participate in the electoral politics in the country. There is one important change the workers themselves brought about: they asserted a change in the nomenclature of their identity. The use of the derogatory term 'coolie' is no longer acceptable and they gave themselves a new identity: *adivasi*. However, in successive elections they end up becoming a vote bank for any political party which makes promises to improve their lives. They may have heard about the farmers' agitation in Northern India from the media but they have no contact with this agitation.

Contemporary research literature on Assam tea-plantation labor reveals a very pessimistic picture of workers' lives. As with their experiences with colonial labor laws, the potential benefits promised under the PLA rarely reach the labor force. They are still paid subsistence wages supplemented in kind. They still live in poverty and families living in the plantations cannot support themselves on the wages they earn. Their illiteracy, poor socio-economic and political conditions, harsh and unhealthy living environment in the labor lines expose laborers to various infectious diseases and malnutrition. Nutritional problems leding to children being underweight and to thinness among adults, and micronutrient deficiency disorders like anaemia are widespread. Common infectious diseases are worm infestation, respiratory problems, diarrhoea, skin infections, filariasis and pulmonary tuberculosis. The health conditions of women laborers, who constitute nearly 50% of the labor force in the tea plantations, have remained the most vulnerable.

I believe one of the major consequences of a prolongedly immobilized residential existence left the laboring communities isolated from the

Assamese society outside the plantations. And despite the settlement of a very large number of time-expired labor on land in the vicinity of plantations, this isolation remains an important phenomenon. While the forced enclave existence left them socially and politically isolated, this was further reinforced due to the general attitude of indifference, by the Assamese intelligentsia and political leadership, towards the tea-plantation laboring communities, both during and after colonial rule.

7. Building on this last question, and also thinking specifically of labor histories that have been analyzing global labor regimes in their multiple declinations of "freedom" and "unfreedom" (e.g., Marcel Van der Linden), how can your historical work shed light on contemporary waves of labor migration, liberalized labor markets and the role of the state (and other agents) in governing such processes, in India and beyond?

Labor has undergone tremendous changes in India during the last three decades. One of its largest industries, textiles, collapsed during the 1980s. The closure of nearly all the textile mills in Ahmedabad, Bombay, Kanpur, Delhi, Amritsar and other industrial centers of India during the last quarter of the twentieth century led to the dismissal of hundreds of thousands of workers. A similar fate fell on several other industries, both in the private and public sectors. Trade unions suffered a severe decline of their influence as the size of organized labor shrank hugely, down to 8% of the entire labor force. These dramatic changes in the organization of the industry took place within the context of a state policy that was introduced in 1985 and which gave priority to the liberalization of the economy and increasing flexibility of the labor system. In the guise of labor reforms, under pressure from the growing private corporate sector, several labor laws were amended or altogether removed from the legal system by the Indian state. The start of a new industrial policy gave rise to a second and even more substantial round of retrenchment. Today 92% of Indian labor is employed in the unorganized informal sector, a large section of them rural migrants to the urban world. The informal sector and even some of the organized industries have grown a practice of hiring and firing that indicates labor is not protected by legal regulations. The ideological shift from the idea of state-regulated capital-labor relations towards 'unfettered markets', following the neoliberal reforms initiated in 1991, further pushed an ever larger pool of the Indian labor force into the expanding informal sector. The unprotected nature of informal-sector labor is loosely linked with the inability of the workforce to protect itself by organizing. They find all kinds of rudimentary opportunities—menial service jobs, street occupations, part-time employment, often finding multiple sources of income. 'Self-employment' is the buzzword ruling—class politicians convey to India's laboring poor.

Migration in the nascent industrial experiences of the developing world has shown the emergence of a huge urban underclass who did not get absorbed into the mega-industrialization process. Migrants populate urban slums in large numbers. Many among the plantation laboring communities in Assam have begun to migrate to Indian metropoles in search of basic livelihood in the informal sector. For this, children (particularly girls) become vulnerable to trafficking. Scores of young women and children have been trafficked out of the Assam plantations with the promise of work and education. Many end up in prostitution. It is ironic that, after being transported for nearly one and half centuries to work in the Assam tea plantations, men and women now are increasingly pushed to travel to Indian metropoles to seek work for livelihood. Under these circumstances of labour lives one wonders whether the debate on free and unfree labor has lost its relevance in the contemporary world.

PART V

Afterword

CHAPTER 14

Afterlives: The Recursive Plantation

Deborah A. Thomas

How do we give a capacious account of the centrality of the plantation to modernity without falling prey to the fictions of what Michel-Rolph Trouillot called North Atlantic universals (2002)? How might we understand shifting and overlapping modes of empire, moments of political alliance and rupture, changing notions of selfhood and belonging, and elaborations of social, racial, ethnic, and cultural hierarchy in ways that open up the conceptual frames of ecology and affect, and not just those of political economy? The authors in this volume offer up answers to these questions, and read together, their essays allow for a kaleidoscopic layering, historically and in the present, of the recursive afterlives of plantations.

What this volume so beautifully demonstrates is that older imperial dispossessions never quite disappear; one form of colonialism, its power dynamics, its constructions of space and time, is never fully displaced by another. Where Western modernity inaugurated plantation time across the space of the Atlantic World, new notions of the "human" emerged,

D. A. Thomas (✉)
University of Pennsylvania, Philadelphia, PA, USA
e-mail: Deborah.Thomas@sas.upenn.edu

C. Le Petitcorps et al. (eds.), *Global Plantations in the Modern World*, Cambridge Imperial and Post-Colonial Studies,
https://doi.org/10.1007/978-3-031-08537-6_14

notions that marked the boundaries between Europeans (who were human), Indigenous peoples (who were not-quite-human), and enslaved Africans (who were non-human). Alongside the plantation, however, as Sylvia Wynter and others remind us, was the plot, the space for the elaboration of community, or human-ness, among the enslaved. The Cuban War for Independence shifted imperial time to that which would ultimately become the developmentalism that characterized the Cold War, and to a space that was defined by the long reach of the United States across both the Atlantic and the Pacific. But this time and this space was also punctuated by the non-aligned movement, a third dimension of anti-colonial space-time. While 1989 brought neoliberal time to the fore, the space remained that of the United States, and it is only now, with the intensification of Chinese investment throughout Africa, Latin America, the Caribbean, and Southeast Asia that we are entering a new time, and potentially new spaces (those of the maritime Belt and Road).

What does it mean to think about the afterlives of imperial dispossession when we must also reflect an emergent configuration, one that potentially heralds both the death of the West, and its elaboration through new modes, and via new historical and contemporary channels? If the modern West was built on Indigenous dispossession and slavery through the development of plantation-based agriculture in the early sixteenth-century Caribbean, and if both Indigenous and African-descended populations were excluded from modern personhood, then what will it mean to be human in the wake of the West? In the emergent dispensation, how will the work of racial surveillance and violence, economic accumulation, and sexual cruelty be spatially organized? And where will we locate the spaces of alterity that flourished in the plantation's counterpart? How will we understand and bear witness to these emergent forms of displacement and dispossession, and to the innovative maneuvers people develop in order to live in relation to these new dispensations?

In assembling people to think through these questions, the editors of this volume have privileged the terms sovereignties, ecologies, and durabilities. These terms, I think, exist relationally with three others that emerge as central and overlapping rubrics organizing the assemblage of work in this volume—modernities, mobilities, and mutualities. It is to these latter terms that I would like to draw our attention in what follows, by thinking through the power and perils of the plantation as a universal trope. To do this, I want to return to an essay Michel-Rolph Trouillot published the journal *South Atlantic Quarterly* in 2002, "North Atlantic Universals: Analytical Fictions, 1492-1945."

This essay was published in a special issue organized in relation to the theme of "Enduring Enchantments" at the height of academic interrogations of modernity and its alterities. The various contributions were designed to interrogate our deployment of terms and the attachments these terms create and reproduce. I was just starting my first job when the special issue was published, and as a Caribbeanist interested in both the enchantments and violences of modernity, the collection of essays was both inspiring, and not a little legitimating. Trouillot's article constituted a refutation of those who would locate "modernity" only in nineteenth-century imperial maneuvers. By drawing attention to early Latin American and Caribbean historical experiences, he designated words like progress, development, modernity, nation-state, and globalization as "North Atlantic universals," words that purportedly described ongoing processes but that instead "project the North Atlantic experience on a universal scale that they themselves helped to create" (2002: 847). These words, for Trouillot, "appear to refer to things as they exist, but because they are rooted in a particular history, they evoke multiple layers of sensibilities, persuasions, cultural assumptions, and ideological choices tied to that local history" (ibid.). The seduction of these North Atlantic universals, he argued, lay in their "ability to project transhistorical relevance while hiding the particularities of their marks and origins" (2002: 848). The antidote for such silencing, for Trouillot, was analysis of "the relation between the geography of management and the geography of imagination that together underpinned the development of world capitalism and the legitimacy of the West as the universal unmarked" (2002: 855). It is just this relation that the essays in this volume consider, historically and ethnographically, offering us new insights into the complexities and continuities of the plantation.

Modernities

In my own thinking through the changes characterizing the afterlives of the plantation in Jamaica, I have been drawn to the notion of epochal shift, and of course this is the framing preferred by those who have become captured by anthropocenic discourse. My interest in epochs, however, has been rooted in the stunning continuities between the colonial and so-called post-colonial period, continuities that are themselves the result of the seismic shifts inaugurated by Western modernity. In "North Atlantic Universals," Trouillot defines modernity as a regime of history that is "structurally plural," one that ruptures the planes of past, present, and future only to tie them together again in a linear reckoning that tethers time to space in ways that support familiar hierarchies. "Modernity," he writes, "requires a localization of space:"

> As soon as one draws a single line that ties past, present, and future, and yet insists on their distinctiveness, one must inevitably place actors along that line, either ahead or behind. Being behind suggests an elsewhere both within and outside of the space defined by modernity: outside to the extent that these Others have not yet reached that place where judgment occurs; within to the extent that the place they now occupy can be perceived from that other place within the line. This new regime of historicity requires also a localization of its subject...The modern is that subject which measures any distance from itself and redeploys it against an unlimited space of imagination. (2002: 850)

The plantation—being a modern organization of production and consumption, and of social and cultural life—made "wild" landscapes legible. Sugar, cotton, oil palm, and even citrus all fueled the vision of the rational ordering of people and landscapes. We are reminded here of the continuities that cut across these ordering projects. In the southern United States before cotton became King, in Haiti at the beginning of the U.S. occupation, in revolutionary Cuba, and in neoliberal Sierra Leone's Chinese-driven sugar industry, developmentalist dreams reign(ed) supreme. Commodity agriculture rendered that which was outside its rationalizing schemes illegible. Haitian peasants were perceived as "politically unruly and economically dormant" (Sapp Moore); overseers on southern U.S. tobacco or indigo farms were incompetent (Stubbs); and peasant life in Cuba was isolating and austere (Aureille). Despite the violences that necessarily accompany and produce plantation modernities, and despite the many forms of fugitivity that punctured plantation hegemony, rational ordering (whether imperialist or nationalist) also produces a kind of nostalgia in its wake.

Sitting in the ruins of the citrus plantation, Cubans in Sandino look with hope toward the development of a promised tourism resort. What is at stake here is not merely jobs, but also the continued viability of the revolutionary project, one in which a viable and paternalistic sovereign state "brings" modernity and development to its people. And after the

Civil War, after Ebola, Sierra Leoneans too look back at the history of economic cooperation between Sierra Leone and the People's Republic of China with the hope not only of continued investment, but also of an alternative to Western modes of extraction, accumulation, and aid. "Progress," in these examples, is the purview of the state—whether colonial, nationalist, or socialist—as people face what Nile Davies called "cyclical ruination, abandonment, and long-term precarity." Yet aspirations for "modern" development and upward mobility continue to be tethered to the space of the plantation.

Mobilities

In "North Atlantic Universals," Trouillot reminds us that the massive movement and creolization—of people, crops, animals, ideas, and capital—that are seen to characterize the late twentieth and twenty first centuries were also what inaugurated modern modes of exchange, governance, and socio-cultural expression beginning in the fifteenth century:

> In 1493, when Columbus returned to the Caribbean island he had named Hispaniola, he was on a different mission than on his first trip. In his seventeen ships were not only the instruments of conquest that he carried on his first voyage, but also loads of crops, fruits, seeds, and animals, including sheep, pigs, goats, cattle, chicken, onions, radishes, chick peas, wheat seeds, and grapevine plants. (2002: 840)

As people and animals moved, so did goods:

> Massive flows of gold and silver, of crops and spices, of plants and diseases, from tobacco to coconuts, from syphilis to smallpox, from the mines of Peru to the Kew Gardens sprinkled over the British Empire, enmeshed world populations into encounters and confrontations unrestricted by physical distance. From the beginning Europeans who came to the new world brought along with their slaves a variety of plants, animals, and other living organisms. Horses, pigs, sheep, dogs, chickens, donkeys, cattle, bananas, plantains, and all their parasites moved to the new world. So did measles, whooping cough, bubonic plague, malaria, yellow fever, diphtheria, amoebic dysentery, influenza, and smallpox. The latter alone proved to be a mass murderer of proportions still unmatched for the native population. (2002: 842)

There are two things Trouillot recognizes as novel about Columbus's actions and intentions here. First, it is clear that these crops and animals (and people) were brought in order to reproduce in the Antilles. Second, it appears Columbus was certain that he and others after him would continue to move back and forth between Old and New worlds, not least because among the twelve hundred people on board with him were "specialists in farming, irrigation, and road building" (2002: 841). The desire for wealth and the need for labor to produce and organize it are the main forces propelling these early movements. The later moments interrogated in this volume give us additional insights into the new imperial presences, new forms of management, and new orientations to space and time that emerge in the wake of Columbus's initial conquest and colonization.

Of course, all that is new builds on what was initially established, even as these links between past and present are erased, as Irene Peano shows us through her interrogation of discourses of the "new slavery" within the context of migrant farm labor in Italy. Where media commentators see the conditions of these laborers as reminiscent of an "American south," and where migrant workers themselves describe their labor conditions as "animalization," the *modern* slavery of sixteenth-century sugar plantations is eclipsed, relegated to the past, while a discourse of "new slavery" serves to criminalize migration. The links between contemporary and historical processes are not interrogated, Peano argues, which renders neo-abolitionist ideology merely instrumentalist, rather than illuminating. These elisions and evasions, and the processes by which they are elaborated, raise questions about origins, naming, belonging, and the negotiations surrounding processes of inclusion and exclusion.

What does it mean to be native to a place? Sophie Sapp Moore asks this when she considers what happens when "Sea Island cotton" traverses the Caribbean Sea and pushes up through Haitian soil during the U.S. military occupation, itself occurring in the wake of the America's Civil War and the abolition of slavery. The demise of slave-cultivated cotton in the U.S. south led to attempts at cultivation elsewhere, which were also, of course, attempts to build on previous imperial projects to make otherwise unruly spaces and people legible. U.S. imperial ambition during the nineteenth century and the first half of the twentieth sought to push its "big stick" toward what it understood as its "backyard" in the Caribbean, culminating in the 1904 Roosevelt Corollary to the Monroe Doctrine, but also westward to Hawai'i and elsewhere in the Pacific. Where Sapp Moore shows us U.S. military personnel confronting fugitive forms of sovereignty in Haiti's Central Plateau, Nicholas Miller presents Chinese sugar planters in Hawai'i navigating competing sovereign claims—those emanating from native Hawai'ians, the Chinese imperial government, and the British and U.S. governments attempting to regulate migration and movement. These essays demonstrate the complex and overlapping entanglements of imperialism and plantation development, and also give us a sense of how the kinds of silencing and disavowals with which Trouillot was also concerned operate. Tracking Chinese settler families in Hawaii, for example, demonstrates that "the claims of *haole* settler nativists to racial, cultural, and political ascendancy after 1887 were hardly hegemonic." Imperialism, and the establishment of plantation-based agricultural projects, is therefore shown to be complexly multi-valent.

We know, of course, that while mobility characterizes modern processes, movement is also always monitored, managed, and thwarted. Martino Sacchi and Lorenzo Ravano show us that "colonial society was less strictly compartmentalized than we may expect," and that "its internal frontiers were continuously challenged by slave mobility." Indeed, in Haiti as elsewhere throughout the post-emancipation Latin America and the Caribbean, mobility becomes something to be managed, and managed by a nascent state. This draws our attention to the various reorganizations of governmentality that characterize the long nineteenth and twentieth centuries after the Haitian Revolution. Sapp Moore also reminds us that Haiti's Central Plateau was home to fugitives, *cacos*, and small-scale peasant producers accustomed to freely transgressing borders, and that this mobility posed a problem to U.S policy makers, who, like the French colonial agents before them, associated the high degree of mobility with widespread "banditry." Here mobility is experienced as "wildness," like the plateau itself. It is criminalized; it requires surveillance and management. Today, in places like Jamaica and Trinidad, this management often takes the form of states of emergency and "zones of special operation," legislative designations in which extreme police powers are allowed in areas where criminality is perceived to be rampant, and where gang warfare has been seen to create sovereign spaces outside the control of the legitimate state. Again, there are lines to be drawn between the regulation of the countryside, the maintenance of security, the monitoring of movement (internally and transnationally), and the exclusion of "unruly" Black and Indigenous people from the legitimate parameters of citizenship, historically and in the present.

Mutualities

Like many, Trouillot was interested in the processes of creolization that characterized the making of the New World. The massive movements of goods, people, and capital across the Atlantic Ocean and the Caribbean Sea, and eventually in and through Pacific routes, not only changed the ways political and economic life was organized, but also the ways people understood the world around them and their relationships to it. Trouillot points out that the adoption of new practices was widespread, not only in the New World but also across the Old:

> Some Native Americans quickly adopted the horse from herds that had escaped Spanish ranches. By the time they encountered the first Anglo-Saxon colonists, they had already integrated horseback riding into their daily cultural practices. It took less time for maize to be adopted by Africans on the Angola-Congo coastline in the late sixteenth century than it took espresso to move from the two coasts of the United States and become an accessible commodity in the Midwest or the South in the late twentieth. (2002: 844)

And of course, as people moved, they mixed—often under violent conditions—and these mixtures created "hybrid" people and spaces:

> Not surprisingly, the first moment of globality produced...individuals or groups who saw themselves as belonging to more than one sociocultural unit, as sharing more than one cultural heritage. Seventeenth-century Cambay, a commercial port on the Indian Ocean, linked East Africa, the Middle East, and Indonesia and counted a number of Portuguese residents who erected mansions built and furnished according to Portuguese taste. Was it an Indian, Islamic, or Portuguese city? (2002: 845)

If, as the editors of this volume write, plantations can be considered "sovereign-making machines[s], workshop[s] in which tools of both domination and resistance are forged" through the production of "capacities, intimacies, and relations," then we must probe the forms of relation through which sovereign claims are articulated. That these relations involve not only humans, but also more-than-human entities (including hauntings), is made clear through several of this volume's contributions.

Rodrigo Bulamah, for example, encourages us to think plantation infrastructure through the figure of the creole pig. In his rendering, creole pigs, which were in the seventeenth-century part of the emergent technologies of the plantation regime in Haiti, eventually became members of a commons, sharing life on provision grounds with those who were enslaved (and who would later become peasant cultivators). Bulamah shows us that creole pigs cemented their inclusion in the commons, and their centrality to modern notions of freedom, through their use as mediums in the ceremonies that gave rise to the Haitian revolution. Pigs, then, became part of the architecture of sovereignty, and simultaneously the means toward sovereign claims. And these kinds of multispecies encounters also created new spaces of fugitivity, and new attempts to control them.

Where creole pigs emerge as actors within liberation ecologies, parasites on oil palm plantations in West Papua both mediate and complicate Indigenous Marind engagements with the Indonesian state and the forms of agribusiness it has introduced. Having themselves been displaced to make way for oil palm plantations, Marind villagers, Sophie Chao shows, identify with the fate of native species, seeing these species' flailing or flourishing in the face of an alien and invasive cultivar as refractive of their own position vis-à-vis oil palm, and thus the state. Will oil palm be a lethal and parasitic predator, or will they develop the kind of thriving and positive relations that characterize biodiverse, rather than monocrop production?

Chao also demonstrates how palm parasites can parallel the action (or hopes) of the people who must contend with them. "Unlike the organized and spectacular violence of the Indonesian state," she writes, "the slow violence of parasitism is often invisible to the human eye." These forms of mutualism and metonymy draw our attention to complex and quiet forms of accommodation and negotiation (rather than opposition) in the development of shared worlds. As Chao concludes, "'friends" and "enemies" in the plantation assemblage are neither fixed nor bounded entities, but rather malleable and dynamic relationalities."

Mutualities, of course, not only emerge with more-than-human species, but also in relation to changing ideological and affective circulations. Mariana Muaze shows us how changed ideas about cultured living emerged in Brazil during the second half of the nineteenth century, when slavery had been abolished everywhere but Cuba and Brazil. Wealthy landowners and coffee barons began to value a notion of civilization that was rooted in "etiquette, good manners, and refinement," inspired by

French *savoir vivre* and new notions of order. Etiquette, education, courtesy, and hygiene came to stand alongside the consumption of luxury goods and a valorization of sociality to characterize proper living, in clear contradistinction to the planter excesses and uncouthness often reported regarding planters in the eighteenth-century West Indies. These are late nineteenth-century shifts that not only transform the comportment of plantation owners, but also the lives of those who were enslaved, since it increased the demands on both women and men working as "house slaves."

A different form of mutuality emerges from David Abrampah's archaeological exploration of a plantation in Dodowa, Ghana that was originally established by Danish settlers. His team's excavations show the plantation as "a place of settlement, abandonment, and reoccupation," the latter, in some cases, by elite Africans and others who inhabited these formerly Danish plantation landscapes both during and after the period of active cultivation. Here, mutualities are forged across time as people challenge the social hierarchies created in and through plantation settlement. If our analysis of plantation life must go beyond the "master/slave" dichotomy, as Abrampah argues, then we must also perhaps come to understand both the political economy and the social and cultural dynamics of plantations and their afterlives in terms of waves.

Waves

The focus of my own investigations of the afterlives of the plantation has been on *creating and assembling* archives of violence in Jamaica. This has meant working with existing archives (difficult because these are colonial, or otherwise surveillant), and it has also meant developing new archives, which have been narrative, performative, sonic, visual, or otherwise embodied. These archives, thus assembled, stand as representations of the plantation's afterlives and its new lives, as a kind of fractal tracking of its recursivity. While my focus has been on moments of state violence that have either been forgotten or that are disavowed in various ways, the purpose has been to create different affective relationships to violence, relationships that are themselves tethered to particular places and times. This practice has been geared toward generating difficult conversations about the relationships among personhood, politics, and violence, and to create the conditions for people to think through their own relation to these archives, or to elaborate new foundations for sociality and liberation.

The papers in this volume constitute such an assemblage, moving across time and space to chart the shifts in players, methods, and effects of plantation development. They bear witness to the ways people have attempted to navigate these shifts, and to the complicated affective entanglements that have emerged.

In my own thinking through the afterlives of the plantation in Jamaica, I have attended to the continuities among imperial moments by borrowing Jacqui Alexander's (2005) notion of palimpsestic time. This notion draws attention to the layering of forms of dispossession and oppression, but also turns our eyes to the spaces within which people imagine futures otherwise. One might chart these afterlives within Jamaica like this...During the eighteenth century, Jamaica was the jewel in Britain's imperial crown, with planters and estate managers earning money hand over foot, an extraordinary wealth that gained them the reputation as the cruelest, most debauched, and most backward estate owners in the Caribbean. Jamaica was the testing ground for new imperial policies before and after the abolition of slavery, and during the late colonial period, its governors had all seen service in some of the empire's "hottest spots" like Malaya during the "Emergency," Kenya, or Gibraltar, suggesting that Jamaica was regarded as an area of concern that would require experience both with communist insurgencies and ethnic/racial conflict.

During the post-independence period, Jamaica was a central thorn in the side of the United States due to its history of left-leaning political leaders and its strong faction of communist supporters. This was especially true after Prime Minister Michael Manley developed a friendship with Fidel Castro, became the leader of the Non-Aligned Movement, and declared Jamaica to be a democratic socialist country in 1974, which prompted the elaboration of covert anti-communist operations designed to destabilize Manley's popular regime. Jamaica has also been a primary node in the circulation of Black liberation ideologies that have been anathema to both British and American imperial projects, and the country has consistently drawn the attention of the DEA, due to its location within international distribution networks of illegal drugs and arms.

Now, Jamaica is the Caribbean hub of the Chinese Belt and Road Initiative. However, while the country was central to both British and American imperial projects, its location within the broader scope of Chinese overseas expansion is somewhat more peripheral. Despite plans to build a deep-water port and logistics hub, and the bauxite mining that is currently infringing upon sovereign Maroon lands, Jamaica might find itself to be interchangeable with other small island states, rather than at the center of one or another empire. This is an unfamiliar position for Jamaicans used to a particular significance within global geopolitics, and it marks a kind of epochal shift, one that also requires us to think about how we might imagine our political futures beyond Western parameters, about what sovereignty might look and feel like in a new dispensation, and about the new forms of accountability that will be required.

Thinking in terms of epochal shifts has been a useful way for me to conceptualize the temporal and spatial realignments of these past several centuries. But more and more, I feel that dispossession happens in waves. Waves are disturbances, changes from equilibrium, that travel fractally through a medium from one location to another. Waves involve the movement of a disturbance, but not the movement of matter; they transport energy, but often with no permanent displacement of the particles that make up the medium. Waves, of course, also make it possible for us to see, and to hear, in non-linear unpredictable ways. They are recursive; they repeat. They reflect, but they also refract, and it is in these refractions, diffractions, and interferences that we might find new spaces of possibility. The authors in this volume bear witness to these refractions, diffractions, interferences, and possibilities. They give us a sense of how, as the mediums through which imperial waves transit shift, new alignments are becoming visible.

References

Alexander, J. 2005. *Pedagogies of Crossing: Meditations on Feminism, Sexual Politics, Memory, and the Sacred*. Durham: Duke University Press.

Trouillot, M.-R. 2002. North Atlantic Universals: Analytical Fictions, 1492–1945. *South Atlantic Quarterly* 101 (4): 839–858.

Index

C. Le Petitcorps et al. (eds.), *Global Plantations in the Modern World*, Cambridge Imperial and Post-Colonial Studies,
https://doi.org/10.1007/978-3-031-08537-6

GPSR Compliance

The European Union's (EU) General Product Safety Regulation (GPSR) is a set of rules that requires consumer products to be safe and our obligations to ensure this.

If you have any concerns about our products, you can contact us on ProductSafety@springernature.com

In case Publisher is established outside the EU, the EU authorized representative is:

Springer Nature Customer Service Center GmbH
Europaplatz 3
69115 Heidelberg, Germany

FSC
www.fsc.org
MIX
Papier | Fördert gute Waldnutzung
FSC® C083411

Kolibri 360 GmbH
Ferdinand-Jühlke-Straße 7
99095 Erfurt, Deutschland
produktsicherheit@kolibri360.de